Pause for Prayer

daily devotional

· Cindi Ferrini ·

© 2015

All rights reserved. No part of this book may be reproduced, stored in a retrieval system, or transmitted in any form, or by any means, electronic, mechanical, photocopying, recording, or otherwise, without prior permission of the authors.

Editor: Linda Meixner, Cleveland, OH
Design: Premier Designs, Cleveland, OH
Cover Photo: Courtesy of www.istockphoto.com

Scripture quotations taken from the New American Standard Bible®, unless otherwise noted.
Copyright © 1960, 1962, 1963, 1968, 1971, 1972, 1973, 1975, 1977, 1995
by The Lockman Foundation (www.Lockman.org)
Used by permission.

ISBN: 978-0967761237

Cindi Ferrini
Pause for Prayer
Creative Management Fundamentals
PO Box 360279
Cleveland, OH 44136-0005
www.cindiferrini.com

Printed by CreateSpace, an Amazon.com Company
Charleston, SC

Dedication

I dedicate this *Pause for Prayer* daily devotional to the memory and legacy of Katie Williams.

Sometimes we find ourselves in places we never expected.
I found myself in the company and companionship
of the original voice of *Pause for Prayer*—Katie Williams—often.
It happened in a fun, unexpected, and precious way. Times with her were always like that.
She didn't know it, but she was my mentor. She was a natural.
I have a feeling many women would say the same of our dear friend Katie.
She was available, intentional, and loving.
Today she is missed.

May the prayer ministry she began continue in and through those of us who presently serve
and those who will serve in the future.

Thank you, Katie.

"And My people who are called by My name humble themselves and pray, and seek My face and turn from their wicked ways; then I will hear from heaven, will forgive their sin, and will heal their land."

II Chronicles 7:14

Katie Williams
July 17, 1921 – April 18, 2004

Note On The Dedication

Sometimes we find ourselves in places we never expected. Joe and I found ourselves in the dining room of Howard and Katie Williams in 1990. Katie Williams had been the voice of *Pause for Prayer* (first in small groups and eventually on the radio) for about 18 years the day we first met her. She seemed the perfect voice and they the perfect couple to join us and our local FamilyLife team as we ventured to bring the CRU FamilyLife Weekend to Remember Marriage Get-Away to Cleveland. The team prayed Katie might lend her voice and platform to be our prayer chairman along with Howard. We came to know one another as we chatted about ministry, family, and business and had so much fun that night. We learned of their involvement during the 1972 Billy Graham Crusade, Katie sensing the Lord's direction to continue the prayer movement begun prior to the BG Crusade. She spent a great deal of time seeking someone to do a daily radio spot, someone with the training and expertise. Time and a bit of coaxing were needed for her to realize she was the person for the spot! An added plus of our evening together was meeting their daughter Christie Claypoole, who stopped by after dinner (and most recently helped me with this timeline).

Christie had introduced her parents to Christ and CRU (formerly Campus Crusade for Christ), and their lives were turned upside down when they chose to follow Jesus! They were sold out for Him. Howard and Katie became pillars in the Cleveland community, but their influence throughout the years was international. Time and space won't allow for details, but someday I think we'll all share in rejoicing about the influence, service, and love they shared with many. But that night, we saw only a glimpse. They were under the impression we were going on staff with CCC/CRU and seeking their financial support. How precious and dear it was to us that they would invite us to dinner, knowing we might be asking for financial support—new kids on the block who'd never met them! Instead, we popped the question, asking them to be our prayer chairmen. They were so gracious to excuse themselves from that role, suggesting we needed a younger chaircouple, who could proceed into the future with the team. We left feeling as if we'd known them for a very long time but in reality had just met and made some new and treasured friends.

Yes, sometimes we find ourselves in places we never expected. We dined with the Williamses often during their remaining years. Sometimes we enjoyed fine dining spots; other times we'd meet for a cup of coffee and dessert. Sometimes we met for ministry planning for big prayer events like Concerts of Prayer at the IX Center or simply on our knees in prayer together. A tender mentoring friendship had begun—particularly for Katie and me.

I never expected to be asked by Katie to write and record *Pause for Prayer* segments for months that had a fifth week, perhaps the safe way to determine whether I could do it! I had done a few radio interviews, but I had never written manuscripts to be recorded. Joe and I have always chosen to say "yes" to opportunities in which the Lord was working, so I accepted Katie's request to join the team as the fifth-week person and my first *Pause for Prayer* aired June 15, 1998. I was nervous and unsure of the responsibility, but she assured me she would guide me. She was patient and kind. It was clear she would know how to groom a novice like me because she had found herself in that very place after the 1972 Billy Graham Crusade. When I look back to my first week of *Pause for Prayer* manuscripts, I laugh: They were so elementary. Before long she asked me to join the team as a regular, and I loved what I'd been given to do!

Years later on a cold wintery day in 1999, Katie and I met to talk about *Pause for Prayer* and simply visit.

Katie's aging, fragile, and cold hand beat me to grab the coffee tab. She was strong, and I didn't fight it! Howard's health had become a challenge; she was looking at a few upcoming surgeries and mentioned increasing difficulties in traveling to the radio station to tape. I often had several extra weeks on file for emergencies, so I said to her, "Katie, if you can't get in to tape, just ask Paul [Carter, our trusted and patient producer] to use my recordings for your week if you can't get in." As I vacationed in Florida that spring a short time later, my future son-in-law Cosmin called to tell me I was on the radio that morning and that he hadn't expected to hear me. Neither did I. I cried. I knew that meant Katie couldn't get in. My heart hurt. I knew the voice of Katie Williams would soon be heard less and less often. I got off the phone and whispered a quiet prayer to the Lord, "What can I do for Katie? I'll do anything." To my heart I sensed He spoke, "Whatever she asks of you, just say 'yes.'"

I returned home from vacation to a message on my answering machine. It was Katie. "Cindi, call me when you get home. I'd like to talk some things over with you." I called her immediately and heard her quiet voice, "Cindi, I feel I've said everything the Lord has wanted me to say. My health is becoming challenging. I wonder if you would pray about taking over my position as the coordinator of Pause for Prayer." I responded without delay, "Katie, I don't have to pray about it. The Lord already told me to say yes to whatever you ask. I'd be honored." I found myself once again in a place I never expected.

I had enjoyed and listened to Katie for many years as the voice of *Pause for Prayer*. For years, she alone wrote the approximately 300-word manuscripts and taped the daily spots that aired three times a day, Monday through Friday. For those of us who do this on a once-a-month basis, we remain in awe of that commitment! Eventually, she built a team who shared her heart for and burden to pray by assigning each of us "our week to air." We'd pray for needs of a personal nature, for our neighborhoods, and for the world around us. Her world was expansive. I will always picture Katie in my mind next to II Chronicles 7:14: "And My people who are called by My name humble themselves and pray, and seek My face and turn from their wicked ways, then I will hear from heaven, will forgive their sin, and will heal their land."

Many voices that have come and gone have graced the *Pause for Prayer* team and are now a part of the legacy she initiated. The voice, legacy, and memory of Katie Williams will always be in my heart, and my heart of appreciation for her offer to groom me to be her fifth-week contributor in 1999 will always remain.

Each of us who served with her (and her husband Howard) in the prayer ministry and other ministries count it a pleasure and privilege. They are missed but never forgotten.

Acknowledgments

Writing has been a passion of mine for many years, but getting the words from pen and paper or computer to an edited and graphically designed copy takes more than one who loves to write. This, and all of my projects, would be impossible without others who enjoy their own passions to help me pursue mine.

How very special to have my former high school teacher (and, yes, cheerleading coach), now friend, edit my work. Dr. Linda Meixner of Linda Meixner Edits takes such care of my words, allowing them to sound like me while crafting them with her expertise and teaching me in the process. What a gift, Linda! Thank you.

When I open a roughly drafted attachment of a page layout and say, "Don't change anything— It's perfect!" I know it was done under the watchful eye and by the creative hand of Michele Kasl of Premier Designs. To have someone create exactly what I had in mind but couldn't do myself is a treasure. Thank you for reading my mind and creatively using yours, Michele.

Sometimes we find ourselves in places we never expected. I never expected to coordinate the *Pause for Prayer* segments I had listened to and enjoyed for many years on Moody Radio Cleveland (WCRF 103.3 FM). The voice, legacy, and memory of Katie Williams will always be in my heart, and my heart of appreciation for her offer to groom me to be her fifth-week contributor in 1998 will always remain. I shared the rest of this story in the Dedication, but for this acknowledgement, she was like no other in my life! She was dearly loved and now dearly missed!

Although I dedicate this book to Katie Williams' honor and legacy, I also want to thank and appreciate the past and present voices of *Pause for Prayer*. Their many volunteer hours were and are a labor of love with intentionality and purpose to continue a prayer movement begun in 1972. In addition, I wish to thank WCRF past station managers John Maddex (whom I never had the pleasure of meeting) and Dick Lee for the support they gave to this ministry for many years before retiring. Paul Carter, producer of this radio prayer segment, has seen many changes in technology since Katie began but has faithfully helped each of us work at crafting our words, style, and message. His professionalism is trumped only by his patient and caring ways. I appreciate that he has a sense of humor and will laugh with us when we make mistakes that result in more work for him!

As we move into the future, I appreciate Scott Krus, WCRF station manager, who has embraced *Pause for Prayer*, giving us direction, keeping this spot relevant and exciting for today's radio audience, and, of course, the voices of Katie Williams, Jim Rosenberger, Helga Gross, Kinney Cathcart, Joe Ferrini, Joe Abraham, Nate Hunter, Jannelle Nevels, Delphine Allen, Barb Karayan, John Kerezy, Joy Trachsel, Rob Walgate and David Zanotti.

Day 1 — *Pause for Prayer*

> *"And it came about that while He was praying in a certain place, after He had finished, one of His disciples said to Him, "Lord, teach us to pray."*
>
> Luke 11:1

Sometimes I don't feel like doing a lot of different things like making dinner or doing laundry, running errands, and a multitude of other "chores"; but they simply must be done. I often have to muster up the energy and say to myself, "Just do it!"

Although not one of my household duties, prayer is equally difficult sometimes. It's a spiritual duty that requires discipline, and I know its importance because I've seen answers the results of prayer. For that reason, I must pray even when I don't feel like it because it's so much more valuable and important than chores!

Prayer is often the last resort but should be the first thought. In prayer God helps us make our decisions, and he provides the "next steps" to be determined. In prayer we also seek His approval and direction regardless of our own plans from the One who has our needs, desires, and plans in His hand.

Let's Pause for Prayer

Heavenly Father, the quiet closet of prayer is where ministry leaders are lifted up, where families are embraced and cared for, and where our connections to You, the Creator, are made. All that You give us to do requires prayer support. Lord, show us for whom to pray and situations that need prayer. Give us guidance and direction in how to obey You. We know we need help to be faithful in this area of prayer because we often fall short when we hesitate and wait to pray and when we think we don't need to pray! Show us Your answers that will encourage us to pray all the more and help us to recognize the missed opportunities when we should have prayed. We don't want to miss any opportunity to pray as we seek You. May we see prayer as the work—not just the preparation for the work—and then do it whether we feel like it or not! In Jesus' name we pray. Amen.

What are some things that hinder your prayer? List them for yourself here.

_____

_____

_____

Do any of those reasons sound like valid reasons to keep you from praying? If so, name them and explain. If not, describe your plan to use this devotional to get you into His word and prayer daily.

_____

_____

_____

Day 2

Hungry and Thirsty

"Blessed are those who hunger and thirst for righteousness, for they shall be satisfied."

Matthew 5:6

Sometimes when I'm running errands, I get so hungry that I do the fast food drive through. I generally wish I would have packed a banana or other fruit to carry me through the day because once I eat the fast food, I feel full but not satisfied. Those nuggets are deceiving!

Similarly, although I love to read from the wisdom of others, I'm never as satisfied as when I read from God's word. Nuggets of wisdom from Proverbs or the Psalms are encouraging, often life changing, life giving, and always satisfying.

Nothing quite like a fine meal from appetizer to dessert fully satisfies our bodies, and nothing will replace reading and studying the word of God.

Let's Pause for Prayer

God, may we so hunger and thirst for Your Word that we want to be nourished by it every day. May we drink deeply from the words that encourage and fully satisfy. Thank You for having been given many wonderful authors who write in ways that help us to understand Your word, but may we never neglect time in prayer and reading Your Word daily. Keep us focused on learning from Your word, which teaches us how to live better as we live in obedience to You. Help us want Your word daily so that we don't settle for what might be the equivalent of an appetizer instead of the full meal deal, one that is appetizing and fully satisfying! May we encourage one another to study Your word, hold each other accountable to what You share in Your word, and may we all be encouraged to live it out before others as an example of how You work in our lives through Your word. In Jesus' name we pray. Amen.

Share the last really meaningful scripture you remember reading.

_____

_____

_____

Are you in God's word daily? If not, plan to spend a few minutes daily in an effort to become fully satisfied. Will you start today? Share what you learned that was meaningful to you.

_____

_____

_____

_____

Day 3 — Little Things

> *"He who is faithful in a very little thing is faithful also in much; and he who is unrighteous in a very little thing is unrighteous also in much."*
>
> Luke 16:10

Do you have difficulty finding people you can count on? Folks who are dependable? Does it ruffle your feathers when others are careless about details or completing tasks with excellence?

In *Keep a Quiet Heart*, Elisabeth Elliot tells the story of the headmistress of her boarding school, who could see from where she sat any student who kicked up a corner of a particular carpet at the end of a hallway. When students didn't fix the corner of the carpet, the headmistress instructed them to be concerned and attentive to the "little things" in life; otherwise, those "little things" would eventually trip them up! In this hallway, called "Character Hall" with its small oriental rugs, Elisabeth learned that the little things in life reveal our character. Our responses to little things will make or break us. She learned what many of us are learning: "It's not easy to find children or adults who are dependable, careful, thorough, and faithful."

If we can't follow through with the smallest of tasks, why would we think God would ask us to perform greater tasks? He is looking for those who are dependable, careful, thorough, and faithful.

Let's Pause for Prayer

Lord Jesus, please help me to be faithful in the little things. Prompt and nudge me to follow through with the tasks before me. Help me to avoid distraction, loss of interest, or forgetfulness in completing what I've started. I want to be viewed by others as responsible, caring, and careful. Even more, I want to please You. I want to be used by You to do whatever will further Your kingdom. May I be dependable, careful, thorough, and faithful in every detail, but not so overcalculating or precise as to frustrate or nitpick. Help me act in such a way as to show honor and respect as I work with and for others. In Jesus' name we pray. Amen.

Can people count on you to follow through and be a person of your word? Explain.

_____

_____

_____

Describe a small task that you will work on today with excellence.

_____

_____

_____

Day 4

Sinning Without Shame

> *"Tremble, and do not sin; meditate in your heart upon your bed, and be still."*
>
> Psalms 4:4

In a stirring message years ago, Nancy Leigh DeMoss said this: "Inside the church, we have failed to live by the scripture. We say we have obeyed the Word of God, but how do we explain all of the evidence to the contrary? We are a community of the forgiven who refuse to forgive. We live with unresolved conflicts in our homes, among church and ministry staff, and in the pew. We have ignored or rejected the biblical standards for spiritual leadership. We exalt giftedness over godliness, and elevate men whose lives and homes are far from conforming to the standard of God's Word. We sin without shame. We have lost our capacity to mourn and grieve and weep over sin. In our casual brand of Christianity, there is little sense of the fear of the Lord. How else could millions of churchgoers sit under the preaching of the Word and leave unchanged and unmoved? How else could so-called believers who claim to believe in holiness sit watching television and laughing at ungodly jokes, lifestyles, and philosophies? When was the last time we trembled at the Word of the Lord?"

Let's Pause for Prayer

Lord, keep me still this moment and reveal my sin. Make me uncomfortable in my sin for the way I have dishonored You. Forgive me for compromising, diluting, and ignoring what I know to be true. Lord, I want to mourn over what breaks Your heart and weep over those things that I and others do that displease You. Help me to repent (turn away) from my sin and be renewed by Your strength. In Your strength may I be bold enough to do whatever You ask me to do for Your glory and honor. In Jesus' name we pray. Amen.

Today this sin, from which I will repent and turn away, came to mind:

_____

_____

_____

What I will do about this sin (for example, ask forgiveness or make restitution):

_____

_____

_____

_____

Day 5   *It's Not Easy To Be Still*

> *"Be still and know that I am God."*
>
> Psalms 46:10

I am challenged daily to walk in obedience to God. Sometimes I sense so clearly what He wants me to do, and I sense His direction and guidance. Other times I wonder whether I'm even close. But one thing I know: I want to obey Him, so I listen very carefully.

He reveals His will to us in many ways—sometime quickly, sometimes in ways that we sense His overwhelming presence during a time of waiting. Sometimes it takes so long that we can actually see our faith being tested!

So how do we learn to discern His will so that we can obey it? Circumstances can lead us in one direction, but it's not always the wisest or surest way to confirm God's will. And we have God-given intelligence to help us make decisions. In addition, we can ask the counsel of other Christians who walk closely with the Lord and discern God's will by reading His word daily and through prayer, which is also important. But the Number 1, perhaps most neglected, way to determine God's will for our lives is to take time to listen—to be still and listen.

Let's Pause for Prayer

Heavenly Father, help me to use the mind You have given me as I use common sense and the intelligence You've given to consider what You want me to do. Put in my path those believers who can counsel me and use Your word to guide me. But may I never neglect taking the time to be still in prayer, asking You to reveal Your will to me. May I be still in my heart until You reveal what Your next step for me might be. Help me to be quieted in mind and in spirit, listening carefully, waiting patiently, and making no moves forward until I have heard from You. May I not rush ahead but wait until You lead me to that next step. In Jesus' name we pray. Amen.

Why it's hard for me to be still and wait to hear from God:

_____

_____

_____

What I will do today to listen for His guidance:

_____

_____

_____

_____

Day 6 — *Praying In Public*

"For I am not ashamed of the gospel, for it is the power of God for salvation to everyone who believes."

Romans 1:16

Years ago I sat at a water park while the children played and couldn't help but notice two dads and their young daughters setting out lunch at a table behind us. I heard one dad say, "Well, group, how about if we ask the Lord to bless this food?" His simple prayer of thanks was special. He also prayed about the blessing of being able to serve Jesus. I was not only touched by his prayer, but I was also impressed with the ease with which he prayed in public.

We eventually shared a short conversation in which I encouraged him in his public prayer and the example he was setting for the young children as well as those around him! I learned that he was a believer of two years and his friend for just two months! What an example he was to this new believer! What an encouragement to me! May we all be so bold and unashamed to pray in public.

Let's Pause for Prayer

Heavenly Father, we are able to exemplify Christlike behavior to others both directly and indirectly. Thank you for these two men who led their young daughters by example. Thank you for allowing others to witness their prayer before their meal and to see what Christlike behavior looks like in this small way. Give me the courage to pray in public. Let me be direct in pointing others to You. Keep me from embarrassment when praying at a meal, bowing my head to pray with someone on the spot in public when an immediate need for prayer arises, or holding others' hands as I pray them through a crisis. Let me lead by example so that others see more of You in me and all around them! In Jesus' name we pray. Amen.

Do you find praying in public easy or difficult? Explain.

_____

_____

_____

How will you initiate prayer the next time you have an opportunity in public? What's your plan?

_____

_____

_____

_____

Day 7 — *Disabled Or Able?*

> *"I will give thanks to Thee, for I am fearfully and wonderfully made; wonderful are Thy works, and my soul knows it very well."*
>
> Psalm 139:14

It's difficult for me to listen to commentaries and read articles on abortion. Knowing a person or two who have aborted children because of possible limitations and challenges or because a child at that particular time wasn't a good idea and also realizing the horrific methods used to kill babies, I struggle. I wonder what has happened to our society when we can so casually dispose of a life. We're all aware of pet advocates, who raise millions to care for and protect animals from harm, abuse, or extinction; yet we permit the taking of human life.

Access to abortion in our throw-away society allows many to consider those with limitations to have little worth. As parents of a son with special needs, we have experienced both the hard work and the privilege of learning and growing tremendously as our son has blessed and challenged us. He has taught us to love each individual unconditionally and has shown us that even those with physical and mental limitations can have abilities we could never have imagined as well as the capacity to know our Lord Jesus. May we count each individual as valued!

Let's Pause for Prayer

Heavenly Father, thank You for creating each one of us individually and uniquely. You know us so well, and we are important and valuable to You. Please help me to hold life as sacred and as valuable as You do. I pray for those making decisions to end a pregnancy to think beyond an uncertain future for the child, their own lives and comforts, or whatever fears lie before them. Surround them with people who would love them through a pregnancy and help care for the child. Help us all learn and grow as we open our arms to those who have physical or mental challenges and limitations. In Jesus' name we pray. Amen.

When you look at the people in your neighborhood, church, and family, do you consider them to have great value?

_____

_____

If you've struggled with certain people or certain types of people, what actions can you take to value them in your heart as well as in your actions?

_____

_____

_____

Day 8 — *Serving God Or Pleasing Others*

> *"And whatever you do in word or deed, do all in the name of the Lord Jesus, giving thanks through Him to God the Father. Whatever you do, do your work heartily, as for the Lord rather than for men. It is the Lord Christ whom you serve."*
>
> Colossians 3: 17, 23, 24b

We lose zeal and passion for life, work, ministry, and family when we

- Boast about things we're going to do but have little or no motivation to follow through
- Stay busy but not with our life purpose, mission, or calling in mind
- Rely on our own talents over God-given gifts and abilities
- Go-go-go and forget to stop and rest
- Fail to stay true to our word, forgetting to make our yes mean yes and no mean no!
- Stop having fun and become serious about everything and everyone
- Take things personally and act negatively upon those thoughts
- Think about ourselves and stop or lose focus on serving others
- Want things our way and fail to work cooperatively with others
- Think we're overly important instead of realize we're all part of the puzzle
- Let others steal our joy and contentment
- Seek the advice of others instead of God, doing man's will, not God's
- Quit when the going gets rough, which is usually just before the best is about to happen

Let's Pause for Prayer

Lord Jesus, may I never lose the zeal and passion that You gave me when I first came to know You! I pray for all who lead and serve in ministry—pastors, lay leaders, elders, and all Your workers in the church. I pray for a Godly standard in my life to work at that to which You've called me and to reflect You as I serve. For those who serve in other types of work in the home or community, please help each of them back their words with actions. I want to be called to fulfill a vision, not merely a task. Help me to use the gifts You have given me and not to rely upon what I perceive to be my talents. May I take time to rest so I can and complete Your work refreshed. I pray that my enthusiasm and passion emanate from You. May all that I do be done for Your glory and honor. In Jesus' name we pray. Amen.

Do areas of your life lack zeal and passion? Which ones? What step will you take today to revive that zeal and passion?

_____

_____

_____

Day 9 — The TV In Our Homes

> *"Finally brethren, whatever is true, whatever is honorable, whatever is right, whatever is pure, whatever is lovely, whatever is of good repute, if there is any excellence and if anything worthy of praise, let your mind dwell on these things."*
>
> Philippians 4:8

Summer reruns, oldies but goodies, new programming, even commercials—we welcome them all into our homes. We hear statistics on the number of sexual references, obscenities, and violent scenes onscreen during what was formerly considered the "family hour." I'm amazed what enters our homes, what we allow to enter our homes. We turn on the TV, plop down on the sofa or some easy chair, and like a guest treated to our hospitality, we invite whatever is on the TV screen to entertain us. We watch mindless, sinful, garbage for hours and wonder why our kids and society are the way they are.

Do we throw out our televisions? Do we limit TV viewing? Shall we choose a show or two that's appropriate and look forward to watching it? Do we write television studios and voice our opinions on the types of programs on the air?

Some good could probably come of each of those solutions, but whatever we do, it must start with each of us individually. As Christians we should set a high standard regarding our television viewing instead of following the crowd. It's so easy to let into our family rooms via TV what we would never allow to enter our front door!

Let's Pause for Prayer

Heavenly Father, let me follow Your high standard as given in Philippians 4:8. Please reveal to me when I am viewing something that is sinful, evil, trashy, and without value to me. Please guide my mind and heart to discern immediately what programming is not appropriate or worth my time. May I willingly and obediently turn off the television that very moment instead of viewing entire programs before concluding they're not worthy of my time and attention. May I willingly adhere to Your high standard for Your honor and glory and be an example to my children and others. In Jesus' name we pray. Amen.

As you watch television today and in the coming week, be attentive to what might not be appropriate and hinders your spiritual growth. Can you think of any shows that you might need to remove from your list?

_____

_____

What will you do to replace that time in front of the television?

_____

_____

Day 10

Exposing Sin For All To See?

"If we say that we have no sin, we are deceiving ourselves, and the truth is not in us."

I John 1:8

The customer ahead of me in the grocery store was having quite a discussion with the cashier. She said, "I think anyone who does something like that should have it written on their front door. No, they should have it written across their forehead for all of us to see. It should be like that for all of us; all of our wrongdoings should be written on our foreheads." Since I didn't catch the whole conversation, I just listened, but what I heard certainly got me to thinking; and I wondered how she would really feel once she had something posted on her forehead for all to see? Would she really want her wrongdoings exposed like that?

Imagine if everyone could see all of our wrongdoings (what God calls SIN) by reading them on our foreheads! Would I be more careful to avoid sin because someone would know it so readily? Would my motivation to avoid sin decrease because of the way I would "look" to others? Do I think God overlooks my wrongdoings just because they can be kept secret from others? What does God think of my sin? What happened in the grocery store certainly caused me to pause and reevaluate my heart attitude! How about you?

Let's Pause for Prayer

Dear Lord, we ask for Your forgiveness for being more concerned about what others think about our sin than what You think about it, for worrying more about the sin of others than our own sin, than my sin. I want to please You, Lord, and I need Your help to show me my sin and to develop a heart that is concerned for my sinful ways. I know You see and know my heart. I want it to be pure, but I can only do so with Your help. May I present to You only pure motives and attitudes so that I can reflect who You are in my life. In Jesus' name we pray. Amen.

How would you feel if you had to wear your wrongdoings and sin as a label across your forehead?

_____

_____

_____

What sinful actions or wrongdoing comes first to your mind that you will confess and from which you will turn away? How will you begin to turn away from and stop committing that sin?

_____

_____

_____

Day 11   *How Committed Are You?*

"In the morning, O Lord, Thou wilt hear my voice; In the morning I will order my prayer to Thee and eagerly watch."

Psalm 5:3

As I meet with women (and as my husband meets with men) about their desire to be disciples through God's word, I often ask what their present commitments are as well as how often they spend time when Bible study and in prayer. Knowing that discipline is needed to prepare for a weekly lesson if we're discipling someone, it concerns us that many admit to seldom having a daily time for Bible reading and prayer. When asked why that doesn't happen, the usual answer is "I don't have enough time." They might be active in an array of activities, even weekly Bible study, working full- or part-time beyond their at-home responsibilities, serving others, meeting the needs of their children and spouse, and engaging in church ministry. Not one activity could we say is negative.

But if scripture is supposed to be our spiritual food, why do we choose not to be nourished by it? When was the last time you missed a regular meal? How long do you go without real food? How long could we go without real food? What would it take to be motivated to a committed daily quiet time of Bible reading and prayer?

Let's Pause for Prayer

Lord, if only I could be as motivated to seek nourishment from Your spiritual food as I seek satisfaction from my three daily meals—and snacks! If only I took seriously my personal relationship with you. My life could be full of "if onlys" as I stay busy with life but never learn to know You well. I ask Your forgiveness for neglecting to come to You daily. Help me discern what to change in my daily schedule that seems so urgent that I neglect what You desire most—time with me. May I commit myself to a time of Bible reading and prayer each and every day! In Jesus' name we pray. Amen.

What is keeping you from spending daily time in Bible study and prayer?

_____

_____

_____

What will you do today to recommit and initiate a daily quiet time of prayer and Bible reading and study?

_____

_____

_____

Day 12 — *Gifted*

> *"And do not neglect doing good and sharing; for with such sacrifices God is pleased."*
> Hebrews 13:16

God has gifted each one of us uniquely so that His will can be done at all times for His glory. Those who are gifted in teaching can give of their time and talents by instructing others. Those gifted in administration will organize tasks and keep things running smoothly. A person gifted in serving will delight in doing for others and generally take no credit! We know that we are made able by Christ to use any of His gifts at various times in our walk with Him.

I believe God has given me the gift of encouragement, but using just the specific gift He has given me doesn't mean I shouldn't or can't use other gifts He has bestowed upon all His children. If He wants me to teach, He will allow me to encourage and exhort as I teach. We should employ the gifts when need arises. And where we recognize need and we are willing, He will supply all that is necessary for us to help!

Let's Pause for Prayer

Heavenly Father, thank You for the gifts you have given each of us. How unique it is that You've done this to accomplish Your purposes through us if we are but willing! We pray You would speak to each of us and help us remember to do good and share at all times so that You are pleased with us. Let us also recognize and appreciate the blessing of others having gifts different from our own. Allow us to welcome their gifts and work together to "get the job done"! We don't want to be critical of how or what others do because their gifts differ from ours, but we desire to work together for Your purposes. In Jesus' name we pray. Amen.

What is your primary spiritual gift from the Lord and how do you use it?

_____

_____

_____

If you're not using it, how can you? If you are using it, are you effective? What could you do to use your gift better to please the Lord?

_____

_____

_____

_____

Day 13 — *Always On Call*

> *"Call to Me, and I will answer you, and I will tell you great and might things."*
> Jeremiah 33:3

I enjoy modern technology. I love being able to mass produce copies on a copier, fax info in just a moment's time, email and work on the computer, connect with others through social media or a new phone that practically thinks for me; but my very favorite is an answering device. My answering machine or voice mail takes the calls I can't get to when I'm unavailable. And when I make calls, I love getting the recorded message on the other end! I can leave a brief message and know it will be heard later. I don't love it, however, when I need to speak directly to the person I'm trying to reach—when it's urgent—and I can't get through.

What if we heard a recorded message when we decided to connect with God? What if we heard His voice on a message system, or one of His angels on the recording saying, "I'm sorry, but the Lord can't take your prayer request right now. If you'd like to leave your name and request, He'll get back to you when He has a moment. Thank you and have a nice day." How thankful we can be that He would never put us on hold!

Let's Pause for Prayer

Heavenly Father, we are so thankful that You are always on call—never too busy, never asleep, and always available. I want to practice coming to you for all my needs and for all the joys I experience as well as to talk to you throughout the day about whatever comes to my mind. I am grateful for Your willingness to hear from me no matter what time of day it is. Thank you for always being available to listen. Please help me to be available to hear what You have to tell me because I want to be a good listener, too! In Jesus' name we pray. Amen.

Do you pray daily and even moment to moment to the Lord?

_____

_____

_____

What can you can do today to deepen your prayer life with your Lord and Savior?

_____

_____

_____

_____

Day 14

Our Sexualized Culture

"Blessed are the pure in heart, for they shall see God."

Matthew 5:8

Our culture has become highly sexualized. "Exactly what was that sexy commercial selling?" Joe and I often ask each other. For us, I guess the tactic didn't work. As I browse through magazines, I see people wearing less and less clothing to make some kind of point I'm simply not buying into!

Campuses sponsor Sex Weeks. Engaged couples, more than ever, live together before marriage because they have bought into the Hollywood lifestyle. "Friends with benefits" is a common expression designating a behavior of the high school-aged and younger. Bad habits, or sin, might provide short-term pleasure but also often leave long-lasting consequences. Thinking ahead and making different decisions can spare us the long-term (and often negative) consequences. People often wake up to this sexualized culture and its consequences later in life. We see this phenomenon when we mentor couples who now have trouble dealing with baggage from their past. The remorse and struggle make them wish they could redo what has undone them.

Let's Pause for Prayer

Heavenly Father, in this sexualized culture, we know only You will satisfy any longings we have! I pray for You to protect and guide our children, steering them in the right direction, no matter which direction the culture takes them. Please make them leaders who will stand up for Your ways and help us teach and give them the understanding that they should wait for marriage to "give" themselves to another. Give them a future sense of what "no regrets" will look like someday by making them uncomfortable and uneasy in situations that might tempt and lure them into wrong relationships. In Jesus' name we pray. Amen.

Do you recognize the culture as highly sexualized? How will you counter this cultural trend?

_____

_____

_____

Turn off the TV for a week. Read a book, write notes of encouragement to others, connect with others by making a few phone calls. THEN after a week, turn the TV back on. Share what you find offensive in provocative commercials and shows that you had grown accustomed to but now affect you. What changes will you make as a result?

_____

_____

_____

Day 15

Do The Right Next Thing

"And whatever you do in word or deed, do all in the name of the Lord Jesus, giving thanks through Him to God the Father."

Colossians 3:17

"Do what's right and see what follows" would be a great thought for all of us to consider and practice. Often when our children were making decisions as youngsters or as young adults, we'd tell them to just take the next right step and see what happens. God doesn't lay out all the details and plans of our lives, I believe, so we can learn to trust Him and develop the ability to take one step at a time. Furthermore, when we plan to do the next right thing, we have a better opportunity to steer away from sin, wrong motives, and wrong directions because we're not trying to manipulate the future but seek Him and where He wants us to go. No one will live a life without struggle, hardship, or challenge; but at least if we're seeking the next right step, we'll head in a direction that offers us the satisfaction of knowing we did it with right thinking and motives and with the Lord and His ways in mind! I've heard it said, "I don't know anyone who's truly tried to seek God and who's had a life full of regrets." We might have struggles, but we won't have regrets!

Let's Pause for Prayer

Heavenly Father, I may experience struggles in life, but if I truly desire to seek You, I know those struggles are not the consequences of my sin but lessons from You, allowing me to learn and grow. I know it's easy to step away from Your will and head to the fast lane, wanting my own way; but as I listen and learn from You, I pray to trust You more and more and have less fear in taking that next step. Father, let me take a stand for doing right over wrong, good over evil, difficult over easy, serving over being served, and loving well through it all. Help me lead by example all who are watching. In Jesus' name we pray. Amen.

Write down something that you are praying about, considering, or contemplating. Be specific.

_____

_____

_____

_____

_____

Pray and ask for the Lord's direction and guidance and record what you believe to be the next right step to take.

Day 16

Self Is Ugly

"Do nothing from selfishness or empty conceit, but with humility of mind let each of you regard one another as more important than himself: Do not merely look out for your own personal interests, but also for the interest of others. Have this attitude in yourselves which was also in Christ Jesus."

Philippians 2:3

The sin of "self" is really quite ugly. Most of us can write a long list of that "self" sin we see in others! Sin like

- Taking and having no desire to offer to give or help others
- Wanting only to be heard but never asking others about them
- Spending unnecessary and excessive time on personal care to the point of vanity
- Taking care of one's own needs without concern that someone else might have a need
- Needing and demanding to be the center of attention
- Failing to appreciate, give thanks, or show gratitude

Although it's easy to point out what we see in others, we know that all of us from time to time behave selfishly, want our own way, and find our own actions on the list above. Some practice will be required to detect our own sin and to develop the desire to do something about it.

Let's Pause for Prayer

Heavenly Father, we want to do what You ask of us in Your word. Thank you for Your word, which so clearly teaches and guides us. Lord, help me to consider others first, to ask others about themselves, being sure to listen without reloading too quickly to blast a reply about ourselves or demanding to be the center of attention. Lord, let me appreciate others who've given to me and offered their time, energy, and talents in a giving and self-sacrificing way. I pray I would be sure to thank them and let them know their deed was appreciated. May I observe and listen without interrupting in a way that others know I really care and have concern for them. In Jesus' name we pray. Amen.

Even though it may be tough to admit, what is something you do that is selfish?

_____

_____

How can you take this selfish act and find a way to put others first, talking and sharing with them?

_____

_____

Day 17 — *Sin Draws Us In: To Ourselves*

> *"Therefore, confess your sins to one another, and pray for one another, so that you may be healed. The effective prayer of a righteous man can accomplish much."*
>
> James 5:16

Have you ever noticed that sin has a way of drawing us into ourselves? Perhaps you've observed it in others as well as personally. When people know they're wrong, have sinned, or are in a place of sin, they often stop communicating with others—especially if those others will hold them accountable. They are often embarrassed by their sin, knowing they're wrong.

We can spackle the cracks in our walls, sand them, and cover them with a coat of paint; but if there is a structural issue, the crack will reappear. Sin is much the same: We can put on smiling faces, laugh at jokes, and steer conversations in other directions away from our sin; but the sin will be revealed at some time and become visible. Sometimes the consequence of that sin will be invisible, but God will always expose it.

Let's Pause for Prayer

Heavenly Father, please help us to get out of our place of sinfulness, bitterness, and anger. If I need to confess my sin to another person and to You, please reveal to me exactly to whom and how to make it happen. Give me a gentleness of spirit and humility to make right where I have wronged. Where I have been sinned against, let me forgive even though I want to hold on to that hurt and punish the other person. I know that by holding on to it, I hurt, too. Give me the ability to forgive and grant forgiveness often so that I can be renewed spiritually and have a sense of proper function with the others in my life. I know even my countenance will change when I "get right" with others and You. Nudge me to make the right next choice when I know I am wrong even if my part of the wrong is 1%. Help me make the first move to reconciliation. In Jesus' name we pray. Amen.

What sin came to mind as you read this lesson? Does it involve a person with whom you need to have a conversation and ask for forgiveness?

_____

_____

_____

What will you do to clear this sin from your conscience? When will you follow through and ask for forgiveness? Share what you did.

_____

_____

_____

Day 18 — *Waiting Is Not Easy*

> *"Now faith is the assurance of things hoped for, the conviction of things not seen."*
> Hebrews 11:1

Is there anything in your life at this moment that requires faith?

If you are a believer, I'd like to think that something popped into your mind right away. Are you in a difficult marriage and by faith staying the course to try to make it work? Are you caring for a loved one who is ill, requiring your care and assistance, and by faith walking that journey? Are you without work or waiting to have a child or sitting in a hospital waiting for the outcome of a loved one's surgery or chemotherapy treatment, trusting by faith that someday God will answer your prayer. There seems to be an aspect of *waiting* where faith is concerned. Faith, as scripture points out, involves an element of hopefulness and what seems to be a lot of confidence (assurance) as well as the knowledge that it's something we can't see!

Let's Pause for Prayer

Heavenly Father, it is so difficult to wait for the answer to a prayer. I know it will take the faith only You can provide for me to wait patiently and seek Your will earnestly. Waiting doesn't always bring me hope, but I pray as I learn to better trust You, that I'll understand the beauty of the time I spend waiting. Help me to appreciate what I am learning. Help me to see the beauty of Your design in Your plan. I desire to ask for Your understanding in my circumstances. Lord, I don't want to rush You or test You because the more I know You, the better I know Your timing is perfect and Your ways are pure. In Jesus' name we pray. Amen.

What came to mind that requires you to have faith at this time? Is this time of waiting difficult?

_____

_____

_____

What will you do to put your faith into action today?

_____

_____

_____

_____

Day 19 — Are You All In?

> *"But his delight is in the law of the Lord, and in His law he meditated day and night. And he will be like a tree firmly planted by streams of water."*
>
> Psalm 1:2-3a

Does the Lord have all of you or just part of you?

People who are really "all in" for the Lord are those who are more concerned about others than themselves and want to serve and give even when it's uncomfortable. These people will think about heaven and will be real with God when it comes to their emotions, frustrations, joys, and challenges. They'll want to have a close and vibrant relationship with God.

When you hear this, do you feel that you are all in for the Lord? Is your dedication totally and wholly for Him, or do you feel something is lacking? Is something missing from your dedication? And what will it take for you to be the one who is found serving and giving? Do you see a significant gap in your life? Is it a long jump from where you are to where He wants you to be? Will you choose total obedience or stay comfortable on the sidelines of Christian life?

Let's Pause for Prayer

Heavenly Father, these questions and thoughts are good for each of us to ponder. Total obedience to You will cost me something. It will cost me the loss of myself and what I want. It will mean taking risks to be who You want me to be and to serve those you want me to serve. Father, this can be a frightening place for those who've not totally surrendered to You. Help each of us trust You, knowing You will bring us to a new place of service to You. I want a close relationship with You, not just a commonplace acquaintance. What a privilege to be able to have You, our Mighty God, as our Father and also our Friend! May I find serving delightful and energizing, so I want to do so all the more. Help me to engage with the people in the places You are asking of me so I'll be most effective for You. In Jesus' name we pray. Amen.

Does the Lord have all of you or just part of you?

_____

_____

What will your next step be to assure that the Lord has all of you? Are you willing?

_____

_____

_____

_____

Day 20

Anxiety And Stress

"Cast all your anxiety on Him because He cares for you."

I Peter 5:7

Stress! How do you feel when you're stressed? We may feel our blood pressure rise as our hearts beat faster. We may become so frustrated and upset that we take it out on others. We may even worry.

What do you do when you're stressed? Some people jog or do other forms of exercise. Some talk to friends. Some stop everything and get quiet.

Our lifestyles tend to indicate that we are ALL stressed! Although we can't eliminate stress completely from our lives, we certainly can make a decision about what to do with it!

We often pray as a last resort instead of a first response. The Lord is able to handle all of our stress. He can take our stress and troubles and allow us to focus on what's really important and concentrate less on what is trivial. He can prioritize and balance our lives and help us to see just what He wants us to learn through stressful times. When He teaches us in this way, we learn that stress isn't all bad. He is the one who can change our thinking, our priorities, and even our circumstances. Are you willing to let Him?

Let's Pause for Prayer

Heavenly Father, your word says We can cast our cares and anxieties upon You. When I feel the welling up of an anxious thought or feeling, please help me to remember to call upon You as a first response, instead of a last resort. Let me always recognize Your hand in helping me. And let me remember to thank you for this opportunity to quiet myself before You. Will you please quiet and calm my heart and change my stressful attitude to one of gratitude? Please help me to see Your purposes for me. Help me to see Your will for me, that I might serve You fully. Let me be an example, because I know others are always watching to see how I as believer handle life and its stressors. In Jesus' name we pray. Amen.

How often do you turn to prayer when you are under stress? Is it a first response or last resort?

_____

_____

_____

Think of a stressful area of your life at this moment. Ask the Lord to guide you in your stressful situations. Write it out.

_____

_____

_____

Day 21 *Indifference*

"You call me Teacher and Lord; and you are right; for so I am. If I then, the Lord and the Teacher, washed your feet, you also ought to wash one another's feet. For I gave you an example that you also should do as I did to you."

John 13:15

What kind of examples are we as Christians? Shouldn't we be examples as He was?

I am saddened by the indifference in our society. We have become indifferent to divorce, abortion, suicide, homicide, assisted suicide, lying, cheating, and so much more. Watching the news and people offers little hope when we hear of scandals, deception, faithlessness, and lies from public officials, many claiming to be Christians.

Sports figures are no exception. We indifferently turn our heads while those who should be positive role models are arrested for drug possession, abuse, and numerous other crimes.

We bring the indifference right into our own neighborhoods, schools, and homes as we turn our heads from the needs of those around us, pretending not to see broken marriages and troubled children.

This attitude troubles me. If we are indifferent to the behavior of international and national leaders and turn our heads when athletes exhibit antisocial behavior, we can easily fail to notice problems in our own spheres of influence—and in our own lives.

Let's Pause for Prayer

Lord, we apologize and ask for Your forgiveness for our indifference to the sin in our own lives and the sins of those elected to run our country at all levels. We want to follow the kinds of example You have been. Help us, help me to be an example. We pray for our leaders to come to know you as Lord and Savior and to serve as public servants, not politicians. We pray for sports figures or actors in the public eye to live morally and uprightly. For those who are to be the role models of our era in the public eye, may they take up the important role of living as the believers they claim to be. Lord, start with me. Show me my sin. I pray to be faithful and to be a role model to my family, my community, and anywhere You'd have me serve. In Jesus' name we pray. Amen.

What area of sin keeps you from being the kind of role model you could be to your family and friends? Confess that sin, turn away from it, and share what you will do to be a better role model.

_____
_____
_____
_____

Day 22

But I Didn't Want Flowers

"Bless the Lord, all you His hosts, You who serve Him, doing His will."

Psalm 103:21

My husband is great about following through with tasks like phone calls and correspondence and especially faithful about following through with what I put on the to-do list at home.

How would I feel if after looking at the to-do list, he brought me a bouquet of flowers instead of completing the tasks on the list? I know how I would feel! I would feel as if he didn't care about my request, which was important to me. I would feel that he just wanted to do something that looked good as opposed to accomplishing what was needed. Thankfully, he isn't like that.

Aren't we sometimes like that with God? We know He is asking us to do something, and yet we decide that it's not exactly what we want to do—so we choose something else that looks better. Well, at least for whatever reason, we think it looks better. Aren't we merely handing the Lord a bouquet of sorts, something that outwardly looks good but doesn't meet the need that He had in mind?

Let's Pause for Prayer

Lord, Jesus, I thank You that I can humbly come to You and ask You to reveal to me what You want me to do. May I listen so carefully and obey so fully that I will sense Your blessing as I serve You in whatever capacity You choose. I don't want to hand You a bouquet of good works that looks good outwardly to everyone but You. Thank You for the way You will use me to further Your kingdom. May I be faithful! In Jesus' name we pray. Amen.

How might God want to use you and even bless you if you simply chose to fulfill His requests?

_____
_____
_____
_____

What do you miss by choosing your own way?

_____
_____
_____

Day 23 — *Concern And Compassion?*

> *"Put on a heart of compassion, kindness, humility, gentleness, and patience; bearing one another."*
>
> Colossians 3:12-13

Sadly, two qualities—concern and compassion—seem to be in short supply these days. In fact, I wonder in my own heart how much concern and compassion I truly have.

We commonly ask questions like "How are you?" and hear the programmed response, "Fine." We ask other questions like "What's new?" and get more programmed responses. Do we ask questions because we want to appear kind, or do we ask because we are truly concerned and compassionate?

Some people don't even ask those typical questions. Have you noticed? Do they not want to know the answers? After all, how would we respond if someone told us honestly how they were? Would we ask the next question that encourages people to share their hearts, or would we avoid doing so, not wanting to take the time to care or become involved? And what would happen if their responses caused us to have to do something, perhaps take some type of action? A deeper level of friendship and commitment would be required.

Let's Pause for Prayer

Heavenly Father, when I brush off standard questions like "How are you?" and quickly move to the next meaningless question, I do not really encourage an honest response from others. Please help me this very day to show genuine concern and compassion for others by asking them how they really are and expressing patience and care as they tell me. Help me to take further action, if needed. May I not be rushed to do what I need but to take a moment to see how I might fill the need of another. Give me genuine concern for others. Give me passion and compassion to help and serve others. I desire to show Your concern and compassion. In Jesus' name we pray. Amen.

Can I accept the challenge to show true Christian concern and compassion? Am I willing to do so today? How?

_____

_____

_____

_____

Day 24 — *Procrastination*

"He who watches the wind will not sow, and he who looks at the clouds will not reap... Sow your seed in the morning, and do not be idle in the evening, for you do not know whether morning or evening sowing will succeed, or whether both of them alike will be good."

Ecclesiastes 11: 4, 6

Procrastination—a fault to avoid just as we try to avoid what we know we should do! Many procrastinate because they fear failure. We sometimes procrastinate because we don't want or like to do the very thing we should. Sometimes we procrastinate by putting our least favorite activity at the bottom of the list, conveniently never having the time to do it. Sometimes we wait for perfect conditions that will allow us to do the job. No matter how we look at it, procrastinating is avoiding; and if we are avoiding what God is asking us to do, that is sin.

We can't know what will happen as a result of our obedience, but we know that if we are faithful in doing what He asks, He will allow that activity to succeed and be of use and purpose. May we not procrastinate or hesitate to do whatever He asks us to do.

Let's Pause for Prayer

Heavenly Father, I am so sorry for procrastinating and putting off the very thing you have clearly told me to do. I desire to follow through immediately when I sense You are guiding and giving me direction. I don't want to wait for what I expect will be perfect conditions. Help me to be faithful to do Your will this moment and no longer make procrastination my way of life. I truly want to do anything and everything that You ask because I know You have only the best in mind for me. I don't want to question, be overly concerned, fearful, or afraid of anything You give me to do. In Jesus' name we pray. Amen.

Can you admit that you procrastinate? What are the tell-tale signs that you are procrastinating? How does it look?

_____

_____

_____

What one thing will you do today that you've had on your list and have been putting off and procrastinating? When will you accomplish it?

_____

_____

_____

Day 25

Upside Down Way Of Life

> *"My little children, I am writing these things to you that you many not sin. And if anyone sins, we have an Advocate with the Father, Jesus Christ the righteous: and He Himself is the propitiation for our sins; and not for our sin only but also for those of the whole world."*
>
> I John 2:1-2

Indeed the Gospel seems to be UPSIDE DOWN:

- It's a call to sinners not to the righteous.
- Even those who are good still need a Savior to save them from their sin.
- It tells us to give without expecting to receive.
- Loving your enemies is a key.

This kind of Gospel is taught by example. We need to show others how to love an enemy instead of merely telling her or him how to do it, teaching how to give and serve with gladness—and without expectation it will ever be returned. It must all be modeled. To appear as if we have it all together isn't righteousness but self-righteousness. No Christian has it all together. We are sinners who need Jesus Christ to save us from sin.

Let's Pause for Prayer

Heavenly Father, although we may try to hide our sin to appear righteous and as one who has it all together, we know that we are not perfect and need a Savior. I need You. May I face my sin, own up to it, admit to it, and confess it. I need to share with humility and transparency that I have failed, confess to others (and You), and repent (turn away from my sin) as an example to others and to show You that I'm serious about my relationship with You. Forgive me when I act like a know-it-all, who admits no mistake or error or sin. Show me when I sin. Keep my mind on my own sin and not the sin of others. Deal with me, and I'll let You deal with others. I thank You that You tenderly teach and guide us. I don't want to be arrogant or self-righteous in dealing with what I know to be sin. In Jesus' name we pray. Amen.

What sin has God brought to mind for you to confess? (Be specific.) How will you confess it to Him? If you've wronged someone in the process of this sin, how will you confess it to her or him?

_____

_____

_____

_____

_____

Day 26 — *Lead*

> *"But whoever wished to become great among you shall be your servant."*
>
> Matthew 20:26

Leadership happens through servanthood. Those who want to be the kingpin seldom become real leaders. It's when we're willing to do any and all of the work that needs to be done that leadership skills are developed and servanthood is then shown by love in action. It's not entitlement, which demands elevation to a position and even status. Without work, serving others, and taking on responsibilities, all of which are necessary for a servant–leader, one will not become a leader in the true sense of the word.

Let's Pause for Prayer

Lord, thank You for Your word, "But whoever wishes to become great among you shall be your servant, and whoever wishes to be first among you shall be your slave; just as the Son of Man did not come to be served but to serve and to give His life a ransom for many" (Matt. 20:26b-28), which teaches us to humble ourselves before You and before others. Help us, Lord, to desire to be servants like you were. May we show love toward others by caring for and about them through serving, performing acts of kindness, noticing needs, and recognizing when we can provide what someone else needs. We want to serve like You served and with total willingness. May we honor others before ourselves and learn to be humble by implementing more of others, less of ourselves; more of Jesus, less of us. Let us recognize maturity isn't about being the kingpin but instead about being one who is willing to do whatever is needed whenever it's needed. We want our hearts, souls, and minds to be surrendered to You so that in every situation we will surrender our wills to Yours and humble ourselves to do what You ask. In Jesus' name we pray. Amen.

Think of someone who has served well in a leadership role. Jot down a few qualities that made them a good example of a leader.

_____

_____

_____

_____

Pray for those in leadership over you (at work, in ministry, etc.), and if you are the leader, pray for God to help you to do the best job you can.

Day 27   *Mind Your Own Business*

"Like one who takes a dog by the ears is he who passes by and meddles with strife not belonging to him."

Proverbs 26:17

"Mind your own business!" cascaded from my mother's lips like a waterfall when we were kids. The expression covered a variety of areas of life: learning not to tattle, spread gossip, or meddle into the affairs of other people when they didn't concern us. Mom didn't stick her nose into the dealings of others, and she set a good example! It takes time and practice to mind our own business, learning from our mistakes.

Let's Pause for Prayer

Father, we appreicate Your instruction in Proverbs 26:17, "Like one who takes a dog by the ears is he who passes by and meddles with strife not belonging to him." We strive to be in Your word, studying it in such way that we learn to live as You want us to live. We want to take note mentally and spiritually about what we should or shouldn't do. We want to mind our own business so that we will be people of integrity, not desiring to know more information than what concerns us and certainly not giving advice or telling others what to do when it's not our concern. When others ask our advice, may we come in prayer to You so that our words to them will be Your business and not ours. Help us lead others to You so they can learn to do the same. May we not take information others have shared with us and share it without their permission. May we not snoop and pry into the affairs of others just because we want to be in the know, or worse, because we want to use information to unfair advantage over others. Help us mind our own business because we know we have much on our own plates to keep us plenty busy without interfering in the lives of others. In Jesus' name we pray. Amen.

Think of a time you meddled or tried to work things out to your own advantage. How did it go? Did you learn anything from the lesson?

___

___

___

___

How can you or will you mind your own business if failing to do so has been a problem for you?

___

___

___

Day 28

Comfort And Routine

> *"Woe to those who are at ease."*
>
> Amos 6:1

Sometimes we get so set in our daily routines and comforts that we can say we're at a point of maintenance. This verse from Amos warns people who are at ease and comfortable but need to pay attention to what might happen to their city. I can't truthfully do so all the time, but I love being able to say, "It's comfortable" or "It's predictable" even if only for a short time. It's pleasant but unrealistic for the long haul. We can't live in ongoing maintenance, but it certainly would be nice if we could. We need to pay attention.

Let's Pause for Prayer

Father, we want to enjoy those moments when life seems to be at a point of maintenance: All is going well and smoothly like the well-oiled cogs of a machine. It's nice to have those times, and we are grateful for them because they give us time to regroup, refresh, and then reengage in real life. Lord, help us to recognize when You want us to reengage in the mission You have for us, whether it's helping a neighbor in need, a family member requiring assistance, or a coworker or ministry partner who needs attention. Let us be mindful of intentionally moving from maintenance to mission, from comfort, ease, and fun to fulfillment and purpose. Let us get our coasting vehicle out of neutral and use the gas pedal to get moving in the mission to which You've called us—in our day and in our life. May we not grow comfortable in such a way that we refuse to be challenged or feel content to sit and watch others in the game. Let us be fully involved and engaged in Your work. Bring us alongside like-minded others and help us to be good leaders as well as good followers. Wherever You put us, let us be about serving even if it's not comfortable, easy, or fun. In Jesus' name we pray. Amen.

Consider a time when you might have been "sliding" in life with everything going smoothly. When life is easy and comfortable for you, are you happy there or do you look for ways to serve at that time? Share a prayer that can prepare you to serve.

_____

_____

_____

_____

_____

Day 29 — *Balancing Life*

> *"A false balance is an abomination to the Lord, but a just weight is His delight."*
>
> Proverbs 11:1

Not everyone agrees with the idea of balancing life. I admit to being one who thinks balance is worth working toward. For me it's not a matter of perfection, total stillness, or absence of trouble or challenges but a state of peace. It's making sure there's joy and laughter alongside the hardship and tears. It's working to play as hard as we work, and it's reconciling time with people and projects and time alone. We have balance in nature, and we balance our checkbooks. Why not life?

Let's Pause for Prayer

Lord, we choose to honor You with our lives in all ways, accepting all You send us and also accepting that which You withhold. We want to observe the ways You teach us to balance lives that lack balance because of sin, ignoring You, or simple lack of awareness of how to work at keeping life in balance. We know that Your word says, "A false balance is an abomination to the Lord, but a just weight is His delight" (Proverbs. 11:1). Whether we're talking about money, time, or life, we know You want us to experience joy-filled days and to embrace hardship, knowing You'll see us through it. We know You will guide us through the times we're not seeing clearly or making the right choices. Help us recognize when we need to take a break and let us not feel guilty when we do. May we be thankful for the fun we enjoy and may we also give thanks for trials because we know you'll guide us through them. Help us to keep life in perspective, in balance, and allow us to welcome and fully accept all that comes from Your hands to ours. We want to keep in step with You so we aren't tipping the balance too far to one extreme or the other. Keep us balanced with thankfulness and appreciation. In Jesus' name we pray. Amen.

Do you feel you can or cannot work at balancing life?

_____

_____

_____

In what ways would you like to see more balance in your life? Ask the Lord specifically in prayer to help you in problem areas.

_____

_____

_____

_____

Day 30

Writing Of Books Is Endless

> *"Beyond this, my son, be warned: The writing of many books is endless, and excessive devotion to books is wearying to the body. The conclusion, when all has been heard, is fear God and keep His commandments because this applies to every person."*
>
> Ecclesiastes 12:12-13

If the writing of books is endless, consider all the words on our computers! The writing of blogs and information sent on social media is literally endless. Blogs are enjoyable and often informative. Books are wonderful. Stories can be entertaining, even give us the how-to in dealing with difficulties in our lives. They can inform, instruct, and encourage us. But with all the works on bookstore shelves, one we must never neglect is also entertaining, informative, and encouraging and gives us all the how-to we need in life. It's the Bible.

It's often easier to sit down at our computer, pick up a novel or newspaper, and let the Bible sit. Perhaps it's because the Bible, which is God's word, has a way of getting into our heart and teaching us things that can be difficult and challenging. But if we're going to read words that are meaningful and helpful, we must not neglect reading from God's word.

Let's Pause for Prayer

Heavenly Father, I desire to learn and grow. Enjoyable authors may help me do so, but please let me never neglect Your word, the Holy Bible. Please help me desire to read your word daily. Give me a hunger and thirst for what You teach in Your word. I want to so desire it that I can't live without it. I want it to be food for my soul. I might enjoy the computer and books, but I want most of all to enjoy what I read in Your book. I want to make it the first and top priority of my day to hear from You! In Jesus' name we pray. Amen.

Are you more devoted to other reading material than you are to the Bible? What is your weak spot?

_____
_____
_____

What will be your plan—starting today—to read from God's word daily?

_____
_____
_____

Day 31

In God We Trust

"Trust in the Lord forever, for in God the Lord, we have an everlasting Rock."

Isaiah 26: 4

Our forbearers incorporated God into political writings, religious hymns, and most importantly—everyday life. They even put "In God We Trust" on our currency! They recognized that America needed to surrender to Him in order to prosper and succeed as a new nation. They came to this new land to be free—in their religious expression and in life. The names God, Jesus, and Lord were everyday words.

Today when we say the name of God, the Lord, or Jesus, opposition and uncomfortable feelings are often the result. Have you noticed that Christian celebrations like Christmas or Easter are going through a transition? Now Christmas vacation is winter break. Easter break is spring break. Anything religious or related to God is no longer politically correct.

Libraries defend their right to have questionable literature, even pornography on the Internet, claiming freedom of speech and ideas. When I've been asked as a Christian to speak in public libraries, I've also been asked not to share my faith too openly; yet time and time again, people will ask just the right questions, leading me to share my faith. In a few cases, after meetings, I have been able to share Christ with them. God will always have His way!

Let's Pause for Prayer

Heavenly Father, as Christians, we need to take a stand and be bold in our speech and actions as we defend You everywhere! I don't want to shrink back when I can defend my faith. We not only have a right but also a responsibility to use our freedom of speech to be bold for You, Lord! I want to be as bold as our forefathers to defend the name of Jesus! Lord Jesus, I exalt Your name above all names. May I not be ashamed of Your name or your message. In God we trust! In Jesus' name we pray. Amen.

Are you embarrassed or reluctant to say or use the name of Christ, Jesus, or Lord in public? Why or why not?

In what ways can you share your faith and use the name of Christ with others? When and how will you put that into practice even today?

Day 32

How Will They Know?

> *"For whoever will call upon the name of the Lord will be saved. How then shall they call upon Him in whom they have not believed? And how shall they believe in Him whom they have not heard? And how shall they hear without a preacher? And how shall they preach unless they are sent? Just as it is written, 'How beautiful are the feet of those who bring glad tidings of good things!'"*
>
> Romans 10:13-15

I recall reading an article about a young girl who had lost both her parents in a tragic car accident. After their death she attended a neighborhood church and learned the way of salvation and eternity in heaven with Jesus. Upset to realize that her parents had probably never made the decision to know and serve Christ, she wrote a letter to the church saying that even though they lived close to the church, NO ONE ever came to tell them about Jesus. She then called them hypocrites. I'm not sure if the congregation lacked concern, compassion, time, or the proper tools to share Christ with this family, but clearly there was a missed opportunity.

The kind of letter this gal wrote to her neighborhood church should call us to action!

We really have no excuse. God Himself calls us to share the Good News with others. In addition, we have films, brochures, tracts, classes, and churches nearby that can encourage people to learn about Jesus; but without someone to share the message, how else might one know about Him?

Let's Pause for Prayer

Lord, we want to see others come to know You. Show me the words to share, the tools to use, the compassion to show that I care and love others; and reveal to me personally those individuals or groups to whom You would like me to reach out. May no one in my sphere of influence die and go to hell because I didn't reach out to tell them about You! Please help me to have the concern, compassion, and time to tell others about You! Show me the points in my day that give me the time to pursue others. I don't want to have any shallow excuses when I stand before You for my failure to share You with others. In Jesus' name we pray. Amen.

Has the Lord brought to mind anyone with whom to share His gospel? Who is it?

_____

_____

What is your next step in developing a relationship and sharing the Good News with others?

_____

_____

_____

Day 33 — *Playing It Safe*

> *"Praise the Lord! Praise the Lord from the heavens, praise Him in the heights!"*
>
> Psalm 148:1

Heights never used to bother me until one day I traipsed to the end of a natural stone bridge while vacationing in Arizona. From my viewpoint, it looked perfectly safe. My husband's viewpoint was quite different—he could see the drop—and it was not safe for me to be where I was. He kept gently and calmly trying to get me to come back to safety. All the while I was being silly, thinking he was trying to spoil my fun! All he wanted me to do was play it safe and have me return to safety.

"Playing it safe!" is a phrase that often conveys much wisdom and may be a good warning for some things in life; but when it comes to sharing the Gospel, it is definitely not applicable! In such cases, we must take that leap of faith and overcome obstacles with perseverance, even standing in a place with no safety net, where we are able to offer others the opportunity to see the beauty we see.

Let's Pause for Prayer

Heavenly Father, I am so thankful that I know You and can enjoy the beautiful things in Christian life that You have given me. I want to share it with others. I want others to know You as I do and understand all that You do for us. Help me to have the courage to share my faith, to stand in places that might be a little frightening, to be open with people with whom I might not normally have contact, and to serve in new places where I can share my faith. Would You please help me to take the next challenging step, perhaps out of my comfort zone and place of safety to share Your Gospel with others? I want to pursue the course less traveled to a deeper level of commitment to you, and I want to be excited about where You will take me. Thank you for the privilege of being able to serve You and share You! In Jesus' name we pray. Amen.

Are you playing it safe? What obstacles are keeping you from sharing the Gospel with others?

_____

_____

_____

Do you share the Gospel just far enough to feel good about it but never ask for a decision, thus missing the beauty of seeing a new life in Christ?

_____

_____

_____

Day 34

It's Never Too Late

"For he will not often consider the years of his life because God keeps him occupied with the gladness of his heart."

Ecclesiastes 5:20

This Bible verse makes me think that we won't have to worry about growing older if we stay occupied doing His will. As we remain active in God's work, it will never be too late to start new and stimulating activities that will actually give us excitement and energy!

Golda Meir became prime minister of Israel at 71. Grandma Moses started painting at 80; then she went on to finish 1,500 paintings, a quarter of them after her 100th birthday. Thelma Pitt Turner of New Zealand completed the Hastings Marathon in 7 hours and 58 minutes at the age of 82. Jessica Tandy won an Oscar for Driving Miss Daisy. She was 88.

So what are we waiting for? It may not be to hold public office, paint a masterpiece, run a marathon, or win an Oscar; but we can pray for our neighbors, take time to listen to someone's heartache, or meet a need for someone we find unlovable. It's never too late to seek what He's calling us to do. No matter our age, we don't know how many days we have left. We can be young with only days to live—and that makes us very old in life.

Let's Pause for Prayer

Heavenly Father, You don't tell us how much time we have, but whatever amount of time You've given me, I desire only to do Your will today and every day so that I don't look back with regrets at what might have been and say, "It's too late." Lord, please redirect and reprioritize my life in the areas that I need. Allow me to see life in a new and different way so that I can see needs around me or even take a new direction of learning and growing and meeting others so I can share You with others! Lord, it's never too late until my days are over. Even when I am old, I may have many more years to live. Let none of us waste those precious years! I may be young and not even realize it! Help me serve You with gladness and enthusiasm until You call me home. In Jesus' name we pray. Amen.

Are you an older person but feel very young and vibrant or a younger person who feels old and "done" with life? Express those thoughts.

_____
_____
_____

What is God telling you to do while He is still giving you the time to do it?

_____
_____

Day 35 — What's My Assignment?

> *"And whatever you do in word or deed, do all in the name of the Lord Jesus, giving thanks through Him to God the Father."*
>
> Colossians 3:17

It may be years since we've been in school and asked to complete an assignment. Do you remember when you had course descriptions and syllabi to show you what you had to complete? Have you considered that although you may not see your assignment on paper, you do indeed have one for this very day?

Why do you live where you live? Do you live there simply because you can afford it or perhaps because you can't afford anything else? No, it's because God has assigned you to be a lighthouse to your neighborhood and you are assigned there.

As Christians we need to know that wherever we are is our assignment! We might not be sent out as missionaries to a foreign country, but we are in our neighborhoods, in schools, in workplaces, and in community affairs because God has assigned us to share His love and His Gospel right where He put us. Our assignment is to show that Christ lives in us and that we are dedicated to tell about Him to everyone who will listen. That is our assignment and our job description!

Let's Pause for Prayer

Heavenly Father, please help us to recognize that where You have placed us is our assignment. Please help us to realize that we are to meet the needs of others in our spheres of influence and to tell others about You. Would you help me look for ways to pray for others and show others that I care about them? I don't want the needs of those around me to elude me, so please help me to see what I might be missing. Use the abilities and gifts You've given me to share my life and treasures with others. I want to recognize a need and strive to meet it with Your help and guidance. May I complete the assignment You have given me with grace! In Jesus' name we pray. Amen.

Why do you think you live and work where you are? Do you participate in community and civic affairs, neighborhood committees, school clubs, or other activities?

_____

_____

_____

Are these service venues or the assignments God has given you? How will you find your assignment in these places, and what will you do?

_____

_____

Day 36

SIN!

> *"For all have sinned and fall short of the glory of God."*
>
> Romans 3:23

Wearing the oldest pair of tennis shoes I had to a rainy Cleveland Indians game seemed better than wearing a new pair of walking shoes. The bottoms were worn but good for rain! Walking through puddles and in the rain, I realized that my right foot felt cold, then wet, indicating a hole, not just wear.

The hole had developed so slowly that it went quite unnoticed until the moment I walked through a puddle. Remedy: Change my sock and put on a new shoe!

This anecdote reminds me that we allow sin to creep into our lives and take hold. Little by little we disobey. Little by little we think we are getting away with sin. Before long, what may have been apparent to others (and certainly to God) becomes evident to us and we realize that something is wrong. We have a choice to make regarding that sin, and it needs attention NOW. We must make a conscious decision either to let sin have its way or turn from it to let God have His way. Repentance is changing our mind about what we are doing, changing the direction of the mind and heart, confessing the sin, and committing it no more.

Let's Pause for Prayer

Heavenly Father, we know that each one of us sins. Will you help each one of us individually to see clearly the area of sin that has taken hold of our lives and turn away from it? Help me to make the right choices and flee from sin. I know sin is costly: It affects those around me and it affects me. The consequences of every sin, whether we think it's a small or big one, cost each of us. Lord, I desire to confess my sin to You and turn away from it as I follow You. I don't want to hide from my sin but see it as clearly as You see it. I no longer want to hide from You because of my sin but desire to follow and serve You in the light! In Jesus' name we pray. Amen.

Has a particular sin taken hold in your life? Name it. Confess it, turn away from it, and ask the Lord to help You stop the sin cycle. Write out your prayer.

_____

_____

_____

_____

_____

_____

Day 37 — *Restoration*

> *"Then I will restore to you the years that the swarming locust has eaten."*
>
> Joel 2:25

Have you ever experienced summer locusts? Years ago as we moved into our new home with a wooded lot, we were told it was the year that the locusts were returning! They were everywhere, and it was impossible to walk anywhere without crunching them! Their sound was so loud, resembling an industrial air conditioner in full force! It was hard to get out of the car without being bombarded by them. It got to the point that we'd pull into the garage, shut the door, and then turn lights on as they swarmed around them, humming around our heads!

Soon, but perhaps not soon enough, the humming subsided. It then became evident the damage that had been done. Many of the trees had massive clumps of dead leaves. If you looked closely, you could see the many locust shells attached to them.

Joel 2 relates the locusts stripping God's people of everything. God allowed this to happen because of their sin. They needed to confess and repent (turn away from) their sin before God could do what He promised. In Joel 2:25 God said, "Then I will restore to you the years that the swarming locust has eaten." The key word seems to be *then*.

Let's Pause for Prayer

Heavenly Father, we thank You for the ways you speak to us through nature and through Your holy word. Help us to experience the need for turning back to You. Lord, please show me my sin that I might turn away from it and turn to You in full obedience. I know that sin plagues us just as the locusts were a plague upon the vegetation. I want my heart to be whole and pure and not ravaged by sin. I want to be restored and know that You promise that for us, if we ask! Just as trees will require many seasons to be repaired, it might take time for our hearts to be repaired; but we trust they will. Restore us to You, oh, Lord! In Jesus' name we pray. Amen.

What damage have I done through sinful behavior that later became clearly evident?

_____

_____

What would God restore in my life if I confessed and repented of my own sin?

_____

_____

Am I willing to repent of my sin so God can restore in my life what the sin has damaged?

_____

Day 38

Cooperation

"And whatever you do in word or deed, do all in the name of the Lord Jesus, giving thanks through Him to God the Father."

Colossians 3:17

It doesn't matter whether we are talking about adults or children, the truth is this: We all need to learn to work together!

If you knew how to swim and noticed someone drowning, would you sit by and watch? Would you casually walk and look around for the lifeguard until you found her or him and then point out the drowning victim? No doubt, you'd be yelling and gathering as much help as you could, lifeguard or not!

When it comes to serving others and performing ministry in the name of the Lord, when we see a need, we must put aside egos, ideas, and programs and work together to unify the body of Christ. Not until that happens can we then reach out to those around us. Christians and non-Christians alike are watching to see how Christians work together. How are we doing? (On second thought, don't answer that question. Just get busy!)

Let's Pause for Prayer

Heavenly Father, we are guilty when in our own communities we don't join together with other ministries for Your sake to share the love and salvation of Jesus with others. Please help each individual, each Christian church, organization, and parachurch ministry to work together in unity, helping to complete, not compete with one another. Challenge those who desire to promote their ideas and programs instead of promoting and sharing Jesus to a new sense of urgency to work with others who share the same faith. And on a personal level, let us include others with a cooperative spirit that says we are all worthy to be a part of the "plan"! Help me, Lord, to be inclusive of others, not "selecting" only those I like or only those who "fit in." Let us purposefully and actively support one another in love. In Jesus' name we pray. Amen.

As a Christian am I willing to work alongside another ministry, even if the ministry I represent doesn't get the credit, even if my ministry isn't front and center? Can I rejoice with other ministries and the people in them as I work with them, or will I watch from the sidelines, waiting for them to fail because the workers are too few?

_____

_____

Do I include or exclude others? Here is how I'll make a change:

_____

_____

_____

Day 39 — What's In A Name

> *"The name which is above all names... that at the name of Jesus every knee should bow... and every tongue should confess that Jesus Christ in Lord."*
>
> Philippians 2:9-11

A few years ago, to satisfy my own curiosity, I read about the origin and meaning of family crests. The crest served as a means of distinguishing individuals and thus, their family lines, name, birth order, and specifics about the individual.

Although family crests were displayed and worn by royalty, I thought it would be a fun family project to create our own! Although we would never qualify for royalty in the eyes of the world, we know from scripture that those who have received Jesus (the King) become His heirs. James 2:5 says, "My beloved brethren: Did not God choose the poor of this world to be rich in faith and heirs of the kingdom, which He promised to those who love Him?" We are royalty through Jesus Christ!

An artist friend rendered a crest for us that now hangs in our foyer as a constant reminder of who we are in Christ. Our prayer is that our family name would reflect our desire to live for Jesus and also reflect not who we are, but whose we are.

Let's Pause for Prayer

Lord Jesus, thank You for choosing us as Your heirs because we love and accept You. I am grateful that someday each one of us will bow to Your name. May I daily bow down to Your name. I am grateful that I can know You, the King of Kings as I pray to You, as I seek You, and as I serve You. I am grateful that although I am not royalty here on earth, I have inherited great gifts, salvation, and a place in heaven because of Your sacrifice on the cross and my acceptance of Your gift. In Jesus' name we pray. Amen.

Are you prepared to kneel before the Lord someday? If you have accepted Christ, did you know that you are royalty and an heir to Jesus Christ?

_____

_____

_____

Knowing now your position in Christ, how will you live differently?

_____

_____

_____

Day 40

No Greater Joy

"I have no greater joy than this, to hear of my children walking in the truth."

III John: 4

When we were young parents, we worked hard to point our children in the right direction. As young Christian parents, we guided our children in learning to pray, to make decisions in light of knowing Christ, and to seek after Him in all ways at all times. We wondered what our efforts would look like in the future.

My youngest, a recent college graduate asked whether she could have some friends over for the evening. I can't think of a time Joe or I ever said "no" to inviting others over, so of course we said, "Sure!" She then added, "Good, because we want to pray and need a place to hang out!"

My first thought was, "Wow, how wonderful that these young gals want to seek the Lord!" My second thought led me to the fourth verse in III John, which states, "I have no greater joy than this, to hear of my children walking in the truth." What a blessing it is to watch our children seek the Lord and walk in His truth!

Let's Pause for Prayer

Heavenly Father, thank the You for making Yourself real in the lives of our children. Please cultivate in their young and tender hearts a love for You and a desire to please You in all ways. As they mature and grow, may that love be rooted more deeply so they can serve You more fully in the professions or ministries to which You call them. We thank you for choosing us to raise them, but we give You all the glory for how You've helped guide us in the process of loving and caring for them through the years. We know we are, in and of ourselves, unable to adequately parent; but with You, all things are possible. Whether we are parenting young children or emptying our nest, give us the right words to encourage them to seek You. May we be an example to them, directly or indirectly, of walking with You and standing firm in you. In Jesus' name we pray. Amen.

Whether or not we are parents, we are "influencers." Answer this question: How am I influencing young people to pray?

_____
_____
_____

Am I an example of one who prays? Here is what I'm going to do be a better example of one who prays:

_____
_____
_____

Day 41 — *The Meaning Of Our Names*

"A good name is to be more desired than great riches, favor is better than silver and gold. The rich and the poor have a common bond; the Lord is the maker of them all."

Prov. 22: 1–2

"What's in a name?" Do you know the meaning of your name? Our names are important. They identify us. They tell a lot about us. Sometimes we choose to name our children after others because of the strength of their character. Sometimes we choose not to name our children after others whose names have negative connotations to us. We select a name carefully and desire to have the child grow into their given name.

The name of Jesus has so many meanings! Here are a few:

- Creator Comforter
- The Alpha and the Omega
- Son of Man
- King of Kings
- Lord of Lords
- Redeemer
- Savior
- Mighty God
- Everlasting Father
- Lamb of God
- All-Sufficient One
- Friend
- Wonderful Counselor
- Prince of Peace
- Most High
- Deliverer
- Healer
- Provider

We may not always live up to the name we are given, but we know that He has lived up to every one of His given names. "Holy and awesome is His name!" (Psalm 111:9).

Let's Pause for Prayer

Heavenly Father, although we may know Your name and recognize You as Truth, even know You as Deliverer, at some point, either now or in eternity, we will bend our knees as we submit ourselves to the King of Kings. Lord, help us to know You personally in all aspects of Your name. Help us to submit to You and serve You because You are a Mighty God. In Jesus' name we pray. Amen.

If you know the meaning of your name, share it. Do you live up to the meaning of your name?

_____

_____

With which name of Jesus do you most identify and why? What do you appreciate about that name?

_____

_____

_____

Day 42 *Getting Caught*

"Do not be deceived, God is not mocked; for whatever a man sows, this he will also reap. For the one who sows to his own flesh shall from the flesh reap corruption, but the one who sows to the Spirit shall from the Spirit reap eternal life. And let us not lose heart in doing good, for in due time, we shall reap if we do not grow weary."

Galatians 6: 7–9

My daughter's friends shared with me a situation when they got caught. They were sitting outdoors in a park—praying. As the night grew cold, they decided to hop into their van and huddle in the back to continue their prayer time. A while later, the police arrived and told them the particular area was closed and they would need to get moving! When asked what they were doing, the girls said, "Oh, sorry, officer, we lost track of time. We were praying." The surprised look on his face said, "Oh sure, you were praying." But when the girls prepared to drive away, he saw their open Bibles and said, "Wow, you really were praying!" I loved the policeman's surprise because I suspect he might have thought they were up to no good. I also suspect this might have been a really good example to the girls and the policeman of a different way to get caught!

Let's Pause for Prayer

Heavenly Father, we love when we can make You known. How sweet that these young ladies shared the importance of You in their lives without even setting out to do so! So innocently and honestly they were able to "get caught" in prayer. May I live life so openly and transparently that I'll get caught doing the right things for the right reasons. May I also take advantage of every opportunity to make You known to others and share with them who You are. May I leave others questioning whether they have the kind of faith in and relationship with You that is real and vibrant or whether they need to find You to achieve that relationship. May I not be ashamed to pray to You privately and publicly, and may I always take a courageous and bold stand for You! In Jesus' name we pray. Amen.

Are you able to pray openly and aloud? Why or why not?

_____

_____

Are you able to pray in a group or do you pray privately to the Lord in the quietness of your heart?

_____

_____

What might the next step be for you to deepen your prayer life?

_____

_____

Day 43

That Was A Lie!

> *"Also, do not take seriously all words which are spoken, lest you hear your servant cursing you. For you also have realized that you likewise have at times cursed others."*
>
> Ecclesiastes 7:21

Have you ever been accused of saying or doing something that simple wasn't true? Have you ever received a note or letter that was left unsigned, leaving you to draw your own conclusions as to the identity of the writer?

Most of us can probably say that each of those things has happened to us. How did you respond? How should we respond if we know and love the Lord?

I believe we can follow some principles when we have been accused of things or when we receive anonymous notes or letters. First of all, I personally do not read anything that comes to me unsigned. I throw it away and pray that the person who wrote it would have the courage to come to me in person. I, too, have been tempted to write a business or individual about something and leave it unsigned. But I also realize that God would not want me to do something that could potentially hurt others or leave them without a plan of action or help, which I should be willing to provide if I am taking the time to write them.

I also realize that scripture has something to say about what others say about us: "Also, do not take seriously all words which are spoken, lest you hear your servant cursing you. For you also have realized that you likewise have at times cursed others" (Eccl. 7:21). And because of this, we must all learn the value of Eccl. 3:7b—"A time to be silent, and a time to speak."

Let's Pause for Prayer

Heavenly Father, I pray that You would give me the courage of my convictions to speak to others—a close friend or one who curses me. May I be straightforward and not seek to be anonymous. I ask for forgiveness for saying things that are unkind or untrue. Please help me to right that wrong and ask forgiveness of those I have wronged. Give me the encouragement needed to help instead of hinder the work of fellow believers because of words used improperly or wrongly. Help me to promote unity among believers by building up instead of tearing down. In Jesus' name we pray. Amen.

Has someone told lies or gossiped about you? Describe the situation and how you felt.

_____

_____

If there is something you have done to hurt others, write it down, pray about ways to correct it, and go to that person and ask forgiveness. Share what happened here.

_____

_____

Day 44

Is Self-Prayer Selfish?

"Oh, that Thou wouldst bless me indeed, and enlarge my border, and that Thy hand might be with me, and that Thou wouldst keep me from harm, that it may not pain me!"

I Chronicles 4:10

Do you pray for yourself, or do you think that praying for yourself and asking the Lord for something for you is selfish? What does the Bible say about praying for yourself?

Tucked away in a lengthy genealogy is the prayer of Jabez as recorded in I Chronicles 4:10: "Oh that Thou wouldst bless me indeed, and enlarge my border, and that Thy hand might be with me, and that Thou wouldst keep me from harm, that it may not pain me!"

It is Biblical to ask the Lord to bless our work, our home, and any other situations we face.

It is Biblical to ask God to increase our ministry. It is from Him that we will be given the power, strength, and desire to do His will. Prayer is a key ingredient.

It is Biblical to ask to be kept from harm. As God expands our ministry, He sends us into enemy territory.

We need His protection from enemy attack. Let's come to the Lord and ask for what we need in our own lives.

Let's Pause for Prayer

Heavenly Father, thank you for loving me and caring for me in such a way that I can come to you about anything. I come to ask your blessing upon the places where you are using me to minister for You. Thank you for protecting me from harm, from people who wish to do harm, and from all that would hinder Your work. Please expand the borders of where I now minister and allow me victory over my enemies. Thank You for Your loving hand, which is always upon me to give power, strength, and guidance. As I serve You, please keep me on the right path to do Your will. In Jesus' name we pray. Amen.

What are you asking and trusting the Lord to do in your heart and in your ministry?

_____

_____

What are your present "borders" in life and ministry, and how might you recognize whether and when the Lord expanded that territory?

_____

_____

Day 45

Time Marches On

> *"There is an appointed time for everything. And there is a time for every event under heaven."*
>
> Ecclesiastes 3: 1

Fast flipping through the months of a calendar is a fun scene in a movie, but sometimes I feel as if real time is moving that fast! The passage of time is quick.

When we approached the new millennium, we all thought about the passage of time! One day, as I sat in my car waiting to pick up one of the children, I watched familiar people coming and going from the building. One young boy drove up to pick up his younger sister. I distinctly remember him in my daughters' kindergarten class, which seems like only yesterday. A woman I remembered from a committee on which we served limped into the same building, when just a few years ago she seemed so young and healthy!

Evidence of growth and aging in our physical bodies is not always apparent in the day to day, but it appears suddenly later on down the road. When it comes to our spiritual growth, are we able to identify growth daily so that even others might see those changes in us in our Christian lives?

Let's Pause for Prayer

Heavenly Father, daily we desire to have evidence of our spiritual growth that You and others might recognize! Please help us to show the fruit of the Spirit (love, joy, peace, patience, kindness, goodness, faithfulness, gentleness, and self-control) to others so that our lives would be a growing and glowing example to others of our love for You. As time marches on, may we move in the direction of deepening our relationship with You, studying Your word, and serving as an example to others. In Jesus' name we pray. Amen.

Am I stronger in my faith than I was a year ago?

_____

_____

Do I spend more time in prayer and in reading from God's word than I ever have before?

_____

_____

Do I exemplify the fruit of the Spirit to draw others to the Lord?

_____

_____

Day 46

Three Years Of Thursdays

"Whatever you do, do your work heartily, as for the Lord rather than for men: knowing that from the Lord you will receive the reward of the inheritance. It is the Lord Christ whom you serve."

Colossians 3: 23 –24

Every Thursday for about three and a half years, I had the precious blessing and privilege of helping care for my father. Along with my two sisters, one taking Tuesdays, and the other being there in the evenings because she lived with my folks, we cared for him through numerous stokes, diagnosis of Alzheimer's, hospital stays, months in and out of rehabilitation and nursing homes until he came home needing full-time care, sharing his desire for that to occur in his own home.

I know I wasn't alone in caring for someone who needed full-time care. Mom was there *all* of the time except for when we came on our days to give her a break. The responsibility of caring for that special someone in our lives is very important. Although many frustrations and challenges accompany the care of those who cannot care for themselves, many wonderful blessings may come to caregivers as well.

We can be thankful for the time—and in many cases we see it as extra time the Lord has given us—to have time with this person. We can rejoice in knowing that we have served someone who will never be able to do the same for us. We can experience firsthand what it means to serve the Lord without any expectations of what it will do for us.

Let's Pause for Prayer

Heavenly Father, I pray for those who shoulder the responsibilities of caregiving and perhaps and have little time away from the care they give. Allow them to treat the one they are caring for with love, respect, and dignity. Please encourage them to give You thanks for the privilege of serving others in long and difficult situations. Please bless and refresh each caregiver with a sense of Your peace and Your presence. Help them find things to refresh themselves so they can better care for their loved one! In Jesus' name we pray. Amen.

If you are caring for a loved one, share what that care looks like.

_____

_____

_____

How can I, as the caregiver, pray for the one I love, myself, and others? Share the prayer.

_____

_____

Day 47 *Watch Your Tongue*

> *"For you were called to freedom, brethren; only do not turn your freedom into an opportunity for the flesh, but through love serve one another. For the whole Law is fulfilled in one word, in the statement, 'You shall love your neighbor as yourself.' But if you bite and devour one another, take care lest you be consumed by one another."*
>
> Galatians 5:13–16

How we work together with others will reveal much about us as individuals. When we work with people with whom we get along well, things go smoothly, and we may actually have fun. But sometimes we find ourselves in extremely challenging situations with others. If two personalities conflict, not only may we run into turbulence, but the work is also no fun!

Challenges occur in our families, with our friends, with coworkers, and yes, even in ministry. How we respond to difficulty will show to others who we really are.

We have the freedom to serve one another, not to bite and devour one another. Are we serving where we are working and ministering? Or do we need to have our way? When we don't get our way, do we bite and devour one another?

Let's Pause for Prayer

Heavenly Father, please help me to serve others around me. Please help me to find the good in others so that we have true freedom in serving. Help me to speak sweet and kind words to and about others for their encouragement. Keep my words honest and true, yet loving and kind. Allow me to show kindness when others are unkind or misuse words and cause hurt. Make me an example from which others will learn and build better relationships. May the body of Christ be a uniting force as we together serve one another. In Jesus' name we pray. Amen.

Do you feel you speak kindly and with encouragement, or do you need some work in that area?

_____

_____

_____

How can you change to speaking more kindly? Can someone hold you accountable? Someone you can ask to keep you on the right track? Perhaps someone you can also pray with?

_____

_____

_____

Day 48 — *Those In Authority*

> *"Let every person be in subjection to the governing authority. For there is no authority except from God, and those which exist are established by God."*
>
> Romans 13:1

Someone sent me an email *years* ago that told of all the crimes of the present United States Congress. Further research showed it to lack verifiable facts, but when I watch the news, I see many men and women in various positions of authority who have been caught in doing wrong. Some include spousal abuse, sexual acts outside marriage, affairs, sexting, assault, drug-related charges, lying under oath, drunk driving, and the list goes on.

These are the people in authority over us. With what we hear in the news today, we must definitely pray for those in authority because they are the lawmakers who make the rules by which we are to live.

Let's Pause for Prayer

Heavenly Father, we desire to diligently pray for those who are in authority over us. I pray that You would become real to those making the rules and laws in this country. Thank You for the freedom to pray for them. Thank You for the freedom they have to come to know You, serve You, and acknowledge You before all men. And I pray that they would. In Jesus' name we pray. Amen.

This is how I usually react when I hear the news of someone in authority being arrested or caught doing wrong:

_____

_____

_____

This is how I will pray for our leaders in authority now (before I hear bad news about them) and also how I'll pray when I hear bad news about their actions:

_____

_____

_____

_____

Day 49 — *Choices*

> *"The way of a fool is right in his own eyes, but a wise man is he who listens to counsel."*
>
> Proverbs 12: 15

We all have choices. Those choices determine consequences and outcomes that might affect us in the future.

During the 70s (when I was in college) the trend toward coed dorms took root. I never experienced them but remember all the talk about them—both positive and negative.

Decades later a different type of living arrangement was made available to college students. "Iowa State University has established a dormitory in which students are not allowed to smoke, drink alcohol, have sex or let their grades slide," says the Des Moines *Register* (Aug. 23, 1999). A residence director was quoted as saying. 'They said nobody was going to live there. . . . We could have filled three buildings with the students who wanted in'" (Focus on the Family, *Citizen* magazine, Oct. 1999).

All these years later, some college students may still have this choice, but for those students at universities where such a choice is unavailable, the pressures are great; and for those who refuse to conform, the pressures are perhaps even greater. Responsibilities for those who desire to live according to Christ's teachings might seem almost impossible in these types of situations.

Let's Pause for Prayer

Heavenly Father, we confront pressures around us everywhere to conform to what the world says is right and OK. We pray for Christian college students, some of whom are away from home for the very first time, to be able to stand firm in their faith and resist what they know is not of You. We pray that they would be confident examples to their unbelieving college friends. We pray that others would come to know You as Christian students lead by example. In Jesus' name we pray. Amen.

Have you ever been pressured by temptation in a particular setting like college to stray from your beliefs? How did you handle it?

_____

_____

_____

How can you pray for the young adults in this situation? How might you help?

_____

_____

_____

Day 50 — *Storing Up Treasures*

"Do not lay up for yourselves treasures upon earth where moth and rust destroy and where thieves break in and steal. But lay up for yourselves treasures in heaven where neither moth nor rust destroys, and where thieves do not break in or steal; for where your treasure is, there will you heart be also."

Matthew 6: 19-21

"There once was a rich man near death. He was very grieved because he had worked so hard for his money and wanted to take it with him to heaven. He began praying that he might be able to take some of his wealth with him. An angel heard his plea and said to him, 'You can't take *anything* with you to heaven.' The man asked the angel to see whether God might make this one exception. The angel returned and said, 'God will allow you to bring just one suitcase with you when you are called to heaven.'

"Overjoyed, the man gathered his largest suitcase and filled it with pure gold bars. He died and met Peter at the gates of heaven. Seeing the suitcase, Peter said, 'Hold on, you can't bring that in here!' The man explained that he had received permission and asked Peter to verify it with the Lord. Peter returned and said, 'You're right, but I'm supposed to check its contents before letting it through.'

"Peter opened the suitcase to inspect the worldly items that the man found too precious to leave behind and exclaimed, 'You brought *pavement*!?!!'"

Let's Pause for Prayer

Heavenly Father, in our short-sightedness we store up for ourselves things of this world that have no value and that will not last. Help us to want to know You better and serve You faithfully instead of accumulate things. Help mold us according to Colossians 2:2-3: "That their hearts may be encouraged, having been knit together in love, and attaining to all the wealth that comes from the full assurance of understanding, resulting in a true knowledge of God's mystery, that is, Christ Himself, in whom are hidden all the treasures of wisdom and knowledge." Thank You for giving us Your treasures of wisdom and knowledge. We will accept them and use them for our work and service to You! In Jesus' name we pray. Amen.

What do you treasure here on earth that has far less value than you're putting on it?

_____

_____

What change will you make as you prepare your heart for all eternity?

_____

_____

Day 51 — Unimportant Words

> *"Pleasant words are a honeycomb, sweet to the soul and healing to the bones."*
>
> Proverbs 16: 24

I'm learning the unimportance of most of what I say. When I'm in conversation with others, and if I'm interrupted, my goal is to stop and let the other person finish what they began. Sometimes the conversation doesn't come back to me, but on those occasions when it does, I've often already forgotten what I was going to say! Then I ask myself, "How important was that thought or idea of words if you already forgot what you were going to say?"

I suppose the greatest lesson to be learned here is to be sure that what I want to say and what I actually say actually matter. But when I consider most of the conversations I hear and in which I participate, I'd say a lot of our words are just not that important or meaningful or helpful or informational or even interesting!

Let's Pause for Prayer

Heavenly Father, I pray that You would use my words, our words, to glorify You and to bring You honor. Even if we are simply chatting about our day or what is going on in life, we want our words to have some value. May we encourage others through the words we use. May we lift the spirits of others when they are down, lonely, or in need. May the words offered be kind, caring, and uplifting. Help us to notice when others need encouragement to keep them going in life, and help us not take too seriously the words from others that were meant to help but didn't. Help us to learn to appreciate the heart of a person first and their words second. Thank you for those people you put in our lives who know the right thing to say, when to say it, and how to say it; and help me be that person for someone else! In Jesus' name we pray. Amen.

Do you feel your conversation is all-important or do you give others a chance to share?

_____

_____

How can you be mindful of what you are saying and how you want to say it?

_____

_____

What will you do differently today to make your words count?

_____

_____

Day 52

Door 1, 2, Or 3

"But every decision is from the Lord"

Proverbs 16:33

Life has so many choices, which can sometimes be great, but as in *Let's Make A Deal*, the TV show popular in the 60s and 70s, we seldom know what is behind door Number 1, 2, or 3!

When we choose the surprise behind any of the doors, we might not be happy about the choice we made and wish we'd chosen the other door that held a better surprise or prize. Real life can be a little like choosing one of those doors; we have to make our choices and live with them; however, as Christ's followers we have the opportunity to pray before we make choices. As we yield to God, spend time in His word and commit ourselves to Him, He will help us make choices, both big and small. If we follow His lead, He will see that we are faithful in the small things, and He'll help us to be faithful in the big things as well. As He allows us choices, He'll lead and guide us to differentiate the good from the bad and the best from what seems good.

Let's Pause for Prayer

Heavenly Father, we are thankful that we can come to You, pray to You, and seek You in any and all situations and circumstances as we make choices in life. Lord, may I become an excellent listener as I bring before You requests, questions, decisions, and choices. I pray that I will listen well and learn to discern Your ways from my ways, Your will from my will, and Your best from what I think is best. As I learn and grow, help me to bring everything to You, big and small, so that I can have full assurance that I've included You in helping me make right choices. May I make the kinds of choices that will result in good because I've wanted to serve and please You. May I honor You in all ways. In Jesus' name we pray. Amen.

Lord, if I had included you in my decisions, I would have made some different choices in my past; but I did not include You then in my decision making. I pray now to do things differently, which include the following:

_____

_____

_____

What I will put in place to include the Lord in my future decisions:

_____

_____

_____

Day 53

Whack-A-Mole Life

> *"Whatever your hand finds to do, verily, do it with all your might."*
> Ecclesiastes 9: 10

Whack-a-mole. You know the game. Whenever a little mole head pops up, you try to whack it and score some points. The problem is that the heads keep popping up faster and faster, and it's hard to hit them all. Playing it in an arcade brings laughter and fun, and I love the game; but when the game makes its way into real life, it sure can be frustrating. My prayer is that my hands would keep busy in the work of the Lord, but at times I feel I have more chores than time, more emails to reply to than the desire to answer, more work to do than energy, and then I feel as if I'm playing real-life Whack-a-mole.

As a time manager, I know the things I need to do to calm life down. I need to prioritize, to ask for help, to delegate, and to say yes or no to certain things; but sometimes life catches up with us, and we get stuck playing an unwanted game of Whack-a-mole.

Let's Pause for Prayer

Heavenly Father, thank you for the many opportunities You give us in this life of service to You. Help us choose carefully from the good things that are placed before us by others as we learn to choose that which is best—and that which is from You—for us to accomplish. Bless the work of our hands according to Ecclesiastes 9: 10: "Whatever your hand finds to do, verily, do it with all your might." In whatever we engage, in whatever we choose to do, may we accomplish that which is from Your hand. We don't want to waste the time You've given us, the talents or gifts You've bestowed upon us, or the resources You've given. Help us to manage what You've given so that we'll be faithful to Your call. Let us be attentive to Your priorities. In Jesus' name we pray. Amen.

If life seems too busy or out of control for me right now, what three things can I apply to get it under control with proper priority?

_____

_____

_____

If my life is in a stagnant place, what must I do to be in God's will, doing the things He is calling me to do?

_____

_____

_____

Day 54 — *The Matter Of Giving: A Heart, Not Pocketbook, Issue*

> *"Honor the Lord from your wealth, and from the first of all your produce."*
>
> Proverbs 3:9

In his book *Grace is Enough* the late Pastor Ken Radke, our dearly missed friend, said this: "We are commanded not to worship money, but nor are we to glorify poverty." Wealthy individuals are needed to help provide for the work of the Lord. The work of the poor, who are equally capable of doing the work of the Lord, might just look a little different from the work of the wealthy. Governments can make the wealthy give to the poor, but not until God is over us and in our finances can we become generous in our giving. Whether we have little or much, the matter of giving and generosity is of the heart, not the pocketbook. We must consider our attitudes toward wealth, giving, and providing.

Let's Pause for Prayer

Heavenly Father, we don't want to worship money. Help us to open our hands, not tightly clench them, so that we can be generous givers as well as willing receivers. We know that all we have is directly from You. Whatever You've given us, let us recognize it came from Your hand; and if You ask us to release it, may we be willing to do so. Let us recognize and claim Your word, Philippians 4:19, "And my God shall supply all your needs according to his riches in glory in Christ Jesus." And let us, as stated in Proverbs 3:9, "Honor the Lord from [our] wealth, and from the first of all [our] produce." May we give You the first of all we have so that Your ministry might be accomplished, so that others will hear of You, accept You, and desire to serve You! Father, we don't want to withhold from You or others. May we offer to You and others our resources, our money, time, and talents. In Jesus' name we pray. Amen.

What are you withholding from the Lord? What is the first thing that came to mind?

_____

_____

_____

What can you offer to the Lord? Will it be your time? Your talents? Your money? How will you put giving into action?

_____

_____

_____

_____

Day 55 — Leaving Cash Or A Legacy

> *"Therefore be careful how you walk, not as unwise men but as wise, making the most of your time."*
>
> Ephesians 5: 15-16

Do we want to leave a stash of cash or a legacy of a life well lived for our kids? The better, but more frightening question might be "Do our kids want us to leave them money or a solid God-honoring legacy of a life well-lived?" The answer would certainly be telling, wouldn't it?

Having lost both my parents just shy of five days apart in 2001, I can tell you that I'd far rather have them here than to have what they left us monetarily. Even so, what I most cherish is the legacy they left: 51½ years of marriage to their one and only as well as Joe's parents' legacy of 55 years of marriage. They left a legacy of wonderful memories of family vacations, fishing, boating, swimming, skateboarding, and laughing. What they poured into our lives—values, morals, ethics, life, and God-lessons—is invaluable.

Let's Pause for Prayer

Let us with purpose be mindful about what we're really leaving to our kids. We pray we are making memories for them that are of great value. We pray that they would take with them memories of parents (and grandparents) who got along, enjoyed time with the family, and through hardships stayed the course as great examples of loving You. May we persevere with endurance, teaching them the values that will help them through life, showing them how to prioritize, living a godly life of service to You. If we leave them anything of worldly value, including money, may they treasure it for your kingdom's use because they first learned that principle from us. Give them wisdom in the decision-making process when using that which is left to them. Give them discernment and grace to bless others and not just themselves. Give them a clear vision of the way You would like them to use the monetary blessings and the blessing of the legacy that was left. In Jesus' name we pray. Amen.

What are you actively pursuing in terms of leaving a legacy for your children and grandchildren?

_____
_____
_____

How can you prepare your estate, your memory, and your legacy with purpose?

_____
_____
_____

Day 56

Letting Go

"Behold, children are a gift of the Lord; the fruit of the womb is a reward. Like arrows in the hand of a warrior, so are the children of one's youth."

Psalm 127: 3-4

Parents encounter many difficulties. One challenge is letting go. We learn to let go in small doses, hoping that letting go will be easier when significant departures occur; but I haven't found that to be the case! We let go when our children are learning to ride a two-wheeler. Pretty soon they're riding on their own around the block and to the homes of friends. Later, we let go when we hand them the car keys and let them drive off to high school activities and then off to college! Soon we're waving good-bye as they leave our home for marriage, ministry, or careers!

If we are raising our children "as unto the Lord," we want their love of and for Jesus always to be evidenced in obedience; however, it might not be for us to know how that obedience looks in their lives. Enter prayer!

Let's Pause for Prayer

Heavenly Father, how thankful we are that through every step of letting go we have the privilege of praying for our children! We are so thankful that You know our hearts and that our hearts are for our children to love and serve You faithfully. Please help us to guide them in their formative years as we teach them to learn how to call upon You and as they learn how to hear from You. Let us, as we equip them and disciple them in Your word, encourage and teach them not to fear the future but embrace it wholeheartedly because You have gone before them. As we let go, allow our children to have fond memories of the past. Help them set their eyes ahead and not look back with regret, sorrow, or disappointment, and in their own way let go to be able to follow You in obedience. No matter their ages, we can (and should) pray them through a life of obedience! Then, let us enjoy watching them make decisions and live lives in the fullness of knowing You. In Jesus' name we pray. Amen.

If you have children, in what ways have you had to let go? Share small and big ways.

_____

_____

_____

If you don't have children, consider times in your own life when you had to let go and move on to the next step that God had for you. What situations have caused difficulties on letting go?

_____

_____

_____

Day 57 — Face To Face

> *"Since then no prophet has risen in Israel like Moses, whom the Lord knew face to face."*
>
> Deuteronomy 34:10

According to some online statistics

- Over 2.1B people across the globe have access to the Internet
- 1.15B use Facebook
- 500M use Twitter
- 70M use Pinterest

Along with knowing how many people use social media, knowing how much time individuals spend using what is so easily accessible would be equally interesting. And even more interesting would be the amount of time we choose not to spend with others face to face because we feel our emotional needs are met through the Internet.

The Internet has made us comfortable. We feel engaged and connected with friends with the simple click of a Like button. Unfortunately, we often miss the story within the story, which may be far different from the sugar-coated version we find in Facebook posts or pictures.

Let's Pause for Prayer

Heavenly Father, how very thankful we are that we have access to our smartphones, computers, the Internet, social media, and current modern technology. We appreciate being able to connect to those next door and around the world with the click of the reply or send button, but we pray we will never miss opportunities to learn more about and care for others as we enter into one another's lives in deeper and more meaningful ways. Help us be creative in finding ways to meet with others one on one and face to face—to listen to one another's stories as we learn to rejoice with those who rejoice and weep with those who weep (Rom. 12:15). As Moses spent time with the Lord face to face and knew Him (Deut. 34: 10), let us find interest in things beneath the surface of simple and friendly conversation that mean something to others. From what we learn, let us pray for one another. In Jesus' name we pray. Amen.

When was the last time you reached out to people to meet them face to face and get to know them better? What will you do this day to make time for someone else in person?

Day 58 — *No Mistakes*

> *"Wonderful are Thy works, and my soul knows it very well."*
>
> Psalm 139: 14b, c

Differences are divine. God made us all different so we can accomplish His purposes on earth. He made us special and unique and each of us for a purpose. For several years I had hoped to get out west to visit a restaurant in Albuquerque, NM: Tim's Place. His advertises comfort, food, and hugs! When interviewed on national TV shows, Tim said, "I'm more like you… than different." Tim has Down syndrome. Everyone who walks into the restaurant gets a hug from Tim, and at the time of our visit the "official hug counter" showed he's given over 72,000! Although we missed meeting Tim and didn't get an official hug, we enjoyed good service and food.

Let's Pause for Prayer

Lord, thank You for creating each one of us differently and so very uniquely. Thank you for making us more alike than different and for allowing our differences to be used for good and more importantly for Your glory. Thank you for people like Tim, who have parents who support him in running his restaurant, as he strives to be used of You in ways that others would never imagine he could be. Thank you for the specialness about him (and others with special needs) that is intriguing and delightful. Help us to recognize that those who are different from ourselves are according to Psalm 139:14 "fearfully and wonderfully made" and that we are, too. Father, let us be patient and helpful when those differences are difficult to understand because they're not a part of our lives. Let us look at others as being important, worthwhile, and made in Your image. Help us to take time to understand our differences but also to make time to understand our similarities. Through each of our differences and similarities, may we bring You glory and accomplish Your purposes on earth! In Jesus' name we pray. Amen.

When you see people with special needs, do you tend to feel sorry for them or look for the uniqueness in their specialness?

_____

_____

_____

How might you embrace (in your heart) someone with special needs? How might you pray for the one with special needs and her or his family?

_____

_____

_____

Day 59 — Just Jesus

> *"And He called a child to Himself and stood him in their midst, and said, 'Truly I say to you, unless you are converted and become like children, you shall not enter the kingdom of heaven.'"*
>
> Matthew 18: 2–3

Years ago I went through the process of becoming the guardian for our then 18-year-old son. Joey has a number of physical, mental, and health challenges that will require him to be cared for all of his life. Someone from Probate Court came to our home with papers for Joey to sign and talk to him about guardianship and get the process in progress. In front of this woman and Joey, I explained to him what it meant. I explained that I wanted to become his guardian and that meant that I wanted to be the one to take care of him. I asked him whether he wanted me to be his guardian, and he said, "Yes." I then asked him if there was anyone else he would want to take care of him besides me. I expected him to say Daddy or Grandma or one of his sisters or aunts. But he very quickly and to the point said, "Just Jesus." While he may have some challenges, he doesn't seem to suffer from any spiritual challenges!

When meeting with our lawyer to finalize the details, he showed me that Joey's words were written in the court document, seen by the magistrate, file clerks, and others working on this case. He asked me, "May I have your permission to share Joey's story and words with others?" With a hearty "yes" I consented, and I believe Joey is sharing the Gospel like we never imagined he would.

Let's Pause for Prayer

Heavenly Father, we pray that each one of us would teach our children and those with childlike abilities to know You. May we diligently teach them to follow You so that they will always have You as a source of strength when we are not with them. May we become like children with humble and pure hearts to know You and to love You simply and purely. Father, thank you that our children—little ones in age and ones with limited abilities—can know You and serve You in ways we'd never expect or imagine. Thank you for putting them in our lives to teach us. In Jesus' name we pray. Amen.

Can you trust Jesus in such a simple and decisive way?

What will you do today to trust and depend on Him?

Day 60 — Voted Off The Island

> *"For I have no one else of kindred spirit who will genuinely be concerned for your welfare. For they all seek after their own interests, not those of Christ Jesus."*
>
> Philippians 2:20-21

All through school I remember my awareness that someone was being left out, forgotten, or purposely excluded or eliminated from some group or activity. We called that blackballing, which is voting against membership, especially to exclude from membership by casting a negative vote.

Today that word isn't used much, but I hear the word *dismissed* when similar things happen. *Dismissed* is defined as being sent away, put aside, or out of mind. (You know. It's like being voted off the island!) It's hard being blackballed or dismissed from an activity in school when kids are young, but it's quite another story when it happens in the workplace or worse yet in the church, where we should experience grace, love, and a sense of belonging and purpose. Sadly, it happens even there. Being blackballed or dismissed is not much different from being bullied, no matter where it happens.

Let's Pause for Prayer

Heavenly Father, if we profess to be Christians, we need to make the choice to represent ourselves in ways that show love, care, and concern for others, to show grace and love to all with whom we have contact, never dismissing others because they are no longer of use to us because they think differently or for any other reason. Help us to make right choices to include the lonely, those who are different from us, those whose ideas differ from ours, and those who are still trying to find their way and purpose. Help us to invite others into our group, go out of our way to meet someone new, serve someone who doesn't represent some purpose, agenda, or immediate use in our lives. Help us also to recognize that sometimes, being voted off the island gives us a chance to meet new (and often nicer) people, become involved in new things, and serve You in ways we'd never have expected. In Jesus' name we pray. Amen.

Who will you reach out to and include in your life today? Ask the Lord to identify someone in whom you can become interested and for whom you can show concern. Pray for the individual, and then ask the Lord for the next step.

_____
_____
_____
_____
_____

Day 61

Rest Or Rust

"It is a sign between Me and the sons of Israel forever; for in six days the Lord made heaven and earth, but on the seventh day He ceased from labor and was refreshed."

Exodus 31:17

The famous opera singer Placido Domingo was asked in an interview (per my memory!), "When you go on vacation, do you rest your voice?" His response interested me. He said, "If I rest, I rust. I cannot allow myself too much time off without my voice getting out of shape." If we take a Christian perspective on his comment, we might conclude that if we take too much time to rest, we will get out of shape in our service to the Lord! If we rest, we will rust!

We definitely need to take time to rest. The body, mind, and spirit need it; however, too much rest will cause us to rust. We will grow complacent about the things for which we have responsibility. When we become comfortable in our complacency, we will easily settle into disobedience and stop doing what God is asking us to do. When we disobey, we rust.

How interesting that we see in scripture (Exodus 31:17) that even God rested and was refreshed.

Let's Pause for Prayer

Heavenly Father, we pray that we would never be found resting to the point of rusting in our service to You. Please help us always to listen to Your voice, which guides and directs us. As a piece of iron that is rusted must be sanded before it can be used again, we pray that You would gently smooth off our rough edges so that we can be used by You for Your purposes and glory. In Jesus' name we pray. Amen.

Are you able to rest to be refreshed? What provides refreshment for you?

_____

_____

_____

In what ways have you disobeyed God and need Him to sand the rough edges to smoothness to return from too much resting and serve Him once again?

_____

_____

_____

_____

Day 62 — *Discouraged, Dismissed, Disregarded*

"Not that I speak from want; for I have learned to be content in whatever circumstances I am."

Philippians 4:11

Can you embrace the place and situation where you are right now as the scripture above expresses?

Recently someone shared with me that she felt discouraged, dismissed, and disregarded in a particular area of her life, yet what I found remarkable was that she was so very content where God had her. Although her tears flowed, she showed such gratitude as she recognized that God was in the business of protecting His own, and she believed that despite feeling dismissed and discouraged, she was also quite protected—and even spared!

God wastes nothing—not time, not relationships, not work, not service—so He will use whatever of our life situations He needs to teach us; and if we are willing, we'll see things from His perspective instead of the world's or our own skewed views.

Let's Pause for Prayer

Thank You, Father, for the way You teach our hearts and the way You can fill us to the fullest even in times of discouragement. Thank You for Your word, which points us to look to and for the right things according to Philippians 4:8, "Finally brethren, whatever is true, whatever is honorable, whatever is right, whatever is pure, whatever is lovely, whatever is of good repute, if there is any excellence and anything worthy of praise, let your mind dwell on these things." Thank You for training our minds to dwell on those things that when we truly desire to seek and serve You, we are content where You have us. Thank you for "the peace of God which surpasses all comprehension, which guards [our] hearts and [our] minds in Christ Jesus" (Phil. 4:7). Let us always recognize Your protection and sovereignty and then let us show our appreciation by being thankful and grateful as we embrace the place where you have us! In Jesus' name we pray. Amen.

Describe for yourself a situation where you've felt discouraged, dismissed, or disregarded. How did you react or respond at first?

_____

_____

How can you look at things differently in light of what today's scripture teaches? How will you put that answer into practice for yourself?

_____

_____

_____

Day 63 — I Didn't Finish All I Wanted

"And whatever you do in word or deed, do all in the name of the Lord Jesus, giving thanks through Him to God the Father."

Colossians 3:17

Chances are I'll never get to visit every person with whom I'd like to spend time. I'll not get to write all the ideas onto paper (or computer) that are constantly popping into my head. I'll probably not get to travel to all the places I find interesting. I'll likely never get to do all the projects that seem as if they'd be fun to do—or at least try! But the good thing is this—If I listen to and obey the Lord, I'll visit, travel, write, and work on projects only as He wants me to.

At the end of our day, few of us will say that we were able to do everything we wanted, with whom we wanted, and for the length of time we wanted. But we can rest at the end of that day with a sense of satisfaction that the work of that day is done and it was completed knowing God gave the direction.

Let's Pause for Prayer

Heavenly Father, we are so thankful for Your word to guide us: Colossians 3:17, "And whatever you do in word or deed, do all in the name of the Lord Jesus, giving thanks through Him to God the Father." Oh, Lord, may we seek You to do what You have in mind for us. May we look to You for direction about where we should serve, where we should visit, where we should spend our time and talents—and most importantly those people with whom we should invest our lives. Make us recognize the importance of using wisely the time, talent, or treasure You've given us on tasks that will show and bring You honor and glory. Father, use us up to the very last drop so that we can look back and recognize a life well lived—without regret and knowing we completed just what You wanted us to. In Jesus' name we pray. Amen.

Seek the Lord in prayer for the way He would like you to prioritize your time with people and activities. Express it here:

_____
_____
_____
_____

In what way will you take a step in doing only what the Lord instructs?

_____
_____
_____

Day 64

Do What's Right

"For let not that man expect that he will receive anything from the Lord, being a double-minded (doubting or hesitating) man, unstable in all his ways."

James 1:7-8

Are you one who finds the decision-making process difficult or easy? Do you have a process by which you come to a final decision? Perhaps it's more fun to make decisions that are simple "no brainers." Those difficult challenges that require decisions can be very trying emotionally, spiritually, and sometime physically. Sometimes a written pro and con list can be helpful, but most definitely we need to take time to pray about them.

Let's Pause for Prayer

Lord, in this day, help me to approach decision making with Your will and ways in mind. I want to come to You in prayer first and then listen well and carefully for Your guidance. When needed, may we seek wise counsel. May we listen to You, make choices, and then rest in them. We don't want to be like the person described in James 1: 7-8: "For let not that man expect that he will receive anything from the Lord, being a double-minded (doubting or hesitating) man, unstable in all his ways." We pray we'll make decisions in mind, in heart, and in step with You and not let the comments and control of others steer us in the wrong direction. We want to be stable in our thinking and praying and cautious in our listening. We want to be confident and not doubting, moving forward when we know we should and not hesitating and missing opportunities You have planned for us. May we listen intently so when You speak, we hear and will not wonder whether we heard correctly. We will just know. Life as a believer is exciting, Lord, but seldom easy. We want to be a good example to others, so we know we must be discerning and careful as we make the choices in life that will lead to the next step and to the next. We want to be sure we're in step with You. In Jesus' name we pray. Amen.

What decision are you considering that you know you must make in order to do the right thing and see it through?

_____

_____

_____

What action will you take, that is a right decision toward your next opportunity or decision?

_____

_____

_____

Day 65 *Suicide*

> *"Let your speech always be with grace, seasoned, as it were, with salt, so that you may know how you should respond to each person."*
>
> Colossians 4:5

Suicide affects everyone. Its journey and end are heartbreaking, and it's life changing for those who are left trying to fit all the pieces together, often unsuccessfully. Because it is one of the top causes of death, we need to learn to recognize the signs of potentially fatal depression and intervene.

I am quite certain that each person reading this knows of someone suffering from some type or degree of depression. Many, if not all, readers know someone personally who has taken her or his own life. Although national strategies for suicide prevention have some benefit in educating the public, nothing is as important and crucial as prayer for individuals who struggle with depression or suicidal thoughts and actions.

Let's Pause for Prayer

Heavenly Father, we pray for those we know and love who struggle with depression. Help us not to be judgmental because of our lack of understanding. Help us faithfully pray for their recovery. Help us be observant and aware of signs that call for us to get them the help they need. Help those who might contemplate taking their own lives to stop, listen to this prayer, and ask Jesus to take control of their lives. Give them a strong desire and purpose for living—to tell others of Your goodness! In Jesus' name we pray. Amen.

Privately on your own, write down the names any person who comes to mind and pray for him or her.

_____

_____

_____

Ask the Lord how you can be helpful in the life of this person—quiet prayer or a next step of action—and note it for yourself.

_____

_____

_____

_____

Day 66

Never Stop Praying?

> *"Pray without ceasing."*
> I Thessalonians 5:17

"Praying is boring."

"There's too much to pray for, so I just can't pray."

"I have no one to pray with."

"I'm too sleepy to pray."

"I don't have time to pray."

"I'm too lazy."

"I don't think God will answer."

"I have other important things to do."

These are all reasons we hear—and have perhaps personally said—for our failure to pray. Each is merely an excuse because we can truly pray anytime and anywhere and certainly *all the time!*

We can dismiss all the excuses we have used that have kept us from prayer as we simply and boldly pray!

Let's Pause for Prayer

Heavenly Father, we are so sorry for neglecting our communication with You through prayer. We are sorry when we act as if it's hard work, when you have commanded us to pray and we know doing so is essential for a growing relationship with You. I am sorry that I have sometimes chosen other things to fill my time even though you have shown me the benefits of prayer. Please forgive me. Please restore me to a fresh and vital prayerful relationship with You! Please call to mind people and situations for which You would like me to pray. Please use my waking hours to center on prayer to You! In Jesus' name we pray. Amen.

Have you ever used any of the above excuses not to pray? List them for you to see.

_____

_____

_____

Starting right now, what will you do to pray without ceasing?

_____

_____

_____

Day 67 — *Gossip In Prayer*

> *"Let no unwholesome word proceed from your mouth, but only such a word as is good for edification according to the need of the moment, that it may give grace to those who hear."*
>
> Ephesians 4:29

We may never have pondered the link between prayer and gossip, but when praying aloud in our families or communities or among friends, we may unwittingly invite gossip, share incorrect news, shocking comments, or even brag. When we approach the Lord in prayer with our family and friends, we need to consider the words we say so that we are sharing from a heart of compassion, humility, honesty, and love. A few tips that could help us as are follows:

- approach certain topics with caution
- check with the person or family whether a particular prayer concern should be made public
- let the family give surgical or diagnostic details privately at their discretion
- pray to God, not at others, and
- recognize privacy and delicate subjects or topics.

Let's Pause for Prayer

Heavenly Father, please help us to be sensitive and thoughtful to the needs of others as we publicly pray for them. Keep our voices silent when we don't know the specific details or when the specific details should not be shared publicly or privately. We ask you to put in our hearts those who need prayer, even when we are not aware of their specific or deepest needs. Let us realize it is our prayer, not the knowing of every detail, that is enough. May we always be humble in asking requests of You and as we share victories in ministry in Your name. Thank you, Lord. In Jesus' name we pray. Amen.

Have you ever felt the challenge of letting gossip slip into prayer?

_____

_____

_____

What have you or can you do to keep prayer pure?

_____

_____

_____

Day 68

Providing A Need

> *"And we know that God causes all things to work together for good to those who love God, to those who are called according to His purpose."*
>
> Romans 8:28

I qualified the call to our youth pastor (years ago) by saying, "I'm not yet volunteering but was wondering about any needs for the upcoming ministry trip with the teens?" He said, "We're short at least one driver and need room for about four more youth." Gee, that was just what my van would hold in addition to my being available that week. One glitch: I get sleepy behind the wheel, and this was a long trip. After talking it over with my husband and praying about the long drive and the week's stay, we decided the Lord was leading me to volunteer. I requested an adult female front-seat passenger who could hold a good conversation for a long period of time. If that could be provided, I thought I could provide the van, the seats, and my time. They did and I did.

That trip was such a learning experience for me. It was a great opportunity to serve, for sure. It was a great way for me to develop a sweet, new friendship with a woman I knew but got to know a whole lot better on this long trip. Finally, but perhaps most importantly, it gave me a front row seat as I watched how the youth directors worked, served, and blessed others. And it gave me new ways to pray!

Let's Pause for Prayer

Heavenly Father, I thank you for those who serve in youth ministry. Thank you for their willingness to pour their love, energy, and spiritual wisdom into these young adults. We ask you to bless all youth workers with continued strength, endurance, patience, and Your wisdom and love. Thank you for calling them to a life-changing ministry at such a crucial time in the lives of these teens. Bless them and their families for the sacrifices they make to do Your will. May we take the opportunity to help them serve when we have the time or talents to do so. Use us to encourage them. In Jesus' name we pray. Amen.

Have you ever volunteered to serve in a ministry for which you felt unqualified? How did it go?

_____

_____

_____

Name some places where can you offer your time or talents that are new, different, or unusual for you. Will you? Write for yourself your plan of action.

_____

_____

_____

Day 69 — The Scratched Up Wedding Band

> *"With all humility and gentleness, with patience, showing forbearance to one another in love"*
>
> Ephesians 4:2

As our friend Tom showed my husband and me the scratches and nicks on his wedding band, he said with pride, "I know some people like to get their wedding bands polished from time to time to keep them looking new, but I want everyone to see the wear and tear on my ring. I don't want anyone to think I'm newly married. I want everyone to know that Sue and I have been married a long time and that we are committed to each another."

Joe's parents had celebrated 55 years of marriage, and mine celebrated 51½ years. For the occasion of their 50th anniversary, my mom wanted a new wedding band. Because my dad's failing health was such that he could not help her choose one, my sister helped Mom. The new band was shiny outside, and the inscription inside testified to their commitment: "Love ALL ways." The phrase expressed not only many wonderful years but also experiences they hadn't planned on—Mom's caring for Dad, who could no longer express love in word or deed. She saw him through Alzheimer's, serving him in ways she'd never expected as his body and mind failed. She loved all ways. Commitment. Sacrifice. Legacy.

Let's Pause for Prayer

Heavenly Father, we thank you for those in our lives who have weathered the storms of marriage and are still committed to their spouses. Thank you for the legacy they are leaving their loved ones. Help each one of us follow Your example of love and commitment as we desire oneness in our own marriage. I pray that our marriage will be such that others will be encouraged and find hope and purpose in working on theirs. May we enjoy the benefits of a Christ-centered marriage (personally) and may the church (the body of believers) be strengthened (corporally) as we go the distance in our marriage. May we love all ways. In Jesus' name we pray. Amen.

If you had the chance to renew your vows, would you?

_____

_____

_____

How are you caring for your spouse in a way that says you love all ways?

_____

_____

_____

Day 70 — We Teach Directly And Indirectly

"And you shall teach [the commandments] diligently to your sons and shall talk of them when you sit in your house and when you walk by the way and when you lie down and when you rise up."

Deuteronomy 6:7

I remember reading about a teen drug addict, who used to smoke marijuana with his father as a way for them to bond and become buddies. The son said he learned that it's more beneficial in the long run for parents to be parents.

I have difficulty imagining that scenario, but we may be oblivious to other ways that we as parents appeal to our children to be their buddies instead of their parents. We must teach and train them as we spend time with them in all ways of life to learn what is right and wrong and what is permissible or not. We can't allow them to do things, act certain ways, or continue in types of wrong or sinful behavior because we're afraid to discipline and correct them for fear that they won't like us or be our friends. As parents we will teach them by our own actions—whether we think they're watching or not—and we need to show them by action and words the ways they should behave. They are learning directly or indirectly from us, their parents. We need to consider our own behavior.

Let's Pause for Prayer

Heavenly Father, we desire to be loving and guiding parents. We ask for you to reveal to us if there is anything that we are doing or allowing in our relationship with our children that will draw them away from you. Let us be mindful that they are watching the subtle things we do. Help us to see the wrong direction of our ways so that we will be proper examples to our children of Christlike living, character, and integrity. And let us be mindful of the obvious: teaching them to tell the truth, to work hard, and to be kind as we train them by our example. In Jesus' name we pray. Amen.

What do you recognize as subtle and indirect ways that you teach your children or the children of others?

_____

_____

_____

How can you be proactive about directly teaching through your example?

_____

_____

_____

Day 71　　　　　　　　　　　　　　　　　　　　　　*Praying In Place*

> *"With all prayer and petition, pray at all times in the spirit, and with this in view, be on the alert with all perseverance and petition for all the saints."*
>
> Ephesians 6:18

Sometimes I catch myself praying for someone or something because of where I am. Years ago I noticed a sign across from the gas station, plain white background with bold red letters: PSYCHIC. Each time I needed to get gas and every time I drove past that sign, I prayed that the people who owned the psychic business and the individuals who frequented the establishment would have a very real uneasiness about what they were doing as they participated in ungodly practices. I prayed specifically that they would sense the need to know Jesus Christ and His Holy Spirit, not the evil spirits they encountered. Ultimately, I prayed that the shop would close.

Just a few months later the sign was gone! No more cars were in the lot. I don't know whether the business is gone or simply relocated, but I've not seen the sign anywhere else. I am trusting that the business has closed up and that some of the clientele have come to know Jesus or will come to know Him someday.

Let's Pause for Prayer

Heavenly Father, we are so thankful for Your answer to prayer as we petition you where the need arises. Our prayers may concern business, business owners, communities, our loved ones, our churches, or any relationships; and we know You will answer the prayers of our hearts according to Your will. Please put before us the situations about which You want us to pray regularly. We are willing and want to sense Your direction. Give us humility—even a broken heart over the situations for which You call us to pray. In Jesus' name we pray. Amen.

What people or situations do you regularly pray about?

_____
_____
_____

If you've not been one to pray regularly, what will you do to start praying in this way?

_____
_____
_____

Day 72 — Work, Train Or Quit?

"For I am confident of this very thing, that He who began a good work in you will perfect it until the day of Christ Jesus."

Philippians 1:6

A life-changing book for me was *Seeking the Face of God* by Gary L. Thomas, who says, "Salvation is free, but maturity comes with a price." Do we care enough to want to be mature in the Lord? Do we try for a month or so and then just quit saying, "This was a good idea but just not realistic for me." We set goals to mature in Christ, but are we really willing to train toward them? When we quit trying, do we quit relying on Christ to help us change and mature? Or is doing so merely an element of insincerity in our lives?

Maturity in Christ is the spice of life and the true essence of a Christian's existence. We can become respectable and even well-mannered, but that simply is not enough. Our faith and growth to maturity in Christ should be our primary concern, and that means we must invest the time and energy necessary to become better, more mature Christians, intimate with Christ.

We can study, apply and even exercise in worldly matters and yet remain dull, negligent, and unimproved in our devotion to Christ. We know we cannot succeed in school, marriage, parenting, and life without purposefully applying ourselves to moving forward, yet we often fail to realize the same is true of our spiritual growth.

Let's Pause for Prayer

Heavenly Father, we desire to become more like You and ask You to change us and mature us as we apply Your word to our lives and as we seek Your will in our lives. I ask you to mature me deeply, not just so I can look like a good, well-mannered person but to be molded in ways that I become keenly aware that You are doing this work in me. And as You do this work in me, please work through me to share with and care for others. Make me an example that others will want to follow as I lead them to You. In Jesus' name we pray. Amen.

Do you find yourself wanting to look good as a believer on the outside but not really caring about your heart attitudes and issues?

_____

_____

_____

What will you do today to take a step forward as you work at and train for the maturity you desire in your walk with Christ?

_____

_____

Day 73 — *Grow Up!*

> *"Speaking the truth in love, we are to grow up in all aspects into Him, who is the head."*
> Ephesians 4:15

Occasionally, names will come to mind of people we knew (or know) and to whom we wish we (or someone who knows them well) could have said, "Grow up!" Maybe you know that person, too, the one who quits because a better situation came along—work, an adulterous affair, a hobby—or the one who was so frustrated by a situation (or a person) that she or he decided simply to throw in the towel and quit.

Perhaps you are that person, experiencing the frustrations of being a father and husband or wife and mother, and are contemplating running away from it all. Perhaps you are the spouse who has been left behind to raise the children on your own or you are a child trying to figure it all out. More than likely, we all know family members, friends, or neighbors struggling to keep their families together. Sometimes they need our prayers or our help or to grow up and take on the responsibilities they've been given. Let's take a moment on behalf of these people to pray for them and for ourselves not to fall victim to our problems.

Let's Pause for Prayer

Heavenly Father, we lift up men today as we pray. Please give them the strength they need to follow through on their commitments and responsibilities to their wives and children. Lord, please give them the direction they need to make the right decisions. Allow them to decide to follow You so that they can remain with their families and not become a statistic of divorce or desertion. For women who are contemplating leaving or quitting, give them the strength to take the next step to right thinking and right living so they can go the distance in their marriages and with their families. Please remind each of us to continue to pray for those who we know are struggling at this time. And Lord, we know we've all had times when we've wanted to throw in the towel and quit because we've had enough. Help us. Remind us that You are there for us, and give us clear mental, physical, and spiritual pictures of what we need to do to stay right with you. Help us to grow up not only in maturity as a person but also as a Christian who wants to follow in Your steps. In Jesus' name we pray. Amen.

If you're honest, you know you've said, "I've had it. I am not taking it anymore." As you remember that time, write down for yourself what it was like and what kept you going. If you're in the midst of wanting to quit, write down your frustrations and then seek the Lord to find His way, not your own. Ask Him to guide you. Don't move yet. Listen.

_____
_____
_____
_____
_____

Day 74

Growing Older

"For he will not often consider the years of his life because God keeps him occupied with the gladness of his heart."

Ecclesiastes 5:20

Are you one who hates getting older, or do you look favorably at your maturing years? I can't quite lean to one side or the other. I appreciate what I'm learning as I grow and mature in Christ, but the aches and pains of aging aren't quite as agreeable!

"Here is what I have seen to be good and fitting: to eat, to drink and enjoy oneself in all one's labor in which he toils under the sun during the few years of his life which God has given him; for this is his reward. Furthermore, as for every man to whom God has given riches and wealth, He has also empowered him to eat from them and to receive his reward and rejoice in his labor; this is the gift of God. For he will not often consider the years of his life because God keeps him occupied with the gladness of his heart" (Ecclesiastes 5: 18–20).

This passage from Ecclesiastes tells me that I need not fret or worry about getting older as long as I remain occupied doing the things He wants me to do, and He will give me joy as I do it. And let's face it! We are all aging. We may as well enjoy it.

Let's Pause for Prayer

Heavenly Father, we desire to use that which You've given us to work for You. We desire that You keep us occupied so that we will have joy and gladness of heart in doing Your will. Allow us to see work that needs to be done, people who need to be encouraged, ministries that might need our financial help; and may You be the One to guide us and initiate our involvement. We give thanks to You that as we obey You, we will not be consumed with negative thoughts about our aging but instead simply find joy in continuing to serve You and walk with You for as long as You give us life. How exciting the later years of life can be if we continue (with joy and gusto) to serve You with our whole heart, mind, soul, and body! In Jesus' name we pray. Amen.

No matter what your stage in life, do you feel you're giving life your all?

_____

_____

_____

What can you do to have and give full strength in your later days with joy and gusto?

_____

_____

_____

Day 75 — *Please, Listen!*

> *"Let everyone be quick to hear, slow to speak and slow to anger."*
>
> James 1:19

I needed to make quite a few phone calls the other day. By the time I had made it through about half my calls, I must admit I was totally frustrated. I'd finally get through the many rings or busy signals and then be put on hold without being asked whether or not I was able to hold. I listened to music, repeated voice prompts, and sales pitches that added to my frustration. When I finally spoke to someone and explained what I was calling about, she or he would abruptly say, "One moment please." Holding yet another time, a new person would answer, "Hello, so and so speaking." At first I would explain the reason for my call, but after numerous interruptions to send me elsewhere, I would just say, "Yes?" I would wait to see whether this individual knew anything about my call from the previous person or whether my call had just been transferred to him or her. I was secretly hoping that this person had already been notified of the reason for my call, that they had been given the information needed to help me in my quest. The repeated ordeal made me realize each person was acting rudely by quickly sending me on to someone else, never really listening to what I needed to accomplish with this phone call.

In my frustration, I asked the Lord to allow me to be patient, a good listener, kind, courteous, and even helpful to anyone with whom I might talk or come in contact. I realized that at times I do the same thing and don't even realize it. Perhaps they didn't realize it either. What a lesson for us to become better listeners before we speak!

Let's Pause for Prayer

Heavenly Father, please help each of us understand Your word: "Let everyone be quick to hear, slow to speak and slow to anger" (James 1:19). Help us to listen attentively as others speak, allowing them to realize we care about what they have to say. And guide us as we help others in a courteous way, thinking of them, not ourselves, first. Help us be more like You when it comes to caring about someone more than ourselves and putting their needs above our own. In Jesus' name we pray. Amen.

Think of a time you were quick to speak when you should have been quick to listen. Write it down for yourself to think about.

_____

_____

How will you make it a point to be a better listener and not jump into the conversation too quickly? (Be specific.)

_____

_____

_____

Day 76

Christian Comfort

> *"Make my joy complete by being of the same mind, maintain the same love, united in spirit, intent on one purpose. Do nothing from selfishness or empty conceit, but with humility of mind let each of you regard one another as more important than himself."*
>
> Philippians 2:2–3

How do you serve? Are you totally in the picture to serve others no matter the time, no matter the situation, and no matter the cost? Or do you serve with reservation: half-hearted, halfway, and half the time? Christians have said to me, "I don't like or want to get to know others too well or they might expect me to get involved and help." Ouch. Really? I thought that is what we were supposed to do as believers.

When we focus on others, we won't be so concerned with ourselves; we'll actually experience joy in serving instead of being served. We'll find satisfaction in putting the needs of others above and before our own, and we'll actually realize we're doing that to which God has already called us.

Let's Pause for Prayer

Heavenly Father, we are sorry for the times we've lacked the desire to help others, to listen to others, to serve others. We recognize we've wanted our own comfort and ease and have ignored the sufferings and needs of others. Forgive us for being so selfish and uncaring. Forgive us for walking past the needy, not even letting our eyes meet those of others who we know might need someone to listen or a helping hand. We are sorry for turning away and comfortably going in our own direction. Father, for those hearing us pray and recognizing they are guilty of ignoring others and not helping when their assistance is needed, allow them (and us) to be honest and do something about it. After our admission, help us take a step toward action. Show us how we can sacrifice our time, talents, gifts, treasures, and energy and help someone who is lacking right now. Let us be proactive and not wait until we're asked but serve immediately when we see a need. In Jesus' name we pray. Amen.

Share the ways you serve. If you are more of a taker than a giver, decide to serve someone today.

_____

_____

_____

_____

_____

Day 77 — Trials Are Not Trivial

"Therefore, my beloved brethren, be steadfast, immovable, always abounding in the work of the Lord, knowing that your toil is not in vain in the Lord."

I Corinthians 15:58

Through trials, God reveals Himself to us. I have watched Him reveal Himself as He unfolds a trial or challenge and as He calls me to action. In the process of revealing who He is, He also reveals who I am. I seldom like trials, so whether my response is just in my thinking process that no one knows about or whether I'm responding in word or deed in some way during these times, He's usually showing me how I'm missing the mark of understanding who He is, His role in my life, and the reason for the trials. I admit it's not always a pretty response He gets from me, but I know, as I seek him, I eventually come to understand and recognize what He is trying to teach me as well as His lordship in my life. I have so much to learn. As I learn and as we learn how to respond to the lordship of Christ in our lives—

Let's Pause for Prayer

Heavenly Father, we want to stand before you someday and hear you say, "Well, done my good and faithful servant." We know those words from You will encompass our acts of service and kindness and our words or lack of words as well as our responses to the trials you've allowed in our lives. Oh, Lord, I know this world is temporary, so help me realize how fleeting these trials are in light of all eternity. Help me readily accept all that is from your hand—the good, the bad, the ordinary, the extraordinary, the short and long durations, and the lessons learned. I want to be a student who has learned my lessons well. I desire for others to see that I've weathered the storms of life well because I knew and trusted You to get me through them. Help us all to trust You so deeply and genuinely that we have no questions, no second guesses, and no doubts about what You're doing in our lives as You mold us to becoming more like You. In Jesus' name we pray. Amen.

What trial are you going through right now?

_____
_____
_____

How will you learn, honor the Lord, and grow from this trial?

_____
_____
_____

Day 78 — *Mirror, Mirror, On The Wall*

"And put on the new self, which in the likeness of God has been created in righteousness and holiness of the truth."

Ephesians 4:24

Perhaps you've heard this little rhyme: "Mirror, mirror, on the wall, I am my mother, after all!" Sometimes I look at my hands and see my mom's. Occasionally, I'll catch a glimpse of myself in the mirror and see an expression or sagging skin like hers, or I'll even catch a look my dad might have made on my own face as I'm getting ready in the morning in front of the mirror. Every so often I laugh, and in that laughter I hear the sound of my mom's laugh.

We'll all take likenesses from our parents—like them or not—but our goal in this life should be to mirror Christ in our behavior, values, and conduct. We hope we'll catch glimpses of ourselves acting like, speaking like, thinking like, and responding like Jesus as we become the expression of God to others, of who He was and is.

Let's Pause for Prayer

Heavenly Father, we are your children, and we want to be just like You. We want to look like You in every thought, word, and deed. We want You to be proud of us because we've followed in Your footsteps and acted kindly or spoken gently. We want to be like You as we listen carefully and respond thoughtfully to what others say to us. We hope to emulate your gentle ways, Your careful responses, and Your wisdom. Lord, make us wise to share and say only what is necessary and helpful and not what will cause hurt or sadness. Father, we know that sometimes even in the best of situations, we try to do the right thing, and it still comes out wrong; so teach us to observe the right way to do things, the best and right ways to respond, ways to mirror who You are to others. Oh, Lord, Help me to be a good and godly example. In Jesus' name we pray. Amen.

When you think of Christlike behavior, what does it look like to you?

_____

_____

_____

How will you put into action (be specific with examples) some of these Christlike ways?

_____

_____

_____

Day 79 *For Whom Do You Pray?*

> *"I thank my God always, making mention of you in my prayer."*
>
> Philemon 1:4

Do you find it hard to pray? If you answered yes, you're not alone. Some don't like to have to pray out loud, but some simply don't know even where begin a prayer. Next to me on my desk, I have a list of over 30 people to pray for, not individual names but categories like the following:

- Neighbors
- Coworkers
- Family
- Friends
- Teachers
- Those involved in pornography
- Those involved in drinking
- Those who purpose to do evil
- For those who don't know Jesus
- For those whose marriages I know are struggling

The list could be endless. I find the key ingredient to praying is caring enough about the people or topic to want to pray. I never miss a day praying for my husband, children, and other loved ones in my life.

Let's Pause for Prayer

Heavenly Father, as we list so many different people and needs around us, we recognize that we have a lot of things for which to pray. As you put different people in our path, let us listen to them as they share their needs and consider how we can pray for them. When we know of troubled marriages or difficult family situations, nudge us to pray for them in their times of challenge as we hope others will pray for us in our times of challenge. Keep me mindful to pray for them without sharing details with others, keeping confidences. May I be faithful to walk with them in prayer for however long it might take. Thank you that we can be there for one another, whether or not we know all the details. Nudge us to pray when others might not want to ask. Let us remember that although we do the praying, You are the One who will provide the outcomes. The outcomes are in Your hands. In Jesus' name we pray. Amen.

For whom to you regularly pray? If you don't pray regularly for others, begin a list of those for whom you'll pray.

_____

_____

_____

_____

_____

_____

Day 80

Slow Down

> *"Love is patient, love is kind."*
>
> I Corinthians 13:4

I remember reading a newsletter about a 16-year-old high school student with special needs who was told she could not join her classmates for a trip because of her disability. Apparently, she occasionally required the use a wheelchair or some rest to get through a strenuous day. She was told she could not go on the trip because a teacher feared her medical condition would present a burden to the travel group and that her disability would slow the group down.

As a parent with an adult child who needs help dressing, shaving, and showering, I am saddened to hear that others express their impatience and feel inconvenienced when slowed down by a handicapped person. How sad that we don't stop to think how slowed down handicapped people might be as a result of the disability and what patience they learn because of it or how slowed down their caretakers are. God teaches us through people He puts in our lives. I have never learned as much as I have and as much as I do daily by caring for someone who will never be able to be on his own. Have I been slowed down? Definitely, but believe me, the lessons have only been to my advantage!

Let's Pause for Prayer

Heavenly Father, we thank You for those you have put into our lives to help us learn more about Your love for us. Thank you for slowing us down by teaching us to serve and care for the needs of others. Help us to serve with gladness of heart and not resort to sinfulness by showing our frustration or impatience because of our selfishness. Allow us to consider others who might need help and to offer kindly. Help those who are impatient to recognize the challenges that others may have that they don't see because they just want to "keep moving" and not be bothered by others. We all need help. Help us, help me. In Jesus' name we pray. Amen.

Have you ever been frustrated by someone with special needs because she or he held you up and slowed you down?

_____
_____
_____

What might be an action for you to take the next time that happens to you?

_____
_____
_____

Day 81 — *Ease, Fun, And Comfort, Please*

> *"For my yoke is easy, and my load is light."*
>
> Matthew 11:30

Without much thought and after much observation of many people, I can say most of us if we had a choice would choose ease, fun, and comfort. Many people I know have learned as I have that my greatest lessons have been learned during and through hardship, not ease; challenge, not fun; and hard times, not comfort. In *Seeking the Face of God*, Gary Thomas says that wanting comfort and ease is not only "unrealistic, but [also] a lie from Satan and a temptation to make us bitter toward God. It would simply allow us to remain shallow and unrooted in our personalities and our faith. When we learn to see difficulty as the path of growth, [everything] will change." He references John of the Cross with these words:

"Endeavor to be inclined always

not to the easiest, but to the most difficult;

not to the most delightful, but to the harshest;

not to the most gratifying, but to the less pleasant;

not to what means rest for you, but hard work;

not to the consoling, but to the unconsoling;

not to the most, but to the least;

not to the highest and most precious, but to the lowest and most despised;

not to wanting something, but to wanting nothing."

Let's Pause for Prayer

Heavenly Father, we realize that what we think we want is not always best for us. Please help us to find contentment in the hard and difficult times, knowing that You have placed them in our lives to teach us to trust You and knowing that You will help us to carry the load You've given. We desire to thank You in and through those tough times, and we desire to continue serving even when doing so is a challenge. Help us recognize the blessings in those challenges and the joys and the victories (although they might be small) along the way. Help us to call upon and trust in You. In Jesus' name we pray. Amen.

If you had a choice, would you choose easy or difficult, comfortable or uncomfortable?

_____

What have you learned through the fun, easy, and comfortable times of your life? As you've gone through challenges and hardship, what have you learned?

_____

_____

Where have you learned more?

_____

Day 82

Isolation

> *"And be subject to one another in the fear of Christ."*
> Ephesians 5:21

Years ago, while observing several people and families isolate themselves because of depression and other mental challenges, children with special needs, and even sin—because hiding is what most people when they sin—I did some reading. I read that isolation can be destructive, both physically and mentally. For Christians, isolation *should be impossible*. If we meet the needs of our family, friends, and church members as the Lord put it on our hearts, no one would ever suffer from isolation. If we sought out others simply to get to know them, others would not suffer from isolation. Should we open our homes for fun and fellowship, others would not suffer from isolation. And sometimes, those others might be us. Simple obedience to the Lord would allow us no excuse to be isolated from others. Perhaps our physical and mental health depends on it!

Let's Pause for Prayer

Heavenly Father, we ask You to put on our hearts someone to whom we can reach out to this very day, especially if we have allowed ourselves to become isolated from the fellowship of others. And if we should be so blessed to receive a call from someone today, could we be strong enough to make that effort to get together with them in Christian fellowship? We know that even with the best of efforts, others might turn us away, but let it not be for lack of trying. As we obey You, Lord, please strengthen us both physically and mentally to serve and honor You in all ways. In Jesus' name we pray. Amen.

Have you ever been in a place physically or mentally when you chose to isolate yourself? What did that time of life look like for you?

_____

_____

Did you have others reach out to you and how did you respond?

_____

_____

Can you reach out to someone today who might need to be included? Write for yourself your plan of action.

_____

_____

_____

Day 83 *Kindness*

"Therefore encourage one another, and build up one another just as you also are doing."
1 Thessalonians 5:11

Kindness goes a long way to encourage someone in the body of Christ. Probably one of the easiest ways to identify kindnesses to do for others is to ask yourself what you'd enjoy having someone else do for you or say to you. Here are a few ideas, and none will cost you anything but a moment of your time!

- Send an encouraging card or letter to someone you appreciate
- Help someone do repair work on the house, yard, or car, perhaps an older person or single mother, or the neighbor who just had surgery
- Offer to take someone's place in the church nursery as a helper
- Babysit for a single parent or couple so they can have some free time
- Stand in for someone who is caring for an invalid or a child with special needs
- Invite someone who is single or who's lost a spouse to join you at your home for dinner

None of these are very difficult. The challenge is saying yes to the challenge. May I challenge you?

Let's Pause for Prayer

Heavenly Father, we desire to show someone kindness this week. Help us to go out of our way, to be unselfish, to show love and concern, to encourage someone for Your glory. Please help me personally to accept the challenge of showing kindness to another, not because I want to be blessed in return but because I want to bless and encourage another. May You be glorified in the process! And might each person who is shown kindness show others the same! In Jesus' name we pray! Amen.

Can you think of something to do this day to uplift someone who might need a little encouragement? Who will that person be and write exactly what you'd like to do.

_____
_____
_____
_____
_____

Day 84

Left Alone

"Little children, let us not love with word or with tongue, but in deed and truth."

1 John 3:18

As I look around in my own church, at conferences at which my husband and I speak on marriage and family, and at the lives of others around me, I see many single parents, second (and more) marriages, numerous step-relationships, and large numbers of people left alone to survive after engaging in infidelity, tiring of being married, and experiencing other situations that may have been avoidable.

Broken marriages break my heart—and the hearts of so many involved. The husband of one young lady left just as she was about to give birth to their child. Another man left his wife because he had fathered another woman's child, and he was emotionally torn about his obligations. One gentleman with whom my husband and I do business was left by his wife a number of years ago: She left the children with him to pursue a fast-paced youth-oriented lifestyle! I was amazed that she could do that, but I am equally quite wonderfully amazed at the great job he is doing alone as a single father. In another case a wife's husband wants nothing to do with the Lord, even though he professed to be a Christian when they married.

As we look at each of these scenarios and most broken marriages, the problem boils down to pride or selfishness or both. Think about it and let me know if you find a situation that differs.

Let's Pause for Prayer

Heavenly Father, we know that people with broken marriages have broken hearts and homes in one way or another. We ask You to give each one the strength to make it through the day as they try to do the job of two people in one, as they try to put one foot in front of the other when their hearts are so broken they can hardly lift their feet. We pray that You would gently speak to the heart of each one and encourage them with Your love. Allow us to be sensitive to their needs and to offer them assistance if we can help in some way and if they are willing to accept it. Please put in our hearts a way we can specifically pray for them? Help us to discern how we can be useful to them for Your glory. In Jesus' name we pray. Amen.

Do you know anyone for whom you can pray as she or he goes through the devastation of a broken marriage?

_____

_____

How can you offer prayer or care to this individual to make her or his load a little lighter?

_____

_____

_____

Day 85

Just Who Are You?

> *"When Jesus entered Jerusalem, the whole city was stirred and asked, 'Who is this?'"*
>
> Matthew 21:10

Wouldn't it be wonderful if people saw in us—as a result of coming to know and serve Christ—such a change that they would ask, "Just who are you?"

A friend from high school had accepted Christ in his late 20s. His life was so radically changed, all in good ways, that one day his son answered the phone and said to his father's friend, "Did you want my old dad or my new dad?" That is how much his behavior, attitude, words, and actions changed. His young son noticed.

It's only when Jesus was asked into the heart of that individual that He was able to help the man make the changes that would affect families, workplaces, and whole communities! Those of us who know the Lord and have been in the process of change and growth in our walk with the Him can attest to the excitement when we see the positives that happen as a result of our obedience to Him.

We can see those positive changes in our lives, in our marriages, and in the lives of our families when we take seriously our relationship with Jesus, who can make those changes in our lives. If you don't have a relationship with Him, would you like to? There's no time like the present. You simply need to ask Him.

Let's Pause for Prayer

Heavenly Father, I thank You that I can come to You, the Living God, and ask You to enter my heart. I confess to You my sin, which keeps me from truly knowing you, and ask you to forgive me of my sin. Please come into my heart and make the changes in me that are needed in order to make changes in my family, my work, my life, and even my community. Thank You for what you have done for me through the death and resurrection of Your Son, and help me to be all I can be for Your glory! In Jesus' name we pray. Amen.

What changes have you seen in your life as a result of trusting in the Lord? What changes have you seen in the lives of others who've come to know Christ?

_____

_____

_____

Is there a next step for you so that the Lord can work to cause change that matters in your life?

_____

_____

_____

Day 86 — *Does Prayer Make A Difference?*

> *"Therefore He [God] said that He would destroy them [idolaters], had not Moses, His chosen one, stood in the breach before Him to turn away His wrath from destroying them."*
>
> Psalm 106: 23

Sometimes I forget that my prayer can make a difference. Sometimes I wonder whether God hears and considers my requests, yet scripture has a way of showing me the reality of what prayer can do if I obey God and do it. Psalm 106: 19-23 presents a retelling of the story of His people making and worshiping an idol in the form of a golden calf in Horeb. "They forgot God their Savior, who had done great things in Egypt, wonders in the land of Ham, and awesome things by the Red Sea. Therefore He [God] said that He would destroy them had not Moses, His chosen one, stood in the breach before Him to turn away His wrath from destroying them."

Even when the people forgot God, He did not forget them. God considered the prayers of Moses and did not destroy the people because of his prayers. We should consider the many ways we have built idols and forgotten the God of our land who has done great and mighty things. We hope we will be the ones to pray for those who've forgotten and trust that God will restore. Our country is in a place right now where prayer could help. Will you be one who would stand before the Lord on behalf of our country?

Let's Pause for Prayer

Heavenly Father, thank You for hearing our prayers. We pray that you would allow us to be as Moses and stand in the breach before You, asking You to turn Your wrath away from destroying our land. Please forgive our disobedience to Your word, our building of idols to people and things, and our lack of concern over what must break Your heart. Help us to know Your heart and pray for what You desire for us as individuals and for our country. In Jesus' name we pray. Amen.

After reading this devotional and prayer, where did your heart turn to pray?

_____

_____

_____

As you pray about that particular issue, situation, or challenge, ask the Lord what you might do to take action. Write it down for yourself and take the next step.

_____

_____

_____

Day 87

Living Day By Day

> *"Then the Lord said to Moses, 'I will rain down bread from heaven for you. The people are to go out each day and gather enough for that day. In this way I will test them and see whether they will follow my instructions.'"*
>
> Exodus 16:4

Andrew Murray's *Abide in Christ* (Day 14) has been enjoyable for me to read. Every sentence is packed with truth from God's word and often needs to be reread!

As I was reading about abiding in Christ day by day, I was struck with the realization that many of us don't live that way even though God wants us to. Are we different from the Israelites in the time of Moses?

Andrew Murray says, "We are so easily led to look at life as a great whole and to neglect the little today, to forget that the single days do indeed make up the whole, and that the value of each single day depends on its influence on the whole. One day lost is a link broken in the chain, which often takes more than another day to mend. Each day of faithfulness brings a blessing for the next, makes both the trust and the surrender easier and more blessed. And so the Christian life grows: As we give our whole heart to the work of each day, it becomes all the day, and from that every day… and the days make up life."

Are we borrowing troubles from tomorrow, worried or anxious about the future over which we have no control anyway, fretting over some difficulty or problem that if we simply take it to the Lord in prayer, He would resolve it?

Let's Pause for Prayer

Heavenly Father, please help me to be content in today, trusting in You to meet my every need just as you did with the Israelites. I desire not to complain about what I think I should have or do, knowing that You have given me this day and the joys and challenges of it for a specific reason. I want to trust in You, and I thank You for the way you will teach me that trust this very day. In Jesus' name I pray. Amen.

What struggle or concern do you have today that you will turn over to the Lord?

_____

_____

_____

What will you do today to let the Lord have control of all the minutes of your day?

_____

_____

_____

Day 88

Off The Treadmill

"For it is God who is at work in you, both to will and to work for His good pleasure."

Philippians 2:13

A major turning point comes for most of us when we realize we've been listening to the voice of our inner critic and not the voice of God. Longing to be loved and affirmed, seeking approval yet feeling unworthy, performing for others, wanting to please others, and doing and doing puts us on a treadmill of sorts. We find the fast and compulsive pace of life can often mirror what we have come to believe in our hearts—even if we know better. All of our efforts and performance-based actions will not gain for us God's love and acceptance of us.

We need to get off the treadmill of life, stop, and listen until we hear His voice speak to our hearts and learn what new direction He has planned for us.

Can you relate? I have a feeling most of us can.

Let's Pause for Prayer

Heavenly Father, we pray that we would take this moment to pause from the busyness of the day and ask You to direct us. Lord, if I am pursuing mostly good things, but they are not the best to accomplish Your work, please show me. Please redirect me so that my life is filled only with the work You would have me to do. Lord, guide me and my family in pursuing Your work for Your glory and not for the vain glory of man. I want to be in the center of Your will, doing only what you expect of me, so that someday I will look back with no regrets. In Jesus' name we pray. Amen.

Do you sense this frantic fast-paced life is yours? In what way? Describe it.

_____

_____

_____

_____

What will you do to change? Write out a prayer to pray today.

_____

_____

_____

_____

Day 89 — Don't Leave Home Without It

> *"The effective prayer of a righteous man can accomplish much."*
> James 5:16b

If you are in Christian leadership, you know that a spiritual battle rages every moment of every day on every front. No matter what God asks us to do, a battle awaits. Even if you aren't in Christian leadership, you certainly see battles raging in your own life and in the lives of members of your family and colleagues at work as well as in the ministry opportunities you have.

For years we prayed about all those struggles and even asked others to pray for us, but in 1996 Joe and I asked some close friends and family to pray for us as we enlisted a prayer team.

This group was asked to pray for us regularly, and we pray for them. We send them a monthly prayer request letter, and many of them do the same for us so that we can be in prayer together. It is very satisfying to know that others are praying for us when the going gets rough and rejoicing with us when the way is smooth. Although the monthly prayer request letter covers the activities of the month, we occasionally may call or email an urgent request for prayer.

We have found this to be very beneficial for us as individuals, as a couple and a family, and in both work and ministry. We know we are not alone in the daily struggles that come our way.

Let's Pause for Prayer

Heavenly Father, please help each of us desire to take part in the lives of others by praying for them. We know life is full of surprises and glitches, joys, and fears, good relationships and testy ones, hardships and victories; and having one another to pray through those is such a blessing. Please show me for whom You would like me to pray on a regular basis. Thank you for the prayer partners you give us, for prayer requests we can pray about and watch You answer, and for being there for one another in prayer! In Jesus' name we pray. Amen.

Do you have someone who you know is praying for you? Do you pray regularly and faithfully for anyone?

_____

_____

If not, perhaps this might be the nudge you need to take that step to develop a prayer team of your own. Who might you ask?

_____

_____

_____

Day 90

Anytime Prayers

> *"Sow with a view to righteousness, reap in accordance with kindness; break up your fallow ground, for it is time to seek the Lord."*
>
> Hosea 10:12

Like many of you, I spend quite a bit of time in the car. Getting my son to and from his place of employment, running errands, and traveling all add up to hours in the car. I have learned to make good use of my time in the car by doing a number of mental activities.

I mentally go through what my day has in store, what is on my shopping list before I get to the grocery store, who I'll meet, and how I will respond to them. I think about my husband and children, their friends, our extended family and others. I think about topics I would like to write about, and I think about memories from the past that bring me joy.

What I like best about those mental activities is that they are not really just mental activities. They are opportunities to pray. I pray for the produce workers and checkout clerks, many of whom I have come to know over the years, shopping in the same grocery store. I pray for those I might meet whom I didn't expect to meet—the good meetings and the ones that aren't quite so pleasant. I pray for my husband and his day at work, the children and their families and careers, their friends, and also their coworkers. And then, I pray in a spirit of thanksgiving that I am able to drive, think, and serve the Lord as a wife, mother, and ministry leader.

Let's Pause for Prayer

Lord, thank you that our commutes can be quite filled! Our commutes do not have to be tedious, nor do they have to feel empty because You are there with us. Thank you for days filled not only with activities but also much prayer support. And I am thankful that I can pray all day to You everywhere I go. I don't need any technology to have conversation with You, Lord. Thank You for filling our moments of commuting time with precious time with You! In Jesus' name we pray. Amen.

Have you considered using your commute and other quiet time to pray?

_____

_____

For whom will you pray? What situations and people come immediately to mind?

_____

_____

_____

Day 91 — Call Home

> *"Do not fear or be dismayed. Be strong and courageous."*
>
> Joshua 10:25

As the morning unfolded the day of 9/11, I wished my whole family had been together, something I think many of us feel at a time of crisis; but I was heading to the radio station for a meeting that would soon be canceled and I'd return home—where I wanted to be!

Entering my home, I headed first to the phone, delighted that each of my family members had called home and left messages about where they were. Our youngest (age 12) called from school to ask whether a friend could come over after school because no one would be home at her house. I said, "Absolutely, and we'll keep in touch with her parents." But then she said, "Mom, we're really scared. Will you bring us home right now?" I asked if she was sick or hurt. She said, "No" to both. I then said, "How about if I don't pick you up. You have a job to do at school. You need to show the peace and love of Jesus. If you, knowing the Lord, are afraid and want to come home, why would any of your fellow students want to learn about your Lord? Honey, this is a battle. Our country has been attacked physically, and that is one battle. But you are now in a spiritual battle. You are on the front lines. So let's pray that you will be a light in a dark place for your classmates." Then on the phone we prayed, and she said, "OK, I can do it."

Let's Pause for Prayer

Heavenly Father, we come to You, desiring to serve You and to make You known to others. We pray knowing you have all the answers, power, and authority! We pray Joshua 10:25: "Do not fear or be dismayed. Be strong and courageous." Father, help us to stay on the front lines, praying without ceasing, no matter where we are. Please keep us focused on being a good example to others. We know when we call upon You, we are calling home. Help us to share with others whenever opportunities present themselves—in crisis and in peace. In Jesus' name we pray. Amen.

Do you call upon the Lord in crisis? How about in times of peace?

How can you show others the strength you have in the Lord today?

Day 92

High Alert Status

> *"Devote yourselves to prayer, keeping alert in it with an attitude of thanksgiving."*
>
> Colossians 4:2

You've probably heard news reporters say, "Our country is on high alert status!" Or you've heard an emergency system blaring to get your attention or a police car or emergency vehicle zooming past you, and you knew you had to pull over and stop.

Suddenly, our mundane routines—momentary or daily activities—stop for us. We'd never have believed we could devote an entire day to rearranging our day or stopping what we thought was so urgently important about our daily business. But we stop. We stop because our mundane daily routine no longer seems so important. Nothing is presently as important as it was 24 hours ago.

Suddenly, we realize that although God cares about all of our concerns, what is happening during a crisis, tragedy, or emergency grind to a halt. And that is when even our prayers go into high alert status!

Let's Pause for Prayer

Heavenly Father, we are sorry for the times we haven't come to you or were just too busy to pray. We apologize for failing to recognize and realize that we *always* have a reason to pray and time to pray when we see it as *top priority*. Father, we are on high alert status, coming to you to pray for our country, our families, and our personal journey with you. We don't want to let our guard down and be prayerful only when a siren calls us to pray. We pray for your protection and guidance for the leadership of this country, for the leaders in our homes, and for us to lead by example. Let us remain on high alert status, praying as you lead us. In Jesus' name we pray. Amen.

Is your normal prayer attitude one of taking action in crisis, tragedy, or emergency? If so, how do you take action?

_____

_____

_____

How will you take action to pray moment to moment and throughout the day so that it's not just an event in an emergency? Write out a prayer to get started if that will help.

_____

_____

_____

_____

Day 93   *Fashionable Prayer*

> *"Give ear to my prayer, O God; and do not hide Thyself from my supplication."*
>
> Psalm 55:1

It is very encouraging and even energizing to hear secular as well as Christian radio and television announcers say, "We will be praying" or "They have our prayers" or other prayer-related comments. When disaster, crisis, or tragedy occurs, it's amazing how fashionable prayer becomes. At some crisis points, the Christian radio stations have had full day-long prayer times. Sometime people will gather at churches or outside public places to pray during times of disaster. I've even heard of businesses offering times of prayer over lunch hours.

It's sad that it often takes horrible tragedy to call us personally and as a country into an attitude of prayer. But it's wonderful that when those times come, we are allowed to pray and people make the effort to pray. We have reason every day to continue praying, but wouldn't it be great if at those times of urgent need, prayer would be sustained through that time and beyond? It is exciting when emphasis on prayer continues with individuals who make an impact with their fearlessness and pray publicly. And at those times, I have been amazed that I have never heard of anyone asking another to stop praying!

Let's Pause for Prayer

Heavenly Father, we rejoice that many take a stand to pray, whether at work, in churches, at home, or in public places. How thankful we are that we can pray as faithfully and diligently in our hearts as we can out loud! Please keep quiet those who might hinder prayerful efforts. Continue to instill in all those who pray, the boldness to share You, to pray to You, and to be courageous as we proclaim You as Lord. Never let us be shy, afraid, unsure of our abilities, worried, or in any way fearful of proclaiming You, Your Word, and the power in your name. In Jesus' name we pray. Amen.

Are you one who can and does pray in public? Why or why not?

_____

_____

_____

What is one step you can take to feel comfortable praying publicly (for example, at dinner when in a restaurant, in church during prayer time, with friends)?

_____

_____

_____

_____

Day 94

In God We Trust?

"I will put my trust in Him."

Hebrews 2:13

Do you feel secure in these times of unrest in our country and in the world? Where have you placed your trust? Is it in your savings account? Is it in a trust fund? Is it in the stock market? Or have you trusted and put your security in the Lord Jesus?

Everyone one of us trusts in something. As Christians we need to be ready to share with others our faith in Christ as the only means of security anyone will ever need. I believe the situations that engulf us in our country—the lack of transparency in our government, the bullying, and the mean-spiritedness—as well as all that is happening around the world either make us fret and worry or call us to fall on our knees and pray as we trust in Him to help us through whatever challenges and crises occur. It would be great to see a renewed interest in spiritual matters that should have us ready as Christians, willing and able to share our faith with everyone who has a question, a concern, or a worry!

Let's Pause for Prayer

Heavenly Father, we thank You for Your words in scripture that assure us of our security in You. John 5: 24, "I assure you, those who listen to my message and believe in God who sent me have eternal life." We rejoice in knowing that we are safe and secure in You forever. Let us not be ashamed, shy, or reluctant to share that certainty with all those who are in our circles of influence. In Jesus' name we pray. Amen.

In what or whom do you honestly put your trust?

_____

_____

_____

Are you prepared to help others, using the overflow of your trust in Jesus to help them put trust in Him?

_____

_____

_____

_____

Day 95

Overflowing Gratitude

"For all things are for your sakes, that the grace which is spreading to more and more people may cause the giving of thanks to abound to the glory of God."

II Corinthians 4:15

We are often encouraged to be positive, look on the bright side, or realize that every cloud has a silver lining; however, being thankful for difficult people and being thankful in difficult circumstances does not derive from psyching ourselves up to have a good attitude. Instead, our gratitude must flow from a more reliable source.

In II Corinthians 4, Paul said that the source of our gratitude is "faith in the grace of God." In faith we believe and speak because we know that the Father has poured, is pouring, and will continue to pour out His grace upon us. It is His grace that caused "thanksgiving to overflow to the glory of God." Let's ask Him by faith for His grace to be able to say thank you at all times and in all things.

Let's Pause for Prayer

Heavenly Father, we thank you—yes, we thank you—for that difficult situation, difficult person, or disappointment in our lives that deeply challenges us. By faith we ask that You give us the grace to be able to appreciate that you have given all things, and we ask that we should be able to embrace this challenge so we can learn and grow. Transform our hearts so that we will be grateful for all you have given. In Jesus' name we pray. Amen.

Are you having a hard time with a situation for which you will give thanks? What is that difficulty, disappointment, or challenge? Name it.

_____

_____

_____

Write out a prayer of thanksgiving that you can daily pray.

_____

_____

_____

_____

_____

Day 96　　　　　　　　　　　　　　　　　　　　　*Hidden Calling*

"Make it your ambition to lead a quiet life and attend to your own business."
I Thessalonians 4:11

Good people and the extraordinary ways God uses them are usually hidden. God doesn't always put on display the works He most treasures.

Some people are called to a kind of serving that is noticed and seen by thousands, but many are called to live quiet lives that others consider unremarkable, uninteresting, hidden, or even invisible. Serving in hidden ways does not mean that we're forgotten by God. He places us, as Oswald Chambers writes, "where we may bring Him the most glory, and we are no judges of where that is."

Sometimes being noticed is, in fact, a spiritual hazard. The longing that some feel to be noticed is evidence enough that such notice would only harm us spiritually.

Perhaps you serve in a ministry of prayer or serve meals or write encouraging notes or make telephone calls. Perhaps few people know you even do those things. Let's rejoice that while our high calling may go unnoticed, it is still very important!

Let's Pause for Prayer

Heavenly Father, we pray that you would instill in our hearts the desire to serve You no matter who we are, no matter where we are, and no matter who notices. Help us let go of the idea that we need to be noticed, thus freeing us to serve You wherever You call us. Help us to recognize the gifts and responsibilities to which You've called us and to be content in serving in both quiet and hidden places as well as in the open and more noticeable venues You've placed before us. We want You and You only to be pleased. In Jesus' name we pray. Amen.

Is your service to the Lord in a hidden or visible ministry? Write out what you believe He has given you to do. Is change needed? If so, what is the change you need to make and how will you make that change?

_____

_____

_____

If you are in a more up-front and visible ministry, did you put yourself there or did God? Share your thoughts to reread later and to pray about.

_____

_____

_____

Day 97

Authority Over Me

> *"Pray on behalf of kings and all who are in authority."*
> I Timothy 2:2

What comes to mind when you hear the word *leader*? The president, elected officials, kings, perhaps your pastor? Yes, each of these is a leader, but I wonder whether we could take this thought a few steps further and consider the leaders in our lives who are not quite so public as those noted here.

I Timothy 2:2 says that we should "pray on behalf of kings and all who are in authority." As I reflected upon those who have been or are authorities in my life, the list became pretty long—my parents, teachers, principals I worked with, a former boss, my husband, pastors, and even heads of committees. I was quite surprised to realize the number of people (for one reason or another) who have been leaders in authority over me. How about in your life? Perhaps your authority is a choral director, a youth pastor, a parole officer, a judge, a piano teacher, or even a bus driver or someone else who is in charge.

Have we prayed for those in authority over us? I would say at times we might choose to rebel and not pray for them possibly because we don't like the idea that they have the responsibility to lead us and are in authority over us; but if God put them there, we are instructed to pray for them.

Let's Pause for Prayer

Heavenly Father, we pray for each person You have just brought to mind who is in authority over us. Thank you for that teacher or boss or other leader who takes the time to train us, teach us, and lead us. Help us to appreciate the role that they have in our lives, and give us teachable hearts open to learning from their leadership. Lord, may I be receptive to their guidance and care. And in the case of one who is not using her or his authority properly, may I be the one to pray for that individual to come under Your authority and seek to do what You have asked. In Jesus' name we pray. Amen.

Do you pray regularly for your leaders?

_____
_____
_____

What one thing will you do today to support someone who is in authority over you?

_____
_____
_____
_____

Day 98   *Money*

"He who loves money will not be satisfied with money."
Ecclesiastes 5:10

Both big businesses and smaller privately owned businesses struggle during economic downturns, which may be difficult for many people to get through. Many will have to make cuts in their personal budgets to make it month to month, and as the economy goes, so go businesses.

How many of us have said, "God has everything under control"? In challenging and stressful times, however, we are really put to the test of whether what we say is what we truly believe.

I have been reminded recently of a few things that blessed and encouraged me:

1. God owns everything, and I am merely His money manager.
2. My heart always goes where I put God's money.
3. Giving is the only antidote to materialism.
4. Heaven, not earth, is my home.
5. God may prosper me, not to raise my standard of living but to raise my standard of giving.

No matter where God has placed us presently in our financial status, we can take responsibility for the way we use, save, and give the money He has allotted us.

Let's Pause for Prayer

Heavenly Father, we know You are in control of our finances. Please help us to respond accordingly. Help us save as good stewards, spend wisely, and give sacrificially. Help us to be mindful of others who may have needs in times of economic uncertainty and act responsibly in caring for them in their time of need. May we give to Your causes, knowing that those investments will last for all eternity. Show us those who need help, leading us to do what would honor and please you and help them. In Jesus' name we pray. Amen.

What part does money play in your everyday life?

_____

_____

Consider someone who has a need. How might you fill that need anonymously?

_____

_____

Day 99 — Aging Gracefully?

"And even when I am old and gray, O God, do not forsake me, until I declare Thy strength to this generation, Thy power to all who are to come."

Psalm 71: 18

I have always been aware of aging. I remember even as a little child wondering why we couldn't get old and then get young again. Aging parents gave me a perspective as well, one that I will probably share with my children. As I watch those around me whom I love, I realize the importance of growing old gracefully, and I thank the Lord for giving me some beautiful examples from which to learn.

Having attended a seminar a number of years ago on the topic of aging, I recognized that the Lord might be trying to impress upon me some important lessons at that time of my life! A few things I learned from that meeting and from others teaching me about growing gracefully are as follows:

1. We must have hope! If we don't have hope, we won't live long, and we certainly won't live happily.
2. We should (even now) develop a spirit of gratitude, optimism, and forgiveness every day.
3. We need to employ the spirit of empathy, walking in another's shoes instead of assuming a critical attitude.
4. We must continue to reach out to others, not withdraw, isolate, or hide ourselves.
5. We can't prevent that which is inevitable: Our bodies and minds are changing!
6. In aging, there is much wisdom to share—if one has lived to gain wisdom. You can't share what you don't have.
7. We all know that we are aging even at this moment. Let's consider how we can do so gracefully.

Let's Pause for Prayer

Heavenly Father, thank You for reminding us that we are aging. We are grateful that aging causes us look to You to soothe us when we have aches and pains, that we become more focused on heaven as our eyesight dims, and that we can look around at others as examples of growing old and know that we, too, can grow old gracefully! Help us to be examples to others around us as we desire to finish well. Help us to live out Psalm 71:18: "And even when I am old and gray, O God, do not forsake me until I declare Your strength to this generation, Your power to all who are to come." In Jesus' name we pray. Amen.

Who in your life is an example of someone who is growing old gracefully? Write about why she or he is an inspiration. Consider whom you will be able to influence and guide as a result of the wisdom you will gain as you grow older if you continue to walk in the ways of the Lord. What do you hope others will learn or gain from you and your example?

_____

_____

_____

Day 100

Taking For Granted

"It is good to give thanks to the Lord, and to sing praises to Thy name, O Most High."

Psalm 92:1

Years ago Joe and I spoke in Colorado Springs, staying at the historic Antlers Doubletree Hotel. In 1893 a young woman named Katherine Lee Bates, an English teacher from back East, visited Colorado for the first time and stayed at the same hotel. One view from the hotel is the beautiful Pike's Peak. For those of us from the East, the sight is difficult to put into words. But as Katherine Lee Bates saw the view and then climbed to the top of Pike's Peak (reaching the summit of the 14,000-foot peak), the beauty of the majestic panorama before her struck her as awesome. She hurried back to her hotel room, where she penned the first three stanzas of "America the Beautiful."

Do you suppose those who wake up every morning to that view throw open the window and break into song? Perhaps some do, but I would guess the majority take for granted what is in their own backyard.

Likely, we all tend to take for granted what's in our own backyard. We take for granted our backyard view, our marriages, and our children, freedom of religion, or perhaps even our jobs and ministries. At one time, each of these was brand new, and we were astounded by the panorama before us. But now, we take it for granted.

Sometimes we need to climb the mountain again and take in the view as if we were seeing it for the very first time.

Let's Pause for Prayer

Heavenly Father, thank you for the beautiful things you have given to us—the sunrise and sunshine, the rain and snow, the warmth and cold, and the many views we take for granted. Thank you for our friendships, our marriages, our families, and our jobs and ministries, which we know are gifts from you. We pray that You would show us a fresh view of all that You have provided for us so that we do not take any of it for granted or become bored or simply ungrateful for all that You have provided. We humbly thank You. In Jesus' name we pray. Amen.

What view had you once thought awesome that you now take for granted?

_____

_____

Make a list of the people, things, or situations that you feel you take for granted. Pray a prayer of thanksgiving for all God has given, allowed, and provided.

_____

_____

_____

Day 101 — Silence Is Golden

> *"My soul waits in silence for God only."*
> Psalm 62:1

The April after 9/11 I was honored to accompany the Strongsville High School music groups as a chaperone to New York City. We enjoyed many sights and tours. The students had the distinct honor of receiving instruction from the director of the orchestra for *Les Miserables*, preparing them to perform in a church the Sunday morning before our return home. I was amazed to hear the pieces they played, some of which were original scores, and the beautiful voices of these talented young performers.

But what struck me most wasn't the talent of the teens, the tours or activities of our five days away, or that our public school students were performing music of Christian origin in a Christian church. What struck me most was our time at Ground Zero, then called The Pit, which was right next to our hotel. From certain windows, we could see The Pit, observe workers day and night, and we could see another building next to ours with many windows blown out, some boarded up, some wide open, and some with lights on inside as if someone lived there.

One morning all 110 of our tour group members went to place a wreath at the site of Ground Zero. The orchestra director said, "None of us knows how we will respond when we get there, so if you are unsure how to respond, please respond in silence." To my amazement, amidst the busy street and the honking of horns there was extreme silence. Some wept, some knelt in prayer, some just stood quietly while our tour guide, who had seen the second plane crash into the second tower, sobbed. She said, "Not a day goes by that I don't think about what happened and the people we lost."

The impact of what happened back in September (9/11) took on a new meaning for many of us. Although some have moved on with life, it stopped at Ground Zero for countless families. Let's not forget them or where our country is right now as a result of that day.

Let's Pause for Prayer

Heavenly Father, please help us to remember the grieving families who have lost loved ones—then and presently as a result of terrorism, hate crimes, and tragedy. We pray for those serving and fighting in our armed services to protect the freedoms we continue to enjoy; we are thankful for the way You have worked in our hearts since then. May we always remember what it means to sacrifice, for those who've done so have paid a great price—civilian and service men and women alike. In Jesus' name we pray. Amen.

What does sacrifice mean to you? Have you ever had to sacrifice something for another person? Explain.

Day 102

Approved

"Be diligent to present yourself approved to God as a workman who does not need to be ashamed, handling accurately the word of truth."

II Timothy 2:15

It would be so freeing to be ruled neither by people's opinions nor public opinion but concerned only about God's opinion.

We often spend a significant amount of time concerned with what we think others think about us! We want the approval of others and strive to get it. Jesus said, "He who speaks from himself seeks his own glory; but He who is seeking the glory of the one who sent Him, He is true, and there is no unrighteousness in Him" (John 7:18). How much better it is to be free from the pressure of pleasing others and strive only to please God!

Let's Pause for Prayer

Heavenly Father, we pray that You would help us to care most about people but not to be concerned about their opinion of us. May our words be kind, true, and encouraging to all with whom we are in contact. May we say the words that we know You would say even when it needs to be corrective and instructive. May we not keep silent when we know we must speak yet speak in love. Help us to know the right time for words and the right time for silence. In Jesus' name we pray. Amen.

Do you feel the need to please others? Write down a few examples for yourself.

_____

_____

Can you take action about seeking first the Lord for His approval instead of seeking the approval of others? How will you take action to make this happen?

_____

_____

_____

_____

Day 103

Manners Matter

"Every good thing bestowed and every perfect gift is from above, coming down from the Father of lights, with whom there is no variation, or shifting shadow. In the exercise of His will He brought us forth by the word of truth, so that we might be, as it were, the first fruits among His creatures."

James 1:17–18

Manners matter. Saying please and thank you is important in showing kindness and gratitude. It seems few people feel the need to write thank you notes anymore. I'm not sure why. Let's consider the giving of a gift. The giver must first consider what to give, then search for the gift, purchase or make the gift, wrap it, and present the gift. Just adding up the time it took should encourage the receiver to at least say, "Thanks for the effort!" But in saying or writing a thank you note for a gift, we are acknowledging the giver's kindness in both thought and in action. What might take the giver hours to complete can be acknowledged by the recipient in the 5 minutes it takes to write a thank you.

Let's Pause for Prayer

Heavenly Father, we pray that we can transfer this simple lesson of gratitude to the larger realm of what You have done for us. May we teach our children to recognize and thank You for the many ways You have blessed us, the way You've bestowed gifts upon us, the way You've provided and protected us. And by expressing thanks to others, may our children learn how much more important it is to thank You, too! May we be an example of the way we want our children to respond and act. In Jesus' name we pray. Amen.

In what ways do you wish others would show appreciation when you've given a gift?

___

___

___

Do you thank others when they've given you a gift?

___

___

Have you shown thanks and appreciation to the Lord for what He has provided for you? If so, how; and if not, how will you go about making it a practice?

___

___

___

Day 104 — *Laughter And Tears*

> *"Even in laughter the heart may be in pain, and the end of joy may be grief."*
>
> Proverbs 14:13

Following the deaths of my mom and dad a number of years ago (around the Thanksgiving holiday), I went through the routine of a normal day yet experienced deep sadness. As I completed my errands at the grocery store, I thought, "This grocery clerk has no idea of how I am feeling because I am smiling and carrying on as usual, but nothing feels usual right now." I remember looking at the clerk and thinking, "I wonder what she is going through that is causing her pain, and yet she is smiling." My eyes were opened to a different perspective as I went about my day.

People often carry some specific pain, some memory of difficulty, a circumstance that will never change, or a life change that prevents life ever from being normal again; and few others around them know it. We carry on as usual, but nothing is usual and never will be again. Knowing this has helped me to pray for others whom I know are experiencing difficult times as well as to pray for those who hide pain and suffering beneath their smiles while I remain completely oblivious.

Let's Pause for Prayer

Heavenly Father, we thank You that we can pray for one another through times of difficulty. We pray for those who have recently lost loved ones, knowing that life will never be the same for them. Please give them strength. We pray for those who are experiencing pain from their past and ask that you would be their comfort. We pray for those whose present situation has changed their lives so radically that nothing will be as it once was. Please help us be aware of others for whom to pray and care and with whom to share Your love. In Jesus' name we pray. Amen.

Have you experienced a time when you sensed a combination of sadness and joy or laughter and tears at the same time? Write about the experience you recall and tell how you felt.

_____

_____

_____

How can you pray for others today? Is there someone to call or reach out to whoever might need a word of encouragement or understanding? If so, who is that person and when will you contact her or him?

_____

_____

_____

Day 105

Does Anyone Stay Married Anymore?

> *"Let marriage be held in honor among all."*
>
> Hebrews 13:4a

A while ago I overheard a short conversation of several people who did not seem to know one another. Somehow they discovered they were from the same town and began a friendly conversation. The couple asked the man what brought him to town, and he sheepishly laughed and said, "Divorce." The woman of the couple said, "Does anybody stay married anymore?" All three laughed uncomfortably.

I know people divorce for many reasons, but I wonder how many marriages could be worked out if both partners worked toward oneness instead of isolation. I also wondered how many marriages could have been saved had both partners kept the promises they made in their wedding vows!

Let's Pause for Prayer

Heavenly Father, we pray for all marriages—that we would honor them and hold them up in high esteem. We appreciate seeing a marriage that has stood the test of time and is on its way to leaving a legacy for the next generation. May those contemplating divorce or separation recognize what is being severed. Lord, we know that not only the marriage will be severed but also the family, extended family, and even relationships with friends. Please help all couples to work hard at marriage by giving them stamina and endurance as they come to You for help and guidance. In Jesus' name we pray. Amen.

Do you know of one or more couples struggling in their marriage? List ways you can pray for them.

_____

_____

_____

_____

In what ways can you offer help to them? How can you help them go the distance in their marriage?

_____

_____

_____

_____

Day 106 — *The Last Time*

> *"I will be with you; I will be with you; I will not fail you or forsake you."*
>
> Joshua 1:5b

High school and college seniors get excited about finishing their last final, anticipating their last day of school, and then come to the realization that commencement just might be the last time that they will see many of their classmates. It is such a bittersweet experience, isn't it?

Some of us have had to let go of relationships following difficulties (sometimes death) and recognize the last time we'd be with our loved one.

We leave jobs, ministries, churches, neighborhoods, and a goodbye is always involved that last time we are together. We hear voices echo, "I hope to see you soon" and "Let's keep in touch"; but the sad reality is that all will go their separate ways, and if any keeping in touch is to be done, it will take a lot more effort than they think it will.

Let's Pause for Prayer

Heavenly Father, we pray for those in situations in which goodbyes are a part of change. May You give each one a sense of accomplishment for all they have endured and achieved in each relationship. For those who know, follow, and serve You, we pray these last opportunities with friends, classmates, and neighbors present the occasion to make a decision for You, Lord. For those who do not know You, we pray that someone will be courageous and tell them about You so that they will go on their way with You. Whether they are able to keep in touch or not, let them know they will see one another again. In Jesus' name we pray. Amen.

When have you had to say goodbye to someone? Write for yourself as many remembrances as you can.

_____
_____
_____
_____

What can you do to prepare for a goodbye or last time with someone? How would that look if it worked out ideally?

_____
_____
_____
_____

Day 107

Yes, Even God Needed Rest

"For in six days the Lord made heaven and earth, but on the seventh day He ceased from labor, and was refreshed."

Exodus 31:17b

Do you ever feel the need to refuel and refresh yourself? With family obligations, ministry opportunities, work responsibilities, and everyday life, it's easy to come up empty at the end of the day. When those days turn into weeks, months, or possibly years, the absence of rest and refreshment in our lives can cause us to crash and burn!

We all need to take time for rest. Doing so is not a sin, but we are so wrapped up in busyness and activities that we may think it's wrong to rest! Taking time to reflect upon each day and taking occasional vacations to rest are essential to refueling, which we need in order to do our best with all that is on our plates.

It's OK for us to stop and get refreshed, and the Lord gave us that permission with His own example in Exodus 31:1b.

Let's Pause for Prayer

Heavenly Father, we desire to be recharged and thus refreshed in the process. Will you, dear Lord, allow us to rest by showing us how to remove ourselves from busyness and constant moving and doing, taking time to reflect upon Your call to us? Please recharge and refresh us with rest so that we are ready, able, and willing to serve You. In Jesus' name we pray. Amen.

What causes you to be busy, to be in an agitated state of mind, to feel frustrated with all that is going on in your life?

_____

_____

_____

What is the one task or obligation you can remove from your list to initiate the process of becoming refreshed? What can you remove next from your daily rat race to reduce stress and exhaustion? When can you remove them?

_____

_____

_____

_____

Day 108

I Want It My Way

"And put on the new self, which in the likeness of God has been created in righteousness."

Ephesians 4:24

I find that going through life wanting to have our own way is easy, but when others want their own way with us, we are frustrated and irritated. We should, however, see such times of frustrations as opportunities to share Christ with others, giving us a new outlook on an old frustration.

Which of us hasn't at some time wanted or demanded our own way? Which of us hasn't felt someone has been a bother or nuisance to us? I can't even imagine how these attitudes of selfishness must sadden the Lord.

I think of times that we sense we should do something for someone who has a need but stay in our own comfort zones because helping would be a bother, cramp our style, or make us sacrifice time, energy, money, or our talents to do something for someone else. I think of times that we simply want to do our own thing, you know, something more fun, more adventurous, more thrilling than actually meeting the needs of someone who may not be lovely or easy to love.

But if we reach out of our comfort zones, God can use us to minister in such a way that others will clearly see Him. When we take that step to do something difficult or help someone who is difficult to love God is reflected in that service; and others can see Him work through us.

Let's Pause for Prayer

Heavenly Father, thank You for Your love. We know that we are not easy to love, and yet we set our own standards of measure of who we think deserves our help. May we look at each person as one to whom we minister, showing Your unconditional love. May we put aside our selfish ways and not merely see but actually look for the needs of others so we can meet those needs. As we follow Your lead, may You be honored and blessed. In Jesus' name we pray. Amen.

Can you recall a time when you were frustrated because someone wanted his or her own way and was demanding? Can you remember a time you were demanding and selfish?

_____

_____

_____

How can you respond (instead of react) to someone the next time he or she shows demanding selfishness? What can you do to stop yourself from being demanding or selfish?

_____

_____

Day 109 — Silence Isn't Always Golden

> *"My soul waits in silence for God only."*
>
> Psalms 62:1a

I have always liked the saying "Silence is golden." I love the peacefulness and tranquility of my wooded backyard and enjoy the silence. I have enjoyed quiet times resting by a lake or pond or taking a walk through a beautiful area. I remember the silence of a sleeping child in my arms and how pleasant those moments were. Times of waiting for the Lord have also been special in many ways.

Recently I became aware that silence is not always golden. Some people use silence in a way that becomes destructive. Sometimes it hides our fears, sins, hurts, and insecurities; shows our rudeness and impatience; or can be an excuse not to do what we know we should. It is clear that when used strategically, our silence can hurt more than our words. This kind of silence isn't productive, isn't healthy; and using silence to hurt others is most certainly not how we should conduct ourselves as Christians.

Let's Pause for Prayer

Heavenly Father, we desire to be silent when our words could hurt or when we really have nothing of importance to say, but please help us to know when we are strategically and secretly using silence to hurt, be rude, or ignore others? Help us then to confess that sin to You and to turn away from our prideful and selfish ways in order to follow You and treat others with respect, also confessing to them. In Jesus' name we pray. Amen.

Ask the Lord to reveal a time when silence was used in an unhealthy, hurtful way? What was revealed?

_____
_____
_____
_____

What action might you take to make sure that your silence isn't hurtful or unhealthy?

_____
_____
_____
_____

Day 110 — *Are You Sorry, Or Sorry You Got Caught?*

"They should repent and turn to God, performing deeds appropriate to repentance."
Acts 26:20b

Although the following definitions are not from Webster's dictionary, I think you will, as I have, relate to them.

- Conviction is God telling me "You did it and you were wrong."
- Guilt is me saying, "I know I did wrong."
- Embarrassment is me "knowing you know my sin"!
- Repentance is me owning up to my wrong, confessing it, and getting back on the right track with God.

As unfortunate as it is, sometimes what makes people respond and repent is embarrassment. We may sense God's conviction and our own guilt, but unless we are actually found out, we will not take care of the issue. Sometimes we think, "I'm not sorry I did it, I'm just sorry I got caught." And more and more often in the news, I actually think some people want to be found out for the wrongs they're doing because of the way they flaunt what they have done and seem to enjoy the publicity.

The only way to rid ourselves of our wrongdoing or sin is to confess it and repent or turn away from it. That confession and repentance are what will spark the fire of revival in our hearts and throughout our churches.

Let's Pause for Prayer

Heavenly Father, please allow each of us to understand that Your heart grieves when we sin and try to cover it up. We want to learn to repent and fully turn away from all sin. Deal with each of our hearts so that we will answer honestly when you convict us of sin, admit to the wrong doing, and show willingness to do all we need to do to repair whatever damage has been done. In that way may we glorify You. In Jesus' name we pray. Amen.

Is there a sin God wants You to confess? Write out for yourself a prayer of confession and own up to the sin and recognize that God noticed it.

_____

_____

_____

What will you do to repent (turn away from that sin) and what will you do to make restitution for the sin?

_____

_____

Day 111   Get Plugged In!

"I am the vine, you are the branches; he who abides in Me, and I in him, bears much fruit; for apart from Me you can do nothing."

John 15:5

"I need to get my battery charged!" We may have said the same when we're weary and tired from the work we do. I can certainly understand that we need time to be rejuvenated and refreshed, but can we compare our Christian lives—our spiritual lives—to getting recharged when we run out of power? The lives we lead in Christ resemble a plug in a socket. We have a direct connection to Jesus, and we simply need to be plugged into Him as the source of our being filled with His Holy Spirit! He is always connected to us. His Holy Spirit will flow through us, provided we stay connected to our power source: Jesus Christ. He can but doesn't often use jumper cables to get us going. He continuously provides the Holy Spirit, who is always there to supply the power. We simply must be plugged in!

Jesus said, "I am the vine, you are the branches; he who abides in Me, and I in him, bears much fruit; for apart from Me you can do nothing" (John 15:5). Apart from Him, without Him, we can do nothing. That is how we get plugged in!

Let's Pause for Prayer

Heavenly Father, we thank you for your Holy Spirit, who resides in those of us who have asked You to be Lord of our lives. Thank You for never fluctuating or changing. Because You do not change, we can depend on You. Thank You for being all sufficient so that we don't need to rely on our own self-sufficiency. We ask You to be the Lord of our lives because we desire the peace that comes only from You. In Jesus' name we pray. Amen.

Do you recognize when you are plugged into Your heavenly Father? Do you sense when you've pulled the plug? Share examples of each.

_____

_____

_____

What will you do to get plugged into your Lord and Savior and how will that look as you walk with Him today? What changes will you and others be able to see?

_____

_____

_____

Day 112 — *Unrealistic Expectations Of Pastors And Leaders*

"For who among men knows the thoughts of a man except the spirit of the man, which is in him? Even so the thoughts of God no one knows except the Spirit of God."

I Corinthians 2:11

Sometimes, no matter what pastors and leaders do, they end up in the wrong. Sometimes they just can't win! Here are some examples:

We want our pastors to guide their congregations and help members grow, but heaven forbid, if they make any changes in the usual routine!

We want our ministry leaders to have perfect families; they must never miss an evening meeting and must be on call whenever someone needs an ear to listen.

Some people can become angry with leaders, who must nevertheless tolerate and accommodate them. Pastors and leaders must always show concern but never ever criticize anyone for anger directed at them.

Ministry leaders help a couple with their marriage in crisis and then they turn on the leaders because the pair didn't like having their sinful behavior pointed out.

You may be able to cite many other examples. I am quite sure pastors and leaders have all been in these no-win situations at one time or another. If instead of imposing unrealistic expectations, everyone showed respect, stopped expecting the impossible of others, and owned up to their sins and inconsistencies, what would happen? When this happens, I believe others will be drawn to know Christ.

Let's Pause for Prayer

Heavenly Father, we pray that we would be careful of our words at all times but especially when we use our words to impose unreasonable expectations upon our pastors and leaders. Help us to recognize that their position of leadership requires them to make decisions that can't and won't please everyone. Give them the desire to seek You only so they know and we will see that what they do is from You and for You. Allow us to be good followers as we help in the Kingdom work so that Your name will be glorified. In Jesus' name we pray. Amen.

Do you encourage your pastors and church leaders through your words and actions? If not, what will you do to make that look different in your life? How will you do that with a pure heart instead of merely the desire to look good?

_____

_____

_____

_____

Day 113 — On The Job

> *"Servants, be submissive to your masters with all respect, not only to those who are good and gentle but also to those who are unreasonable."*
>
> I Peter 2:18

The job market seems to be tight right now, yet I can't think of a time in my life when that hasn't been true! It seems many are having a difficult time finding employment, but some who have secure jobs complain because they don't like their job, their boss, their pay.

Two verses of scripture come to mind that might encourage those in difficult job situations, both those who need a job and those who are unhappy in the one they have.

I Peter 2:18 says, "Servants, be submissive to your masters with all respect, not only to those who are good and gentle but also to those who are unreasonable." Verse 13 says: "Submit yourselves for the Lord's sake to every human institution."

Those who have jobs have a responsibility to serve in their positions as "unto the Lord." Those without work may seek to work every day in life as "unto the Lord," waiting for the Lord's perfect timing. No matter where we work or serve, we're always on the job!

Let's Pause for Prayer

Heavenly Father, thank You for the work You give us to do, whether we're earning a paycheck for it or not. Please give us the grace to fulfill our obligations in ways that honor You. May those without work be encouraged to continue their search, knowing Your timing is perfect. Teach us that as we wait, we can depend upon You for every need. May this time be a time of great spiritual growth that will yield a life dedicated and committed to You! In Jesus' name we pray. Amen.

Are you currently employed? Are you grateful for your work? Do you thank your boss for the work you're given to do?

_____

_____

_____

What can you do to improve your present situation? Might you look for a job? Be thankful for the one you have? Work faithfully as a volunteer until a paying position opens up?

_____

_____

_____

Day 114 — *Discouraged*

> *"Nothing is too difficult for Thee."*
> Jeremiah 32:17b

We all experience times of discouragement, even those in positions of leadership. Whether one is a lay leader at church, a Sunday school teacher, or a pastor, each has experienced discouragement. They are often held up to a different standard because of their positions, but their positions do not eliminate hurtful, difficult times that lead to discouragement. Their positions sometimes prevent them from being able to share their discouragement with others privately or publicly because of the harm it would cause.

God knows their challenges and can do anything to encourage them. We, too, can encourage our leaders through our prayers for them.

Let's Pause for Prayer

Heavenly Father, we desire to lift up our ministry leaders and pastors this day. We pray that You would give them the desire to endure discouragement and pursue lives of integrity and godly service. Please give them comfort and refreshment when they are weary, help us to see their needs and assist them through action and prayer, and show us how that would look to each individual. In Jesus' name we pray. Amen.

Do you consistently and faithfully pray for those in leadership and those in authority as pastors in your church? Do you lift them up in prayer when you know they are discouraged or when the Lord puts them on your mind?

_____

_____

_____

How can you show those in leadership encouragement?

_____

_____

_____

_____

Day 115

Hospitable Or Entertaining?

> *"Do not neglect to show hospitality to strangers, for by this some have entertained angels without knowing it."*
>
> Hebrews 13:2

Our busy lifestyles often cause us to realize we lack the time or capacity to entertain or show hospitality, but when we make that extra effort to be hospitable, we can teach our children and learn some very important lessons ourselves. The lessons we learn by showing hospitality (important lessons like sharing, serving, and showing compassion and concern to others) will far outweigh entertaining (amusing or treating) others. Early Christians understood what sharing with others was all about. They shared meals together in their homes with "glad and sincere hearts" (Act 2:46).

Whether we open our homes to one person or to many, our hospitality will encourage others. Consider how this might look.

Let's Pause for Prayer

Heavenly Father, we desire to invite others to our homes so we can show them Your love through us. Please show us what neighbor might have a need, what teacher might need encouragement, or what friend might need a listening ear; and allow us to open our hearts and homes to them. May they feel welcomed, not only during the Christmas holidays but also at any time of the year. In Jesus' name we pray. Amen.

When was the last time you invited someone to your home to bless and encourage them?

_____

_____

_____

Who might be encouraged by an invitation to spend time with you over a meal or cup of coffee in your home? When do you plan to invite her or him?

_____

_____

_____

_____

Day 116

Anxiety

> *"Anxiety in the heart of a man weighs it down, but a good word makes it glad."*
> Proverbs 12:25

At certain times of the year and even certain times of our week or day, we can become overwhelmed with anxiety. It weighs on us. Sometimes it feels as if someone is sitting on our chest—the pressures are so real—yet we can often feel the bounce return to our step when a good word was shared with us or someone encouraged us to make it through the day!

I believe we have all experienced the scripture verse quoted above. I wonder! Even if we don't feel that we have a glad heart, can we make it our purpose to speak a good word to another to make his or her heart glad? Sometimes we just need to get moving in a good and positive direction in doing the right thing to or for someone else before we will have the anxiety lifted from us.

Let's Pause for Prayer

Heavenly Father, we thank You for using us to bring a kind word to others. Help us to encourage someone whose heart is heavy with anxiety today. Help us to lighten his or her load through a kind and thoughtful word. And we pray for those too burdened to be able to think about encouraging another, let alone actually do it. Please bring someone into their lives to speak words of encouragement to them. In Jesus' name we pray. Amen.

Are you feeling weighed down because of life's pressures, people saying unkind things to you or about you, causing you to feel a heaviness of heart?

_____

_____

How do you feel when someone has given you a compliment (and I don't mean idle flattery) or a word of encouragement?

_____

_____

Who is the Lord putting on your heart to encourage with a good word? Your spouse, your pastor, your Sunday school teacher, your coworker, maybe your boss?

_____

_____

Day 117

The Fruit Of The Spirit

"But the fruit of the Spirit is love, joy, peace, patience, kindness, goodness, faithfulness, gentleness, self-control; against such things there is no law. If we live by the Spirit, let us also walk by the Spirit."

Galatians 5:22, 25

I have often heard the verses above described as an outward expression of an inward reality. The verses tell me that how I act and live will be in direct proportion to how I allow the Spirit to live through me. I recently recognized that the fruit of the Spirit is all other-centered, reinforcing that I can't be filled with the Spirit of God and filled with self at the same time.

When I sense I am filling up with self, I am sometimes sad, centering on my disappointments; or angry, centering on wanting my own way; or headed for discouragement when things are not going as I had expected. Although I could cite many more examples, I recognize the slippery slope to self in everyday life. Centering on others through love, joy, peace, patience, kindness, goodness, faithfulness, gentleness, and self-control will keep me from sadness, anger, discouragement, depression, and dwelling on myself!

Let's Pause for Prayer

Heavenly Father, thank you for teaching us through Your word. Thank You for showing me that sometimes I get in the way of living for You. Show me, Lord, when I'm heading down the wrong path and heading for a collision with self. Help me and those praying with me to rely on Your Holy Spirit to show the fruit of the Spirit to others and to find victory in living for You! In Jesus' name we pray! Amen.

Do you feel you exemplify the fruit of the spirit? How?

_____
_____
_____

What can you do today to walk in the fullness of the Holy Spirit, to reflect Him and to walk closely with Him? Can you start today?

_____
_____
_____
_____

Day 118

Open 24/7

> *"Pray without ceasing."*
> I Thessalonians 5:17

When we finish praying, do we brush our hands against each other as if to say, "All done! Catch ya tomorrow, Lord! Same time, same place! See ya then!"? I'm pretty certain that isn't what was meant in I Thess. 5:17—"Pray without ceasing." Although the verse is short and simple, prayer doesn't have to be. Prayer can be ongoing and pleasant and lengthy as we pray without ceasing!

When we're with someone we love, we can talk for hours. We can have conversation and communication that is real, casual, fun, and intentional. We are free to say what comes to our mind and heart: The line of communication is always open.

Praying without ceasing is like that. It's simply turning the dial of our communication system with God to the on position, making possible a two-way conversation with Him at any time. When that communication line is open, we can say whatever we want to Him, and He in turn will do the same. Yes, it's possible to pray without ceasing 24 hours a day.

Let's Pause for Prayer

Heavenly Father, we desire to keep our communication lines with You open 24 hours a day, 7 days a week. We recognize that You are always available to listen and we desire to be available to listen and obey. Help us change the mentality of having only a regular daily prayer time to one of having a continuous, ceaseless, vibrant time of daily communication with you! As you show us answers to our prayers, may it excite us all the more to spend that precious time with you more often. In Jesus' name we pray. Amen.

Do you feel you pray as needed, once a day, or 24/7? Explain.

_____
_____
_____

How can you take a new next step toward praying without ceasing? Write out your plan and a prayer.

_____
_____
_____
_____

Day 119 — *Exhausted*

> *"For just as we have many members in one body and all the members do not have the same function, so we, who are many, are one body in Christ, and individually members one of another."*
>
> Romans 12:4-5

Perhaps we've all had feelings of exhaustion, thinking we're the only one who is doing anything! Yes, it's a gross exaggeration but a true feeling when we're feeling tired and exhausted. When we feel this way, we often need to step back and find a few places where we have to say no to some ministries and projects. If no one rises to the occasion, then that ministry or project will have to wait until someone has the excitement, passion, and direction from the Lord to see it through.

Although all of us who are able and capable should work for the Lord to show how much we love Him, we must be careful not to do all the work, leaving others out or feeling they're unneeded.

Romans 12:4-5 says, "For just as we have many members in one body and all the members do not have the same function, so we, who are many, are one body in Christ, and individually members one of another." Imagine if our hands did everything. We would have no need for our head, eyes, or feet. And likewise if our mouths did everything, we would have no need for our brains or hands, and we would surely get ourselves in a lot of trouble with our tongues!

Let's Pause for Prayer

Heavenly Father, please help each of us who belong to Jesus Christ to purpose in our hearts to minister in some way to be an active person in the body of Christ. Help us to know whether we are to pray, to serve, to clean, to teach, to give financially, or whatever You need for us to do. May we be faithful to what You have asked of us. As we seek You, show us where You'd like us to serve. Please give us our next step in whatever direction You need for us to be of best use. In Jesus' name we pray. Amen.

Share in your own words a time you've felt exhausted, spent, or overworked, and explain what happened and how it felt.

_____
_____
_____

What will you do today to be sure you are doing only that which the Lord has for you to do?

_____
_____
_____

Day 120

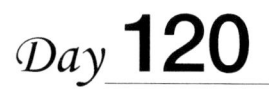

Sin Is Obvious

"There is no health in my bones because of my sin. I groan because of the agitation of my heart."

Psalm 38:3b, 8b

Sin is ugly. When we sin, we are ugly. Sometimes our demeanor and appearance change because of what sin does to us: The consequences of our sin can be evident to us and to others. Psalm 38:3-6, 8 10 says, "There is no health in my bones because of my sin. For my iniquities are gone over my head; as a heavy burden they weigh too much for me. My wounds grow foul and fester. Because of my folly, I am bent over and greatly bowed down; I go mourning all day long. I am benumbed and badly crushed; I groan because of the agitation of my heart. My heart throbs, my strength fails me; and the light of my eyes, even that has gone from me." Through the confession of our sin, however, we can be restored back to spiritual health.

Let's Pause for Prayer

Heavenly Father, we are so ashamed when we have arrogantly taken You on face to face in our sin saying, "Go ahead and punish me. I don't care." God, we know You will not be mocked. We know anyone who says such as this will be in for a horrible reality in this life, and if we choose not to ask forgiveness and repent, we can expect it in the next. May we come to our senses and recognize the sin that keeps us from fellowship with You. But we are so thankful that we can come to You in humility and ask forgiveness of our sin. When we ask You to cleanse us of that sin and give us a new start, joy, and assurance, we know we will be forgiven. Thank you for restoring our confidence, our countenance, and our walk with You. In Jesus' name we pray. Amen.

When have you thought even in your sin that you could take on God, thinking He'd not notice?

_____
_____
_____

If you are in sin, what must you do to get right with God? Write out your specific prayer of confession for yourself to own it and for you to realize that you need to change your ways.

_____
_____
_____
_____

Day 121

Too Difficult For God?

"Ah, Lord God! Behold, Thou hast made the heavens and the earth by Thy great power and by Thine outstretched arm! Nothing is too difficult for Thee."

Jeremiah 32:17

Setting goals is a way of putting the past behind us and taking new steps forward to accomplish new ones, but no matter what we choose to do, even if we think we are the ones making the effort, God will simply never leave us where we are. Whatever efforts we make—losing weight, reading the Bible daily, praying more—it's all good because as we move closer to God, He will move closer to us! He will not leave us where we are but will move us forward, especially when we are willing and able and have the desire to do so. Jeremiah 32: 17 says, "Ah, Lord God! Behold, Thou hast made the heavens and the earth by Thy great power and by Thine outstretched arm! Nothing is too difficult for Thee."

What a delight that we can trust Him to do what we need and how He must be delighted when we do so!

Let's Pause for Prayer

Heavenly Father, we are so thankful for the way You teach us and mold us according to Your will. As we continue to work on what You've asked us to accomplish for this year, please be ever present and allow us to sense Your presence so we know all that is accomplished in the end has come directly from You. Will you nudge and prod us when we need to get moving, and when we've stalled out or thought we might just quit, would you show us the great benefits of doing things Your way? Help us to be faithful to your call, your direction, and the way You want us to lead our lives. We want to look forward, not backward, as we follow You in the plan you have for us. We want to lead others in Your ways as well, so guide us the way You would have us to guide and lead others. Thank you for the way You accomplish Your will through us. In Jesus' name we pray. Amen.

For what one thing are you unable to trust God at this moment?

___

___

___

Write out and then pray the prayer you write to move closer to God, trusting Him for the ways you want to move forward.

___

___

___

___

Day 122

I Don't Know How To Pray

"And in the same way the Spirit also helps our weakness; for we do not know how to pray as we should, but the Spirit Himself intercedes for us with groaning too deep for words."

Romans 8:26

Prayer in the truest form is communion and communication with God. God. Imagine that. Prayer is not rubbing a genie in a bottle and putting our petitions and wishes out there to be granted, but it is coming to, talking to, and listening to God. Sometimes we ask God for what we think we need or want, but we need to come to Him in those instances with an open heart, recognizing that what we want and are asking for might not be His best for us. It's not easy to wait for His best, but when we do, we recognize that He desires good for us, not harm. He will instruct, He will guide, and He will give us a choice if we want to be a part of His plan. This communion with Him is never forceful on His part. It is gentle, kind, and certainly loving. And when we simply don't know what to say or how to say it, the Spirit will help us. Romans 8:26 says, "And in the same way the Spirit also helps our weakness; for we do not know how to pray as we should, but the Spirit Himself intercedes for us with groaning too deep for words." We will never be at a loss for words when talking with God.

Let's Pause for Prayer

Heavenly Father, we desire your instruction, your guidance, and your direction on how to pray to You. We don't want merely to ask for material goods and favors, but we want to come to You to truly know You, to truly understand Your will and your ways and how You work through us. Help us to be attentive and keenly aware of what You're teaching us as we come to You in prayer. Allow us to recognize that we are coming to and speaking with an awesome and mighty God, who is the Creator of the universe. How amazing to try to comprehend! How amazing that You would have such interest in us, that You care for and love us as You do! It's too much, Lord, for us to comprehend, but we appreciate it and thank You for it. In Jesus' name we pray. Amen.

Recall a time you simply could not pray. Write about it.

_____

_____

_____

When similar times come, how will you be able to go to God in prayer?

_____

_____

_____

Day 123

Prayer Is The Work

> *"Be devoted to one another, ... devoted to prayer."*
> Romans 10:10–12

Oswald Chambers said, "Prayer is not preparation for the work, it is the work" (*My Utmost for His Highest*). Prayer is often the last resort but should be the first thought. Do we bathe our decisions and next steps in prayer? Do we seek the Lord for approval and direction for what we're doing, or do we seek his direction only, regardless of our own plans?

I remember someone once telling me, "I wish I had a more public ministry." Nothing wrong with that, but sometimes Christians are more public in their ministry because of the wonderful people who shower that ministry with prayerful support. Ministry leaders need prayer support. Ministry decisions need prayer support. All that the Lord gives us to do needs prayer support. May we see prayer as the work, not simply the preparation for the work.

Let's Pause for Prayer

Heavenly Father, thank You for giving us personal gifts with which to carry out the work You give us to do. Let us not neglect prayer as the first work. Let us not neglect praying for others, lifting them up in prayer as You direct us. Let us be about the work called prayer. May we be unhindered as we pray so that we'd be free to hear from you, unbridled as we pray so that we might pray in any direction we feel You are leading and uncompromising as we pray so that we are open vessels receiving Your word and then praying it through, recognizing that this work called prayer is vital, important, serious, and best. We want to start with prayer, continue through with prayer, and end with prayer for wherever You are leading and directing, and for whatever You are calling each of us to accomplish for Your name. May we be faithful. In Jesus' name we pray. Amen.

Think back to a time when you didn't even consider praying about situations in your life. Write it out and share what has changed from then until now.

_____

_____

_____

Can you be satisfied in knowing that your prayer, though not public in ministry, can accomplish great results? Share how you would like to see your prayer life change now, recognizing that prayer is not simply the preparation for the work but the work itself.

_____

_____

_____

Day 124 — Aging Isn't The Reason Or The Excuse

"Whatever you do, do your work heartily, as for the Lord rather than for men, knowing that from the Lord you will receive the reward of the inheritance. It is the Lord Christ whom you serve."

Colossians 3:23-24

"As God adds more *years* to your life, ask Him for more life to your years." Although I'm not sure who to credit for this quote, it certainly captured my attention!

I once had the privilege of meeting and working with Katie Williams, who originated Pause for Prayer in the early 1970s. What impressed me about her was that she started the ministry of Pause for Prayer at age 60. She didn't go into her elder years fading; she added more life to the years God gave her!

Joe and I agree: We don't want aging to be a reason (or worse yet an excuse) to slow down or stop doing what God has given us to do. As we turn the pages of our calendar, we want to be sure we add more life to the years God gives!

Let's Pause for Prayer

Heavenly Father, as You grant more days and years to our lives, will You stir in us the excitement to continue serving You with zeal and passion? Please help us to recognize whether we start coasting in our service to You. Please nudge us tenderly to remind us that our work is not yet completed here and that we should not take a back seat, sit on the sidelines, or stop moving forward in that which You've given us to do. Show us when we are holding onto sin, grudges, mismanagement of time, or anything that would hinder our service to and for You. Show us Your way for us individually, and for those of us who are married, as a couple. Although we recognize that age, health, and life have ways of creating change we don't always anticipate, we desire to serve You full steam ahead "as unto the Lord" for as long as You give us years! In Jesus' name we pray. Amen.

Should God grant you more days and years to your life, how do you wish to use those days? Be specific.

_____
_____
_____

What one action will you do today to add more life to the years God gives you? Do it!

_____
_____
_____

Day 125

"It's Just The Way I Am!"

> *"Therefore if any man is in Christ, he is a new creature; the old things passed away; behold new things have come."*
>
> II Corinthians 5:17

Have you ever said something like this: "This is just the way I am" or "I can't change. I've always been like this"?

In *Seeking the Face of God*, author Gary Thomas challenged my thinking about why I have said those types of things. He tells us that saying "This is just the way I am" is a confession of slothfulness, not humility. It's admitting we're too spiritually lazy to change, too selfish. We are indifferent to the way our weaknesses and our lack of virtue create casualties.

How easy it is for us to justify our human frailties and sin! How easy it is to claim rights to our needs, wants, sin, preferences, and desires! We know, however, that God doesn't want us to settle into habits that do not glorify Him.

The author's words sent me immediately to prayer.

Let's Pause for Prayer

Heavenly Father, we are so sorry for thinking we can excuse our behavior, attitudes, or actions because we feel that's just how we are. Thank you for your words in II Cor. 5:17: "Therefore if any man is in Christ, he is a new creature; the old things passed away; behold new things have come." We desire to please You before ourselves, to seek Your way above our own, and to live according to Your will over our own. Please make us new as we rely on You to do so, as we are obedient to the process, and as we sense victory in the finished process. In Jesus' name we pray. Amen.

In what area of change might God be seeking and nudging you? Write for yourself the area in which you sense God challenging you.

_____

_____

_____

What will you do to make the changes God has asked of you? What is your next step?

_____

_____

_____

_____

Day 126

The Quiet

> *"Then they cried to the Lord in their trouble, and He brought them out of their distresses. He caused the storm to be still, so that the waves of the seas were hushed. Then they were glad because they were quiet; so He guided them to their desired haven."*
>
> Psalm 107:28–30

Do you remember feeling as if you were going from one crisis or storm to another, from one activity to a crisis to another activity, wondering whether you could ever really enjoy a moment in the quiet eye of the storm? Do you long for the quiet?

Sometimes we need to look for the times we can slow down and rest and gather our wits to get back on track!

Here are some times I realize I need to slow down. When I

- lose my sense of humor,
- mentally stop prioritizing and lose my sense of priority (God, family, work, ministry, fun!), and
- feel I must do certain tasks and don't feel any freedom in decision making.

Let's Pause for Prayer

Heavenly Father, we pray that you would help us to see when we are headed for the storms of life by getting too busy for our own good. Help us learn to be still in Your presence even when the difficulties of life make doing so a struggle. Thank You for desiring the best for us. Help us to see when we are headed for self-destruction, and help us to focus on You. In Jesus' name we pray. Amen.

If you can relate even occasionally, write out some times of ongoing challenges you've experienced and how you handled them.

_____

_____

_____

If you were unable to find quiet and rest amidst these challenges, what will you do the next time you're going from crisis to crisis to find that place of quiet and rest? Perhaps write a prayer of intent and action.

_____

_____

_____

_____

Day 127

Purity In Marriage Relationships

> *"Let marriage be held in honor among all, and let the marriage bed be undefiled; for fornicators and adulterers God will judge."*
>
> Hebrews 13:4

Before and after marriage: purity. Hopping in and out of bed with partners isn't what makes sex or marriage (someday) satisfying.

Married couples long to be satisfied in their marriage: emotionally, spiritually, and intimately (sexually) with their mate. Hollywood movies and television, however, seduce us into thinking that we can enjoy all those benefits outside marriage—and without consequence.

Movies and television imply that if you are attracted physically, that's a good start; and if you can develop emotionally together, that's great. If you and your partner happen upon spirituality somewhere in that relationship—hey, that's even better. No wonder so few people stay together in marriage relationships! Getting off to the wrong start doesn't facilitate getting on track to a happy and healthy marriage relationship in the future.

Seeking God's best for marriage relationships is the place for a good start; we simply can't rely on Hollywood for answers on how to make marriage go the distance. Few good examples and track records are found there.

Let's Pause for Prayer

Heavenly Father, please help our young people to obey Your word and maintain sexual purity so they will someday enjoy a wonderful marriage. Help those of us who are married to be faithful to our marriage partners and thus show our faithfulness to You. When our eyes or minds stray, nudge us back to reality to work on the relationships we have so that we can go the distance. Keep us pure in our marriages. Thank you for Your Word that teaches and guides in the area of pure relationships that will honor and glorify You and satisfy us. In Jesus' name we pray. Amen.

If you have a past that includes sexual relationships outside marriage (fornication = sex before marriage; adultery = sex with someone other than your spouse while married), ask yourself what God thinks about it and what He has instructed you. Have you obeyed His instruction?

_____

_____

What are some of the consequences of sexual immorality? For yourself, write down lessons you've learned and any thoughts you might be able to share someday with others to keep them from the consequences of sexual immorality.

_____

_____

Day 128

Simple And Special

> *"The testimony of the Lord is sure, making wise the simple."*
>
> Psalms 19:7b

Do you have a special person in your life right now? I hope everyone can answer yes, but more specifically I'm wondering if you know anyone with a special need? We all can probably answer yes to that as well because we all have in our lives or know of others who are in the midst of difficulties requiring special needs during tough times. Even more specifically, I'm thinking of special needs in terms of a person's mental, physical, or other disabling condition.

In addition to our son Joey, who has special needs, another young man comes to mind. Both have a special ability that would easily be overlooked or go unnoticed by others. These two young men are often the first to recognize that someone has been left out or mistreated. In addition, they are often undistracted by anything around them and without any shame or embarrassment raise their hands, clap them, and clasp them in prayer and worship when others of us want to refrain from certain outward actions that others might notice. Not so with these young men. They freely worship. For years my friend has made it his responsibility to keep a cup of water filled for our pastor as he speaks. I wonder how many of us thought about that need. When I realize that I am sometimes inhibited in worship or neglect some of the most obvious ways I can serve, the tender acts of worship and service that I observe in those with special needs make me wonder which of us really has a disability?

Let's Pause for Prayer

Heavenly Father, please help each of us to open our eyes to look around us and see how needy we are in our walk with You. Help us to see who and what we have neglected, including our worship and devotions to You, because we are so distracted by our selfishness. Show us how to serve and worship in a pure and simple way. Thank you for showing us through two young men with special needs the simplicity of obedience and the special need we all have to know you deeply and to serve you simply and with joy. In Jesus' name we pray. Amen.

Recall a time where you recognized (after the fact) how you missed the mark on a simple act of worship or service because you were distracted because of your selfishness. Be honest with yourself. How will you be able to use the example above the next time you are in worship or other group setting to be wise and simple at the same time?

_____
_____
_____
_____

Day 129 — *Please And Thank You Go A Long Way*

> *"In everything give thanks."*
> I Thessalonians 5:18

Do you say please and thank you as a regular part of your everyday vocabulary and conversation? Do you say please when making a request, or does it sound more like this: Give me the paper. I'll take the salt. Call me back. Just adding a simple please adds a polite and pleasant dimension to any request.

When a waiter or waitress serves you coffee, do you respond with a pleasant thank you, or do you just go on reading the paper or talking? When someone does you a favor or for that matter, routinely does something for you, are you in the habit of offering a polite thank you? Or do you just assume they know you appreciate it?

"In everything give thanks" (I Thess. 5:18). America has become a thankless and entitled nation. If we took a personal inventory, we would have to agree that we need to own up to our ingratitude, repent of it, and ask the Holy Spirit to work in us to develop hearts of sincere gratitude, appreciation, and thankfulness. Imagine what would happen if that attitude would sweep our homes and our country. The Lord desires that we have thankful hearts.

Let's Pause for Prayer

Heavenly Father, please help us to see the many things for which we should be thankful and give thanks. Please forgive us for the times we have treated others rudely and thus offended them or disregarded them by forgetting a polite please and thank you. Please help us to see where we can show this simple kindness in word and deed. And we thank you for the way You will show us! In Jesus' name we pray. Amen.

Do you recognize your own ingratitude? Think of some ways you've failed to express appreciation to people and to God and write them down for yourself.

_____

_____

_____

How and when will you share your gratitude and appreciation? What will be your next or perhaps first act of appreciation? Write out how you will express this gratitude, to whom, and for what.

_____

_____

_____

_____

Day 130

Accidental

> *"And everything you ask in prayer, believing, you shall receive."*
>
> Matthew 21:22

A number of years ago one of my husband's employees called from the hospital after a chunk of cement came through her windshield, hitting the steering wheel and just missing her face. It likely spun off from the tires of the car in front of her, that driver having no idea what happened behind her or him. When Joe spoke with her, she was shaken, realizing how easily her life could have ended in that brief moment.

Days later, we received news that a patient of Joe's (someone we had known years earlier) had been killed instantly in a fatal car crash.

Often when I listen to the morning rush hour traffic report, I'm tempted not to pay close attention. I'm not usually headed out on the highways during rush hour, so I'm not intent on deciding which route is the best to take. I appreciate the traffic announcer, who adds to a report, "Let's remember those involved in these accidents in prayer." It is a gentle reminder that someone out there has a need and we can be a part of the outcome of that situation.

In the case of the two accidents I mentioned above, I wondered whether I had unknowingly prayed for them, not even knowing for whom I was praying. We can pray at all times. Prayer need not be accidental but purposeful.

Let's Pause for Prayer

Heavenly Father, thank You for the technology to broadcast programs, music, weather, and even reports of traffic on our roadways! Remind us to take the time to pray for those who have been in accidents as well as for those who might be patiently or impatiently waiting in stopped traffic, wondering why it's not moving. Thank you for showing us how we can be used to pray for others whom we may or may not ever know; furthermore, allow us to be used of You in ways that the recipients of our help might never know. In Jesus' name we pray. Amen.

For whom might you consider praying today?

_____

_____

_____

In what situations will you determine to be faithful to pray?

_____

_____

_____

Day 131

Prayer Is Who I Am

> *"Devote yourselves to prayer, keeping alert in it with an attitude of thanksgiving."*
> Colossians 4:2

Often we think of prayer as something we do, but if we are praying the way God instructs us to pray, prayer should be who we are.

I love to pray. I would say that I pray throughout a good portion of the day. I see the sin and needs in my own life and recognize the need to confess those in prayer. I see the needs of my family, in my neighborhood, and in our country. I pray for people, for situations, for relationships, and for anything else the Lord brings to mind; yet I must recognize the need to stop occasionally and ask myself whether prayer is who I am or whether I simply pray when a need arises. I'm not sure that I can find a quick answer to my question. Perhaps the answer will come as I devote more time and energy not simply to the task of praying but also to the vision of what prayer truly is.

Let's Pause for Prayer

Heavenly Father, we desire not only to be about prayer but to make prayer who we are. Let us be consumed with prayer for others. Let us hear clearly from You. Let us know how to pray in every situation, giving us Your vision of what Your heart is so that we can pray as You desire us to pray. Thank you for allowing us the opportunity to communicate with You through prayer. Help us not to take for granted what You have given us. In Jesus' name we pray. Amen.

Are you able to determine whether prayer is who you are? How so?

_____

_____

If you are not one who identifies yourself in terms of prayer being who you are, what steps can you take to make prayer more moment to moment as you seek for prayer to be who you are?

_____

_____

_____

Day 132 — You Can't Hide From God

"No one can serve two masters; for either he will hate the one, and love the other, or he will hold to one and despise the other."

Luke 16:13a

I couldn't believe what I was reading on my computer screen. Sometimes I can't believe a lot of what comes to us that we didn't ask for, didn't pay for, and do not want.

This is what I was reading on my screen: "You are being watched! You need the Privacy Protection that XYZ [product name] provides! Protect: Your Privacy, Your Future, Your Reputation! Stop your private web-surfing from coming back to haunt you! Imagine what would happen if

- your employer sees what's on your system,
- your relatives discover what is on your PC, or
- your computer needs to be repaired?"

My first response was, "Well, if I don't want anyone to find out about what I view and do on the computer, maybe I shouldn't be doing it!" I already know I am being watched. I am being watched by a heavenly Father who will correct and discipline me. My incentive is not to assure I don't get caught but instead to be sure I don't ever get onto a path that will dishonor Him. If I dishonor Him, I dishonor my family, my friends, my ministry coworkers, other coworkers, and all the body of Christ. None of us should ever think that a computer cleanse will solve the problem of what we are doing and viewing. The problem to be solved is an attitude of the heart and the need for cleansing.

Let's Pause for Prayer

Heavenly Father, forgive us for thinking we can hide anything from You. We know and understand that covering up what we view on our computers is foolishness because You see, hear, and know all. We pray that You would instill in each of us who believe in You and desire to live for You, the will to live pure lives in every aspect of our beings. For those thinking they are hiding what they're viewing, I pray they would be exposed, that You would find them out, and guide them to pure living so that they can enjoy the abundance of the good things that you have promised! We know that You will not be mocked (Galatians 6:7), and we recognize we are surely mocking You if we think You will turn Your head to our sin. May we all desire to be pure and cleansed in every area of our lives! In Jesus' name we pray. Amen.

If this Pause for Prayer makes you a little uncomfortable, tell why. What action, what next step do you have to take to live purely and in purity?

_____

_____

_____

Day 133　　　　　　　　　　　　　　　　　　　　　　　*The Value Of A Life*

"Then the Lord God formed man of dust from the ground, and breathed into his nostrils the breath of life; and man became a living being."

Genesis 2:7

Although medical killing has been practiced for decades, I read an article about the Netherlands proposing to legalize euthanasia (Suzanne Daley, "The Dutch Seek to Legalize Long-Tolerated Euthanasia." *New York Times*. June 20, 2000). The proposal was to extend the supposed right to euthanasia to sufferers of Alzheimer's and terminally ill children as young as 12. I don't know what the outcome of that legislation was, but I know the bill included an advanced directive so that patients in the early stages of degenerative disease or dementia could designate conditions under which to be euthanized. In the early 90s people said, "We'll never promote euthanasia for dementia, how dare we suggest we will go that far?" But look where we are now.

Life has become disposable. We hear of newborn babies being thrown into trash bins as their mothers pick up where they left off with life before giving birth. Could it be that they really have no remorse, sadness, or conscience? Could we so easily dispose of a terminally ill family member because of the inconvenience they are to us?

Caring for my father and then my mother-in-law with Alzheimer's and a son with cerebral palsy and mental challenges has taught me lessons far beyond what I could ever have learned in a book. I don't always do things right, and I often have to readjust my thinking, my attitude, and my goals; but God has used both of these situations to teach me how to love others even when it is difficult. Their lives, each one, is valued and of value.

Let's Pause for Prayer

Heavenly Father, it's sometimes hard to thank you for the difficult situations you allow in our lives, but we recognize that doing so will cause us to call upon You for strength and guidance. Please give us a sense of the value of each and every life as You teach us such valuable lessons as patience, kindness, gentleness, and love. Let us value what we learn, and may we teach our children indirectly so that someday they will choose to care for their elders when they are unable to care for themselves. In Jesus' name we pray. Amen.

Have you had the privilege of caring for one who could not care for himself or herself? Describe the situation and record things you learned. If you've not cared for another, have you had opportunity but chose not to participate? Ask the Lord for direction on how you might serve another, writing a prayer of your desires below.

___

___

___

___

Day 134 — Appearances Can Be Deceiving

> *"Even in laughter the heart may be in pain, and the end of joy maybe grief."*
> Proverbs 14:13

It's very easy to judge or in many cases misjudge others—seeing what we want to see and not what really is.

One evening years ago at one of my daughter Kristina's piano recitals, a man sat with his cell phone on his lap. I couldn't help but think, "How important is any phone call that you need to have the phone on your lap during your child's recital?" It never rang, but he seemed intent on making sure it was on and available to him.

About half way through the recital, he slipped quietly to the side of the auditorium, with the phone in his hand and pushed a button. Of course, I was thinking, "You aren't going to make a call now are you?" Without uttering a word he focused the phone on his child as she played her piece. As her performance ended and the applause sounded, he quietly turned it off and returned to his seat.

I was humbled. Suddenly, the narrative had rewritten itself. Was the call to one of the grandparents who couldn't be there, a sibling away at school who wanted to hear a little sister; or was it someone too ill to attend?

As my eyes welled with tears at this sweet scene, I asked the Lord to forgive my judgmental attitude. I thanked Him for that quiet lesson given to my heart, showing me that every story has two sides.

Let's Pause for Prayer

Heavenly Father, thank You for the quiet and tender ways You teach us. Help us to see both sides to a story before we judge. May we give others the benefit of the doubt when we judge what seems so obvious to us. And we pray that others might give us the benefit of the doubt when what we are doing isn't at all as it might appear. We need to learn to be gracious in all our dealings with others and others with us. We appreciate Your Holy Spirit guiding us and leading us to right thoughts and actions in each and every case. And help us, Lord, to see what might not be so easy to see—the one with the hurting heart behind the smile and the one whose joy is soon to be turned to sadness. In Jesus' name we pray. Amen.

Share a time when you were judgmental way and describe how you came to know the truth of the situation. Write a method (perhaps in a prayer) of new thinking to allow you to stop judging without knowing all the facts.

_____

_____

_____

_____

Day 135 — *Choices*

> *"How blessed is everyone who fears the Lord, who walks in His ways."*
>
> Psalm 128:1

The authors of various online and print articles claim that 21% of men and 13% of women admit to having sex with someone other than their spouse, and the average age range of one third of those is 45–60.

Statistics don't always mean much to us unless we become a part of that particular population. Sometimes we don't intend to become a statistic, but our choices of lifestyle lead us in that direction. And yes, becoming a statistic by carrying on an extramarital affair is a choice. Those who find those words difficult to hear may have preferred me to say, "One third of men between 45 and 60 drift into, fall into, move into, or are forced into extramarital affairs." But the truth is that although some drift, fall, move, or seem forced into these affairs, the only way they happen is by choosing to pursue a relationship outside marriage.

If you have had a relationship other than with your spouse, if you are presently contemplating, pursuing, or in the midst of an extramarital affair, you cannot simultaneously pursue oneness in your marriage; and you can certainly not pursue fellowship with God. If you are willing to make the choice, you can stop where you are, turn around, and learn how to pursue oneness in your marriage.

Let's Pause for Prayer

Heavenly Father, we thank you for Your word, Your Hope, and Your plan, which are taught in scripture and at numerous Christian marriage conferences. We pray for those who will choose to pursue oneness in their marriage by attending one of these conferences, by reading their Bibles, and by working at the challenges encountered in all marriages. We pray that you will strengthen those marriages that are hurting as husbands and wives choose to pursue You and oneness in their marriage. And we ask that you bless those marriages that bloom and thrive so that husbands and wives can mentor and guide others to what will be helpful in their marriages. In Jesus' name we pray. Amen.

Whether you are married, single, widowed, or at any other place in life, we can join together to pray for our own marriages or for those marriages around us. We might be the only person praying for these marriages. Who might the Lord put on your heart for whom to pray?

_____

_____

Write out a prayer that you can come back to on occasion to pray for others and their marriages.

_____

_____

_____

Day 136 — Tears

> *"And He shall wipe away every tear from their eyes."*
> Revelation 21:1a

When was the last time you cried? Were they tears of sadness, anger, or joy? Isn't it amazing that for different emotions we shed the same tears?

An article published January 8, 1984, in *The News & Courier* by Knight-Ridder Newspapers showed that all tears comprise mostly water and salt, but tears of sadness, anger, fear, and joy all vary chemically. They even vary chemically from those tears shed when the eyes are irritated by onions! The article stated that emotional tears may be nature's or, as I see it, God's method of removing chemicals built up by stress from the body that helps relieve pain.

Some of us have been told or taught not to cry, yet crying may be the very outlet our body needs in order to heal emotionally and physically as well as to relieve the stress in our lives. The author of the article stated that people who suppress their crying may lose contact with their feelings. Certainly those of us who have had a few really good cries know the relief that crying brings. Conversely, when people remain in a state of sin, their hearts are hardened and tears don't flow very easily. What a lesson for us!

Let's Pause for Prayer

Heavenly Father, we thank You for giving us tears to shed in times of sadness and frustration and in times of joy! Thank You for the creative ways You have in allowing tears to help relieve the stress and tension in our lives. Help us to release these emotions in a healthy and productive way. Help us not to be ashamed or embarrassed to shed the tears you have given us. Father, let us know whether our hearts are hardened because of sin, and help us to come to You and ask for forgiveness and then repent, turn from our sin, and find joy in You! In Jesus' name we pray. Amen.

What generally makes you shed tears, and do you let them flow or stop them?

___

___

How do you generally respond when others weep?

___

___

What steps will you take if someone in your presence cries? And will you allow others to take the same steps if you need to cry in their presence?

___

___

Day 137 — Ask, Seek, Knock

> *"Ask, and it shall be given to you; seek and you shall find; knock and it shall be opened to you."*
>
> Matthew 7:7

Often I think and pray for people but never follow through to let them know they were on my mind and in my heart and my prayers. One day, while texting someone to let her know I was praying for her, the auto correct on my phone substituted the word *pursuing*! How interesting, I thought, that *pursue* would replace *pray* and how relevant that word is to prayer! The definition of *pursue* is "to seek to accomplish; to engage in; to carry out." Pursuing is exactly what we do as we pray. We pursue God asking Him to hear our thoughts, prayers, yearnings, desires, frustrations, rejoicings, and so much more! We seek Him to hear and accomplish what we request. We engage Him to hear our prayers, which speak to our heartfelt desires to Him. I hope we'll pursue an attitude of pursuing God.

Let's Pause for Prayer

Heavenly Father, how right it is that we pursue You in prayer! You say in Your word, "Ask, and it shall be given to you; seek and you shall find; knock and it shall be opened to you." How wonderful that You have given us access to You through this awesome and powerful act called prayer! We know You hear our hearts, our thoughts, and our words. May we pursue You as the King of Kings that You are and as the Lord of our lives. How wondrous that we have the right as well as the responsibility to pursue You in an act as intimate as prayer! We recognize the times we feel as if prayer bounces off the ceiling, but we know that as we keep asking and keep praying, we are pursuing all You have for us. We must be ready and willing to listen to all You will tell us. May we then pursue acting upon that which You've called us to do. May we be faithful to the way You direct and guide us as we pray. In Jesus' name we pray. Amen.

What are you praying for presently that you will now pursue in prayer more fervently?

_____

_____

Share in a prayer, what specifically you are praying and what it might look like when God answers.

_____

_____

_____

_____

Day 138

Pay Attention To Parents

"Hear, my son, your father's instruction, and do not forsake your mother's teaching."

Proverbs 1:8

Someone posted on Facebook: "Parenting—I hope I get this right." Ultimately, the love we have for our children is such that if we have a desire to get it right, we'll likely try to make the right choices in the process of doing a great job as a parent; yet as parents we must understand that our children have free wills just as we do. They might make choices that make us look like bad parents. I've known of lousy, absent, and neglectful parents whose kids turn out just as we all wish our kids would; and I've known wonderful, dedicated, and caring parents whose kids made wrong choices. In each case, the parents really can't take the credit or the blame for the way their children turned out! That is why we have the privilege of praying for our children and the children of others—like my Facebook friend.

Let's Pause for Prayer

Heavenly Father, thank you for the immediate and undivided kind of love you give parents for their children. We pray that You would speak to young parents, giving them direction and guidance. We pray that they would listen carefully and act quickly when You've spoken to their hearts. As parents whose children are grown, may we take the time to pray for these younger families to know and serve You. We pray that children obey their parents, not for either of them to look a certain way to others, not to be commended for great parenting or any other false accolades but for them to understand and reap the benefits of obedience to you as Lord of their lives. Thank you for humbling us through our children who are not perfect because we as parents are not perfect. Allow us to recognize all that is important, and that which is not as we mold the character and wills of our children. May it all be done in Jesus, name with love, tenderness, and confidence. In Jesus' name we pray. Amen.

How do you pray for your children or the children of others?

___

___

___

What actions will you take to change direction in your parenting and prayer?

___

___

___

___

Day 139 — *You Have Things To Work On*

> *"Iron sharpens iron, so one man sharpens another."*
>
> Proverbs 27:17

I've always said that in marriage, we smooth out one another's rough edges; and if children come along, they hack off anything that's left! Scripture says it like this in Proverbs 27:17, which states, "Iron sharpens iron, so one man sharpens another." Indeed, we all need each other to help fine tune our character traits, solve our personality issues, and make us more of what we could be for one another, ourselves, and ultimately the Lord.

It's not always easy to hear from others that we have something to work on in our lives, but if we have healthy and loving marital relationships, where the most transparent interactions take place in correcting, reproving, loving, and helping one another and our children deal with the realities of everyday life, then hearing them out and lending an ear to their suggestions for our self-improvement and working together are healthy ways to respect, care for, and be honest with one another.

Let's Pause for Prayer

Heavenly Father, we thank you for those in our lives who love us enough that we can be transparent with one another and work through character flaws and personality issues that require fine tuning. Thank you for friends and extended family with whom we have close and meaningful relationships and who can and will do the same for us. Help us to be thoughtful and kind, listening carefully when others come to us to address what needs correcting. Help us to be reflective and responsive, not reactive or unwilling to hear or respond. Make us careful, cautious, kind, and true, no matter which side we are on. Thank You for the way You can use others to help teach and correct us out of a heart of love for us. Let us differentiate between those who have sincere heart motives to help us from those whose desire is to hurt or hinder us in our walk with You. May we ever pursue excellence in our walk with You. In Jesus' name we pray. Amen.

Do you have someone in your life who helps smooth out your rough edges? If so, how do they help do so?

_____

_____

_____

Write a prayer to the Lord about how you will work on what is brought to your attention about your personality, actions, and attitudes?

_____

_____

_____

Day 140

Obey God Before Man

> *"We must obey God rather than men."*
>
> Acts 5:29

There's a difference between listening and obeying. Any high school kids can tell you that or—better yet—show you. That look in their eyes that say, "I'm listening!" Their mouths may even agree with you, but no way they plan to obey! It's all for show. They just make you think they will. Perhaps you've seen it in your toddler. They're so smart, aren't they? They can figure out just how to get around your request. They might be listening, but they will not obey.

We are probably not much better at obeying either because we all tend to want our own way. It's so easy to point the finger at someone else who is stubborn and won't obey, but how easily we want to ignore our disobedience and give ourselves a pass by making an adjustment for ourselves! God is not humored. Just as we see the high schooler rebelling and the toddler resisting, He sees us doing the same.

Let's Pause for Prayer

Heavenly Father, it seems we all want our own way and will do whatever it takes to get it. Lying, cheating, pretending, hiding, blaming—you name it, we've tried it. Please forgive us for thinking we've somehow tricked You into believing we're so good and righteous and right. Father, when we read and hear Your word, help us immediately to understand how we must obey it and how we can take the right next action or step instead of manipulate and maneuver life to get what we want. We ultimately know You want only the best for us, so help us understand what You are teaching us through Your word. We need to delve into Your word, study it, and then listen to You as we pray for You to use it in and through us. When we start that process of making an adjustment to Your word to get our way, please stop us in our tracks. Make us feel uncomfortable to move forward in selfishness and disobedience. In Jesus' name we pray. Amen.

When you hear from the Lord do you instantly obey or justify why or why not you should do what you've been told to do?

_____
_____
_____

Pray a prayer (write it out) for how you will approach, and obey the Lord as He teaches your heart.

_____
_____
_____
_____

Day 141

Meeting Needs

"Do not withhold good from those to whom it is due when it is in our power to do it."

Proverbs 3:27

Saying you care is different from showing you care. Quite honestly, it seems easy to tell the difference in everyday life. Take, for instance, the person who says, "Yes, I really hope that Susie does well with her surgery coming up. I'll be praying for her." Prayer is great, and always the first thing we should do; but that is the prayer part. How might the care part look? Sending a note in the mail? Offering to prepare a meal? Asking via a phone call when you might stop by to do some cleaning she can't do postsurgery? I know we are not all called to do everything, but we are certainly called to do what we can. Proverbs 3:27 says, "Do not withhold good from those to whom it is due when it is in our power to do it."

If we are able, and certainly if we are willing, we can make an offer to do something good for another. Let's look for that opportunity today.

Let's Pause for Prayer

Heavenly Father, needs are everywhere and all around us. We know we can't do everything, but we can certainly sense when You nudge us toward or call us to provide for another. Please help each of us to listen and not turn our heads. Help us to discern Your voice and not harden our hearts because helping others is inconvenient or not what we want to do at the moment. We talk about how lovely the willing heart is and how beautiful those acts of kindness are in reflecting Your love played out in acts of service, but yet we often stop short of the doing because it's just not what we want to step out to do. Oh, Lord, may we be ashamed of ourselves for such selfishness. Open our ears to hear from You, our minds to be willing to do what you ask, and our hands and hearts to serve with gladness. In Jesus' name we pray. Amen.

Whom might you serve today and show you care? What will you do?

_____
_____
_____

Is the subject of helping others easy or difficult to think about and why? What does your answer tell you about yourself?

_____
_____
_____
_____

Day 142 — *Life Is Short*

"As for the days of our life, they contain seventy years, or if due to strength, eighty years."

Psalm 90:10

Our lives are much like commercials. They're brief with a limited amount of time to say what is most important and what will be remembered. Although we may live to be 70 years old, which Psalm 90:10 calls "the days of our life," or 80 years, which Psalm 90 says is what is given to us if we have been particularly strong, we often remark about the small number of years we feel we actually have. Many passages in scripture describe our lives as but a breath in the realm of all eternity. So indeed, life is short and we must be purposeful about what we want to accomplish and for what we hope to be remembered.

Jesus, although his life was but a brief 33 years, said and did that which was important and that for which he would be remembered. His life was intentional, impactful, and full of meaning and purpose.

Let's Pause for Prayer

Heavenly Father, thank you for sending your Son Jesus to live on earth the short time He did yet accomplishing Your will for each of us. Thank you for His understanding and intentionality in following through with the purposes You had for him. Thank You for His death and resurrection, which provided eternal life for each of us who receives Him into our hearts and lives for Him. Thank you for the assurance that we will spend eternity with You as we have received You. Please help us to make good use of the lives You've given us as we desire to be examples of Jesus to others. In Jesus' name we pray. Amen.

What do you believe is the purpose God has given you here on this earth?

_____
_____
_____
_____

If you know your purpose, how do you live it out? If you aren't sure what it is, what will you do intentionally to find out the answer?

_____
_____
_____
_____

Day 143 — "Selfism"

"For you were called to freedom, brethren; only do not turn your freedom into an opportunity for the flesh, but through love serve one another."

Galatians 5:13

On August 22, 2002, I heard and later read an edition of BreakPoint, featuring Chuck Colson in a broadcast he titled "It's Not My Fault." He told several bizarre stories of people who were in the wrong, blaming others, claiming to be victims, and winning their court cases. He summarized these situations as cases of "selfism," making them members of the Victim of the Month Club. He noted no shortage of categories: victims of racism, sexism, addictions to sex, alcohol, cigarettes, and gambling, and even victims of shopping, eating, and chronic lateness syndrome. He said it would be funny if it weren't so serious but that the real problem is obsession with individual rights instead of establishing our Christian duty and responsibility. The selfist claims, "I'm a victim." The Christian acknowledges, "I'm a sinner." The selfist says, "What's in it for me?" The Christian wonders, "How can I serve others?"

I believe only one person was the ultimate victim, blamed yet never responding to accusations, wronged but never retaliating, ridiculed but never uttering an unkind word. That person is Jesus.

Let's Pause for Prayer

Heavenly Father, as we think of Jesus' death, and the selflessness of it, may we respond in such a way that our lives would be changed forever more to worship and serve You! May we stop complaining about how we have been wronged and thank You for providing eternal life for us through Your death and resurrection. Instead of seeking what's in it for us, may we seek ways to serve others as You have served us. In Jesus' name we pray. Amen.

Think of a time you demanded something, wanting your own way or not admitting what was truly your fault. Make restitution for that selfish act if you are able, and write out a prayer for yourself that illustrates your desire to yield to and serve Jesus.

Day 144

Blessing Of The Day

> *"This is the day which the Lord has made; Let us rejoice and be glad in it."*
>
> Psalm 118:24

After a two-month hospital stay and nursing home rehabilitation, Joe's mom came to stay with us for three weeks to continue home therapies and recuperation. No easy feat for an 81-year-old!

Caring for her was difficult for our family and extended family members. Continuous adjustments were necessary challenges for everyone involved. Her mind and body were both failing, and determining her needs and how to meet them was a challenge for us.

Although she had been a very positive and uplifting person, she had become negative and sometimes unpleasant even though we tried to do everything possible to help her. In an effort to keep her mind focused on the good things that happened instead of how much work everything was for her, we decided to have a time of sharing at our kitchen table. We decided everyone needed to share two things: first, the blessing of the day; and second, what each of us had done for another person to bless them. If someone had been unable to do, they could state whom had they prayed for instead.

Those questions prompted us to remain focused on serving others and celebrating good things instead of complaining about what we didn't like, what didn't seem fair, and the negatives of life—of which we could cite plenty!

Let's Pause for Prayer

Heavenly Father, we thank You for the way You work in our lives to cause us to look to You for strength and endurance. Please remind us as we care for one another to be mindful of the blessings in each day as well as how we can serve others or pray for them. If we don't have a family member or friend needing a caring and giving hand from us right now, would you please show us someone who might need a tender helping hand when we're able to serve in that way? In Jesus' name we pray. Amen.

Name a blessing you experienced today? Sometime it's difficult to find one, but breathing and enjoying the day count!

_____

_____

_____

What have you done for another person today to bless her or him? If you are unable to do, for whom have you prayed for today?

_____

_____

Day 145   *How Will We Be Remembered?*

"And he departed with no one's regret, and they buried him in the city of David, but not in the tombs of the kings."

II Chronicles 21:20

Stopped at a red light, I realized I would be further delayed by a funeral procession. The delay did not bother me because I took the opportunity to pray for the family and friends of the deceased, understanding that their grief may have been difficult to bear. On occasion I've had a pretty lengthy prayer time! But in this case, besides the hearse, only two cars were in the procession. Along with surprise, I felt sadness. Was the person so elderly that he or she had few family or friends still living? Or was the deceased a loner who never had or tried to make friends or simply an unloved person because of selfishness or a mean spirit?

King Jehoram, early in his reign, had killed all his brothers and other rulers who were potential rivals. He led the nation to worship false gods and then died from a terribly painful disease. This account, found in II Chronicles 21:20 states that "he reigned in Jerusalem eight years, and he departed with no one's regret." What a sad commentary! To be so visible and so powerful, but no one was sad to see him die.

The pastor who married us and who was a dear friend died in his mid 50s from cancer. Ken Radke was a wonderful pastor, dear husband, tender father, and fun friend. The church was packed for his memorial service. The funeral procession seemed endless. What a testimony to a "life well lived," honored and remembered. How will you be remembered?

Let's Pause for Prayer

Heavenly Father, we pray that You will begin anew in each of us today the desire to make an impact on the lives of others who would allow us to be remembered as loving You and serving You as well as others. Help us to love and serve You first so that we will overflow with what You give us. We desire to impact our family and friends with Your love in such a way that we do not question where that love came from. Thank You for freely giving. May we freely open our hearts and hands to the gifts You've given us that we might use them to serve, bless, encourage, and teach others about You. In Jesus' name we pray. Amen.

How do you hope to be remembered? Write a brief epitaph that you would want on your tombstone.

_____

_____

If how you are living isn't in sync with how you hope to be remembered, what changes will you have to make? When will you take the first step to do so?

_____

_____

_____

Day 146

Medicine For Our Neighbors

> *"A joyful heart is good medicine."*
> Proverbs 17:22a

As a child I remember playing outside in the summer, running from yard to yard and house to house with the kids in the neighborhood all day long. None of us had air-conditioning, so the evenings were spent outside on the porch or visiting neighbors who were outside as well. Getting to know the people in the neighborhood was wonderful.

The convenience of air-conditioning that we enjoy today makes staying inside on hot days and evenings very easy. Although this modern convenience has hindered us from getting to know our neighbors in the same way as when we were children, we enjoy an evening walk when the sun isn't so hot and try to allow some time to stop and visit with our neighbors if they're also walking or if they're working in their yards. Sometimes we encounter someone we don't know who may be from another neighborhood as they're walking in ours. Some seem happy just to smile and say hello; others are eager to engage in conversation, and still others barely grunt hello or make eye contact. We enjoy the times we get to connect with those we know and personally like to use those opportunities to pray for our neighbors as we walk. We hope to bring joy so that they don't mind seeing us coming! We want to share in our demeanor our love for Christ even if it's not part of our every conversation.

Let's Pause for Prayer

Heavenly Father, thank You for the opportunities we have to speak with our neighbors. May we greet them with smiles, kind words, and pleasant conversation. Please let us use those opportunities to get to know them better and to pray for them when they have needs as well as when they are rejoicing. Help us to listen to the needs they might have and then meet those needs as a way of showing the love of Christ. Help us to be an example of your love and goodness to them. In Jesus' name we pray. Amen.

How well do you know your neighbors? How can you get to know them better?

_____

_____

_____

_____

_____

Day 147 — Going For The Gold—In Life!

> *"Do you not know that those who run in a race all run, but only one receives the prize? Run in such a way that you may win."*
>
> I Corinthians 9:24

Joe and I really enjoy the Olympics; however, the last time we watched them, the commentators seemed excessively critical of the athletes. With all the training, competition, preparation, expertise, skill, and stamina that each athlete requires to reach the Olympic level of competition, we were astonished by the commentators' harsh criticism of the competitors' style, performance, and routine.

We wondered what a commentator might say about how we "do" life. I imagine the commentator would say something like this: "Well, Joe and Cindi have been at this for a while; however, they still need work on a few of those finer points. Training has been good for them, but these fine points are critical to how they'll come out in this competition. They need to keep their eye on their goal."

Let's Pause for Prayer

Heavenly Father, we thank You for being the ultimate loving and caring coach and guide. For those of us who desire to "finish well" in life, we look to You for the stamina, perseverance, and skill to see us through this life until we meet You face to face at the finish line. Thank You for your support despite our mistakes and sins and for your loving reproof when needed to guide us to making better and right decisions when we come to You in humility and repentance. Help us to take times of rest to get back into the game of life when we're too tired to go on. As we learn and grow, we want to be able to help others do the same. As we perfect our walk with You, may others desire to do the same. Help us to be mindful that others are watching, observing, and paying close attention not only to how we are doing life but also how we'll finish. May we all finish well. In Jesus' name we pray. Amen.

In the race of life, do you feel as if you've kept up the pace God has asked of you, or are you lagging behind?

_____

_____

_____

What will it take (and what will you do) to get back into the race to finish well? When will you do it?

_____

_____

_____

Day 148

One Step From A Bad Decision

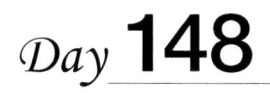

"Listen to counsel and accept discipline, that you may be wise the rest of your days."

Proverbs 19:20

We are all one step from a bad decision. It's amazing, but many of us (yes, even Christians) justify a wrong and bad decision when we feel we've been wronged, aren't happy, or want better or more than we have.

In reality we make decisions all day long. We sometimes think the frivolous and seemingly small decisions—like what to wear or where to go to lunch—are inconsequential, right? Wrong! Even our choice of what to wear can lead us to a next (and wrong) decision. Where we go and with whom can lead us to make a choice we didn't think we ever would.

Our every decision makes a difference because with each one we inch our way toward the fine line that (as I used to tell my children) separates fun from foolishness and right from wrong.

Let's Pause for Prayer

Heavenly Father, help us to be mindful of stepping over that fine line into the wrong and the foolish. We are often already headed in the wrong direction when making the decisions that lead us over the line. We recognize that each decision, each step we take lead us somewhere. We don't always think ahead to where somewhere is, so help us to take notice. Sometimes, Lord, we think if we've made a wrong decision we cannot turn back, but that is wrong thinking, too. Help us make the right decision without fear, without thinking we need to fill some void in our lives. Help us to grow up. We know that You will not be mocked. "Do not be deceived, God is not mocked; for whatever a man sows, this he will also reap." We can't plant apples and expect oranges. Help us make good decisions and choices that will honor, not mock, Your name. In Jesus' name we pray. Amen.

Are you contemplating a decision that is troubling you? Write your thoughts.

_____

_____

Now, pray and ask the Lord to help you recognize whether the struggle is sin and if it is, your decision should be to turn away. What will be your action point to turn away?

_____

_____

_____

Day 149 — Aging Gracefully

"For he will not often consider [remember] the years of his life because God keeps him occupied with the gladness of his heart."

Ecclesiastes 5:20

Joe went first, and then it was my turn to hit one of the milestone birthdays. It was amazing how many conversations made their way to the subject of old age. "We're really not that old, are we?" we said. When looking across the room at an older person, we asked, "Do we look that old?" Well, folks, the answer to both is yes! Some might look better for their age than others, but whether we're 40, 50, 60, or older, we look our decade. We can't hide it!

We prefer to ask ourselves different questions, for example, How are we doing at this age with the time He's given us, and how will we use the time that's left? We want Him to use us until we're used up! We don't want to be found sitting around, waiting for life to happen. We want to be busy serving, rest when needed, and get busy again because He has us here for a reason.

Let's Pause for Prayer

Heavenly Father, thank You for words that encourage us to understand that aging can be a joyous process. Ecclesiastes 5:20 says, "For he will not often consider [remember] the years of his life because God keeps him occupied with the gladness of his heart." Let us be so busy doing Your work that we won't even worry about our age and the aging process because we're doing what You has asked of us! Keep us moving straight ahead and not looking to the right or to the left to distract us from the work we're to do. Thank You for Your concern about our hearts and attitudes and not so much about how old we are. Thank You for the ability to accomplish in elder years things that could not have been done when younger. Father, we don't want to regard our age as a stumbling block in the way of accomplishing Your will. We simply want to be faithful to the end. In Jesus' name we pray. Amen.

Do you feel (no matter your age) that you are happy where you are and as you're getting older? Why or why not?

_____

_____

_____

How can you pray that yourself (and others) will experience the joy of aging gracefully? Write a prayer for yourself and someone else.

_____

_____

_____

Day 150 — Don't Let Go

"For the Lord your God is the one who goes with you. He will not fail you or forsake you."

Deuteronomy 31:6b

As I approached a very busy intersection, I was taken by surprise by a young man walking across five lanes of very busy early morning traffic, holding the hand of a child, who was about four years old. I thought, "That father sure is brave to walk across all those lanes of traffic (not at a cross walk) with such a little child." But my second thoughts went to the child. I saw in that small child the kind of trust we should have in our heavenly Father when life seems hectic, unsafe, and even uncertain.

The father watched the road so the little boy didn't have to. He held the little boy's hand tightly, making sure he didn't move too fast into traffic or lag behind because he was too slow. I could see he was talking to his son, but I could only imagine that his words were something like, "Hang on, Son, stay with me. I will get you across safely. Just hold onto me. Don't let go of me. Keep your eyes on me, and don't turn to the right or to the left. I will get you where you need to go."

Let's Pause for Prayer

Heavenly Father, if only we could respond to You with such trust as this little boy's. What issues, Lord, are you trying to get me to understand? That You are there for me to trust in You for the solution? Have you already walked me through an unsafe situation? Do I just need to trust You in the midst of it? Lord, am I trying to get somewhere on my own and ignoring the fact that You are holding on to me until You get me there safely? Thank You for allowing us to trust You with our very lives. Thank You for providing Your guidance and direction in the midst of the very busy traffic of life. Thank You for holding our hands firmly and lovingly. In Jesus' name we pray. Amen.

Where do you lack trust in God or ignore His hand upon you in your life?

_____

_____

_____

What will you do to make a move (with Him, not ahead of Him) to get to your destination?

_____

_____

_____

_____

Day 151 — Burn Out

"Commit your works to the Lord, and your plans will be established."
Proverb 16:3

Contemplating a quotation I often hear and know I have said myself—"I am burned out!"—I wonder what that really means. Sometimes I expend considerable energy on a task as well as a good deal of time and feel totally recharged, motivated, and even contented! But other times an activity or responsibility leaves me feeling overloaded. Analyzing these two extremes has me searching for that sense of motivation, contentment, and enjoyment instead of winding up feeling burned out.

At least for me, I recognize that I don't get overloaded or burned out from doing too much; I get overloaded and burned out from doing too much of nothing or better said, too much of what God didn't intend for me to do. When I am using the gifts He has given me, when I am certain that I am doing His will, and when I am obedient to His lead, I am content. I'm not fighting against what He has for me to do. I can do much, but if it consists of what He has asked me to do, that's how I will avoid overload!

Let's Pause for Prayer

Heavenly Father, thank You for creating each of us for certain purposes. Help us to learn just what that means for each of us individually. We thank You for giving us a purpose and gifts to use to see that purpose fulfilled. Please help us to learn to use the gifts You've given us for Your glory and to benefit Your kingdom here on earth. Guide us to work for You, not against You, so we won't become overloaded, overburdened, and burned out from doing what You have not asked us to do. In Jesus' name we pray. Amen.

Do you sense that you are doing too much and are headed for burnout? Describe what life looks like for you right now and how you sense what's headed your way.

_____

_____

_____

If you sense burnout is about to occur, how can you stop yourself in your tracks right now and change course? What action will you take?

_____

_____

_____

_____

Day 152 — *What's The Right Thing To Do?*

> *"Whatever you do, do your work heartily, as for the Lord rather than for men."*
> Colossians 3:23

My husband had a unique opportunity in March 2003 to be a part of a White House briefing at which John Ashcroft stated, "When President Bush meets with his cabinet to make decisions, he listens to all the various discussions, ideas, and possible outcomes. Then, he asks the cabinet, 'What is the right thing to do?'"

When you are in the midst of making decisions, are you able to end the thought process with that same question? Doing the right thing doesn't necessarily mean it will be fun, comfortable, or easy. In fact, doing the right thing is often more difficult than what we would naturally choose to do to stay in our comfort zone!

Let's Pause for Prayer

Heavenly Father, thank You for preparing our hearts and bringing to our minds that which you want us to do. Thank You for providing a way for us to be obedient to Your will in order to do what is right even when it may be very difficult for us. Help us to care for the one who is difficult, to spend time with the one we know needs special attention, to stay in a job or a marriage that isn't easy or pleasant, or whatever You've asked us to do. Help us to make the right decision even when others will wonder and question how we could ever make such a choice, knowing in our hearts that it is the right thing to do. Thank You for giving us the strength to do the right thing. In Jesus' name we pray. Amen.

Is God calling you out of your comfort zone to do the right thing? Write out your situation and how you know what the right thing is for you do to.

_____

_____

_____

_____

What will be your first step in the right direction? Write it out or write a prayer to express it.

_____

_____

_____

_____

Day 153

For Evil Or Good?

"And as for you, you meant evil against me, but God meant it for good in order to bring about this present result, to preserve many people alive."

Genesis 50:20

Joseph spent 20 years in Egypt after his brothers sold him into slavery. I guess it took that long for him to prepare to be in charge in order to save his family from famine those many years later. Have you ever wonder what those 20 years were like for him? Do you think they were fun, pleasant, or easy? He was without his family; he was persecuted, jailed, mistreated, slandered, and falsely accused. He was victorious because he kept his eyes off himself and on the Lord. He was able to see that his sufferings were really momentary afflictions and a part of God's greater plan in his life.

When I complain or hear others complain about momentary afflictions or minor discomforts, I sometimes wonder just what God must think! We have such a way, don't we, of grumbling about issues that are so small. We complain and gripe about situations much less intense than what Joseph endured!

Let's Pause for Prayer

Heavenly Father, help me to focus on You instead of myself and my problems this very moment. Help me to take my eyes off myself and look around me to see beauty in what You have made and to rejoice that You give us only what we can handle and only for our good in order that You are glorified. Help me see the world from Your perspective as Joseph did! Help me to give You praise and to let my life, even through difficulty and pain, reflect Your love and kindness. In Jesus' name we pray. Amen.

Has any person in the past ever purposed to do evil to you? If so, can you now see that God turned the situation around for good? Write the incident out for yourself and reflect upon it.

_____

_____

If nothing from your past comes to mind, are you perhaps in the midst of a situation in which you feel you've been wronged? Write it out for yourself.

_____

_____

Are you able to wait upon the Lord for Him to turn this situation around? What does your waiting pattern look like right at this moment?

_____

_____

_____

Day 154 — Fear

"Finally brethren, whatever is true, whatever is honorable, whatever is right, whatever is pure, whatever is lovely, whatever is of good repute, if there is any excellence and if anything worthy of praise, let your mind dwell on these things."

Philippians 4:8

Whenever someone shares with me a fear that troubles him or her, or whenever I fear something, I immediately repeat to myself the scripture above. I let my mind dwell on each of those words and list a detail for each phrase. When fear, anxiety, or uncertainty prevails in my mind, I search in my mind for what I know is true:

- God's word
- God's love for me
- God's protection

    I then go to whatever is honorable (characterized by integrity, that is, soundness, completeness)
- God's will

Next, I consider whatever is right, pure, lovely, and of good repute (or consideration). By the time I work myself through the list, my fears have subsided and I am resting in the Lord.

Let's Pause for Prayer

Heavenly Father, thank You for allowing us to change the way we feel about and respond to fear simply by letting our minds dwell on pure and good things from You. Help bring to mind this verse when we have drifted into an unhealthy way of thinking. Let us keep our eyes focused on You and Your goodness! In Jesus' name we pray. Amen.

What do you naturally do with fears when you can't get them out of your mind?

___

___

After reading Philippians 4:8, are you able to find peace? Write out the verse and the truths God shows you for your particular fear.

___

___

___

___

Day 155   *We Need Direction*

> *"The mind of a man plans his way, but the Lord directs his steps."*
> Proverbs 16:9

I've heard it said that much can be told about us by the checks written in our checkbooks. I've also heard it said that "how we spend our time is the life we lead." Much can be revealed about us by the way we spend our time.

Do we spend time

- on people or projects?
- with family or friends or coworkers?
- to rest, or are we always working?
- to have fun? to work? to sleep?
- having others over to our homes, or do we wait for an invitation to go to someone else's home?
- playing sports and enjoying hobbies at the expense of our families?

If someone were to see all the ways we spend our time, would they say we are balanced, obedient, and wise?

Let's Pause for Prayer

Heavenly Father, thank You for this day You have given us. Help us to use it wisely for Your glory. Help us to balance rest and work, people and projects, serving and being served. We pray that we will not waste the precious time You've given us. We ask You to keep us focused on where we should spend our time as we know that the time You give us here is limited. We want to be sure to use it carefully and responsibly. In Jesus' name we pray. Amen.

Do you know where you spend your money and time? (On which do you think you have a better handle?)

_____

_____

If you think one item, tangible or intangible, would help you make better use of the time God has given you, what is it? If God gave you that item, how would you put into action a plan to make better use of your time?

_____

_____

_____

_____

Day 156 — *Bad Company*

> *"Do not be deceived: Bad company corrupts good morals."*
>
> I Corinthians 15:33

Recently purchasing potatoes, I thought everything looked fine from the outside; but even before I opened the bag, the smell of one bad potato was pungent. Dumping the whole bag into the sink did not instantly reveal which potato was bad. When I found the soft and moldy bad potato, I realized that two others did not look too good either—right next to the very bad one.

I remember my parents telling me who I spent time with would influence who I became. I remember hearing from them, "One bad apple spoils the whole bunch." I Cor. 15:33 says the same: "Do not be deceived: "Bad company corrupts good morals."

If we spend time in bad company, we can expect to look like, smell like, and act like those with whom we spend time. As close as those potatoes were in the bag, the good one had no other choice but to become like the bad one next to it.

Taking inventory of who we're spending time with and determining whether the individual is a good influence or not, encouraging good behavior or urging rebelliousness, and most importantly, whether the person encourages us to grow in the Lord, read from His word, and pray to Him consistently and often throughout the day are what we need to do to ensure the best in our friendships and relationships.

Let's Pause for Prayer

Heavenly Father, we desire to be more like You. We desire to spend more time with others who also want to be more like You so their good ways will rub off on us. Help us to be strong enough to keep ourselves from bad company, recognizing those whose ways are neither pure nor of You. May we stay in Your word and closer to You! In Jesus' name we pray. Amen.

Whom are you becoming most like? Is this a good or a bad thing?

_____

_____

_____

What changes might you have to make to spend time with the right people, who will help you to grow in the Lord?

_____

_____

_____

Day 157 — Push!

> *"Pray without ceasing."*
> 1 Thessalonians 5:17

Do you sometimes pray and pray and pray until you get the feeling that perhaps it's just no use? Well, God has instructed in various places of scripture that we should, in fact, keep praying and praying.

Luke 18:1 tells about Jesus, "Now He was telling them a parable to show that at all times they ought to pray and not to lose heart." In I Thess. 5:17 we are encouraged to "pray without ceasing."

We are to persevere. We are to continue to pray even when we haven't received the answer yet. In my husband's Bible, next to the word pray is the word push: P-U-S-H or "pray until something happens."

That something might be God telling us "yes," "no," or "wait—the time is not right." The holding pattern of prayer is not easy, but it is necessary!

Let's Pause for Prayer

Heavenly Father, we thank You for allowing us to come to You in prayer and make requests of You, the mighty God of the universe. Let us not take for granted that You can and do hear each of us and that you can and will answer each of our prayers. May we be patient as we wait to see our prayers through to the answer You give. Help us not lose heart as we wait upon You for direction and the answers that will emanate from Your perfect will. In Jesus' name we pray. Amen.

For what are you praying through right now that you feel you must wait upon the Lord?

_____
_____
_____

If you have to PUSH, are you willing to wait until something happens? Write a prayer that you can review daily (if needed) about that which is on your heart.

_____
_____
_____
_____
_____

Day 158

Love Your Enemies

"But I tell you who hear me; love your enemies, do good to those who hate you, bless those who curse you, pray for those who mistreat you."

Luke 6:27–28

Do you relate at all to this passage? Do any of the following apply?

- ☐ A coworker is confrontational with me.
- ☐ A neighbor is always angry with me.
- ☐ A family member criticizes me even when I do good.
- ☐ A person who I thought was my friend is very nasty to me.

I remember someone sharing the following at a conference: "One third of the people you'll meet will love you. One third of the people you'll meet won't like you at all. One third of the people you meet could not care less about you. So why do we work to please the two thirds?"

We can all probably think of someone who is upset with us or perhaps even hates us. How we treat that two thirds, however, is very important! Do we react to them or respond to them? The Bible gives us a clear way to respond, and that is to continue to do good to those who hate us.

Let's Pause for Prayer

Heavenly Father, we pray for those who mistrust and even hate us. Show us ways we can bless others. We don't want to be doormats who ask for mistreatment, but we want to respond to mistreatment in ways that show You are in control of us and that You allow us to return a blessing instead of an insult, unkind word, or an action in anger or strife. Please help us to show Your love even though it's sometimes difficult to do so. Please help us to obey Romans 12:21: "Don't be overcome by evil, but overcome evil with good." In Jesus' name we pray. Amen.

Can you think of someone to whom you know you need to respond more positively? Has it been a long process to go from reacting to responding to him or her? How did you come to do or learn that?

_____

_____

_____

If you're still struggling with a particular person, what will you do to respond positively to him or her in the future? Write out your course of action for yourself.

_____

_____

_____

Day 159 — Why?

"'For My thoughts are not your thoughts, neither are your ways My ways,' declares the Lord."

Isaiah 55:8–9

When you experience a frustration or disappointment, do you ever wonder why the particular situation has occurred? Of course, you do. I believe we all do! Do you dare ask God why?

If we were to be honest with one another and with God, I believe we ask why more than we think we do! I also believe God eventually answers us but perhaps not in our time frame or in the way we think He will! And I think He can handle it when we are so bold to ask why.

This scripture attests to the larger plan God has for us as well as what He has to say about His plan. I suppose it is a lesson for all of us to recognize that God's perfect plan doesn't necessarily include telling us what it is or cluing us in on how He's going to see it through. We just have to be diligent to seek Him in the midst of it.

Let's Pause for Prayer

Heavenly Father, we don't know exactly what You have planned for us, but we know You will do just what is right for what we need. Help us to remember Psalm 138:8: "The Lord will accomplish what concerns me," so when times of doubt and discouragement haunt us, we learn to lean instantly upon You, thank You, and know that Your ways are beyond anything we can imagine. Help us to trust in You for the outcome, knowing it will fit perfectly into the plans You have for us. Help us not to doubt Your ways. In Jesus' name we pray. Amen.

What first came to your mind regarding asking why?

_____
_____
_____

Do you feel as if you need to pursue your situation with God, or are you able to rest in whatever He has for you? What is your next step of action?

_____
_____
_____
_____
_____

Day 160 — Waiting In Line And In Life

> *"Wait for the Lord; be strong, and let your heart take courage; yes, wait for the Lord."*
>
> Psalm 27:14

"A study by The Fortino Group in Pittsburgh found that over the course of a lifetime, the average person spends five years waiting in line" (*AARP*, March/April 2004).

Well, that statistic really made me want to reevaluate how I spend my time. How about you?

I have noticed lately how often I stand and wait. Perhaps I notice it because sometimes I feel frustrated doing so, frustrated that I can't do anything about it! So instead of allowing myself to feel that way, I've brought things with me to occupy my time while standing in line. I keep a few pieces of easy-read mail in my purse along with small brochures and short magazine articles; catching up on my emails or texts on my phone or other readable material to help pass the time and give me a sense of being productive with the time God has given me.

I also have been known to start a real conversation (face to face) with someone also waiting in line, but when that doesn't happen, I've also begun asking the Lord for whom or what I can pray. I am amazed at the people and situations He brings to my heart while I am waiting.

Let's Pause for Prayer

Heavenly Father, I am amazed how quickly time passes when You put in my mind someone for whom to pray! As we wait in traffic, in line at the school to pick up or drop off our children, or in an office waiting for an appointment, please remind us to use this time to pause for prayer. Thank you for these moments of waiting that we can use to pray to You for the things You put in our hearts. Thank You for our loved ones for whom we should pray more and for situations in life, in our community, in our nation, and in our world that we can bring before You as we find ourselves waiting. May we use the time You have given us to pray and learn to patiently wait in line and in life for answers. In Jesus' name we pray. Amen.

Do you feel you spend much time waiting in lines (and in life)? Explain.

_____

Have you ever considered taking things to read, praying, or starting conversations with others during that wait time? Which comes easier for you to do? Would you be willing to leave your comfort zone and try something different?

_____

_____

What would something different look like in terms of what you'll do the next time you're waiting in line?

_____

_____

Day 161 — Slambooks Of Yesterday Are The Facebook Of Today

"A man has joy in an apt answer, and how delightful is a timely word!"

Proverbs 15:23

Slambooks—do you remember them? Did you have them or did you write in them in junior high school? They were books that mostly girls put together in binders, each page bearing the name of a different female classmate followed by questions that others could answer about the person. Some questions were fairly tame, but some were worded to motivate others to write unkind remarks about the girl whose name was at the top of the page. The Slambook of yesterday is the Facebook of today: a place where we can hide behind our comments and pretend no one will know we said them.

Let's Pause for Prayer

Lord, in this modern age of social media, we come to You for guidance and direction before we post, comment, like, or dislike on our walls and pages, tweets, and Instagrams so that we do not purposely or unknowingly hurt others, tear them down, or make untrue, mean, or nasty statements or cause others to be critical. As we compose our thoughts, help us to weigh our words carefully, to ask You for guidance as to whether or not our words will encourage or hurt, and then to choose carefully what we actually write. We know we have choices, and it's just as easy to be nasty as it is to be nice. It takes no more effort to say kind words instead of harsh or vicious ones. Help us to recognize when our words are hurtful, and then help us make a wise choice about whether or not to use them or wait for an opportunity to craft them better so they come from a heart of caring and compassion, not revenge. Help us to recognize our negative tendencies and choose better because others in social media, including unbelievers, are watching us and wondering whether they even want to get to know our Jesus based upon what they see and hear from us. Let us not hide behind paper and pen or the computer but be cautious and encouraging in our words to and for others. I pray we would put ourselves in the shoes of others and try to feel how they might feel if negative comments were said to or about us. May our words not come back to hurt us as we try to live by Proverbs 15:23: "A man has joy in an apt answer, and how delightful is a timely word!" In Jesus' name we pray. Amen.

Do you pray before you post, tweet, Instagram, or otherwise make statements on social media?

_____

_____

Write out what you want to do (think, pray, consider, write, and review) before you post on social media and pray about following through with it.

_____

_____

_____

_____

Day 162 — Limited Sight Distance

"O, taste and see that the Lord is good; how blessed is the man who takes refuge in Him!"

Psalm 34:8

We all have limited sight with regard to some areas in our lives. We might not see our own personality quirks and habits that are irritating and obvious to others. At the next level are our blind spots—character flaws that are not only irritating and obvious to others but might also be sinful. In both of these cases, when someone lovingly points them out to us and if we are willing, we can work on those quirks and habits and turn from our sin.

But when we recognize individuals in deliberate, willful, intentional sin and we or others have lovingly pointed it out to them but they continue in that willful and disobedient lifestyle, we can say that they are blind. Spiritual blindness is dangerous and causes ripple effects that extend a great distance: to our immediate family, friends, coworkers, even ministry partners—and if no sincere repentance is forthcoming—throughout successive generations.

Let's Pause for Prayer

Heavenly Father, we can rejoice in the death, burial and resurrection of Your Son Jesus because our sin has been removed and forgiven. If we simply come to You and ask for You to reign in our hearts, we can enjoy the fullness of Your spirit living in us. Help us to identify our quirks and habits, our character flaws that are sinful and may cause others to stumble. Help us to avoid the spiritual blindness some of us may experience because we've not surrendered to You. We pray we would not mock You by saying, "It's just who I am" but instead be willing to change so that we can lead others to You by example. We pray we would be open and bold enough to point out to others these blind spots and weaknesses so that we can all walk closely with You. May we, Father, be open and willing to hear this from others as well. May we hear it first from You and hold one another accountable. In Jesus' name we pray. Amen.

Do you recognize a flaw in your character? Have others shared with you a flaw that you choose to ignore? Write it out here.

_____

_____

How will you or did you handle someone's telling you of a character flaw they saw in you?

_____

_____

Write a prayer for taking the next step in asking God to help you with this sin or flaw.

_____

_____

Day 163

It's All About Me!

> *"As you therefore have received Christ Jesus the Lord, so walk in Him."*
>
> Colossians 2:8

We all know the saying and perhaps have even said it: "It's all about me." We use it sometimes in jest, but a hint of truth often underlies it. Sometimes we wish people would say it because in our minds that's exactly what we're thinking about them. The person who is thoroughly self-absorbed, self-centered, and selfish, concentrating only on what she or he wants and needs (without a good reason such as illness or special needs), wears on others; and sometimes others isolate him or her. The taker, the one who is "all about me" sucks the life out of life.

God clearly teaches in scripture the need for all of us to give instead of receive.

Acts 20:35 states: "Remember the words of the Lord Jesus. That He Himself said, 'It is more blessed to give than to receive.'" Many of us have wandered from what He has taught, wanting our own comfort, our own way, and to have life be "all about me." We must contemplate the selflessness and sacrifice of Jesus on the cross.

Let's Pause for Prayer

Heavenly Father, we are so thankful that Your son Jesus did what You asked of Him. Thank You for Jesus' death on the cross, which provided forgiveness of sin and the hope of eternal life. Thank You for providing salvation through You. We pray that many, especially when we celebrate Your death, burial, and resurrection, would fully come to know who You are. May we all put aside the "it's all about me" attitudes, submit to You, and recognize that our introspection into our sin is what "It's all about me" should mean. Let me, let us, search our hearts, own up to our sin and separation from you and confess our sin to You that we might live in such a way that it's no longer "all about me" but instead "all about You"! In Jesus' name we pray. Amen.

Are you more of a giver or receiver? Explain.

_____

_____

If you are more of a giver, what next steps can you take to become more of a receiver? If you are more of a receiver or taker, what can you do to give more? Explain.

_____

_____

_____

_____

Day 164

Do I Want To Know The Future?

"Jesus, knowing that the Father had given all things into His hands, and that He had come forth from God, and was going back to God."

John 13:3

Do you remember a time when you contemplated whether or not you'd like to know your future and what would happen next? Of course, when we play that idea out, we may discover that perhaps we wouldn't want to know what's next. Knowing the pain, suffering, and even the surprises around the corner might not be what we'd really want.

Jesus was one who knew what was next. He knew that Peter would deny Him and that Judas would betray Him. He knew He was being sent to the cross to return to the Father. John 13:3, "Jesus, knowing that the Father had given all things into His hands, and that He had come forth from God, and was going back to God" relates to us that Jesus was fully aware of His mission here, His surrender to God, and His future. He knew He would be crucified, would die, be buried, and that He would be resurrected from the dead. He knew His mission to save us from our sins would once and for all be accomplished. Do you know it?

Let's Pause for Prayer

Heavenly Father, Your Son Jesus knew His mission on this earth and did not sway to the right or to the left but remained on the straight and narrow to accomplish it. Your will was His will. Your way was His way. Thank You for His obedience to the way of the cross and dealing with the penalty of sin on our behalf by His death on that cross. We praise You for the resurrection, which reminds us of the new birth and life in Jesus Christ when we surrender our hearts and lives to Him by asking Him into our hearts. We pray for those who don't know Jesus as their Savior to study the scripture, seek God, and realize that although we can't know what will happen to us on a daily basis, we are assured of a future in heaven with Him someday because of His obedient ascension to the cross on our behalf and our knowing and living for Him. Thank You, Lord. In Jesus' name we pray. Amen.

Jesus knows what will happen next in your future. How willing are you to trust Him for it?

_____

_____

_____

Jesus knew His mission was to submit to and complete what the Father had ordained. What might your mission and the completion of it mean for you?

_____

_____

_____

Day 165

Repeating: Over And Over And Over

> *"'I tell you that in the same way, there will be more joy in heaven over one sinner who repents, than over ninety-nine righteous persons who need no repentance.'"*
>
> Luke 15:8

When I tape my segments of Pause for Prayer in the radio studio, I come prepared to do the best job I can. I have prepared my script, practiced reading it, and then I'm ready to record. Occasionally, I get through all the scripts without a mistake or two or three! I am thankful that the Pause for Prayer producer can edit out the mistakes I've made—no matter how awful they are! And sometimes when recovery is impossible, I get to start over and try again.

In one taping session, I kept getting stuck on one phrase. I allowed the usual pause in my speaking to leave space for a break so that later the producer would be able to edit out the mistake. Sometimes we both get to laughing, but other times it is frustrating when we both know I've practiced this over and over.

On my way home, God used that taping session to show me what He had done for me. Yes, I tend to repeat some mistakes—even sins—and get stuck on them. I can try with all my might to get it right, but sometimes I find myself repeating the same sin. The difference between the mistake of getting stuck on a phrase during a taping session and sin in real life is that I don't laugh about the latter. I recognized that just as the mistake in taping can be edited out, so does our Father, when we ask Him, erase our sins from the slate of our lives.

Let's Pause for Prayer

Heavenly Father, thank You for forgiving me of all my sin. Thank You for forgiving when I fail You. Please help me to call my sin what it is—sin—not just a mistake. Help me to humble myself and ask for Your forgiveness. And most importantly, may I be repentant, turning away from committing that sin again. Help me to recognize that my sin hurts You and that it is a poor example to others and a hindrance to those who might come to You. Let me be quick to ask forgiveness of others when I've sinned against them, to come to You and do the same, and help me to stop doing what is wrong, sinful, hurtful, prideful, and staying stuck in the same place. I know You can help me. I need You. In Jesus' name I pray. Amen.

Do you find yourself repeating a sin? Name that sin out loud as you write it here.

_____

_____

How will you conquer that sin? Are you willing?

_____

_____

_____

Day 166

The Battlefield

> *"The horse is prepared for the day of battle, but the victory belongs to the Lord."*
>
> Proverbs 21:31

All over the world men and women serve our country. Some actively fight and some stand ready to be sent into a conflict at a moment's notice. Those on the battlefield experience circumstances that many of us will never see or truly understand.

Every Christian, however, knows about and understands the battlefield of the heart, a place where many battles against temptation and sin are won or lost. In *Seeking the Face of God*, Gary Thomas writes of an area of temptation and sin over which he felt he had victory. While he was driving home after sensing a particular victory, however, he said that God showed him that he had really merely avoided one sin to fall into another. The other sin was self-righteous pride. He realized he did not go from "strength to strength" but from "sin to sin."

Thomas recognized that a performance-based Christian says, "I want to do this, but I know I shouldn't. I must not do it or not get caught." He then recognized a new perspective of his relationship to Christ, asking himself, "Do I want to be more in love with Christ or my sin?".

Let's Pause for Prayer

Heavenly Father, we see clearly that our heart is the one battlefield that really matters to each of us as individuals. We see that the state of our heart is the true state of our virtue and our standing with You. We confess to You that we have sinned and we want to commit our hearts and lives to You in a fresh, new way. Help us to resist yielding to the temptations that come our way. May we seek Your face during temptations and be victorious because we have chosen Your way, not sin. In Jesus' name we pray. Amen.

Each of us can recognize our own sin and battlefield and carry on a discussion with God. Can you courageously come to the battlefield of your own heart and seek the face of God in prayer?

_____

_____

After prayer, what will be your next practical and intentional step of faith?

_____

_____

_____

_____

Day 167 — Are You A Prayer Warrior Or Worrier?

"For though we walk in the flesh, we do not war according to the flesh, for the weapons of our warfare are not of the flesh, but divinely powerful for the destruction of fortresses. We are destroying speculation and every lofty thing raised up against the knowledge of God, and we are taking every thought captive to the obedience of Christ."

II Corinthians 10:3–5

One day as I contemplated a particular situation, I found that all I was really doing was reviewing, reconsidering, rehearsing, and yes, even worrying about it; but I wasn't praying as I know I'm called to do. Humanly, I think this can easily happen. When evil is done against us, when life isn't smooth, when concerns overwhelm us, it's sometimes easier to let our minds wander, let our emotions drift, eventually finding ourselves somewhere we didn't intend to go—a place of worry.

I am still in the process of learning. When my mind wanders to worry instead of prayer, I stop the negative thoughts and feelings and dwell instead on the Lord. I refocus my thinking to focused prayer. I prioritize my problems and spend time praying about each one. I talk with the Lord, thanking Him for blessings of the day, not concentrating only on the problems happening in my life but also asking for forgiveness when I was a part of the problem instead of the solution. I take responsibility for my thoughts and actions and let God deal with others for theirs. But it's still a process—a process of letting go of worry and spending time with God in prayer.

Let's Pause for Prayer

Heavenly Father, thank You for teaching us the importance of coming to You in prayer. We are so grateful to You for showing us that we do not have to worry because You have provided for all of our needs. Thank You for Your word, which says, "And do not seek what you shall eat, and what you shall drink, and do not keep worrying" (Luke 12:29). Help us put every situation in Your hands—our concerns, our thoughts, our words—for You to direct us and to use us for Your Glory. Help us to be prayer warriors and not worriers. In Jesus' name we pray. Amen.

When do you worry the most? Explain.

___

___

___

Can you place your cares and worries upon the Lord? How will that look for you?

___

___

___

Day 168 — The Pain We Can And Can't See

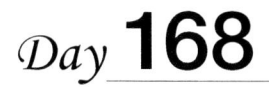

"Shall we indeed accept good from God and not accept adversity?"
Job 2:10b

Those of us who have chronic pain or bouts of reoccurring illness or injuries that result in pain take comfort in prescription and over-the-counter medicines that sooth or quiet the pain. Relief from constant and reoccurring deep pain is welcomed and many times desperately needed, but I believe we are a culture that generally doesn't want to be inconvenienced by even the most minor pain. We want instant relief from the tension headache caused by the stress we allowed into our lives. We want instant relief from other general aches and pains that we in some way or another might have easily prevented with a balanced life style and a conscious effort to maintain that balance.

Emotional pain is not so easy to recognize. We are a hurting people but with a loving and healing God who cares for us in all ways! Coming to Him first might alleviate some of the unresolved pain and also help us deal with the right ways to live to relieve the pain that is physical.

Let's Pause for Prayer

Heavenly Father, we thank You for being the ultimate Healer. We pray for those we know who are dealing with and living with pain today. Please comfort them in a way that they understand that the relief from pain and suffering comes from You. We pray to rely upon You to meet our every need. We thank You for scientists, researchers, and doctors who find ways to treat us through medicine, therapy, exercise, and counseling; but we pray that our ultimate dependence is on You in all situations. In Jesus' name we pray. Amen.

Have you had or do you have chronic pain (physical or emotional) that is difficult for you to handle on a daily basis?

_____
_____
_____

How have you sought the Lord in this regard? Write a prayer that includes thanksgiving as well as asking for His direction and guidance in the matter.

_____
_____
_____
_____

Day 169 — *Good News Sticks*

> *"It is a trustworthy statement, deserving full acceptance, that Christ Jesus came in to the world to save sinners, among whom I am foremost of all."*
>
> I Timothy 1:15

At our local National Day of Prayer gathering, Joe and I had the privilege of praying for families. Joining in prayer for many others—our firefighters and the police force, our nation, our city, and our youth—was wonderful.

The highlight of that evening for us was what happened afterward. A woman holding a Bible came up to us and said, "I just had to come up to you and tell you something. I once came to your door with another person to share with you what I believed, and you invited me in to talk to you. Even then I couldn't believe you would invite us in because most people didn't even talk to us, but you did; and you shared Christ with me. At the time I didn't want to hear anything of it, but as time passed, I thought about what you shared with me; and I saw that what I taught to believe was untrue. I searched the scriptures for more answers. I just want you to know that I am now a Christian, and I know that I have eternal life. I wanted to thank you for what you did for me!"

Interestingly, neither Joe nor I remembered her or inviting her into our home. We often had people in our home to talk when they came to our door, but honestly, it never seemed to go anywhere. Many times we felt as if our words simply scattered into the wind. Who would have known that this woman would now walk closely with the Lord?

I don't suggest that we should let everyone who comes to our door into our homes, but at times we could certainly talk at our threshold to someone who comes with incorrect views and share with them the good news of the Gospel.

Let's Pause for Prayer

Heavenly Father, thank You for the joy of hearing the good news that this woman is a believer in you! Your good news adheres to our hearts, and we are thankful for it! Thank You for allowing her to dive into Your word to learn more, to seek You, and to ultimately find You; and in turn she is leading others to you! May we each be faithful in sharing the good news of Jesus Christ even if we may never know the results. In Jesus' name we pray. Amen.

Have you had the opportunity to share your faith at your doorstep with someone who stopped by? How do you greet these guests?

If you don't feel confident sharing or defending your faith, can you learn how to do so from someone or from a book someone might share with you to strengthen your faith to be able to share with others?

Day 170

Change

> *"For I, the Lord, do not change."*
> Malachi 3:6

What do you think of when you hear the word *change*? Change is defined as "to put or take a thing in place of something else, to exchange, to make different, to alter, to substitute."

Much comes to my mind when I hear that word. I think of loose change, lane change, change your mind, change of life, and change of heart. I don't usually think of change as good. I like stability, normalcy (although I don't really know what that means!), and routine. I can't think of many people who really like change, but I know that many of us are changed by change.

Sure, we'd all like change if it meant we could drop those extra pounds without any effort or if it meant we could hire someone to do the jobs we didn't like or can never seem to start and finish. We could handle that change. I believe, however, that most of our growth as Christians is the result of change in our lives, which in turn caused us to change, one can hope, for the better and to make us more like Christ. Hardships in my life have caused major changes for and in me. Some of those changes have been in my heart attitude, some in the way I see people or situations that I might not have otherwise noticed. Even though the road to change is often challenging, it can be good. Change is more normal than we think normal is!

Let's Pause for Prayer

Heavenly Father, thank You for showing us through change what an awesome God You are. Thank You for developing our hearts, our attitudes, our reactions and responses to be more Christlike as we learn to live for You. Help us to view change as a way to learn instead of as a time to rebel or quit. We love You and want our hearts to be changed to look like Yours. We thank You for Your steadfastness, never changing but helping us through our changes. In Jesus' name we pray. Amen.

What kind of change has entered your life? Write out specific examples.

_____

_____

Did you embrace that change? Run from it? How did you respond?

_____

_____

How can you allow God to help you the next time change comes your way?

_____

_____

Day 171 — Our Words Have Power

"Therefore encourage one another, and build up one another, just as you also are doing."

I Thessalonians 5:11

I was surprised to find in my purse a note that had been placed on top of everything, unnoticed until I arrived home. The note was from the person sitting next to me, encouraging me with her words! I don't know whether she had any idea just how timely her kind words were to my heart!

A week earlier after church someone thanked me with tears in her eyes for a note I had written to her years earlier. I remembered the situation only vaguely but was nevertheless very appreciative to know that she had been encouraged all those years before.

We all have the capacity to be an encourager or a discourager. Without even really trying, we all utter words that can discourage another person. Philippians 2:1-5 states, "If therefore there is any encouragement in Christ, if there is any consolation of love, if there is any fellowship of the Spirit, if any affection and compassion, make my joy complete by being of the same mind maintaining the same love, united in spirit, intent on one purpose. Do nothing from selfishness or empty conceit, but with humility of mind let each of you regard one another as more important than himself; do not merely look out for your own personal interest, but also for the interests of others. Have this attitude in yourselves which was also in Christ Jesus."

Let's Pause for Prayer

Heavenly Father, we thank You for those who have come alongside us and encouraged our hearts. May we now ask You to bring to our mind someone we can encourage by our written or spoken words. We thank You for those who've lightened our load of cares with a spoken word of encouragement. Thank You for allowing us to look to the interests of others and encourage them, thereby pleasing You! Nudge us to give verbal and written encouragement to those who need it when we might otherwise miss the opportunity. In Jesus' name we pray. Amen.

Share a time when someone encouraged you with spoken or written word.

_____

_____

How have you encouraged others?

_____

_____

If you have not intentionally tried to encourage someone recently, take a moment today to ask the Lord to bring someone to mind to encourage, and then speak words of encouragement to her or him or write an encouraging note.

Day 172 — Who's Praying For You?

> *"And everything you ask in prayer, believing, you shall receive."*
> Matthew 21:22

Listening to the lyrics of "Somebody's Prayin' Me Through" gives me hope! When we experience difficulties in life or when we need guidance as we make decisions, I wonder what would happen if people weren't praying for us.

Joe and I asked a group of family members and friends whether they would be willing to be on our prayer team. The idea behind having a prayer team is to have a group of people who accept requests for prayer for upcoming ministry events and opportunities, family prayer needs, and prayer for general needs. We asked that they commit to one year of participation. Each month we mailed or emailed our requests and also asked them for their requests. Thus, we'd be in prayer for one another, not merely expecting one-sided prayer! Although names on our prayer team have changed from time to time, we have a few people who have asked to be "lifers," continuing to pray over the long haul. We are so very thankful for each one who prays, and we are delighted to pray for their needs as well.

Let's Pause for Prayer

Heavenly Father, I thank You for those who pray for others. Please bless them today as they find something wonderful in your word from and for which to pray for others. Thank You for giving us fellow believers who will hold us up in prayer as we in turn will do the same for them. We are encouraged in knowing that "somebody's prayin' us through" today. Thank you for those who pray us through whatever challenges and joys may come our way and for the times others pray when You've led them and they don't even know the circumstances of their prayers. Thank you for the mightiness of prayer. Thank you for the humbleness of prayer. In Jesus' name we pray. Amen.

Do you know whether others are praying for you? If so, who?

_____

_____

_____

If you don't have someone praying for you regularly, consider asking a friend or family member to be your prayer partner so you can both share your heart and pray for those issues together. Who might you be able to ask, and when will you do so?

_____

_____

_____

Day 173 — *Swept Under The Rug*

"For nothing is hidden, except to be revealed; nor has anything been secret, but that It should come to light."

Mark 4:22

Do you sweep information, problems, or situations under the rug? I know some children, when in a hurry to do their chores, might sweep dust under the rug; but I'm thinking more about adults who think that if we don't see or talk about our troubles, trials, and deep hurts, no one else will see or talk about them either. A great danger lies in such thinking. When we continue to hide issues, sweeping them under the rug, eventually lumps in the rug become pretty obvious; and everyone around us can see the trouble spots! They walk around the lumps to avoid tripping over them. Sometimes they even pretend not to see them, but they become so big that no one could miss them! Sometimes those lumps are issues we wish no one would ever know about, and other times they are sins we think we can hide away undiscovered.

Lifting the rug, we expose everything. God does that to our hearts. He tells us that He sees and knows everything. We might think we are protecting ourselves and our loved ones by sweeping our spiritual refuse under the carpet, but nothing can be hidden from God.

Let's Pause for Prayer

Heavenly Father, we are so thankful that You are aware of all of our difficulties, trials, troubles, deep hurts, and yes, sins. Please meet as at our place of need. Help us to share our struggles with others who can help us and pray with us through these challenges. Help us to be available to others who are in tough spots in life. In addition, when sin is involved, let us in humility confess to You how we have displeased and dishonored You. Let us go to others against whom we've sinned and make it right. Help us, Lord, to keep that rug smooth so that our lives are not a danger to others who might be looking to us examples of Christian life. In Jesus' name we pray. Amen.

Do you recognize some things that are causing your rug to get bumpy? Write out for yourself what those bumps are for you.

_____

_____

_____

What will you do to take the right next steps to smooth out the lumps and bumps left by what you swept under the rug?

_____

_____

_____

Day 174

Garbage

"If we say that we have fellowship with Him and yet walk in the darkness, we lie and do not practice the truth, but if we walk in the light as He Himself is in the light, we have fellowship with one another, and the blood of Jesus His Son cleanses us from all sin. If we say that we have no sin, we are deceiving ourselves, and the truth is not is us. If we confess our sins, He is faithful and righteous to forgive us our sins and to cleanse us from all unrighteousness. If we say that we have not sinned, we make Him a liar, and His word is not in us."

I John 1:6–10

I was driving behind a garbage truck, close enough to the truck to read the warning, "Keep back 100 feet." My guess is that they wanted vehicles far enough away from the path of the truck so that if something came flying out, the debris would hit the vehicle behind it. Drivers of vehicles must keep their distance for a very good reason!

But I thought of another reason. The odors emanating from the truck were pretty strong. I thought to myself, "I need to get away from this truck. The odor is getting to me." Somehow my mind went immediately to the idea of sin!

I want to avoid people who know they are sinning and yet continue to live in their sin, engaging in improper relationships, withholding their sins from one another, waffling on resolving sinful situations. And of course, I recognize sin in my own life and the ugliness of it as well. We need to admit to God that we have sinned and confess to Him the wrongs we have committed.

Let's Pause for Prayer

Heavenly Father, we confess that we can easily find sin in others, but we also see how our sin keeps us from right fellowship with others and with You. We know that we must first be concerned about our own sin, confessing to You that we have wronged others and You. Please hear our confession and help us to turn away from sin and walk closely with You. May we live for and serve only You. In Jesus' name we pray. Amen.

Do you recognize an area of your life where sin has taken root?

_____

_____

How will you get rid of that sin? Confess it now and share what you plan to do to keep it from returning to the mainstream of your life.

_____

_____

_____

Day 175

God Will Not Be Mocked

> *"Fools mock at sin."*
>
> Proverbs 14:9

Listening to and reading various media, I am amazed that people mock God and yet expect a blessing even though they fail to walk according to what His word, the Bible, says.

I have heard people in adulterous relationships make light of it and even rationalize what they are doing. Some claim, "God wants me to be happy," a line I've never read anywhere in scripture. They might even discuss what a blessing their lover is and how they feel so complete. They have failed to grasp God's word and the possible consequences of their sin. Sometimes they don't even seem to care that a consequence might follow their sin. They seem to say, "Bring it on, God, I can handle it," a response as blatant, foolish, and ridiculous as the sin they are committing.

Gossips share untruths or half-truths about others and think doing so is acceptable because they need to make sure they're the ones in charge, letting others know how much they know. Liars don't care about the truth, only making themselves look good and demeaning others. Those who can't or won't bridle their anger offer reason upon reason showing that you're wrong and they're right. Murderers justify their acts because, of course, in their own eyes they had every reason to commit their crimes.

God's word defines sin clearly, and if we don't confess our sins and repent (turn away from them), we will suffer the consequences somewhere down the road. God will not be mocked; whatever a man sows he will reap.

Let's Pause for Prayer

Heavenly Father, Proverbs 14:9 says, "Fools mock at sin." Galatians 6:7 says, "Do not be deceived, God is not mocked; for whatever a man sows, this he will also reap." Help us to make those verses real in our lives as reminders not to slide into sin and be irreverent to you and irresponsible in our walk with You. We thank You for speaking to our hearts and reveal to us our sin. We desire, as we recognize that sin, to repent and turn toward You in obedience. Thank You for forgiving us when we confess our sin. In Jesus' name we pray. Amen.

Are you sowing seeds in your life in such a way that you (and surely Jesus) will be pleased with the outcome?

_____

What sin do you feel you must confess and turn from? Do it now. Write out your confession and ask God to keep you from repeating it.

_____

_____

_____

Day 176

We're Hypocrites

"You hypocrite, first take the log out of your own eye, and then you will see clearly enough to take the speck out of your brother's eye."

Matthew 7:5

None of us is perfect, and I suppose to some extent we're all hypocrites. If we had to be perfect to go to church, churches would be empty; yet what keeps a Christians from being hypocritical is first admitting their sin and then doing something about it, which is called repentance, that is, turning away from sin. The prodigal son in Luke 15 acknowledged his waywardness, came home to ask his father's forgiveness, and changed his ways, even saying he'd serve the father as a hired hand. He was repentant, broken, sorry, and wanted to make things right.

Many sitting in the church pews week after week walk out the doors and stray from God Monday through Saturday. When we recognize our sin (whether we hear it from the pastor, a friend, a relative, or hearing God's voice through His word), we need to seek the Lord to learn how to end our sinful ways. To sit in church and listen to excellent teaching about following Christ and the importance of being an example to others by doing what He's asked and then putting on a show of piety and holiness one day of the week before returning to our blatant sin mocks God. Yes, we need to take the log out of our own eyes when we see our own sin because God is not pleased.

Let's Pause for Prayer

Heavenly Father, forgive each of us when we ignore Your word, when we ignore the instruction of others in our lives who care about us enough to confront us about our sin. May we not be haughty about our sin, thinking we can fool You or hide from You. May we individually seek You for the right way to live, the power to live an abundant and fruitful life, directed and empowered by Your Holy Spirit. May we put aside missions, soup kitchens, serving the poor, teaching Sunday School, and even sitting in church if we are doing these things to appear holy to those around us but have another life outside the church. Shame on us for thinking you won't notice. Shame on us for thinking others won't notice. Shame on us for thinking we can act one way and live another. Break our hearts, restore us to Yourself, Lord. We want to be more like You. In Jesus' name we pray.

Take off the blinders and be real with God. What sin are you dealing with that you must conquer?

_____

_____

What steps are you willing to take to get real with God and forsake your sin? Write out your prayer and vow to Him.

_____

_____

_____

Day 177

Satisfied Or Satiated?

> *"They would not accept my counsel, they spurned all my reproof. So they shall eat of the fruit of their own way, and be satiated with their own devices."*
>
> Proverbs 1:30–31

The two short verses above invite me to contemplate whether or not I really listen to the Lord when He reproves me and what life will look like if I don't listen and obey. What does it look like to be satiated with my own devices?

The first thing that comes to mind with regard to the word satiated is eating too much resulting in fullness to excess. I'd rather simply feel satisfied (contented and gratified) after a meal than so full that I feel sick or nauseated. I want to be content and gratified in the Lord, knowing I've listened and obeyed, because I don't want to feel satiated with the things of the world and my own devices. I know it will make me sick at some point. I'd rather be obedient from the outset and avoid demanding my own way and the consequences that result.

Let's Pause for Prayer

Heavenly Father, with sadness we realize that sometimes we want our own way and worldly goods. How easy it is for us to go the way of the world for what it seems to offer! At some point, however, we know it won't satisfy us, and we will feel too full of it. Lord, we will be full of the foolishness and the ugliness of sin; we'll want to be content and satisfied, but it will be too late because we will have demanded and received just what we asked for. Lord, show us now the right way to live, the right ways to serve You, and give us the power to make those right choices. Help us to recognize when we choose wrong ways so that we will avoid their consequences. We know You have our best interests at heart, so we ask You to show us how to make right decisions and live in right ways. We know we can never have too much of You! In Jesus' name we pray. Amen.

When and why do you insist on having your own way?

_____
_____
_____

Are you willing to trust God enough to forsake worldly goods to follow Him? Write out a prayer to share what your next step will be.

_____
_____
_____
_____

Day 178 — Waiting

"I wait for Thy word."

Psalm 119:81b

Sometimes when we pray for something specific, I wonder whether we quit too soon?

A while ago, I prayed with someone who had set aside a certain period of time to pray through something particular. About halfway through that time, she sensed no answer from the Lord and wanted to quit. I urged her to continue through the time frame that she had planned, expressing to her that the Lord might have something very interesting at the end of that time of prayer. And indeed He did. Had she stopped when she wanted to quit, she would not have seen the unique answer the Lord had for her.

Waiting for the Lord is difficult when we want an answer. Our human nature wants to hurry things along, but God isn't a drive-through window. He is one who wants to give us something special and at the right time. He doesn't make mistakes. I've heard it said that He is never late or early but right on time.

Let's Pause for Prayer

Heavenly Father, we seek You because we trust in You. We pray to You because we love You and we know You have our best interests at heart. Help us to recognize that Your answers are worth waiting for and that Your ways are worth seeking. When we want to hurry Your answer to us, help us to recognize that You are always right on time whether the answer to our prayer is "yes, no, or wait a while." Help us to be patient as we pray for Your wisdom and an understanding of Your will in our lives. We don't want our impatience to hinder what You might have for us! May we develop trust in You so that times of waiting will become precious times with You in prayer. Let us watch, wait, and experience Your goodness in the waiting room of life. In Jesus' name we pray. Amen.

Think back to a time you were in the waiting room of prayer over a specific issue. Perhaps you're praying through a particular situation right now. Share it.

_____

_____

_____

Have you or do you ever feel you want to rush God's answer? Have you found helpful thoughts or actions to make the waiting seem less difficult?

_____

_____

_____

Day 179 — My Weapon Is Drawn, But I Don't Use It

> *"Let us also lay aside every encumbrance, and the sin which so easily entangles us, and let us run with endurance the race that is set before us."*
>
> Hebrews 12:1

Someone once shared an idea that impacted me. After an Adult Bible Fellowship class I was teaching as a substitute, one gentleman, somewhat new in his Christian faith, said the following to me about anger (the topic of our discussion): "I'm learning to conquer anger. My weapon is drawn but I never use it." I didn't know him well enough to understand all that might have meant to him, but I thought about sin in general. It seems we all have at least one particular sin with which we struggle on a regular basis, but it doesn't mean we have to act upon it.

Maybe it's gossip, sexual sins, adultery, lying cheating, anger, abuse—the list goes on and on. No matter the sin, we have no obligation to act upon it. Just as this gentleman knew his weak spot and conquered it, we too can name our sin and stop acting upon it. The Lord nudges us about our particular sin, and we need to take it seriously.

Let's Pause for Prayer

Heavenly Father, we want to take a stand against the sins we commit. We need You to help us identify each sin, to name it out loud, and then to do something about it. Show us our sin from which we need to repent. May we turn away from and abandon that sin "which so easily entangles us" (Heb. 12:1) in the snares of this world and keeps us from knowing and serving You fully. Lord, we want to rid ourselves of sin and clothe ourselves with Your righteousness, not for the sake of our appearance to others but for the sake of the quality of our walk with you, the importance of doing what is good and right, and the freedom we'll have in You when we do that which You require. Lord, forgive us for thinking we can get away with sin. We want only to honor You in purity in all areas of our lives. In Jesus' name we pray. Amen.

Do you recognize something that you struggle to keep under control? What is it?

_____

_____

_____

Do you recognize how you can trust in God to help you with this struggle? Share your thoughts.

_____

_____

_____

Day 180 — Process Of Elimination Or Priority

"Thus I considered all my activities which my hands had done and the labor which I had exerted."

Ecclesiastes 2:11a

My desk has become the physical place where I
- put things in order,
- make piles,
- eliminate the unnecessary,
- clean up the responsibilities I have one by one,
- prioritize the essentials,
- organize for today and toss from yesterday, and
- plan for the future: projects, meetings, calendar items.

I see my space as the "happening" place! A lot goes on in that 2½ x 5 foot space: plans, changes, discussions, decisions, and cancellations! In this small space I see the importance of prioritizing as well as eliminating.

God wants us to be mindful of our activities and the way we use the time He has bestowed upon us. Note Ecclesiastes 2:11a, "Thus I considered all my activities which my hands had done and the labor which I had exerted" and Proverbs 16:3, "Commit your works to the Lord, and your plans will be established."

Let's Pause for Prayer

Heavenly Father, may we be mindful that the number of days and hours You've given us is very small: Life moves quickly. Whether our lives are short or long, You're the One who gives us that time and You will be the One holding us accountable for the way we used the time You gave us. May we look carefully to You for guidance in what we add to and subtract from our calendars, what to make a priority or not with family and friends, what to eliminate because You may have better tasks in mind for us. Lord, we desire for You to make our schedules Yours, to make our time Your time, and to help us moment by moment to determine how You want us to plan and use our time, whether for work or rest, for people or projects, and for giving or receiving. Might we hear You clearly and reflect Your priorities in all areas of our lives. In Jesus' name we pray. Amen.

Do you recognize the importance of all that you place on your calendar?

What do you need to add, eliminate, and make a priority that you don't have on your calendar right now? How will you do it?

Day 181 — Seasons Of Discouragment, Disappointment, Depression

> *"I am weary with my sighing; every night I make my bed swim, I dissolve my couch with my tears."*
>
> Psalm 6:6

We've all had, or will have, seasons of discouragement and disappointment. Sometimes when we're in the midst of them, no end or way out of it seems to be in sight. The Psalmist David said in Psalm 6:6, "I am weary with my sighing; every night I make my bed swim, I dissolve my couch with my tears." I picture him weeping—maybe because of his own selfishness and sin or because He was out of fellowship with God, having failed Him. I don't know all that was on his heart, but any of us who've experienced this depth of discouragement, disappointment, and even depression understand how heavy one's heart can be.

Perhaps the lesson here is that David indeed cried out to God. The God he disappointed and sinned against is the same God he was crying out to in emotional pain and agony. He says with confidence in verses 8–9, "Depart from me, all you who do iniquity, for the Lord has heard the voice of my weeping. The Lord has heard my supplication, the Lord receives my prayer."

Let's Pause for Prayer

Heavenly Father, we all have sinned. We all have sinned against You, and when we rid ourselves of our pride, we see how we have hurt You; as a result we agonize over it. Lord, break our hearts to our sin. Help us to see it, recognize it, and call it sin. When we own up to it and feel discouraged, disappointed, and even depressed, we know that we have You, the same mighty God against whom we sinned, there to receive our prayer and us. Thank you, Lord, for hearing us when we humbly come to You in repentance. We pray that we would let no sin come between us, that we would want to have sweet fellowship with You and exchange the discouragement for encouragement, the disappointment for satisfaction, the depression for joy. We trust You to make that exchange, but we know we need to do our part to own up to our sin and failings. Thank You for Your unending patience with us and love for us. In Jesus' name we pray. Amen.

Have you ever desperately cried out to God? Under what circumstances did you cry out?

_____

_____

Are you willing to shed your pride and cry out to God about your sin? Share a prayer here for how you desire to have closer fellowship with him as a result.

_____

_____

Day 182

Having The King's Heart

"The king's heart is like channels of water in the hand of the Lord; He turns it wherever He wishes."

Proverbs 21:1

No matter how many times we read scripture, there are those times a verse pops us and impacts us in a new and different way. Proverbs 21:1 did that for me recently.

As I direct my kitchen faucet to move debris to the disposal, I see that I can easily move bits and pieces the way I want and need them to go. The power and pressure of the water determines where the debris is sent. If only my heart were so obedient to serve the Lord in the same way as the king in this verse of Proverbs. I want for God to make my heart be like water that He can direct. I want Him to say, "This is the way I need and want you to go today"; and I want to comply. May we seek His will, His direction, and our place in it all.

Let's Pause for Prayer

Heavenly Father, Your power is mighty and yet we sometimes refuse to yield to it. You can use our willing hearts, but You won't force us or pressure us. We want to say to You this day that we want the power of Your Holy Spirit to guide us like the king in Proverbs. May our hearts be like channels of water in Your hand for You to turn wherever You wish. We wonder in awe what our lives might look like if we were so obedient to You and so willing simply to obey and go with the flow of Your desires and directions for us. Whether You have us on the white waters or carry us through on a slow and steadily moving stream, we want to offer ourselves to You and ask You to be our director and guide today and every day, in all seasons, and in all ways. You are our God, a mighty one who will not delay in using us for Your glory when we are but willing. In Jesus' name we pray. Amen.

Do you sense and feel the Lord directing you freely or are you holding onto your own idea of what you want and need to accomplish?

_____

_____

_____

How will you offer yourself freely to allow God to use and direct You according to His plans?

_____

_____

_____

_____

Day 183

Don't Doubt

> *"The Lord will accomplish what concerns me."*
>
> Psalm 138:8

"Don't put a question mark where God puts a period."

That powerful statement on a sign in front of a church gave me the opportunity to search my heart when I questioned something God had done in my life and ask Him to please help me find resolve if I had any lingering questions.

As fallen selfish human beings, we find it natural to want our own way. We sometimes think God owes it to us to make our lives comfortable or certainly to see our needs as we do. If we truly want to serve Him as Lord and Savior, we must be willing to surrender all. Yes, all.

Let's Pause for Prayer

Heavenly Father, we are sorry for doubting you, questioning you, and thus disobeying you because we thought we knew better. Please forgive us. We want to surrender our thoughts, hopes, dreams, desires, and lives to you. Because of Your love for us, we know that You will, according to Psalm 138:8, "accomplish all that concerns us." Thank you for loving us. Help us to surrender daily and moment by moment to your Lordship in our lives. In Jesus' name we pray. Amen.

In what area do you continue to pursue God where He's already clearly said to end it?

_____
_____
_____
_____

Is it time to surrender and say, "Lord, I accept your will for me"?

_____
_____
_____
_____

Day 184 — *My Sin Or Your Opinion?*

"Then you will discern righteousness and justice and equity and every good course. For wisdom will enter your heart, and knowledge will be pleasant to your soul; discretion will guard you, understanding will watch over you, to deliver you from the way of evil, from the man who speaks perverse things"

Proverbs 2:9–12

Not everyone agrees with all that we do. I've come to take what people say and put it through the following filter: "Is what they are saying to me about my sin or are they sharing their opinion?" That keeps me focused. I hear what they say and pray about it; if it's a sin that I didn't recognize or own up to, then I need to do so. If it's the other person's opinion, I seek The Lord to tell me whether I need to heed their advice (perhaps they are His instrument to show me what I need to consider) or move on in what The Lord has for me; then I rest. I can't be burdened by the opinions of others; otherwise I'd be all over the place and not where I believe God wants me.

As unfortunate as it is, when we do what God created us to do, we might meet criticism. In our hearts we set out to serve God by serving others or working diligently on a project for church. Although many may say it went well, a handful of people will criticize because they didn't like some aspect of what we did or because it didn't align with their style or preference.

I remember once writing someone a letter of encouragement to which the recipient replied, "I didn't think you were sincere in your letter." It made me recognize that we're not called to serve God in a win or lose situation but to use the gifts and talents He's given whether we're commended or criticized.

Let's Pause for Prayer

Heavenly Father, thank You for the gifts You've given us to use for Your glory. May we use them properly as we serve the body of Christ. May we not be the ones to criticize others as they use their gifts that are different from ours. May we do what You have created us to do and serve you however you call us. Let us be mindful to recognize when someone is sharing an idea that we need to consider, but let us sift it through Your filter of what we need to do or change. We know we will never please everyone, so all the better reason to seek only to please You, Lord! In Jesus' name we pray. Amen.

When have you experienced people criticizing you or suggesting you do something differently because they don't like the way it's being done? How did you handle it?

_____

_____

Thinking through the way God will help you filter someone's criticism, how will you choose to respond to others when you don't feel their criticism is valid or true?

_____

_____

Day 185 — *Being Watched*

> *"And there is no creature hidden from His sight, but all things are open and laid bare to the eyes of Him with whom we have to do."*
>
> Hebrews 4:13

Many television watchers have become transfixed by reality TV shows. I decided one day to watch a show a friend had recommended. I lasted about five minutes probably because I didn't really know enough about all that had been going on previously to want to stay involved in watching it! But what intrigued me was what life must be like with a camera and microphones following these people around all day long!? I wondered, "How many people would like to have a camera watching every move made and a microphone recording every word said 24/7? How real is that reality show? Could they possibly be acting the way they typically do? Surely they are more cautious about what they will say because it will be shown on national television. Surely they will be more careful of their actions, reactions, and responses because people are there watching and recording!" It doesn't seem as if the action and dialogue could be as real as what those hidden camera stories show! That is real reality TV!

In reality as Christians we are actually watched and heard by an Almighty, all-knowing God, who is always everywhere! He knows, sees, and hears everything.

Let's Pause for Prayer

Heavenly Father, I want to check my heart and determine whether I am acting, reacting, and responding in ways You expect. I want to be a good example of who You are and who You want me to be. I don't want to displease You in any way. I know You see and hear everything. Help me Lord to surrender every area of my life to You. Please expose every secret thought and sin that I think I'm hiding from You. As I confess and repent of my sin, may I come to know You better, serve You fully, and obey You completely. In Jesus' name we pray. Amen.

With this picture of God seeing and watching all we do, what was the first thing that comes to your mind that you wish He might not see?

_____

_____

_____

If the thought that came to your mind is a sin, turn away from it; and write out your prayer of confession here.

_____

_____

_____

Day 186 — Caught!

"Would not God find this out? For He knows the secrets of the heart."

Psalm 44:21

While planning and shopping with my daughter for her upcoming wedding, we decided to make quick stop at a shoe store because we had a coupon for a certain percentage off and no surprise to those who know us, we made a purchase. We hated not to use that valuable coupon! Leaving the store we spotted a newscaster and videographer. We excused ourselves to get around them, thinking they were working on a story. What we were soon to realize is that we were the story! After they asked us some questions about this particular shoe store, they asked for the spelling of our names. We all shared a laugh as I joked, my name is Cindi Ferrini, but can you put Cindi Smith? I'm not sure I want to be on TV with these shoes! My husband and friends are going to tease me about "getting caught"! Of course, I gave my real name and the correct spelling. I wasn't trying to hide anything, nor was I seriously concerned about my reputation as I left that establishment.

My daughter and I talked in the car about how important it is to keep our lives pure in all aspects so that no matter where we are, no matter what place we exit, no matter who we're with, we are not suspected of sinful or wrong behavior. We discussed why people hide their faces coming out of some establishments when news and media attempt to get a story: the embarrassment, the getting caught, the fact that loved ones might find something out that they were trying hard to hide. This situation made for a great teachable moment for both of us.

Let's Pause for Prayer

Heavenly Father, your word is clear in Romans 2:16: "God will judge the secrets of men through Christ Jesus." Yes, Lord, You know every thought I have, every place I go, and every word I speak. Please help me to keep every area of my life pure. May I not be concerned about getting caught somewhere because I am firmly established with You. I will not go where I will compromise my testimony for You. And Lord, I give You permission to question every secret of my heart so I might always walk closely with you in honesty and integrity. In Jesus' name we pray. Amen.

Do you have a secret you're keeping? What is it?

_____

_____

Perhaps you've not been caught yet, but why not confess that sin now and put it behind you? Pray to the Lord, writing out a prayer, so you'll remember the day you made this area of your life right before Him.

_____

_____

_____

Day 187 — Weighted Down

> *"Behold, the Lamb of God who takes away the sin on the world."*
>
> John 1:29b

As a man tried to run across a busy intersection, he ran as though his shoes were weighing him down. I've had dreams like that, trying to get somewhere or away from someone; but my feet won't move at the speed I need. In a dream it becomes frustrating to move and frightening to try to dodge the cars. In real life, that's what this man looked like to me. Although he tried to move quickly, his feet seemed simply too heavy to lift. He looked frustrated and frightened that he might not get across before impatient drivers would sound their horns. Perhaps he was older than he looked at first glance or had some type of impairment that was slowing him down.

Thus is sin in our lives. The burden of it weighs us down. We aren't so light anymore. Sometimes the burden of sin shows on our faces, and sometimes it's seen when we show our anger; but we can't escape for long from the sin in our lives. It will find us out. But a way to lift the weight of our sin is to confess it and repent of it.

Let's Pause for Prayer

Heavenly Father, I come to You and ask You to hear my sin. Please forgive me for disappointing You and doing things my way. Please forgive me for willfully making choices that I know to be sinful and that are weighing me down because of my disobedience to You. Please help me to repent and turn away from my sin. With Your help, I know I can walk in obedience and live a life pleasing to You. Thank You for allowing me to come to You directly and ask for Your forgiveness. I desire to do what You ask of me. In Jesus' name I pray. Amen.

Is a sin weighing you down today? Name it.

_____

_____

_____

Pray to the Lord as you ask forgiveness and repent (turn away) from that sin. Write out your prayer if it is helpful to you.

_____

_____

_____

_____

Day 188

I'm At My Wit's End!

Psalm 107:23–31

So many people I know are going through some very challenging times. I often like to read this passage of scripture when I experience a difficult or challenging time:

Those who go down to the sea in ships,
Who do business on great waters;
They have seen the works of the Lord,
And His wonders in the deep.
For He spoke and raised up a stormy wind,
Which lifted up the waves of the sea.
They rose up to the heavens, they went down to the depths;
Their soul melted away in their misery.
They reeled and staggered like a drunken man,
And were at their wits' end.
Then they cried to the Lord in their trouble,
And He brought them out of their distresses,
He cause the storm to be still,
So that the waves of the sea were hushed.
Then they were glad because they were quiet;
So He guided them to their desired haven.
Let them give thanks to the Lord for His lovingkindness,
And for His wonders to the sons of men!

Sometimes the things we must go through are very difficult, even what seems too much to bear at times. Although we may never get over the difficulty, God will get us through it.

Let's Pause for Prayer

Heavenly Father, we thank You for bringing us through the storm to a place of quiet. When we struggle and feel at our wits' end, please help us to remember to pray to You as a first response, not as a last resort. Help us to choose to come to You for guidance, help, and direction. Please show us Your lovingkindness, and may we not forget to give you thanks! In Jesus' name we pray. Amen.

What challenges are you going through right now in your life? How long have they been in or a part of your life? Share a prayer for releasing that struggle to the Lord as you verbally recognize that He will help you get through it.

_____
_____
_____
_____

Day 189 — The Fool

> *"The fool says in his heart, 'There is no God.'"*
>
> Psalm 14:1

When the children were little and even now that they're grown, we sometimes try to fool them. We might try to fool each other by making up a story, trying to convince them of something that isn't true, or some other silly joke.

I hope that I taught them that we could have fun! But I also would show them how fun could turn to foolishness in just one thoughtless moment. A fun drive when tempted to speed can turn into a tragedy. Teasing someone in playful fun can turn into hurtful words. The Bible has much to say about the fool. Here are a few verses:

- Psalm 14:1 "The fool says in his heart, 'There is no God.'"
- Proverbs 1:7 "Fools despise wisdom."
- Proverbs 15:5 "A fool rejects his father's discipline."
- Proverbs 29:11 "A fool always loses his temper."
- Ecclesiastes 10:14 "The fool multiplies his words."

The word *foolish* is also used to mean unwise and boastful. Although our words and actions may be playful and full of fun, let's not fall into the trap of the biblical fool.

Let's Pause for Prayer

Heavenly Father, we do not want to be the fool who claims You do not exist. We know You and love You and are happy to proclaim Your name! We do not want to reject Godly wisdom or our father's discipline. Please help us not to lose our tempers and thus be labeled fools. Help us to watch our tongues so we don't say foolish or unkind words. Thank You for all ways You will guide us to Your wisdom instead of to the foolishness of man. In Jesus' name we pray. Amen.

In what ways have you acted foolishly? Have your foolish actions ever brought trouble to you in any way?

___

___

___

How will you determine the fine line between fun and foolishness?

___

___

___

Day 190 — Loss Of Friendship

From Psalm 55

I suppose it happens every day—the sorrowful loss of a friend. Let's read David's prayer when he lost a friend.

(Ps. 55:1–3, 12–14, 16,18)

Give ear to my prayer, O God;
And do not hide Thyself from my supplication.
Give heed to me, and answer me;
I am restless in my complaint and am surely distracted,
Because of the voice of the enemy, Because of the pressure of the wicked;
For they bring down trouble upon me,
And in anger they bear a grudge against me…
For it is not an enemy who reproaches me,
Then I could bear it; nor is it one who hates me who has exalted himself against me,
Then I could hide myself from him.
But it is you, a man my equal, my companion and my familiar friend.
We who had sweet fellowship together,
When in the house of God in the multitude…
As for me, I shall call upon God, And the Lord will save me.
He will redeem my soul in peace from the battle which is against me.

Let's Pause for Prayer

Heavenly Father, we know You will sustain us through the difficulties of challenging friendships. We realize that the loss of an acquaintance doesn't seem to cost as much as the loss of a close friend. We recognize that the time, treasure, and love invested in that person, the friendship, commitment to helping her or him grow, the sacrifice of our time and plans to share it are why that loss hurts us. Investing always has a cost. But Lord, let us not hold grudges against another or desire to retaliate. Let us have the right attitude toward even our enemies and follow what Paul shared when he wrote to Timothy: "At my first defense no one supported me, but all deserted me; may it not be counted against them" (II Tim. 4:16). Lord, help us to promote love and unity as You have shown us by Your example, and as Paul has written. In Jesus' name we pray. Amen.

Have you felt the pain and loss of a friendship? How did it happen?

_____

_____

Have you been one to leave a friendship and hurt another? What have you learned from these times that you wouldn't let happen again?

_____

_____

Day 191 — Obstacles

> *"Teach me Thy ways, O Lord, and lead me in a level path."*
>
> Psalm 27:11

Sitting on the beach, I was fascinated by a bug near me. I don't know the scientific name of the bug, but it looked like what I was told as a child was a water bug. This little creature was quite ambitious. I don't know where it was going, but it was earnestly trying to get somewhere! It seemed to want to get over or around a tiny mound of sand in front of it. It was pushing sand from here to there. It worked fiercely and then stopped, probably to rest. It would resume, quickly turning to the right or to the left to get around this lump of sand. It couldn't seem to get over this particular obstacle. It continued struggling in this very little area for quite some time. It finally snuggled under the sand, and I didn't see it again.

Although I don't know the instincts of this little bug, I saw the whole picture. I could see that the lump of sand it wanted to climb was really not very big at all. Just a step or two more, and it would have been successful; or another step or two around it would have freed the bug to move wherever it wanted. The bug seemed to be defeated by what wasn't really that big: a tiny sand mound. What a spiritual lesson this is for us! God sees every obstacle before us. He sees the whole picture. He sees how hard we work to overcome an obstacle or get away from it, and yet how often we're tempted to quit because whatever it is seems too hard to overcome or accomplish!

Let's Pause for Prayer

Heavenly Father, I am so thankful that You see the whole picture of our lives. Thank You for allowing us to rely on You to put into our lives just what we need, right when we need it. And thank You for Your word that tells us that You will make known to us what we are to do and what our steps should be. Psalm 16:11 tells us, "Thou wilt make known to me the path of life." And Lord, when I don't know where I am going or what I'm doing, please let me rely upon your word for guidance. Psalm 27:11 states, "Teach me Thy ways, O Lord, and lead me in a level path." In Jesus' name we pray. Amen.

Have you felt frustration when you want to overcome an obstacle but can't? Explain.

_____

_____

_____

In what ways can you put your trust in the Lord to make it to your next goal?

_____

_____

_____

Day 192

Live By Faith

> *"But the righteous will live by his faith."*
>
> Habakkuk 2:4

Ten days in Israel allowed for learning, memories, and more information that this mind will ever hold; but we will never forget all that we did and stories we heard. One of the most memorable sites for both Joe and me was Masada. Although it's not written about biblically, it is a historical location that Herod kept as a winter palace (and place of safety) with 18-foot walls, considered to impregnable; but in AD 70 the Jewish stronghold fell to the Romans. The Jews, believing they could not stand against the Romans, chose death over slavery to Rome when the men killed their families and the remaining men killed one another until the last who remained committed suicide. Somehow two women and five children survived.

As we walked down the mountain (some 4,000 walking steps, taking about an hour), I contemplated the endurance and persistence these people had to have in building this place and hauling supplies up and down the rugged terrain. But it wasn't just their physical pursuits but also their spiritual pursuits: persistence, endurance, faithfulness, and obedience.

Let's Pause for Prayer

Heavenly Father, the kind of endurance, persistence, faithfulness, and obedience You gave, You freely give today to those who ask. May we be bold to ask You for the kind of character traits we need to pursue You and the work You have for us. Although the work will look much different from what you gave those men on Masada to do, work nonetheless needs to be accomplished in the here and now. Seek our hearts and nudge us to get busy. May we stop seeking comfort, entertainment, and ease when much work must be done. Help us to see the frivolity we have permitted to take over our lives that has deafened us to You. Father, we know that our obedience is the key to serving You. May we obey. In Jesus' name we pray. Amen.

Who shall we tell about You? Who shall we serve in Your name?

_____

_____

_____

To whom might we be an example showing Your love through our service and care of Your people as we obey You?

_____

_____

_____

Day 193 — Handle The Word Accurately

> *"Be diligent to present yourself approved to God as a workman who does not need to be ashamed, handling accurately the word of truth."*
>
> II Timothy 2:15

The Sea of Galilee is 13 miles long, 8 miles wide, and technically should be more properly described as a lake than a sea. It's where Jesus reportedly walked on the water. Skeptics say He probably walked on stones and not really on the water. That's an interesting thought for one to consider until you see the Sea of Galilee. From the shoreline it drops off quite steeply, signs everywhere note depth. It's 100–150 feet deep. It seems quite impossible that He would have walked on stones.

As we gathered our tour group onto a boat, resembling the kind of boat Jesus may have been in, we enjoyed the view He likely enjoyed. The sea was quiet. No storms for us. How interesting it would have been to listen to Him teach from this vantage point. He had a captive audience, for sure. Would we have listened, amazed, sitting on the edge of our seats, waiting for His next words? Would we have believed or doubted, trusted in Him or politely just listened until we could get to shore? Would we have followed Him?

Let's Pause for Prayer

Heavenly Father, We want to believe in You and in every detail of Your life. May we believe in and trust in the Holy Scripture that tells of Your life, death, and resurrection. We want to live in the assurances that not only were locations real, but your life and ministry were also real. When others throw up roadblocks, unimportant and fabricated stories to make us doubt our faith, let us stand firm in Your word and learn how to point them to the truth, dispelling lies and sharing what we know to be true. We are thankful that we have Your word from which to study and learn. May we be faithful to do so! 2 Tim. 2:15 tells us, "Be diligent to present yourself approved to God as a workman who does not need to be ashamed, handling accurately the word of truth." Help us to study in that way. May we not be ashamed, and may we handle Your word accurately. In Jesus' name we pray. Amen.

Do you study the word faithfully? Describe how that looks for you.

_____

_____

_____

As you study the word, ask God to help you accurately handle His word of truth. Write down a few Bible passages that will encourage you to take the word seriously.

_____

_____

_____

Day 194

Dead

> *"Even so consider yourselves to be dead to sin, but alive to God in Christ Jesus."*
>
> Romans 6:11

The Dead Sea is 35 miles long, 11 miles wide, and 1200 feet deep, the lowest point on the earth's surface. Many have shared stories of floating in those waters. We, too, wanted to take the plunge. Well, actually you don't plunge into the Dead Sea; you walk in, bend your legs, and the next thing you know, you pop up like a ping pong ball to the top of the water. You wouldn't plunge in because the slightest drop of water in your eyes needs to be washed out with fresh water immediately. Taking even a drink of it could kill you at 38% salt and high contents of minerals. (Reference point: The oceans are 2% salt.) Short dips prevent dehydration from the salt and minerals on your skin; showering off is a must. No boats are in the water: They would corrode. Few people are in the sea because you can't stay in long. There are no fish, no plants, no life. Although it's dead, it's also clean and clear, a surprise when one expects the opposite.

Let's Pause for Prayer

Heavenly Father, Your masterpiece of the terrain and waters in Israel are as diverse as Your word and equally provide many teachable examples. Although the Dead Sea is beautiful, it yields no life: We don't want our lives to be like that. We want to yield fruit from our labors for Your glory. Lord, those waters look so pure, yet the possibility of death is very real should we drink of it. May we seek to drink only the living word of scripture and run from things that entice and seduce us yet deliver nothing but death— spiritual, emotional, physical death. We want our lives to be vibrant and exciting as we serve You. Lord, we don't want to appear one way and in reality be different. Let us be real and authentic as one of Your children. Keep us from the sin that takes away our authenticity. We desire to be real and transparent, so others will learn from us as we point to You. May we serve You and minister to others in the best ways possible. In Jesus' name we pray. Amen.

What sin is keeping you from living truly alive in Christ? What is the first point that came to your mind?

_____

_____

_____

How will you get a handle on this sin that causes you to be dead instead of alive in Christ?

_____

_____

_____

_____

Day 195

Culture Changers

"For as the heavens are higher than the earth, so are My ways higher than your ways, and My thoughts than your thoughts."

Isaiah 55:8

The road called the Via Maris (Road of the Sea) stretched some 1,000 miles and was over 3,000 years old. It's where Jesus most definitely walked with all those who followed Him, and we were privileged to walk where He walked. In addition, we were near the spot where Jesus likely gave the Sermon on the Mount. As we listened to Dr. Nyquist read it in its entirety with our eyes closed, we gained perspective on how we are to think, live, and act. The Beatitudes instruct us how to live, yet the reality of living them out is indeed counter to the prevailing cultural—then and now. Jesus says eight times in nine verses that blessedness is found in who we are—poor in spirit, in mourning, meek, hungering and thirsting after righteousness, merciful, pure in heart, peacemaking, and even persecuted (paraphrased from *Where Jesus Walked*). How clear it is that our human minds don't think right unless we have the Lord in us!

Let's Pause for Prayer

Heavenly Father, we are thankful for Isaiah 55:8, which tells us, "For as the heavens are higher than the earth, so are My ways higher than your ways, and My thoughts than your thoughts." Before we choose to follow You, Your way seems so countercultural; yet as we submit to You and ask You to be the Lord of our lives, Your way becomes so clear and our desire to obey You seems so very important. Lord, Help us to discover Your ways through Your word and our growth in our faith. Let the words of Your truth jump from the pages of scripture into our hearts and then flow from us as we surrender to serve You. Thank You for your teaching on the Sea of Galilee that has remained for over 2,000 years. May we continue to teach what You taught and live what You lived out. May we seek to turn the culture around to one that would honor and revere Your name. In Jesus' name we pray. Amen.

What do you see in the culture around you that is so different from what you know is taught in scripture? Share verses that confirm it.

What can you do to be one who helps to change the culture to know Christ?

Day 196

Wisdom Of Men Or Power Of God

"Your faith should not rest on the wisdom of men, but on the power of God."

I Corinthians 2:5

We prayed and expected an answer that we felt was "of the Lord," and all things pointed to an answer in our favor. The prayer wasn't answered as we expected. I was devastated because I was humanly disappointed but also because I had felt so strongly about where He was directing us spiritually.

I questioned the depth and sincerity of my prayer life, my ability to really hear from the Lord: Was I really listening? I questioned whether I was sincerely desirous of wanting His will or whether I was trying to make something else happen? Was I using my own simple wisdom or waiting to see His power?

Months later, after continued time in His word and in prayer, I sensed the answer. I felt that God was saying to me, "This was a test. I wanted to see if this particular desire was withheld from you and your husband, would you would still seek Me." Although I experienced disappointment and frustration, I continued seeking Him, leading to some very good Bible reading, prayer, and growth—growth that doesn't come from the good, fun, and easy times but from the difficulties in life. Eventually an answer came that was far better than what we prayed for initially!

Let's Pause for Prayer

Lord, thank for directing and redirecting us according to Your will. When we don't see the end of the prayer, may we be patient for to watch for how You will work in our hearts to learn what You want us to learn. Help us understand Your perfect timing, to recognize when the answer comes that it is far beyond anything we could have expected or dreamed. Show us Your power so we know the answer is indeed from You. We want you to have Your way. May we be willing to let go of our own desires and let You direct us. May we resist wanting our own way and see a better answer we would never have noticed, expected, or considered. Let us see Your power mightily. In Jesus' name we pray. Amen.

When you pray, do you pray for vague needs or definite ones? And is that because of the lack of wisdom about how to pray, the lack of faith that God will answer, or the reluctance to ask, specifically trusting that He will answer?

_____

_____

Share your most recent answer to prayer that was a disappointment or that was devastating and how you handled it. What do you need to do now that would put you on a track to see His power instead of your own wisdom?

_____

_____

_____

Day 197

Say Something

"A new commandment I give to you, that you love one another, even as I have loved you, that you also love one another. By this all men will know that you are My disciples, if you have love for one another."

John 13:34–35

In my 12 years of public schooling, I don't believe I remember any people telling me they were a Christian or sharing their faith with me. Perhaps someone reached out, but I didn't recognize it or just didn't listen. It wasn't until college at the age of 21 that I first heard about a personal relationship with Christ and the need to take that step of faith in accepting Him on my own, in my own heart, if I wanted that relationship. As an adult, I often pray that those who profess to be Christians would share their faith in public, private, home schooling situations, and neighborhoods to show the love of Christ to those who may not know Jesus.

My prayer is that Christians will show the love of Christ in profound and authentic ways. John 13:34–35 says, "A new commandment I give to you, that you love one another, even as I have loved you, that you also love one another. By this all men will know that you are My disciples, if you have love for one another." Sometimes we speak through our words, other times in our actions.

Let's Pause for Prayer

Lord, we pray that you would use each of us who know You to be a light in a dark place and share our faith in You with others. As adults, may we encourage the children in our lives to be bold and courageous as they the take leap of faith to talk about You. We pray they would look for opportunities to serve others, to show kindness to others, and to pray for those who don't know You. As they see the fruits of their labors, may they be encouraged to continue! Give us the right words to say, and let us always act in loving ways that show others how much we care about them. If I never get to talk to someone about You, may others see You in my actions. In Jesus' name we pray. Amen.

Are you a quiet person when it comes to sharing your faith with others?

_____

_____

_____

How can you show love in practical ways? How can you share in words with others?

_____

_____

_____

Day 198 — *Hurt By Criticism*

> *"Give no offense either to Jews or to Greeks or to the church of God."*
> I Corinthians 10:32

Making fun, ridiculing, treating unkindly, and hurting with words are ways we've all been wounded. It's often through criticism of one kind or another, often by fellow believers—nothing like "friendly fire"! Although I Corinthians 10:32 states, "Give no offense either to Jews or to Greeks or to the church of God," we often take matters into our own hands to cut to the quick, saying what we think needs to be said or resolved, no matter how hurtful.

Words used for intimidation, rudeness, meanness, or harsh criticism are often quick and cutting and hurt, offend, and slow to be forgotten. Leaders, students, parents, board members, business owners, children, administrative personnel, and ministry coworkers aren't exempt from hurting others in their desire to have situations go the way they wish they would. Acting superior and gaining power are part of what hurtful criticism is all about. The ways we can knowingly hurt others have no limits, and when confronted about it, we should take responsibility to ask for forgiveness.

Humility in asking for forgiveness might open a door to share our Lord and Savior as never before. We say we want others to come to Christ, but are we willing to humble ourselves when we know we've done wrong and ask for forgiveness?

Let's Pause for Prayer

Heavenly Father, for those I've hurt, would You please give me the strength and grace to ask them for forgiveness? Would you please call to my mind people and situations where I need to make a relationship right? Help me to be courageous to own up to my failings and to acknowledge hurting others. Father, I desire to be used of You to lead others to You, and I know my sin will keep that from happening; so I ask You to help me to do my part in confessing my sin and correcting the situation. May I make right what I have wronged. May I humbly recognize it, own it, and correct it. In Jesus' name we pray. Amen.

Who is the first person to come to mind who has been hurt by your words? Write out the situation.

_____

_____

Write out a prayer asking forgiveness of God.

_____

_____

How will you pursue asking forgiveness of the person who came to mind?

_____

Day 199 — Ability Versus Disability

"Thou dost scrutinize my path and my lying down, and art intimately acquainted with all my ways."

Psalm 139:3

Having an adult child with special needs (cerebral palsy) and having helped care for several family members during various stages of disability resulting from cancer, Alzheimer's, brain aneurysm, and massive heart attack, I'm aware that abilities may be absent; but much function often occurs in the mind as shown by the many expressions on their faces. "If only I could talk, I would tell you that I hear everything going on." God's word speaks to that as well: "O Lord, Thou hast searched me and known me, Thou dost know when I sit down and when I rise up; Thou dost understand my thought from afar. Thou dost scrutinize my path and my lying down, and art intimately acquainted with all my ways."

There is meaning in all life, whether the person seems distant or present, regardless of the ability level. Perhaps the meaning in that life is to teach us to be compassionate and caring, to teach us to be unselfish, or to show us the awesome way God created the human body. Some of the most meaningful lessons I've learned in life have come from caring for those who have not been able to tell me what they need, to care for themselves, or to help others when they get better. Considering and caring for those who are unable to care for themselves are important lessons.

Let's Pause for Prayer

Heavenly Father, thank you for showing us Your power and might through Your creation. Help us to value all life: the strong, the fragile, those who can't speak, those who speak but we don't understand, those who are perfectly able to understand but are trapped in their own bodies. Help us to be advocates for those who can't act on their own behalf. Let us learn compassion through caring and unselfish actions as we help others. Let us not turn our backs on those who have need in our own families and in our spheres of influence. Give us much grace and love to show others how meaningful and worthwhile their life is. In Jesus' name we pray. Amen.

Do you care for someone with special needs? Write out the details of their abilities or lack of ability. If no one close to you has a special need, name someone you know who comes to mind.

What can you do to reach out to this person? Perhaps it's the one-time fulfilling of a need or an ongoing offer to help that comes to mind.

Day 200 — Infidelity

> *"Be on your guard! If your brother sins, rebuke him; and if he repents, forgive him."*
>
> Luke 17:3

Greeting cards have been personalized for husband, wife, child, parent, aunt, uncle, first-born, brother, sister, or fiancé; but the first time I saw a card for mistress or significant other (not a spouse), I cringed.

Focus on the Family's, *Citizen* Magazine (September 2005) assessed the Secret Lover Collection, "committed to providing a greeting card collection with empathy and understanding, without judgment to lovers involved in a secret love relationship." Sample wording included "I used to look forward to the weekends but since we met they seem like an eternity." For those special holiday occasions, one card said, "As we each celebrate with our families, I will be thinking of you."

The woman behind the collection says she launched it to help the unfaithful express their emotions. *Citizen* criticized the line of cards for cashing in on this market and the card creator for stating, "There won't be a big banner that says Infidelity. They will be displayed under categories like Love Expression and Intimacy."

I did and still do find that quite interesting. I can't help but wonder whether she's ever spent time with a family member or friend whose spouse has been unfaithful to witness the tearing down of trust, love, family, and faithfulness; or whether she has personally experienced that devastating betrayal. It's devastating, not cute. Infidelity doesn't present itself like a neat and tidy greeting card. Unfaithfulness never affects just the two people committing the sin of adultery. It's like the ripple effect of a pebble thrown into the water, affecting family, friends, the church, and the community. If it's happened to you, you know.

Let's Pause for Prayer

Lord, we pray that as Christians we are faithful in our marriages as we live out our vows. We pray that those committing adultery turn from their sin and seek You to live a life of faithfulness to You and to their spouse. Help us to pray for others who experience the pain and devastation of an unfaithful spouse. The betrayal and hurt are beyond comprehension unless one has walked that road. Relieve those walking this road of their anguish as You strengthen and comfort them. Help all parties make their ways right so they can restore their walk with You, restore their family, and better serve You. In Jesus' name we pray. Amen.

Have you or someone close to you walked through this challenge? Write out your perspective of how it affected you. Is there a next step for you to take (if this is your present situation) or a way to help someone else going through the hurt and betrayal of infidelity?

_____

_____

_____

_____

Day 201

War

> *"A time for war, and a time for peace."*
>
> Ecclesiastes 3:8b

I recently shared with several people how oblivious I was as a young woman to what was happening in Viet Nam. I had friends who served there and tried to keep in touch with them by writing, but when I think back to some of the things that my friends shared with me about the war in their letters, I am saddened me to think how unaware I was to the danger, the devastation, and the death all around them. I was at home finishing high school and going to college and had no clue of the kind of sacrifice my friends and others were making on my behalf.

As a grown woman, I've watched some of my friends send their sons and daughters off to war to serve in the Middle East. I see the news. I recognize the sacrifice young men and woman are making for you and me and the freedom they are allowing us to enjoy in this country. When I pray, I pray sincerely and earnestly for those serving and for the families and friends they left behind.

Let's Pause for Prayer

Lord, we offer thanksgiving for those who enlist in the U.S. armed forces. We pray for the morale of the military and for their safety. We pray that you would protect the hearts, minds, and lives of all serving. May each of them come to know you, and for those who do, may they share their faith with others around them. Protect their lives, their marriages, and all relationships back home. We thank you for the sacrifices they are making on our behalf. Bless them, Lord Jesus! In your name we pray. Amen.

Do you have a family member or a friend who is serving in the U.S. armed forces? List their names.

_____

_____

_____

How do you pray for them? And if you aren't currently praying for them, how can or will you?

_____

_____

_____

_____

Day 202

The Needy

> *"For he will deliver the needy when he cries for help, the afflicted also, and him who has no helper. He will have compassion on the poor and needy, and the lives of the needy he will save. He will rescue their life from oppression and violence."*
>
> Psalm 72:12–14a

How many of us have considered doing short-term mission work but haven't had the finances to do it or perhaps can't make the long trip overseas or for another reason have been unable to partake in a mission trip? For those who have desired to help a devastated people, that opportunity might be just around the corner in our very own country.

I realize that all people do not have the same opportunity to stop what they're doing and leave to serve on a mission trip, but many reserve their planned days off, even vacations, to do what they can when crisis or need arises. They're doing what they can for the period of time that they can to make whatever difference they can.

Many groups of people desire to share food, shelter, and medicine and often with the intent also to share the gospel. Before many of the victims (or people in need) will be able to hear the gospel, they will need to have their physical needs met. As those needs are met, I pray that they will be open to hearing that the Lord cares for and loves them and has spared their lives for a purpose that they don't recognize right now in their distress.

Let's Pause for Prayer

Dear Lord, we thank You for providing help for people who have been devastated by natural disaster, homelessness, and other devastation. Please send in the right people to provide medical care and food to sustain the lives of those waiting for help and care. Please send just the right people who will share Your love and word with them. May many come to know You and the purpose that You have for them as they rebuild their lives. May they rebuild upon Your foundation. In Jesus' name we pray. Amen.

Have you ever been a part of a short-term mission trip? Describe it.

_____
_____
_____

If you are unable to participate in a mission trip, how will you pray for those who can?

_____
_____
_____

Day 203 — *Who Am, I And Why Am I Here?*

> *"And we know that God causes all things to work together for good to those who love God, to those who are called according to His purpose."*
>
> Romans 8:28

The Purpose Driven Life by Rick Warren has helped millions of people answer that question. At various times of our lives, we will wonder about and ponder this question.

Early in the book, Warren asks, "What on earth am I here for?" He shares Proverbs 11:28 from *The Message: The Bible in Contemporary Language*, which states, "A life devoted to things is a dead life, a stump; a God-shaped life is a flourishing tree." According to Warren, "the purpose of your life is far greater than your own personal fulfillment, your peace of mind, or even your happiness. It's far greater than your family, your career, or even your wildest dreams and ambitions. If you want to know why you were placed on this planet, you must begin with God. You were born by His purpose and for His purpose."

As I watch the news and recognize the enormity of war, family devastation, and homelessness and then consider lesser issues like personal challenges and crises, I realize how much has been taken from people—life, homes, jobs, possessions, money, and health. All of life's challenges are devastating and often heart-wrenching. How does one find purpose for life in the midst of such personal challenge and worldwide tragedy?

Let's Pause for Prayer

Heavenly Father, the enormity of the all devastation—personal, national, and worldwide—is beyond what most of us have ever or will ever experience. We pray for each individual to come to know You personally. As their needs are eventually met, we pray that they would see You as a merciful God for having spared their very lives and that they would turn to You and say, "If I made it through this horrible tragedy or challenge, You must have a purpose for me. What is my purpose, Lord?" For those who already know you as their Lord and Savior, may they rejoice in their spared lives and share with others the hope they have in their hearts and lead others to You. Please speak to each heart, Lord. In Jesus' name we pray. Amen.

What is your personal crisis right now? Do you see a purpose in it?

_____

_____

_____

Can you pray for someone who will recognize and act upon the purpose God has for her or his life?

_____

_____

Day 204 — Real Life

"For I, the Lord, do not change."

Malachi 3:6a

I'm reminded of a comic strip that I saw a number of years ago. In it a mother stood outside her car stranded on the roadside with a flat tire. The carload of kids seemed unhappy that they'd been sidetracked. The mother said to them in frustration, "This is not a movie. We don't have a remote control to change what we don't like. This is real life!"

We can all chuckle at this dose of reality resulting from a small inconvenience in life like a flat tire, but some people in this country and in our world experience great hardship and even devastation and wish they could simply touch their remote controls and change the station from this tragedy to a pleasant situation. Often in these difficult circumstances we know lives aren't going to change any time soon. Lives can't be rebuilt quickly. Loss, health issues, and challenging relationships take time to rebuild.

In the Old Testament, Job lost everything, yet he did not walk away from God. In fact, he said, "Though He slay me, I will hope in Him. . . . Only two things do not do to me, then I will not hide from They face: do not remove Thy hand from me, and let not the dread of Thee terrify me. But He knows the way I take; when He has tried me, I shall come forth as gold. My foot has held fast to His path; I have kept His ways and not turned aside. I have not departed from the command of His lips. I have treasured the words of His mouth more than my necessary food" (Job 13:15, 20–21, 23: 10–12).

Let's Pause for Prayer

Heavenly Father, please show Your mercy and love to those whose lives are in a difficult place. We know that from time to time, we all wish we could click a button and have our lives changed into new, wonderful, and different ones; but that is fantasy. For those who know You, let them show their Christian love to others who are in tough places right now. May many turn their lives to You as they recognize that they have been put into particular situations or places to be used in some way for some purpose. Help each one hold fast to you and not depart from you. We are thankful that You do not change. In Jesus' name we pray. Amen.

If you could click a button and make a change right now in your life, what would you change?

_____

_____

How will you pray about this situation? What could you do to make life better?

_____

_____

Day 205 — *Lies*

> *"Do not lie to one another, since you laid aside the old self with its evil practices."*
> Colossians 3:9

Several of our friends have run for elected positions. We pray for these individuals as well as for their families. When we see them, we ask how their lives are going so we know how to pray. I can hardly believe what I hear sometimes. I know this person is telling the truth, yet it's hard for me to believe what goes on with elections! Signs are stolen. People make false accusations about the candidates, their records, their families, their lives. It's awful. I know I couldn't tolerate the heat in that arena, so I am happy to pray for our friends, knowing I wouldn't be the right person for public office.

As Christian citizens, we need to be good stewards of the freedom that God has allowed us and to educate ourselves on issues and candidates and become informed about issues on the ballot. We need to elect godly people who will stand up for biblical issues. And we must pray for them. Pray, pray, pray!

Let's Pause for Prayer

Father, we pray that those serving in public office are surrounded with people who will pray for them and that they are protected from lies and false witness. Each time we vote, let us be sure to do our homework and understand the issues, informing ourselves and diligently studying what we can. We pray that You would call to our minds different candidates to pray for as they stand up to represent You in an often cruel and vicious environment. We know those running for elected positions might not have the financial means to distribute literature and such, but Lord, we know that You aren't interested in the amount of money spent or the number of signs in yards. Instead, You are interested people's hearts and desire for Your servants to be used for Your glory. To that end we pray in Jesus' name. Amen.

Have you ever run for and served in a public office? If so, share your story.

_____
_____
_____

Do you pray for yourself and others serving our city, state, and nation? How can you make that a new habit for yourself? Write out a prayer to this effect.

_____
_____
_____
_____

Day 206

Final Words

"For God so loved the world, that He gave His only begotten Son, that whoever believes in Him should not perish but have eternal life."

John 3:16

Possibly one of the sweetest people I've ever met was Mary, who had hoped to celebrate her ninetieth birthday. Instead of celebrating in the nursing home with family around her, she celebrated in heaven. I'm sure no party any of us would have planned for her would have compared with what she had in heaven!

Mary was expected to die on a particular day but lived almost a full week longer. She remained coherent until the very end. As she lay dying, she remained soft spoken and sweet, never complaining about the pain because as she said to one of her five sons, "Jesus endured pain for me. I can endure it for Him." I wondered why Mary lived longer than expected. But as I heard some of her final words, I think the Lord gave her those extra days to give us a glimpse of heaven and to give her a final opportunity to point others to a real Savior in a real place!

Mary one day opened her eyes and said to her son, "Oh it's you. I was just with Jesus, but it is so nice to see you, too!" Another time she said, "I can't believe how beautiful the aromas are there. And the flowers are like nothing I have ever seen here. The colors are beautiful! I saw the cross and His crown and they are bright! And I don't have shoes. I don't need them there!" In her final words she asked her son to lay his head on her shoulder as she said, "I don't want to be alone." With his head on her shoulder, she said, "I'm going to go now. I love you." And with that, she met her Lord and Savior. She left no doubt that heaven is a wonderful place. Mary knew she was going from life to life.

Let's Pause for Prayer

Heavenly Father, thank You for the assurance You give us in Your word that You are preparing a place for us. May we be as ready and prepared to meet you as Mary was. Father, we pray that those who don't know You accept You as their Lord and Savior and live whatever lives they have left for You! I pray that the glimpse of heaven that Mary enjoyed will penetrate our minds and hearts now and also when we come to that day when our final words will be recorded and repeated. In Jesus' name we pray. Amen.

We don't often prepare ahead of time for what our final days and words might be. How do Mary's words help you to consider your own final days?

_____

_____

_____

How can you pray for others as you live for Him today?

_____

_____

Day 207

Not Fair!

> *"I will cry to God Most High, to God who accomplishes all things for me."*
>
> Psalm 57:2

Most of us at one time or another have probably thought or possibly said out loud something like, "That just doesn't seem fair!" or "Why do I have to go through this trouble?" or "That person always seems to come out ahead when I feel as if I struggle and can't get anywhere." I suppose some of us are in the habit of thinking life should go our way and that we should always be comfortable. I have heard it said and have said it myself that I grow in the ways of the Lord the most when I've gone through a challenging, disappointing, or difficult time. It's not easy. It's not comfortable. We don't have to like it. We don't have to understand it, but we must accept it if we want to grow. His word assures us that He has our best interests in mind. Be assured that the Lord has a plan and everything He does—in some way or another—is for our good.

I take comfort in His word as my confidence and security in good times and bad: Psalm 138:8, "The Lord will accomplish what concerns me; thy lovingkindness, O Lord, is everlasting; do not forsake the works of Thy hands."

Let's Pause for Prayer

Heavenly Father, please forgive me when I don't like what is happening in my life or in the lives of those I love. Forgive my anxious thoughts and the times I doubt that You care. Your word is true, and I claim it for my life. Thank You for ordering my life in such a way that it can be used for Your glory if I simply yield to You and all that you have for me. Thank You for accomplishing just what concerns me. Help me to appreciate that truth. May I walk in a way that shows others I appreciate You. I pray that I would by my attitude show that I trust in You and all that You have planned for me: both joys and challenges. In Jesus' name we pray. Amen.

Have you ever told God that the way your life is going for you is "not fair"?

_____

_____

_____

Do you feel you can graciously accept all that comes from God, both challenges and joys? Write out a prayer that shares what is honestly in your heart.

_____

_____

_____

_____

Day 208

The Evil Twin

"There is therefore now no condemnation for those who are in Christ Jesus."

Romans 8:1

I've known several sets of twins and always thought it would be fun to have a twin! In one way, I guess I do have a twin, but she's not fun! In my walk as a Christian, I have been able to recognize the "other" me. I call her my evil twin. As a Christian, my heart's desire is to follow, obey, and serve Jesus Christ, my Lord and Savior. But when trouble befalls me, people treat me unkindly, or life doesn't go as I had planned, I struggle with my evil twin. It's the struggle between a life in Christ and the sinful, self-centered life. It's the struggle between reacting in a sinful way and responding in accordance with what I know in Christ. I wish I could avoid that struggle, but it is real to me; and if you're honest, it's real to you, too.

Paul had the same struggle. In Romans 7:14–17 he shares his agony: "For we know that the Law is spiritual; but I am of flesh, sold into bondage to sin. For that which I am doing, I do not understand; for I am not practicing what I would like to do, but I am doing the very thing I hate. But if I do the very thing I do not wish to do, I agree with the Law, confessing that it is good. So now, no longer am I the one doing it, but sin which dwells in me." Paul shares his resolve in Romans 7:25–8:2.

Let's Pause for Prayer

Heavenly Father, we appreciate the ability to thank You and rejoice that "There is therefore now no condemnation for those who are in Christ Jesus" according to Romans 8:1. Thank You for the death of Your Son on the cross, our acceptance of His releasing us from sin, and our ability to come to You for victory over that which controls us or tries to. We are so thankful that we don't have to live out of our flesh as the evil twin who controls us but as the one who is controlled by You through Your love for us. Help us to respond to all situations with Your love and mercy. In Jesus' name we pray. Amen.

Do some of your thoughts and feelings make you wonder where they came from? Do you blame them on your evil twin?

_____

_____

_____

How will you work through the desires and deeds of the flesh and what you desire in the spirit? How will you work to become all that Christ wants you to be?

_____

_____

_____

Day 209 — Be An Example

"Let no one look down on your youthfulness, but rather in speech, conduct, love, faith and purity, show yourself an example of those who believe."

I Timothy 4:12

I recently read the following quotation on Facebook from *Collective Evolution* by Cory Booker: "Before you speak to me about your religion, first show it to me in how you treat other people; before you tell me how much you love your God, show me in how much you love all His children; before you preach to me of your passion for your faith, teach me about it through your compassion for your neighbors. In the end I'm not as interested in what you have to tell or sell as in how you choose to live and give."

About the same time I was following a Facebook page where posters had become very vocal. People were unhappy about an issue, and their comments were mean-spirited, nasty, and hurtful. I was embarrassed and ashamed at what I was reading from supposed brothers and sisters in Christ. In my flesh and humanness I wanted to respond; in my heart I simply couldn't and didn't.

Let's Pause for Prayer

Father, forgive us for thinking that we know it all as Christians and thus speak to or treat others unkindly on purpose and without considering whether or not our words would hurt instead of help. Forgive us for not praying first to seek You to determine what to say and do. Lord, help us to show compassion in our words and with actions that build up, not tear down, others—both believers and unbelievers. We read and say that "we have the mind of Christ" according to I Corinthians 2:16b, but do we really, when we are mean, vindictive, brutal, and nasty in the way we speak to and treat others? Jesus, Your example was to speak in love. You were never unkind or hurtful. Help us consider others before ourselves and to put ourselves into the shoes of another before we say what we might regret or worse yet, what we simply want to say to get off our chests and never regret because we are not filled with Your spirit. May we seek You first to give us direction and guidance in using our tongues, our voices, our influence, and our "platform" of knowing You in life and on social media that all can see. Help us to put aside our opinions and judgments and encourage one another in love. In Jesus' name we pray. Amen.

Before you make a comment, post on social media, and the like, do you take time to think and consider how your words will affect others? (Do you recognize that even non-Christians will read what is written?) How can you put into practice a routine of checks and balances before sharing your thoughts whether in person or on social media? Write out your plan.

_____

_____

_____

_____

Day 210 — Warnings

"Therefore be careful how you walk, not as unwise but wise men, making the most of your time, because the days are evil. So then do not be foolish, but understand what the will of the Lord is. And do not get drunk with wine, for that is dissipation, but be filled with the Spirit."

Ephesians 5:15–18

Thousands of young adults die every year from binge drinking, their blood level reaching and exceeding five times the legal limit; yet so many who turn 21 celebrate by drinking the same number of shots in a two-hour time span to initiate themselves into the world of so-called adulthood. No wonder their blood levels reach a lethal level.

We might think, "How could they be so foolish? Haven't they heard the way these situations end?" I believe they indeed have heard and seen it all—their parents' warnings, the news stories, their friends in near fatal situations. They may have even lost a friend to death this way, but they might think, "It happened to them. It happens to others, but it won't happen to me." Because they're young, they have a way of convincing themselves that they're invincible, too young, too healthy, too smart and that it couldn't possibly happen to them! But for some thousands it did indeed happen to them.

God may have us to share with a young adult the cautions and concerns of this behavior, but can we go a step further. We can pray for someone we know to make a wise decision when confronted with this choice or will be in the future. We can pray now, but we can keep them in prayer.

Let's Pause for Prayer

Heavenly Father, we pray that You would speak to the hearts of those young adults who think that binge drinking will not hurt them in any way. We pray that You would give them discernment and the ability to stand firm and say no to that which they not only know is wrong but very possibly also deadly. Help them to be an example to their friends. Give them alternative ways to celebrate that are healthy, fun, wholesome, and life-affirming. Give them hearts to obey and serve You! In Jesus' name we pray. Amen.

List young adults for whom you can pray. Pray.

_____

_____

_____

_____

Day 211 — *If I Could Turn Back The Hands Of Time*

> *"And let us not lose heart in doing good, for in due time we shall reap if we do not grow weary."*
>
> Galatians 6:9

People joke about going back to the 50s when life seemed simpler and less stressful, when life seemed less confusing and less chaotic! Of course, we realize how hard it would be to turn back the hands of time to those days, especially in light of where we are in our busy, full, stressed-out lives in the fast lane!

What if we just turned back the hands of time at dinnertime and reclaimed the family dinner hour? We read and hear about how important family time is. That's another scene out of the 50s, isn't it? We often hear that families who enjoy dinner together have better family relationships; in addition, the children tend to be better adjusted, more studious, and less likely to contribute to crime statistics. Over dinner families connect through good conversation, which leads to good communication, which leads to good relationships, which lead to well-adjusted youth, who generally don't get into much trouble. It's interesting that such a simple activity could make a dramatic difference, not only in our homes but also in society. Having dinner hour together as a family—what a concept! Maybe turning back the hands of time to the 50s for dinner hour isn't a bad idea.

Let's Pause for Prayer

Lord, we desire to commit to You our families and the time we spend with them. If you are challenging us to keep our families together at the dinner hour, please show us how to make that happen. Help us to do what is necessary to gather our families at dinner. Help us to see the ways our schedules keep us from spending substantial amounts of quality time as a family. Help us to know how to talk to one another and how to develop the deep family relationships that lead to stability in each life and in the life of the whole family. Let us not grow weary in this endeavor that we might see the results later in our lives! May we be an example to other families around us! In Jesus' name we pray. Amen.

Do you have a daily meal together with your family? Pray for opportunities to make this happen daily.

What kinds of conversation make for good fellowship around the table?

Day 212

Finishing Well

"But now finish doing it also; that just as there was the readiness to desire it, so there may be also the completion of it by your ability."

II Corinthians 8:11

It was very time consuming. It was designed, cut out, marked, and sewed with delicate precision, and it was a labor of love. It was my daughter's wedding gown.

Although I've sewn many projects over the years, including my own wedding dress, my daughter's wedding gown was probably the finest item I've ever had the pleasure of creating and sewing. I was meticulous. I didn't want to make any mistakes. I wanted it to be perfect. I made sure every seam was finished. Each of the 37 button loops fit perfectly over the silk buttons sewn on by hand. Hand stitches on other parts of the dress were so delicate that you couldn't see them. The inside was constructed in as detailed a manner and as beautifully as the outside. Just for fun I tried to keep track of how many hours I worked on it. It took about 150 hours to the point that all I had left was the hem. The final work required approximately 2,000 inches of hand turning the delicate and individual 6 layers of fabric to a tiny 1/8-inch rolled hem. I felt it might get monotonous. At this point I asked myself, "What if I took a short cut here? What if I all of a sudden didn't care about the final detail because I just wanted to get it done? What if I felt it would just be too much work and effort?"

I saw the correlation to my Christian walk. I can be meticulous, doing a very good job in loving and serving the Lord; but how will I persevere when my walk becomes tiresome or maybe even a bit uninteresting? How will I finish what the Lord has started in me? When it came to the dress, I continued as I had begun. I finished the hem with excellence. But I prayed my way through it!

Let's Pause for Prayer

Lord, I pray, that we would all finish this life of service to You with excellence. We pray that when life is monotonous, uninteresting, or difficult, You would sustain us and allow our walk with You to be close. Help us to pray through the times that are dull and not as adventuresome or as much fun as we'd like, and show us how to be appreciative and thankful. Help us to pray for others during those times. In Jesus' name I pray. Amen.

What major endeavor have you started and completed with great satisfaction? Do you see the correlation to your walk as a believer?

_____

_____

How do you hope to finish this life? Write out a prayer.

_____

_____

Day 213 — "They"

> *"And they went away and reported it to the others, but they did not believe them either."*
>
> Mark 16:13

Who is "they"? You know, the nameless individuals in many of our conversations. I hear myself and others say it as we converse with friends. It sounds something like this, "Those people, they sure know how to make life miserable" or "They are always trying to make matters worse" or "They just don't understand." It's that vague group of people or one person whose name isn't revealed as we share a frustrating or troubling situation. We seldom use the pronoun they when speaking positively of a situation or person. For instance, if talking about someone who has been kind or helpful, her or his name is shared and attached to the good deed. "They" are others in our lives whom we don't want to name out loud!

Even in scripture (Mark 16:13 above) we get the idea that not everyone was named. Perhaps it's protective. We're protecting ourselves from what would lead to gossip because we aren't really sharing the name, just the frustration. Perhaps it's protecting us from being a spreader of negative news. But I've had another thought about the "they" people in our lives. I am very likely and most definitely will be a "they" to someone else, yet I desire, as you probably do, to be the person who is remembered for the kind or helpful deed instead of the negative.

Let's Pause for Prayer

Lord, Jesus, thank You for the "they" in our lives. They help us to rely upon You for strength to get through the difficult situation with them! They are the ones who will allow us to be drawn into prayer instead of using their name and spreading gossip. Lord, help me in this area to extend grace to them. And, Lord, may I extend grace so often and so tenderly that when I am the source of frustration to others, they will be drawn to pray for and extend grace to me. In Jesus' name we pray. Amen.

Catch yourself in conversation today saying *they*. What was the circumstance?

_____

_____

_____

Were you trying to protect the "they," or did you have another purpose? Think it through and then write a prayer.

_____

_____

_____

_____

Day 214 — *Defiant*

> *"And if your brother sins, go and reprove him in private; if he listens to you, you have won your brother. But if he does not listen to you, take one or two more with you, so that by the mouth of two or three witnesses every fact may be confirmed. And if he refuses to listen to them, tell it to the church; and if he refuses to listen even to the church, let him be to you as a Gentile and a tax-gatherer."*
>
> Matthew 18:15–17

Happy smiling faces and fun conversation throughout the church, right? But what about those who don't or, worse yet, won't talk to one another? Those who leave the church without a word because they decide to take matters into their own hands, saying, "I know better than those counseling me"? Or those who stay and continue to cause hardship for the very people who wanted reconciliation and forgiveness?

What sadness and frustration as some Christians take steps toward reconciliation while others (who also claim to be believers) will have no part of it! The latter type is insistent that they are right and defiantly choose to ignore their part. Flatly, they disobey direction from their pastors or elders and interestingly walk and live in sin. Unresolved and unrepentant sin abounds. And sadly, sometimes the leadership also chooses to ignore what is wrong.

God's word is very direct about this. Matthew 18:15–17 tells us how we (as a healthy church) should handle these matters. Members of a healthy church will handle it. Members of an unhealthy church will look the other way and ignore all the warnings as well as the sin. These are strong words that should cause us to pray diligently.

Let's Pause for Prayer

Lord, please help us to "pursue peace with all men" as You state in Hebrews 12:14. Help us own up to our faults and not merely ask for forgiveness and grant it but take the action You require and actually reconcile with others. May pastors and elders take seriously the ramifications of unresolved sin in the church. Grant us the wisdom to know how to handle those who are defiant, disobedient, and living in sin. May we be people of grace and truth as we confront when needed, gracious in granting forgiveness, but most importantly truly reconciling to one another. In Jesus' name we pray. Amen.

If a situation has occurred in your life that sounds similar to what is described above, write it out. How will you pray to secure a good and godly response and result? How will you respond?

_____

_____

_____

_____

Day 215   Sin

> *"If we say that we have no sin, we are deceiving ourselves, and the truth is not in us. If we confess our sins, He is faithful and righteous to forgive us our sins and to cleanse us from all unrighteousness. If we say that we have not sinned, we make Him a liar and His word is not in us."*
>
> I John 1:8–9

After my first child was born, I remember thinking I would walk out of the hospital looking the way I did before giving birth. What a shock it was when I realized that it would take some time to get back into shape! Although returning to normal is actually impossible (the body is never quite the same), I had to adjust in my mind to thinking that I had to take one step at a time to prepare to deliver, so it stands to reason I would have to take at least one step at a time to get back into shape again! It would not be an overnight process.

Sin is similar.

We may recognize sin in another, especially deep, obvious sin, and even easily recognize the need to take one step at a time to construct a plan for that person to get back to a godly way of life. But that process is not always so easy to see if we ourselves are the ones who have slipped into deep sin. Others may try to talk to, counsel, and even pray for us; but if we have hardened our hearts, we need time to get back on track. Just as getting into sin takes one step at a time, today let's recognize the first step necessary to get out of it. Let's seek the Lord for that next step of asking forgiveness, repenting, and seeking to reconcile.

Let's Pause for Prayer

Lord, we confess to You our sin. We repent, turning away from what we are doing to separate ourselves from You, and now desire to follow You completely and fully. Help each of us to see every area where we have sinned. Give us the courage to talk to every person whom we have wounded and ask for forgiveness and make it right. We know that at times we will not return to the way things were and that we will not live in sinless perfection, but our desire is to be at peace with all men so that we will ultimately please You and be at peace with you. In Jesus' name we pray. Amen.

What sin do you need to confess? Write out your sin and the actions you'll take to get busy and make the situation right.

_____

_____

_____

_____

_____

Day 216

Ways Of Life

"And be kind to one another, tender-hearted, forgiving each other, just as God in Christ also has forgiven you."

Ephesians 4:32

Years ago when I taught high school, I gave my students an assignment that always resulted in interesting discussion. They had one month to complete this assignment. For one week out of the month, they were to be quiet, talk negatively but not against people, sometimes acting contrary just for the sake of being contrary, and to be unpleasant and selfish—all about themselves. For another week out of the month, they were to be out-going, positive in their outlook and in their speech, kind and caring about others and reaching out to serve them, and generally pleasant in all ways. By the end of the month, they were to write a report, sharing how people responded to them and how they perceived their behavior and others around them. It always proved to be an enlightening assignment, especially when someone made changes because they could see how beneficial one behavior was over the other!

Fast forward: As I have walked the halls of nursing homes from time to time, I have seen the manifestation of years of one of the ways of life described above. One resident who exemplified the negative had few, if any, visitors. After all, who really wants to spend time with someone like that! By contrast, those who were happy, positive, and unselfish exemplified the positive and the pleasant and were thus very well liked. Friends and family visited often and workers enjoyed being with them and caring for them.

Let's Pause for Prayer

Heavenly Father, help us to be more like You. Help us to exemplify positive attributes that will lead others to know who You are because we are Christlike. We realize that a lifetime of negative behavior, attitudes, and actions will not likely blossom into some positive joyous personality without work toward that end. May we work, with Your help, to be joyous, pleasant, courteous, kind, patient, and loving. May we become more like You in this journey of life, and may we have joy in that journey. In Jesus' name we pray. Amen.

With which personality type do you most identify? Are you willing to try the assignment and see what kinds of results you get? Share what happened if you did the assignment.

_____
_____
_____
_____
_____
_____

Day 217 — Devoted

> *"Devoted to prayer."*
>
> Romans 12:12

Although I am not an avid TV viewer, I have been known to work my schedule around a particular program I don't want to miss. I make sure my work is complete and have a stack of things to look through, cut out, and file while watching, so I make use of that time I'm sitting; but the point is this: I work to make it happen. I'm committed to the time and will be devoted to my show. Other shows will not hold my interest, and so I move on.

I see my prayer life like that sometimes, too. I am very committed to praying for some people or situations. I'm devoted to seeing them through. I plan my schedule to meet for prayer, to pray through some specific points, and to see God answer them. And then, for some less pressing issues I say a quick prayer and perhaps don't revisit that prayer again for long periods of time, if ever. When I don't see an answer to prayer in some area, I must be willing to say, "You didn't take the time to pray and connect with the Lord about this, so you can't complain that nothing has happened." It is true, that we can't be committed to pray for everything all the time; but we must be committed to pray for those situations that God puts on our hearts and then obey Him by praying through them often and earnestly. Let's seek Him in knowing how He wants us to pray, and for what He wants us to pray.

Let's Pause for Prayer

Heavenly Father, help me to reschedule my day in order to come to you in prayer. Guide me to know Your heart and for what I should pray. May I come to you often, recommitting my time, devotion, and prayer requests to You. I know you never tire of hearing our prayers. May we never tire of coming to you to present our hearts and prayers. In Jesus' name we pray. Amen.

Are you committed to prayer? How does it look for you?

_____

_____

_____

What can you do to reach a new level of commitment for that which you pray?

_____

_____

_____

_____

Day 218 — *Changed*

"Therefore if any man is in Christ, he is a new creature; the old things passed away; behold, new things have come."

II Corinthians 5:17

Sharing her testimony of coming to faith in Jesus at her baptism, a woman said, "Years ago I became a Christian. I let God save me, but I did not let Him change me." Very interesting, isn't it? Very perceptive also! It caused me to think a bit differently about my own salvation and walk with the Lord.

I trusted Christ as my personal Lord and Savior in 1976. I remember immediately being aware of sin in my life and the realization that it had to change. I can recall responding in ways that were typical of my old self, for example, showing my impatience. I knew that had to be changed if I was to show others that I was a new creature in Christ. I would recognize the sin, stop in my thoughts or actions, ask forgiveness of the Lord or others, and repent of it, asking the Lord to help me not sin that way again. We all know that we are imperfect and that those kinds of sins, sins of our old nature, can creep back into our lives and cause us once again to come to Jesus and say to Him, "Yes, Lord, please change me, help me to be more like you!"

He did His part, saving us by His death on the cross; but are we willing to do our parts and surrender our lives to Him by truly allowing Him to change us? Let's get serious about our parts!

Let's Pause for Prayer

Lord, thank You for Your word in II Corinthians 5:17: "Therefore if any man is in Christ, he is a new creature; the old things passed away; behold, new things have come." Help us, Lord to be fully surrendered to You, totally dependent upon You, fully submitted to You. Let us be an example to others of what You have done in our lives. Thank You for saving us, and thank you for changing us if we are willing to submit to You. In Jesus' name we pray. Amen.

Are you serious about your walk, your example? How would one know? How do you know?

_____
_____
_____

Are you willing to do your part and surrender your life to Him by truly allowing Him to change you? What would that change look like?

_____
_____
_____

Day 219 — *Role Models*

> *"For you have been called for this purpose, since Christ also suffered for you, leaving you an example for you to follow in His steps."*
>
> 1 Peter 2:21

We don't need to subscribe to tabloid media to learn what people in Hollywood are saying and doing. Watching the news and stumbling on an occasional entertainment spot on television, I get more information than expected about famous people who some say are role models.

Broadcasts boast of affairs, the unmarried pregnant star who, of course, remains unmarried, living with her lover. So many of these people adopt children or engage in humanitarian aid. I can't help but ask: Is that to make up for the blatant sin they are exposing to the world? Do they think God will not notice the sins of fornication, adultery, and homosexuality? Do they think that those sins are cancelled if they do these other good deeds?

Probably one of the most interesting stories I've come across regarded a very seductive and bold performer, telling a magazine that she doesn't let her children watch TV or look at magazines. I ask myself, "Does she know what she is saying, and does she realize the example she is giving to her children and the public? Does she recognize the double standard and double talk?"

For those of us who have no claim to fame, do we think that we can't be caught in the crossfire of double talk, poor example, and committing sin in our lives, all while doing good? Double standards and double talk = hypocrisy.

Let's Pause for Prayer

Lord, thank You for speaking to our hearts when we sin. Please lead us to right decisions based upon Your word and direction instead of vain pursuits of wrong relationships, living in sin, and wrong thinking. Allow us the privilege of doing good and worthwhile deeds for You, not for the sake of covering up sin in our lives but for the sake of proclaiming who You are in such a way that we can be believed, trusted, and seen as a true role model for the one we serve. In Jesus' name we pray. Amen.

Do you have a situation for which you are double-talking and promoting a double standard for yourself?

_____

_____

_____

What steps will you take to stop that behavior and become a true role model for Christ?

_____

_____

_____

Day 220 — *Enemies*

> *"If your enemy is hungry, give him food to eat; and if he is thirsty, give him water to drink. For you will heap burning coals on his head, and the Lord will reward you."*
>
> Proverbs 25:21–22

As Christians we shouldn't deliberately make enemies, but if we follow Jesus Christ, we will certainly have enemies; and often they will be self-professed religious people, the kind of people who crucified Jesus. Some people will hate us; others will hate us and curse us, and a few will hate us, curse us, and deliberately mistreat us. That's the way the world (society apart from God) treated Jesus, and that's the way we should be expected to be treated the more we become like Him. If you want to be comfortable in this world, then you can't be conformable in Jesus Christ (Romans 12:1–2).

For Christian believers, to love our enemies simply means to treat them the way the Lord treats us. God listens to us, so we listen to them. God is kind to us, so we are kind to them. God doesn't give us what we deserve (that's mercy), but He does give us what we don't deserve (that's grace); and we should follow His example. God forgives us for Jesus' sake, and we should forgive others for Jesus' sake; but we can't do it with our own natural strength. This kind of Christian living demands a great deal of faith and love, and only the Holy Spirit can provide what we need to have that kind of love" (Romans 5:5).

Let's Pause for Prayer

Heavenly Father, help us to love our enemies and be a loving example to them of Your goodness to us. Lord, please show even those who profess to be Christians but curse us and hate us that their hatred, silence, and passive aggressive retaliation will not accomplish any good for Your kingdom. Let us love as You love. In Jesus' name we pray. Amen.

Have you ever experienced praying for someone who was or is your enemy? Share the story.

_____

_____

_____

When we pray for our enemies, what should we ask God to do? How can we love our enemies, treat them well, and pray for them?

_____

_____

_____

Day 221

Not Budging

> *"If possible, so far as it depends on you, be at peace with all men."*
>
> Romans 12:18

Marital relationships, work relationships, church relationships, and family relationships—can harmony prevail? I John 4:20 says, "If someone says, 'I love God,' and hates his brother, he is a liar; for the one who does not love his brother whom he has seen, cannot love God whom he has not seen."

I'm aware of two people who work closely together but don't speak. One Christian has tried many times to reconcile. The other, simply won't budge. Is that glorifying God? Will their coworkers, who observe them, ever want to know Christ when they see how one supposed Christian treats the other, who is trying to work out the relationship?

What about the ministry leaders who leave fellow Christians strewn along the side of the road of Christianity, having shown anger, told lies, and gossiped yet continue in ministry without seeking the help they need, without truly reconciling, and move on as if all is well? Is it the sin of pride that keeps these Christians from saying, "OK, I don't care for you, but I'll forgive you and work toward reconciliation so that for the sake of Christ we can be examples and in the process lead others to Jesus"?

Let's Pause for Prayer

Heavenly Father, please help me to be at peace with all people by allowing me to be an example of the way You forgave me, by my forgiving others and working toward reconciliation. And, Father, should another Christian say, "I forgive you" but doesn't work toward true reconciliation, help me to surrender those relationships to You, knowing that I can do only what you have asked of me. May I glorify You. In Jesus' name we pray. Amen.

With whom are you at odds right now and have no peace in the relationship? Be real.

_____

_____

_____

What can you do to pursue peace with this person, and when will you do so?

_____

_____

_____

_____

Day 222 — *Abuse*

"For this is the will of God, your sanctification; that is, that you abstain from sexual immorality; that each of you know how to possess his own vessel in honor, not in lustful passion, like the Gentiles who do not know God."

I Thess. 4:3–6

The abuse of children is a serious problem at home and abroad. I suppose it's always been an issue, but it's now so much before us in the news, in movies, in our own neighborhoods, and maybe in the home of someone you know, including your own. We aren't talking about spankings for discipline: We are talking about beatings out of anger and worse yet, sexual abuse for the pleasure of the abuser.

As I've watched sting operations catching sexual offenders play out on TV, I pray these criminals will be caught, jailed, come to know Jesus, and get the help they need. I know that some of these criminals profess to be Christians. Sin is everywhere.

As I take my neighborhood walks and as I drive, I see children playing and wonder whether their lives have been torn apart by verbal, emotional, physical, or sexual abuse? Will this child repeat the sins of perpetrators because she or he knows no other way? Does the child live in a home where parents claim to be Christian?

Let's Pause for Prayer

Heavenly Father, we intercede for all children who are verbally, emotionally, physically, or sexually abused. We pray for God to deeply convict parents and siblings who are abusers to seek help. We pray for individual spiritual revival, for a desire to walk closely with Christ, and for families to be made whole. Lord, remind us to pray for innocent victims to seek someone who will believe them, listen to them, and help them. In Jesus' name we pray. Amen.

Were you ever the victim of abuse? Have you perpetrated abuse on someone? Share your thoughts here.

_____

_____

_____

_____

_____

_____

Day 223 — Changes

"For God sees not as man sees, for man looks at the outward appearance, but the Lord looks at the heart."

I Samuel 16:7

We are a culture of people who want change. I'm not talking about cultural, moral, ethical or spiritual change but physical change.

We have makeover shows that include updating and redoing wardrobes and makeup and revealing the results of surgeries to change what people didn't like about themselves (dentally and physically). In the past most people didn't talk about enhancement surgeries. They apparently wanted everyone to think the hands of time reversed the aging process for them miraculously! Various cosmetic procedures can result in significant improvements, but no matter how good people may look, they still look close to their actual age. They will never look 25 again!

We understand our bodies are temples of the Lord and we need to take good care of ourselves so we can be used of the Lord for His glory, but if we try to change our physical appearance yet neglect changes that can be made to improve our spiritual condition, we have sadly missed the mark. Perhaps you, too, have met someone who is very attractive, but within a short time they no longer appear as attractive as you first thought because of certain characteristics that surfaced like pride, anger, or haughtiness. The reverse is also true: People who are physically unattractive becomes extremely attractive as their gentle, kind, and tender ways show through. Suddenly, they look very beautiful. Regardless of our age or appearance, God looks at our hearts. That is most important.

Let's Pause for Prayer

Lord, please show us what our hearts look like. We know it's not necessarily wrong to make ourselves look better, no matter the means. Help us to be more concerned about our spiritual appearance before You, not just the façade but also the qualities You'd like us to improve upon. Lord, shall we have more self-control, be better listeners, or show mercy? May we develop qualities that make us look more and more like You so that others will see You in us. In Jesus' name we pray. Amen.

What about yourself would you physically change if you could? What would you spiritually change about yourself?

_____

_____

_____

What steps will you take to make yourself more attractive spiritually?

_____

_____

Day 224

Shallow Prayer Life

"O God, Thou are my God; I shall seek Thee earnestly; My soul thirsts for Thee, my flesh yearns for Thee, in a dry and weary land where there is no water."

Psalm 63:1

Most people admit that their shallow prayer life is a result of a lack of time to pray; however, I know from my own experience, that when we find ourselves in a crisis, we have all kinds of time to pray and ask the Lord to help us.

Psalm 63:1 says, "O God, Thou are my God; I shall seek Thee earnestly; My soul thirsts for Thee, my flesh yearns for Thee, in a dry and weary land where there is no water." Acts 2:42 says, "And they were continually devoting themselves to the apostles' teaching and to fellowship, to the breaking of bread and to prayer." When we are so thirsty that only water will quench our thirst, we seek water. If only we had that kind of desire to seek the Lord in a relationship of prayerful communication.

Both verses describe a strong desire to pray. Any strong desire leads us to setting a priority to fulfill that desire. If we want to pray, we need to make prayer a priority. We need to set time aside. We need to designate a prime prayer time. We need to devote ourselves to making it happen.

Let's Pause for Prayer

Heavenly Father, thank You for allowing us to come to You in prayer and communicate with You and You with us. Forgive us for spending so little time with You in prayer. We know we miss out on such wonderful fellowship with You when we fail to make prayer a priority in our schedule. May we not wait for a time of crisis to come to You. In Jesus' name we pray. Amen.

Describe your prayer life.

_____

_____

_____

How would you like to deepen your prayer life? List what you'll do to make it happen.

_____

_____

_____

_____

Day 225

Accepted Sin

> *"Fools mock at sin"*
>
> Proverbs 14:9a

Cohabitation, adultery, sexual relations between homosexuals, abortion, pornography, the use of profanity, gossip, and gambling seem to be morally acceptable behaviors—and that is within the church.

Our church home is full of sin, seldom confronted perhaps because we've developed a habit of turning away and not looking; we are confused and compromise.

We pray vague prayers as if we're asking God to bless sinful relationships, people struggling with addictions, expecting Him to figure out a solution. Do we hold ourselves and fellow Christians to a standard that sets us apart and shows that we are willing to be different because we stand up for what the Bible says is right? Or do we compromise by saying, "God will surely forgive me of that sin even if I remain in it?" Then, we expect Him to answer with blessing and approval.

Let's Pause for Prayer

Heavenly Father, please forgive us for turning our heads and not confronting what we know to be sin in ourselves and in others, for living in sin and acting as if doing so is acceptable. We want to put our trust in You to do what is right in Your sight. Please give strength to unmarried Christians living together to change those relationships and either marry or live separately so they will honor Your word. Help those contemplating abortion, those in homosexual relationships, those involved in gambling, those thinking profanity and pornography are acceptable to stop making excuses for their sin and choose to do what is biblically right. May we all seek help where we sin and find God sufficient for all our needs, so that we Christians can be examples of what God can do with obedient hearts. In Jesus' name we pray. Amen.

Do you have a sense that we've turned our heads, ignoring sin and failing to confront it? If so, what do you think should be done and what can you do?

_____

_____

_____

_____

How can and should we pray for those in sin?

_____

_____

_____

Day 226

Watching Our Words

"The one who guards his mouth preserves his life; the one who opens wide his lips come to ruin."

Proverbs 13:3

The news sometimes features stories about reporters forgetting to turn their microphones off, allowing an entire conversation off camera to be heard over a broadcast. Perhaps like me you've made remarks you might not have said directly to someone, but you said them nonetheless; and they were near you or within earshot.

We feel bad and humiliated when we realize what just happened. A humble apology would be timely, needed, and appropriate. Maybe we haven't been caught out loud, but sometimes we feel the need to share something with our spouse or closest friend; yet no matter what we say, privately or publicly, we will be accountable for those words.

Matthew 12:36–37 says, "And I say to you, that every careless word that men shall speak, they shall render account for it in the Day of Judgment. For by your words you shall be justified, and by your words you shall be condemned." Proverbs 13:3 says, "The one who guards his mouth preserves his life; the one who opens wide his lips come to ruin."

Let's Pause for Prayer

Heavenly Father, please forgive me when I have said things against another person. Help me to be mindful to speak kindly and truthfully with words that bring life to others. Prepare my heart in all situations to think before I speak. Guard my tongue when I should choose words more carefully than I am prone to do. Silence my lips when I am about to say something unkind. Help me to discern whether what I am about to say has any good and wholesome value to it. And thank you for guiding me to say and do what is right in your eyes. In Jesus' name we pray. Amen.

Share a time when you wish you'd not spoken as you did.

_____

_____

_____

What will you do to protect yourself and watch your words in the future?

_____

_____

_____

_____

Day 227 — Better Than The Lead Role And Applause

> *"Preach the word; be ready in season and out of season."*
>
> II Timothy 4:2

Throughout her education, including college, our daughter enjoyed participating in school and community theater. She loves attending shows on Broadway, in downtown Cleveland, and in surrounding communities; but she particularly enjoys being part of the cast! She has enjoyed portraying minor characters and playing supporting roles, and when she hasn't been able to commit to being on stage, she's offered to work back stage and on the sets. She enjoys all aspects of theatre.

Along the way she had the honor of playing lead roles that included vocal solos. She loved every minute of it: working with the cast, the director of the play, and the director of music; and she really loved having the lead part. She even loved the applause. But what she was most excited about was what happened at the cast party following a particular final show.

She was able to lead one cast member to salvation in Jesus as well as help answer some questions of a second cast member who had accepted Jesus a few days earlier from someone else working in the production! With a group of Christian kids from the cast, she then invited these new believers to several youth-oriented outreaches, eventually seeing both baptized within just weeks of their salvation.

Great plays, fun music, terrific sets, costumes, and even applause are all exciting, but there's nothing so exciting as leading someone to Christ and watching him or her grow!

Let's Pause for Prayer

Heavenly Father, thank You for using us wherever You plant us. May we shine for you in our line of work, in community service, and in leisure activities! Thank you for young people who take their Christianity seriously and are prepared to lead others to Christ. May we all be faithful to tell others about You and help establish new believers in their faith. In Jesus' name we pray. Amen.

Consider a time when you led someone to Christ. Share what it was like and how you felt about it.

_____
_____
_____
_____
_____

Take a bold step this week and share your faith with someone who may not have faith.

Day 228   *Who Is My Neighbor?*

> *"But wishing to justify himself, he said to Jesus, 'And who is my neighbor?'"*
>
> Luke 10:29

A certain lawyer in the Bible passage above wanted to test Jesus by having Him answer how He, Himself, would inherit eternal life. Jesus questioned him as to what was written in the law, and the lawyer answered Him correctly saying he needed to do what was written in the law, which is to "love the Lord your God with all your heart, soul, strength, and mind, and to love your neighbor as yourself." He further questioned Jesus asking, "And who is my neighbor?" As Jesus shared the story of the Good Samaritan, describing him as one who "felt compassion" and "one who showed mercy." He then told this lawyer to go and do the same (Luke 10:29–38).

The Good Samaritan showed mercy and felt compassion by stopping for the man who had been robbed and beaten nearly to death. He provided bandages and transportation to where he would then pay for this man to be cared for until he recovered. He picked up the entire tab. This man cared and put his compassion into practice.

How are we doing in that category? Are we caring for those whom God puts before us as the Samaritan cared for the man who was put before him? Or do we keep walking, thinking, "Someone else can do it," "someone else will do it" or "I just can't be bothered or inconvenienced like that—it will take up too much time"? We may not be called to meet every need placed before us, but we aren't supposed to ignore every need before us either.

Let's Pause for Prayer

Heavenly Father, thank You for the times You have clearly put in my life people who needed care and the lessons You have taught me through that care. We come before you now to ask whether You might be calling us to care for someone. Might you be asking us to care for a child, an ailing parent or relative, an orphan, or someone who has special needs? Or perhaps to take a meal to a neighbor in need or make a phone call to cheer someone up? Show us clearly what you would have us to do. In Jesus' name we pray. Amen.

Is God asking you to help someone?

_____

_____

What has God put on your heart?

_____

_____

_____

Day 229

Listen

> *"Create in me a clean heart, O God, and renew a steadfast spirit within me."*
>
> Psalm 51:10

Let's take a little detour. Each of us will take some time today and sit quietly before the Lord. Just listen. Ask the Lord to share something with you that you need to hear. Take as much time as it requires until you feel He has spoken to your heart. Think about and pause to pray through the verses below as you wait upon Him.

- **I Samuel 16:7**
  "But the Lord said to Samuel, 'Do not look at his appearance or at the height of his stature because I have rejected him; for God sees not as man sees, for man looks at the outward appearance, but the Lord looks at the heart.'"

- **Psalm 44:21**
  "Would not God find this out? For He knows the secrets of the heart." I know You see everything. I might think I can hide things from others, but I can't hide anything from You!

- **Hebrews 4:12**
  "For the Word of God is living and active and sharper than any two-edged sword and piercing as far as the division of soul and spirit, of both joints and marrow, and able to judge the thoughts and intentions of the heart." I know if I ask You, You will show me where I have sinned, where I have fallen short of Your glory. I ask You to show me even though it might be difficult for me to accept it.

- **Psalm 51:10**
  "Create in me a clean heart, O God, and renew a steadfast spirit within me." Lord, I am willing to hear from You and willing to make whatever changes You ask of Me.

Let's Pause for Prayer

Father, thank You for speaking to me today. Thank you for the quiet that allowed me to hear from You, and I'm thankful to have listened. Help me to do all that You've asked me to do. In Jesus' name I pray. Amen.

How did the Lord speak to you, and how long were you in a quiet state of listening?

_____
_____
_____
_____

Thank God for the way He's just worked in your life.

Day 230

Truth

> *"Do not let kindness and truth leave you; bind them around your neck."*
>
> Proverbs 3:3

A while ago, I accompanied a friend to court simply for support in prayer. As I waited in the lobby, I prayed, but I could hardly believe how quickly He answered my specific prayer.

I sensed the Lord nudging me to pray for truth. That was simple enough. My prayer went something like this, "Lord I pray for Your truth to be told throughout this proceeding. I pray that no one would be tempted to utter a lie, not even a half-truth. I pray that truth would prevail in this courthouse."

That was pretty much it. As I continued to pray, I heard a conversation in the lobby that totally took me by surprise.

Two men, apparently both lawyers, were walking into the lobby. The older lawyer asked the younger lawyer, "Have you read the papers I gave you, the ones I wanted you to go over?" The younger said this, "Yes, I'm reading them." Then there was a long pause. "Actually, I haven't even begun to read them, but I will begin to read them very soon."

I didn't look up, but I really wanted to! Right there in front of me, this man was confessing that he had not told the truth. Little did I know that my prayer for truth to prevail in the courthouse would be answered by the Lord in this way! Perhaps He did so that I might know He answered my prayer—very specifically! I couldn't help but wonder what else went on that day that I didn't hear!

Let's Pause for Prayer

Heavenly Father, thank You for answering specific prayers. Your swift response reminds me that You care about every detail we pray about. Help us to be mindful as we pray according to Your will and biblical truths. Let us pray carefully and cautiously, realizing that we might just get what we pray for. Thank You for teaching us through the way You answer prayer. In Jesus' name we pray. Amen.

As You come to the Lord in prayer today, ask Him to give you a word from which to pray. What word do you believe He put on your heart?

_____

_____

_____

Later, share the impact or lesson learned today regarding that word.

_____

_____

_____

Day 231 — Even Playing Field

> *"Let us therefore draw near with confidence to the throne of grace, that we may obtain mercy and find grace to help in time of need."*
>
> Hebrews 4:16

Preferential treatment often comes to those who have money, beauty, fame, power, and influence. But in the world of prayer, none of those factors matter. We can all come to God on an even playing field. As we approach the King of Kings, we are all equal.

The passage from Hebrews above says all we have to do is have need, and we can come to Him. Of course, everything about our very existence is such that we have need of Him. Our very breath belongs to Him. No matter how small the request or what time of day or night it is, we can come to Him and He welcomes us. Even so, we are told to come boldly and with confidence to the throne of grace.

It's easy to develop the habit of praying only when we have a significant need or crisis, but He loves us so much that His line is always open and He is always available. We should never neglect the wonderful privilege we have to pray nor the power that we have in prayer through Jesus.

Let's Pause for Prayer

Heavenly Father, we are so appreciative that we can come to You, the mighty and all-knowing God, and make our requests known to You. We can come to You with major issues and challenges in life, and yet we know that You are just as interested in the seemingly minor situations that occur in our lives as well. Help us to remember that You care about everything, Father. We desire to develop a habit of coming to You with whatever is on our heart, not weighing problems to decide whether they are worthy to be brought before You. We know all things are of interest to You. May we strive to grow closer to You through prayer and the reading of Your word and most importantly as we listen to Your answer. In Jesus' name we pray. Amen.

Do you come to God on a daily basis, or do you wait for a crisis in your life before you come to Him and pray to Him?

_____

_____

_____

What is on your heart (large or small) right now? Write it out and then pray.

_____

_____

_____

Day 232　　　　　　　　　　　　　　　　　　　　　　　*Playing Games*

"Doing wickedness is like sport to a fool."

Proverbs 10:23a

Two little boys sat in front of me in church one Sunday. They were about four and five years old. One was held by his father and looked to be falling asleep on his shoulder. The other little boy was standing next to the father, behaving very nicely. I'm pretty sure Dad thought the boy on his shoulder was asleep. But soon, he started tapping his brother on the head. He still looked as if he were sleeping. The "sleeping" brother must have tapped his brother on the head some five times when the brother who was standing became a bit irritated. The dad looked down at the son who was standing, probably wondering what he was fussing about. My daughter and I smiled at each other, wondering how this would play out and how the dad would handle it. The "sleeping" son seemed to get away with something: Dad had no idea the son wasn't really asleep, but we saw it all!

As I watched, I realized that some people, even those who call themselves Christians, play games like that. Maybe they think they can pull a fast one and no one will catch them. Maybe they think they can treat others in some particular way and not be held accountable for those actions. Perhaps when we realize that "they" could be us, we'd take our own actions more seriously and take responsibility for behaving the way God expects us to. We can hide nothing from Him. He sees every action we take, knows our every thought and even our deepest motives.

Let's Pause for Prayer

Heavenly Father, we thank You for the way You speak to our hearts. Please let us individually and immediately recognize whether we have a wrong motive, dwelling on a thought we shouldn't, or whether we're taking a wrong action so that we will make a right choice in the way we will handle each situation. Help me to honor You and favor others as I walk closely with You. Help us to obey You quickly so that we don't sin and regret our actions. In Jesus' name we pray. Amen.

Evaluate your own life and see whether you're playing games, making sport of misconduct. Write out what comes to mind.

_____
_____
_____

What will you do to change your ways and behave properly?

_____
_____
_____

Day 233   *Road To Hana*

"And your ears will hear a word behind you, 'This is the way, walk in it,' whenever you turn to the right or to the left."

Isaiah 30:21

The Road to Hana is considered one of the Top 10 beautiful drives in the United States. The 52 miles of road twists and turns, crosses over 66 one-lane bridges along the lush and scenic landscape of Maui, Hawaii, and takes about two and a half hours to travel from one end to the other. Visitors can stop to rest while viewing beautiful waterfalls, cascades, and bamboo jungles. Actually, people want to stop to see the view along the way because the curvy roads tend to make even the best of passengers experience motion sickness!

The road can be driven by tourists, but the unexpected twists and turns and proper etiquette in driving over the one-lane bridges (all 66 of them) can make the drive quite tricky. The local drivers know this road so well that they often recommend that visitors have a driver who knows the road take them for the ride. And we were glad we did. They knew where all the favorite stops were, when to pause and when to go over each of the bridges, when to honk the horn in areas with poor visibility around a bend, and how to make it safely from one end to the other. In addition, having a driver takes the pressure off passengers and other drivers.

On our drive through life with Jesus, we can offer Him the driver's seat and allow Him to take us through all the twists and turns of life; or we can take over the wheel, thinking we know best. He will guide us on the road He knows so well. We just need to relinquish the driver's seat willingly.

Let's Pause for Prayer

Heavenly Father, we are so thankful that You have a plan for us and that we can rest in knowing You'll guide us through all the twists and turns of life if we simply allow You to have control. Help us not take over and decide we can do a better job at the steering wheel than You. As You guide and direct us, help us to enjoy the ride You have planned. In Jesus' name we pray. Amen.

Have you given control of your life to the Lord? Have you noticed times you've taken the control back?

_____

_____

_____

How can you be more proactive about letting Him have the driver's seat of your life?

_____

_____

_____

Day 234

Look Around

> *"Watch over your heart with all diligence, for from it flow the springs of life."*
>
> Proverbs 4:23

My exercise of choice is walking, especially outdoors, where I can enjoy the fresh air. I have noticed somewhat recently that I intentionally look for specific sights while completely ignoring others.

When walking outside, do you tend to keep your eyes focused on the ground and what is near to you, or do you tend to look all around you? These questions have no right or wrong answer, but as I thought this through, I developed a new perspective on my own personality as well as the personality and needs of the church. If I am looking just around my feet or at what is near me, I am able to see what is happening close to me, being careful to detect what might trip me up; but if I don't look up now and then, I'm missing all the beautiful sights in the distance, and I don't see all that is around me. Likewise, if I'm looking only around me, I can't see what is close to me that might need attention.

We as individuals as well as our individual churches can face the same choice. When we don't look outward and get a better vision of all that is around us, we miss the big picture. When we don't check out what is close to us, we might miss very important situations, which need care.

Let's Pause for Prayer

Heavenly Father, we are grateful that our walks with You can be ever-growing and vibrant as we look carefully at what is near to us and affects our lives. Help us, however, also to be mindful of the broader view that You have for us individually and corporately as a church. Help us to notice others and help one another to accomplish all You would have us do for Your glory! We need you, and we need one another to complete the work You have for us. May we walk closely with you each step of the way as we look out and about. In Jesus' name we pray. Amen.

Do you tend to be one who enjoys the closer view or the broader view?

_____

_____

_____

How does your answer affect your individual life and the part you play in your church family?

_____

_____

_____

_____

Day 235

Like Lights Shining

> *"Among whom you appear as lights in the world"*
> Philippians 2:15

Certain natural features distinguish the various seasons: the strikingly beautiful colors on the leaves of the trees in autumn, the red berry against a new-fallen snow, or a bright daffodil popping up in spring before other flowers have bloomed.

How about us as individuals? Do we distinguish ourselves? I'm not talking about being famous or even being recognized in our community or church. Are we noticed wherever God puts us?

Recently at a dinner with five other women, we shared openly, unconcerned about what was going on around us. As our small group shared around the table in our tiny private room, our waitress saw us caring for one another, laughing, sharing joy, and caring about sadness in each other's lives. She asked us whether we were celebrating a particular occasion. We said, "Yes, friendship. We're here to catch up and find out how we can support and pray for one another." As she came and went from our intimate setting, she shared some aspects of her own life. Each one of us shared with her a point that was unique and different, meeting her specific need. What fun to watch how each one emerged uniquely in a setting that was strikingly beautiful, including the time of prayer we had with her in our group.

Let's Pause for Prayer

Heavenly Father, thank You for the ways you set situations before us to make You known. May we bloom where we are planted, leaving a fresh fragrance of love and always noticed, not for who we are but for who You are in us. In Jesus' name we pray. Amen.

When was the last time you gathered with friends to care about one another?
_____
_____
_____

When was the last time you gathered someone to you to care about him or her?
_____
_____
_____

Pray for those people you just noted, and make it a point to call them or send them notes.

Day 236 — *Purpose*

> *"And we know that God causes all things to work together for good to those who Love God, to those who are called according to His purpose."*
>
> Romans 8:28

Driving my son home from work on the highway every day gives me many opportunities for prayer. It also gives me ideas for my Pause for Prayer broadcasts and this devotional!

One particular day, I noticed a nice car behind me in my rear-view mirror. I liked the color and the style, but I couldn't tell the make of the car. It looked expensive and classy. As the driver approached to pass me, I got ready to look to see what kind of car it was.

To my surprise, as the car passed to my left, I saw that the passenger's side of the car I had been admiring was crumpled and rusty. It had obviously been in an accident and never repaired. The passenger door had no window, and the rust was taking over an otherwise beautiful car. Sure, the car still ran, but could it be used on cold and rainy days or only in optimum weather conditions?

Our lives can resemble that car if we don't take the time to repair what needs to be repaired. When we don't get the emotional help we need when we've been wounded, injured, or abused or the physical help we need when it isn't available, we can fall into disrepair and not be as useful as we could be if we were repaired and healthy. Certainly, we can still be used, but is it only during optimum conditions?

Let's Pause for Prayer

Lord, please allow us to get the help we need when we need it so that we can be useful to You at all times. Help us to be ready to tell others about You at all times. Help us to get healthy and repaired, not so we look good on the outside but so that we are healthy and able to function at our fullest potential at all times. In Jesus' name we pray. Amen.

Do you feel you are healthy and ready to be put into action, or do you feel you are in a state of disrepair?

_____
_____
_____

What will it take for you to be ready to do what is expected of you?

_____
_____
_____

Day 237 — God's Economy

"He who offers a sacrifice of thanksgiving honors Me; and to him who orders his way aright I shall show the salvation of God."

Psalm 50:23

A banker friend of ours in another state reviewed the many foreclosures before him and his team and discussed their plans to handle each one. Business was bad for the bank because of the foreclosures, which resulted from a change in the housing market; and bankers themselves faced financial difficulties.

As they reviewed one specific case, a man on the team reviewing this particular foreclosure said, "This woman is in the midst of some very devastating events. She didn't mismanage her finances or choose not to pay her bills. Life has hit her too many times, and she can't get up and fight. She hasn't asked us to, but I think we need to fight for her. That's what we as Christians are to do for others." The team agreed with him and lowered her interest rates several percentage points. She was thrilled; however, the next day, events took yet another turn. Light was shed on a particular loan situation, and this team was able to drop her loan rate to 1%. When she was told of this new development, she wanted to decline the additional help because she was already so thankful and moved by what they had done for her. She eventually accepted their offer and came to learn that this team of Christian businesspeople were fighting for her to keep her home. She was touched. This Jewish woman, through various other circumstances, was invited to a Christian church and within just weeks came to know Jesus as her Savior.

Let's Pause for Prayer

Precious Father, we could draw many conclusions from this true story. We, the bankers, and this new believer can see that You are One who provides. You are One who desires to make a way when there seems to be no way. You are One who saves and One who cares about each person individually. Help us to be thankful for the way You have provided for each of us. Thank you for all You have done and do for us! In Jesus' name we pray. Amen.

Have you ever been part of a story about "God's Economy"? Share it.

_____

_____

_____

Can you pray for someone who needs to sense the provision of God in an exciting way right now? Write out your prayer for him or her.

_____

_____

_____

Day 238

What We Can't See

"Let your light shine before men in such a way that they may see your good works, and glorify your Father who is in heaven."

Matthew 5:16

As a nontechnical person, I wonder how accurate some measuring instruments actually are. Wires taped onto one's chest measure heart activity, sending results to a little box resting around the person's waist, resembling the obsolete transistor radio. Results are received at an offsite EKG machine; other wires taped to a person's head measure brain activity with an EEG. Eyes are examined by machines that print out colorful and detailed results, telling physicians and technicians details that most of us cannot comprehend. I look at these means of measurement and results and wonder whether they could possibly be real, yet these fascinating ways of testing and measuring, when analyzed by someone who is educated and proficient in using these machines, can discern some very interesting and important details: properly beating hearts, irregularities in the brain like seizure activity, and the likelihood that surgery can be performed successfully on our eyes.

Let's Pause for Prayer

Dear Lord, we thank You for the way you have created us. Thank you for the ways others are able to see what we cannot see. Thank You for giving some people the desire, skills, and intelligence to learn and understand technology, and we thank You for allowing us to be the beneficiaries. We appreciate that others can use their gifts and talents for the good of helping humanity. May they continue to do these good works so that others benefit and you are glorified as strides in technology are made and as others are helped. In Jesus' name we pray. Amen.

Have you been the recipient of good care from a technological standpoint? Explain.

_____

_____

_____

Pray for someone currently under medical care, whose illness might not have been discovered without the use of modern technology.

_____

_____

_____

_____

Day 239

Be Careful, Little Eyes, What You See

> *"Thy word I have treasured in my heart, that I may not sin against Thee."*
>
> Psalm 119:11

As I settled on a plane, the monitors displayed a TV sitcom we never watch at home. The passengers had no choice as to whether we wanted to listen to it or watch it, yet it was right there for all to see. We don't watch this sitcom at home because we don't care for its content or the story line, nor are we particularly fond of the actors. And it's not just airlines that display shows for all to see: Doctors' offices, health clubs, checks-out lines at some stores, and list goes on, do the same.

At home I can simply change the channel, but in a public environment I am forced to listen to programming I had no option to change. An entire episode was shown while passengers were settling into their seats. To my dismay, the same show was played for a second time in flight. Thankfully, I always have plenty of my own writing and reading to do; I don't have to put earphones on if I don't want to, and I don't have to look at the screen. What about families with young children? Even if they aren't wearing earphones, I would not encourage the exposure of young ones to certain messages onscreen. With as many recorded programs as are available, I can hardly believe that airlines choose the ones they do.

Let's Pause for Prayer

Heavenly Father, we ask you to help us live out Your word according to Psalm 119: 11: "Thy word I have treasured in my heart, that I may not sin against Thee." Help us to concentrate on what we know to be right and to dismiss what we know to be wrong. Help us to turn away from programming, photos, and other media not pleasing to you, whether it's the plot, the costumes, or the words. Allow us to take a stand for truth, honor, purity, and excellence at all times for Your glory! In Jesus' name we pray. Amen.

Have you ever felt forced to watch or listen to programming of which you didn't approve or that you didn't appreciate because of the content? How did you handle it?

_____

_____

_____

Consider that scenario and write out a prayer.

_____

_____

_____

_____

Day 240 — Unity, Liberty, Charity

"And God is able to make all grace abound to you, that always having all sufficiency in everything, you may have an abundance for every good deed."

II Corinthians 9:8

"In essential, unity; in nonessentials, liberty; in all things, charity." Augustine of Hippo

Perhaps you've heard the saying above. As believers we should indeed strive for unity when it comes to basic Christian doctrine, standing firm in God's word and truth, not straying from it. From denomination to denomination and from church to church, however, some issues may not be critically and essentially important. When we overemphasize those issues, they divide us. In those nonessential issues, instead of letting them divide us, we should let liberty flourish. *Liberty* is defined as "freedom, an action surpassing the normal limits." Liberty can flourish when we allow others the freedom to believe in those nonessentials as we extend grace.

When we extend that kind of grace, we can help others realize that we are all at different places in our maturity and growth process of knowing and serving the Lord. We are not talking about sin, but differences of opinion, direction, or expression of where we are in the Lord. I'd sum it up as issues about which making a big deal is unnecessary. As I extend grace to others who see life in ways different from the way I do, I would hope they would also extend grace in my direction.

And in all matters we are to have charity, good will toward others, an act of generosity. If sin is present, we must call it sin and deal with it appropriately. If forgiveness is needed, then we seek it and grant it. If a need is apparent, we provide. We always need to look to the best in the other person. Doing so is both simple and complex.

Let's Pause for Prayer

Heavenly Father, guide us as we study Your word so that we may know clearly what You are teaching and expect from us. Help us to know how and when to show others grace when we think differently on nonessential issues. Help us to strive for unity as we all ultimately desire to honor and serve You. Help all who call themselves Christians be more desirous of unity than of focusing on the inconsequential. May we filled with grace in all of our responses. In Jesus' name we pray. Amen.

Have you ever faced a challenge in extending grace to others who think or believe in ways different from your beliefs? How did you handle it? (Write out a prayer.)

Day 241 *Applause*

> *"A man has joy in an apt answer, and how delightful is a timely word!"*
> Proverbs 15:23

Encouragement—we all need it. We all should give it to others, right? But do we?

I used to watch the end of a cooking program as I prepared my own family dinner. I enjoyed trying new ideas on family and friends from time to time; however, an ingredient is missing from my kitchen as I cook: the applause from the audience. There's no applause as I shake just the right amount of seasoning from the container. The oohs and ahs for mixing everything together are missing.

Let's be real: Most of us wouldn't want that kind of attention in our household kitchen, but on TV, those waves of encouragement (likely cued by a stagehand holding a sign) spur the host to perform with excellence. In real life, we need those oohs and ahs, pats on the back, notes of thanks and appreciation, and words of affirmation to encourage us along life's way.

Let's Pause for Prayer

Lord, may we encourage others as you have encouraged us through Your word. Proverbs 15:23 says, "A man has joy in an apt answer, and how delightful is a timely word!" Proverbs 16:24 states, "Pleasant words are a honeycomb, sweet to the soul and healing to the bones." Help us to encourage others in that way. May we encourage those who live daily with excellence in all that You've given them to do. In Jesus' name we pray. Amen.

Share a time when you were encouraged by someone and how it felt to you.

_____

_____

_____

Whom have you encouraged lately? Make a call, send a note, or pat someone on the back to encourage them today and then share what you did here.

_____

_____

_____

_____

Day 242

Competition Or Cooperation?

"And you shall love the Lord your God with all your heart, and with all your soul, and with all your mind, and with all your strength. The second is this, 'You shall love your neighbor as yourself.' There is no other commandment greater than these."

Mark 12:31

In the spirit of competition and good sportsmanship, all types of contests can be fun to watch. We can also participate and learn many lessons. We can play and work hard and learn to be humble winners or recognize and realize when we are out of our league and learn to lose graciously. Competition isn't just for team settings but for individual contests as well. Both offer opportunities for learning.

One group should be free of competition, but seldom is: Christians who are working for the Lord. Their work may have started out as a team effort but somewhere along the way, competition for attention and the spotlight became the focus instead of giving the glory to God or competition for the seat of honor became the prize instead of willingness to work "as unto the Lord." Disunity and lack of cooperation are sinful and manipulative and dishonor God.

Let's Pause for Prayer

Lord, we pray that You would put into our hearts the spirit of unity so that unity would rule our individual lives, our homes, our churches, our places of work, and our communities. May we follow what is instructed in Mark 12:31: "And you shall love the Lord your God with all your heart, and with all your soul, and with all your mind, and with all your strength. The second is this, 'You shall love your neighbor as yourself. There is no other commandment greater that these.'" May we take seriously and apply Philippians 2:3–4: "Do nothing from selfishness or empty conceit, but with humility of mind let each of you regard one another as more important than himself; do not merely look out for your own personal interests, but also for the interests of others." In Jesus' name we pray. Amen.

Have you ever felt competition from someone in a group? How did you handle it?

_____

_____

_____

Have you ever desired and sought attention and accolades above others in a group? How might you have handled the situation differently?

_____

_____

_____

Day 243

Our Name In A Book?

"He who overcomes shall thus be clothed in white garments; and I will not erase his name from the book of life, and I will confess his name before My Father, and before His angels."

Revelation 3:5

Our family had a wonderful vacation, which included visits to Gettysburg, Philadelphia, and Boston. Because of his love of history, Joe particularly appreciated what we learned. I studied American history in school but never took the kind of interest in it that I now wish I had.

While touring cemeteries and learning about leaders, what was said about them was interesting. Many positive details were given, but some leaders were called crooks; others, womanizers, not faithful to their cause, or money makers. Wouldn't it be interesting to hear what they would say in response to those descriptions?

What might others say of us hundreds of years from now if we made a mark on history? I doubt I'll ever make it to a history book, but I know my name is written in the Book of Life as a child of God. It's not so important to me what mere human say of me, but it's very important what God would say of me. Every life has the capability of making an impact. What will ours be?

Let's Pause for Prayer

Father, as we consider our nation's founders and the impact they have had on our country, we thank You for them, and for those who serve our country politically around the world. We recognize the great sacrifice and contribution to our country, and we realize our need to serve You and make an impact on our own little sphere of influence in ways that would bring honor and glory to You. We pray that You find us faithful to You, honest to all, true to our convictions, and walking closely with You so that others recognize the integrity of our walk with You. In Jesus' name we pray. Amen.

It's difficult to comprehend our names being written in God's book of life, yet it's not difficult for it to happen. We must simply confess Jesus as Lord and Savior. Have you done that? Have you asked Him into your life and heart? Share your story.

_____

_____

_____

_____

If you've never considered what you just read, perhaps you'd like to make that commitment today. Pray and ask the Lord to forgive you of your sins, and put your trust in Him.

Day 244

Getting Connected

> *"Thus says the Lord who made the earth, the Lord who formed it to establish it, the Lord is His name, 'Call to Me, and I will answer you, and I will tell you great and mighty things, which you do not know.'"*
>
> Jeremiah 33:3

When cell phones and texting became important to staying connected to others, I held off for as long as I could for two reasons. One, and the most important, is that I wanted to hear the voice of my callers and have conversations with them; two, I didn't want to learn to text. But in order to connect with others and stay relevant, I needed to take the plunge.

In the process of looking information up on my phone, I stumbled upon the feature that showed me how much time I'd spent on calls and how many calls had been made and received. I'd had the phone for a few years, so it was never been cleared or erased. Even so, I was shocked at the numbers: 11,661 calls, 585:41:59 hours chatting in conversation!

I wondered what kind of numbers would show up if God allowed me to see how much time I'd spent with Him in prayer, how many times I called upon Him and He responded, and how much actual chatting time we had together.

Let's Pause for Prayer

Lord, it's such a privilege to come to You and connect at any time. Thank You for all the times You've allowed me to tell You my problems, dump a bag of discouragement at Your feet when verbalizing my frustrations, or cry to You in desperation. And I'm appreciative of the times You've answered those prayers and the prayers of everyday life that are sent up quickly throughout the day. Thank you that you are always available whenever I come to you. May we all never fail to take time to pray to You in Jesus' name. Amen.

Would you describe your prayer life as connected to God? How might you make the transition to growing closer to Him in prayer? (Write out a prayer.)

_____
_____
_____
_____
_____

Day 245

Men: Lead

> *"Likewise urge the young men to be sensible; in all things show yourself to be an example of good deeds, with purity in doctrine, dignified, sound in speech which is beyond reproach, in order that the opponent may be put to shame, having nothing bad to say about us."*
>
> Titus 2:6-8

In spiritual circles we talk about the spiritual battles we encounter. We talk about sensing the attacks of the enemy—Satan—and how we counter those attacks. Sometimes we see the attacks coming, but sometimes we are caught completely off guard.

All who know the Lord are targets for the enemy, but perhaps the biggest target is men. Men are to be the heads of their homes, the loving Christlike example to their children, servant leaders to wives and leaders in the community, at work, and in ministry. If Satan can get a man off balance, he has a good chance to sabotage his example in the community, at work, and in ministry and tear apart his marriage and family relationships. If a way exists to help men stay on target and learn how to oppose the enemy, would they want to find that way?

Let's Pause for Prayer

Heavenly Father, we pray for all men to desire to be the godly men in their homes and to their families, in their community, at church, and at work. We pray that they would not be distracted from their life purposes and goals. We pray they would keep away from the technology that lures them to the wrong places and choices, and that busyness, information overload, and mistrust would not overtake their thinking. In Jesus' name we pray. Amen.

Whatever men come to mind, pray for men as you write out a prayer for them to be godly examples and leaders. Consider praying for them daily for the next week or so.

Day 246

Without Distraction

> *"But one thing I do: Forgetting what lies behind and reaching forward to what lies ahead, I press on toward the goal for the prize of the upward call of God in Christ Jesus."*
>
> Philippians 3:13–14

Sitting outside less than 12 inches from a flowering bush, I could see and hear the loud buzzing of about 75 bees. I don't normally feel safe around bees, but in this case I did. They were so busy they had no interest in stinging me. I doubt they even knew I was there. They were very intentional about the work they were doing. I watched them for quite some time, and they never seemed to tire or grow weary or frustrated at the work they were doing.

They were doing the same thing over and over again, making me think their work was simple but important to the overall scheme of what they were trying to accomplish and without interruption. As I watered some plants on my deck, some of the spray was taken by the wind in their direction and they continued to work in the same way. They didn't stop even when they were interrupted.

Let's Pause for Prayer

Heavenly Father, we thank You for teaching us through all of Your creation. Help us to know the work that You have given us to do, and may we do it diligently. Help us not to become distracted by people who want to discourage us or by all that this life offers to take us from the purpose you have for us, especially when we tire of doing the same things over and over. May we accomplish for your glory, simple and intentional acts of service that keep us focused on You and You alone. May our lives of service to You be continuous and without interruption. Thank you for the privilege of the work you have called us to do. May we faithfully complete it for Your glory. In Jesus' name we pray. Amen.

Do you feel that you are working for a single purpose and doing so without distraction? Ask the Lord for purpose and direction in a written prayer of request.

Day 247 — Staying Till The End

> *"But if we hope for what we do not see, with perseverance we wait eagerly for it."*
> Romans 8:25

Long, drawn out baseball games with little action often have a twist to them if we are patient enough to make it to the seventh inning. If we stick around, we might learn that a no-hitter is due to take place. A no hitter(when the pitcher pitches nine innings without allowing any hits by the other team) gets pretty exciting. A perfect no-hitter occurs when the pitcher allows no hits and has had no walks. Such a game gets really exciting. Unfortunately, only the faithful few who stay are privileged to see the results of that special game.

Such is the game of life. Sometimes we tire of what seems to be a boring life that isn't going our way, and we quit working toward what God has called us to. We don't think God came through with His part of the deal, so we decide to finish outside His will. For those who stay in the game, life becomes increasingly exciting, and we wouldn't want to miss it. How will we finish? Will we leave the game because it seems uninteresting, uneventful, and even boring? Or will we stick it out and be a part of the wonderful and exciting finish?

Let's Pause for Prayer

Lord, we praise You for the ways You teach us through different situations in life. May we be faithful and stay in the game of life and work diligently toward the end goal You have for us. Thank You for the ways You encourage us in our walk even it does not go the way we think it should or the way we want it to. Help us to see that You have an individual plan for each one of us that is exciting, wonderful, and worthwhile. May we not quit early, but work faithfully in the game of life toward the goals You have for us. In Jesus' name we pray. Amen.

Share a time when you wanted to quit walking with the Lord and go your own way. What did you (or will you) do to get back on the right path?

_____
_____
_____
_____
_____
_____

Day 248

Sowing

"Do not be deceived, God is not mocked; for whatever a man sows, this he will also reap. And let us not lose heart in doing good, for in due time we shall reap if we do not grow weary."

Galatians 6:7, 9

We've likely all felt we've been taken advantage of or used in some way. We hear from someone who seldom calls—who doesn't take time to stay in touch with us—now needing our help or a favor. We recognize the one who has taken unfair advantage of us, leaving us feeling hurt or angry. Another with whom we work closely in ministry has taken our position or tried to benefit or gain for themselves from the efforts we have put forth. What do we do with situations like these? There's only one right thing to do. Galatians 6:7, 9 says, "Do not be deceived, God is not mocked; for whatever a man sows, this he will also reap. And let us not lose heart in doing good, for in due time we shall reap if we do not grow weary."

We don't have to judge others, scheme a way to make a plan work out the way we think it should, or be unkind to others for any reason. If their intentions are for ill, God will take care of them and their actions. We need only to be concerned with our own hearts, motives, and responses. When we do what we are supposed to do, in due time we, too, will reap what we have sown.

Let's Pause for Prayer

Dear Lord, we can be easily disappointed, hurt, and even angry; but we ask You to make our motives sincere and honest toward others. Please help us in our friendships at work and in ministry. We want to be there for others even if we feel we have been taken advantage of or wronged in some way. You can work out the details as we walk closely with You in honor and integrity. Guide us to the right ways to respond to people who take advantage of us, oppose us, or want what we have even if it's when we're in the process of doing Your work. Allow us to have an open hand and heart of willingness to serve others no matter the cost. May we honor you in all we do. In Jesus' name we pray. Amen.

Have you ever felt taken advantage of? Share the situation and how you dealt with it.

_____

_____

_____

Did you deal with it in the best way possible? Share the outcome and how you learned from it.

_____

_____

_____

Day 249 — *Clearer Focus*

> *"The Lord will accomplish what concerns me."*
> Psalm 138:8

After our first daughter married, I purposed to find something to do with my time to replace what had kept me busy with all the wedding preparations. Without any previous training or study, I chose to sign up for a watercolor class.

My patient instructor helped me to understand how the mixing of colors brings about the perception of nearness and distance, and by using certain colors in just the right place and in just the right way other colors emerge and become focal points. But what has been the most fascinating is learning about impressionist art. Close up, each tiny marking of paint the artist makes looks messy and of little value until one stops to see the painting from a bit of a distance. All of a sudden, things come into focus, and one begins to see the whole picture.

Life, too, can be unclear, sometimes even frustrating or confusing us; but when we step back, focus, and evaluate, we see the larger picture and perhaps even understand the reason that God has allowed some imperfections and difficulties to come into our lives.

Let's Pause for Prayer

Heavenly Father, Your Word reminds us that You are in control of our lives. Psalm 138:8 says, "The Lord will accomplish what concerns me." Thank You for the plan and purpose You have for each of us. Thank You for making life clearer to us day by day even when we can't see it. Thank You for the ways You put us in the distance until we are needed in the foreground, for the ways you blend the colors in our lives so that life is neither dull nor brilliant all of the time. We will wait to see the larger picture as You are willing to reveal it to us, and may we serve diligently in that process. In Jesus' name we pray. Amen.

Consider a time when you felt that your life's plan was not clear but instead muddied or dull. As you were able to see the situation more clearly, how did you respond? How did you respond to God?

_____

_____

_____

_____

_____

_____

Day 250

Future

> *"Trust in the Lord with all your heart, and do not lean on your own understanding. In all your ways acknowledge Him and He will make your paths straight."*
>
> Proverbs 3:5–6

The drive to Provincetown, the very tip of Cape Cod, didn't seem like a long drive; but once on that journey and on the one road in that direction, it proved to be a longer ride than we had anticipated. It might have seemed somewhat deceptive as we kept driving, thinking we should be there already; but because we hadn't specifically calculated how long the drive would be and because we didn't have an agenda, it didn't matter when we got there or how long it took. We had a goal and started in that direction.

I'd love to approach life that way daily. Wake up, have a goal, get moving, but get there in the time frame God has in mind, allowing Him to direct the twists and turns on the road of life in a calm but precise and direct way. As each of us considers the goal or goals that we might have ahead of us, let's purpose to set out in that direction as the Lord leads.

Let's Pause for Prayer

Heavenly Father, we pray that You would guide, direct, and even redirect us as You see fit this year. We may sense things You'd like us to do and goals You'd like us to accomplish for Your glory, but please help us to be good listeners and receptive to Your leading. At the end of the day and at the end of this year, we'd like to look back with assurance and confidence that we did only what You asked and that our journey was the one you wanted us to take. In Jesus' name we pray. Amen.

Do you feel as if you have a direct and focused approach each day? Or do you get moving and let God control the day?

_____

_____

_____

How might you give the control of your days to the Lord? Give specific courses of action.

_____

_____

_____

_____

Day 251 — Our Adequacy

> *"Not that we are adequate in ourselves to consider anything as coming from ourselves, but our adequacy is from God."*
>
> II Corinthians 3:5

If we've ever met someone we thought was powerful, influential, and very significant, we might have felt a sense of worthlessness or insignificance in those situations. It might have been our own thinking or perhaps the person indeed intended to make us feel that way, but Psalm 62:9 tells us about this type of person: "Men of low degree are only vanity, and men of rank are a lie; in the balances they go up; they are together lighter than breath." I guess we could say they are as light as air. When we feel insignificant, it's our own lack of knowing who we are in Christ that causes us to feel that way. II Corinthians 3:5 says, "Not that we are adequate in ourselves to consider anything as coming from ourselves, but our adequacy is from God."

Let's Pause for Prayer

Heavenly Father, we know that our adequacy comes from You. When we feel insignificant or when we have failed, we want to remember to thank You for helping us use our failure and feelings of worthlessness to claim Your word, which is powerful, and not seek man, who is not. We want to recognize that we are worthy to be called Your children if we have trusted in You. When we feel small and insignificant, help us to realize that each of us plays an important role in Your will and are a piece of the larger puzzle, needing to be obedient to know just what piece that is. Thank You for allowing us to come to You, the Holy One, humbly yet with confidence and pray to You, asking You to speak to our hearts. We want You to guide us, and we want to follow in obedience. In Jesus' name we pray. Amen.

Share a time when you felt inadequate. How did you work through that feeling of inadequacy?

_____
_____
_____

Write a prayer to the Lord asking for His guidance and strength.

_____
_____
_____
_____
_____

Day 252 — Lessons Learned And Prayers Answered

"By awesome deeds Thou dost answer us in righteousness, O God of our salvation."

Psalm 65:5

In C. S. Lewis' Prince Caspian Narnia story, the lion, Aslan is a Christ figure; his narrative is analogous to the story of Jesus. He wants to teach a lesson and says to Lucy, "Why didn't you come to me for help?"

Lucy responds, "I'm sorry, why didn't you come in to save us like last time?"

Aslan replied, "Things never happen the same way twice."

Perhaps you have learned as I have that no matter how many times a new lesson pops up (or an old one resurfaces) for me to learn, I'm taken by surprise that the Lord didn't meet me with an answer similar to one He gave me in the past. In fact, I've noticed from observing newer believers that He often seems to answer their big prayers fast, but those who have known and walked with Him for a longer period of time may pray and wait a long time for an answer to come to what may seem to be a smaller prayer request. Why is that? Perhaps He takes pleasure in answering quickly for a newer believer because He wants that believer to learn to rely on Him. As we learn that He hears and answers and that we know we can trust Him, perhaps He waits a bit longer the next time or answers differently the next time so that we can learn how to be patient.

Let's Pause for Prayer

Heavenly Father, you ask me to wait so that I can learn to rely upon You or to teach me to be patient. Do You know me so well that You are answering just as is necessary for me? I love the way Your word gives me a little glimpse into Your heart: Ps. 138:8, "The Lord will accomplish what concerns me, Thy lovingkindness, O Lord, is everlasting." Thank you, Lord! What You do concerns just me, and whatever You do emanates from Your lovingkindness and concern for me and my life and what You want me to learn. Help me to ask You for help and to be ready to receive it. Help me not to expect a certain answer in a certain way but to learn to be patient in waiting and watching for You to work out details that are especially and specifically for me. Please keep me focused on You as You give me new lessons, and as you occasionally show me that I may still need work on what You've shown me before. Thank You for Your patience with me. In Jesus' name I pray. Amen.

Consider how God answered you in your prayer life as a new believer. Describe. Share the way God's answers might be different now in your life.

_____
_____
_____
_____

Day 253

Taking Time

> *"With the Lord, one day is as a thousand years and a thousand years as a day."*
>
> II Peter 3:8

If you've had a loved one in the hospital even for a week or two, you know that it can seem so much longer. Time might seem to pass very slowly just because we are in a situation that is so very challenging and demanding. When there's a load of work in front of us that we know will take weeks to accomplish but needs to be done in two days, we can sense the stress pressing in on us; and it can be frustrating. But then we have those times when we have a long day to spend with a special friend or loved one, and maybe it's not just a long day, but many days; yet the time goes by so quickly and seems too short.

When I am doing what I love, time goes by quickly. When I am in a situation that is stressful, challenging, or frustrating, time seems to stand still. Those times make me remember that God and I don't have the same time table. Those challenging days that linger in my life may only be a quick blink of an eye in God's view of time. His time is not as ours.

Let's Pause for Prayer

Heavenly Father, Your ways are not our ways and Your time is different from our time. Psalm 18:30 also tells us, "As for God, His way is blameless; the word of the Lord is tried; He is a shield to all who take refuge in Him." We know that Your timing in our lives and Your way in our lives is perfect because You care so much about each one of us. We know that You make no mistakes in what You have planned for us, yet we question You. We ask You, Lord, to help us patiently wait for Your guidance in our lives when we are tempted to hurry things along or slow them down by thinking we can manipulate them. In addition, we don't want to rush through life without learning what You'd have us learn. Let us be mindful and wait, watch, trust, surrender, and rejoice in whatever You give us. In Jesus' name we pray. Amen.

Has time ever gone by quickly yet another time just dragged? If so, how did you handle the situation?

_____
_____
_____
_____
_____
_____

Day 254

The Church Country Club

> *"Let us consider how to stimulate one another to love and good deeds, not forsaking our own assembling together, as is the habit of some, but encouraging one another."*
>
> Hebrews 10:24–25

I've heard it said that the church begins to look like a country club when people huddle in their comfortable groups of friends, act and dress in ways different from their daily habit, and try to impress one another with how well they're doing, when in reality they all have the same issues and challenges as anyone else. I guess we need to ask ourselves, then, why do we need to go to church, why do we actually go, and what do we want to get out of church?

I've heard people express how unhappy they are at how casually people dress for church. They don't like the drums. The music is too loud. It's more like a rock concert than a worship service. Perhaps what we need to realize is that it's not about how the church should make us happy but about choosing the right attitude to worship God and derive some benefits from the message.

Let's Pause for Prayer

Heavenly Father, we sometimes, if not often, fail to see You in the midst of the reasons that we need to go to church and sometimes miss the point of our time there. We desire to put aside the personal issues that keep us from focusing on You, that keep us from getting the most out of what we should gain from going to church. As we spend time in worship, we pray that we would concentrate less on aspects that we don't like or wish would change to our liking and more on who You are and what You mean to us. Help us to focus on the teaching that might be for us and not point a finger at someone who we think needs to hear it. Show us the importance of our heart surrendering to You as we gather with other believers to worship in unity; and keep us from judging or criticizing how we think things should be done differently. Let us worship in spirit and truth as we read the word, sing, worship and learn. In Jesus' name we pray. Amen.

What are your thoughts and feeling about attending church?

_____

_____

_____

Do you feel at all as if you need to improve upon the way you include others and reach out to others in some way?

_____

_____

_____

Day 255 — *Problem Or The Solution?*

"An evil man is ensnared by the transgression of his lips but the righteous will escape from trouble."

Proverbs 12:13

Are we part of the solution or part of the problem? As Christians, we should speak up when a problem arises; but how we do so is of great importance. Do we first ask ourselves whether or not we are the troublemaker or peacemaker? We certainly think about that when someone else speaks up, but do we so easily direct that question to ourselves?

When confronted with situations where we have an opportunity to speak up, we must be sure our intentions are pure and our words are true. We must be prepared to speak the truth even if others do not.

Let's Pause for Prayer

Lord, as we approach a situation where we feel the need to speak up and voice our thoughts and opinions, we desire to be peacemakers, claiming your word and living it out as an example to those we meet. As we read your word, please let it penetrate our minds and hearts that we might reflect You as we meet with others. Lord, help us not to sin with our lips and to present only truth as we speak with others when we need to clarify situations and opinions. Let us use what we have learned from Your word to express ourselves. Proverbs 15:7 says, "The lips of the wise spread knowledge, but the hearts of fools are not so." Father, we choose to be men and women of wisdom and not talk or act foolishly so that we properly represent You. We don't want to look good or speak well to justify or please ourselves but to honor and please You. Fill us with Your Spirit and keep us focused always and only on You as our source of help to be a peacemaker for Your ultimate purposes. May truth always win. In Jesus' name we pray. Amen.

Share a situation in which you could have been part of the problem but acted in such a way that you became part of the solution instead.

_____

_____

_____

Write out a prayer and pray for truth in our hearts, in the church, and in daily interactions with others in various circumstances.

_____

_____

_____

_____

Day 256 — Sin Is Sin

"David behaved himself more wisely than all the servants of Saul. So his name was highly esteemed."

I Samuel 18:30

Appearance and reality often differ. If we seek to understand the truth and what is right, we desire to choose what is right, not what is sin, by formulating our thinking and outcome, ultimately desiring to do what is right in the sight of God, who knows the true and full story.

The people wanted a king to rule them. Even though Samuel warned them about what a king would expect and take from them, they still wanted a king as other countries had. Saul's jealousy over Jonathan and David's relationship, his need for power, and his sinfulness caused him to want to kill David. He resented the way David stood for the Lord and was righteous, and Saul wanted him out of the picture. Saul made a lot of mistakes and committed one sin after another: trying to kill or have David killed many times, indulging in the occult, and repeatedly sinning against God. Others saw it. Even Jonathan knew it. Although it was admirable for Jonathan to remain faithful to his father, his faithfulness did not change what was true: His father was a sinful man. Furthermore, many people were hurt because they dared to defy Saul and stand for what was right. None of us escape the sins we commit even when others cover them. The Lord departed from Saul, and he lost his reign to David. He did not escape his sin and judgment and in the end perished with his three sons, including Jonathan.

Let's Pause for Prayer

Heavenly Father, keep us from sin; yet when we fall, let us be the first to admit our sin, to repent from it, and to walk uprightly with You. Let us love and honor others—when they surpass us, have something we don't have, or are liked better than we are. Let us not side with evil by loving and joining in the sin but instead confronting the sinner in love, desiring ultimately for him or her to learn right from wrong. Expose sin and make us strong in You so that we can exemplify the boldness to stand for Your truth and not shrink when one who leads or reigns over us tries to overcome with evil. Let us show the way by our love for those individuals in choosing what is right and true in Your eyes. In Jesus' name we pray. Amen.

Share a time when you sought the truth and persevered to make it known.

Write a prayer about a current situation that you know requires God's truth.

Day 257

Rest To Refresh

> *"Come to Me, all who are weary and heavy-laden, and I will give you rest."*
>
> Matthew 11:28

We've been caught in it. You've probably been caught, too. We often don't want to admit it. Others who are watching and observing often see what we can't or don't, and thus, they catch us. Are you interested in knowing what we are often getting caught in the act of doing? It's the act of being too busy.

Interestingly, when I ask an audience, "Who would like to be busier," I seldom see any hands raised. Sadly, when we're too busy, we are often too busy even to recognize it! The person who recognizes it is the one who listens and watches from a distance, and can see it in our lives but not in their own.

Let's Pause for Prayer

Heavenly Father, You tell us in scripture to rest, yet Sunday is often the busiest and most hectic day of the week for the Christian who serves the church body. Exodus 31:14–18 records Your creation of the universe and instructs us to pattern our lives after Your example and the way you rested. Help us to determine when we should rest and allow us to see that true rest will bring refreshment. Allow us to experience true rest so we will long for it and seek after it, not in theory but in practice. In Jesus' name we pray. Amen.

Have you recognized the importance of rest and refreshment? How does it look for you?

_____
_____
_____
_____

Let's consider a time when that we will rest and take time to be refreshed so we can do what God asks of us.

_____
_____
_____
_____

Day 258

Leaving An Inheritance Or Family Legacy?

> *"And you shall love the Lord your God with all your heart and with all your soul and with all your might. And these words, which I am commanding you today shall be on your heart; and you shall teach them diligently to your sons and shall talk of them when you sit in your house and when you walk by the way and when you lie down and when you rise up."*
>
> Deuteronomy 6:5–7

We try periodically to take what we call F3 vacations. F3 stands for Ferrini Family Fun vacations. Some may call it bribery, others motivation, but we call it legacy. Here's how it works. Depending on the location, either we (the parents) provide for the travel expenses or everyone provides for their own. But no matter what, we take care of the accommodations and food. We've shared with our children our desire to continue spending time with them and their growing families as we continue to invest in their lives and enjoy spending casual time together. Our desire is to leave a legacy instead simply an inheritance.

We've had great talks around a fire pit and learned how to skeet shoot in the mountains, fly kites at the beach, and spend time with one another, learning the way group dynamics play out in our family. Through all these opportunities we desire to weave in principles of scripture and share our lives. We can do so on vacation, but we can also do so in everyday life.

Let's Pause for Prayer

Heavenly Father, we thank You for Your word, which guides us to make the best of our relationships with our children and grandchildren, both small and grown. Lord, help us to make good use of every teachable moment we have with our children as we look for opportunities in everyday life to instruct them about You and to teach the ways of Your word. Let us teach directly from Your word and indirectly as we set the example. As we see the opportunities You set before us, let us take hold of them and teach so that those who follow us will know how to walk uprightly with You. May we be good examples for them to follow as we seek to follow You. In Jesus' name we pray. Amen.

Do you have a purposeful plan in teaching your children, nieces, nephews, and others?

What are some of the goals, plans, and prayers you have for those you influence directly or indirectly, family or otherwise.

Day 259 — Be Ready To Share Your Faith

"Always being ready to make a defense to everyone who asks you to give an account for the hope that is in you, yet with gentleness and reverence."

I Peter 3:15

On one of our Ferrini Family Fun (F3) vacations, we were all very hungry and found a little town, where we could have dinner. We saw no one walking on the sidewalks and little traffic, but as we all piled out of the car, right in front of us were two men standing like statues, waiting and watching. They were very clean cut, gentlemanly young men; and they asked us questions of a religious nature. I don't think they had any expectation of what was about to happen. We all listened carefully, posed some questions for them, and had some interesting dialog. A few minutes into this conversation, my husband shared in a loving manner, the errors of their faith, supporting his points with scripture. I don't think these young men usually talk to people who know their Bible and have a handle on the scripture as Joe does. They seemed stunned. When we parted company, they said they would seek answers to the questions Joe raised.

The best part, besides all of us praying for them at dinner, was watching our grown children witness their dad in action. He was leaving a legacy as he showed them how he shares his faith, and it was fun to see them so proud of him. He allowed them to see the importance of being prepared for whatever assignment God has for us.

Let's Pause for Prayer

Heavenly Father, we know we must always be ready to share our faith in You. We can never be caught off guard if we have Your word in our hearts and can use it to defend our faith. We are reminded in I Peter 3:15 to be ready to share our faith. May we diligently study Your word so we can share with others who search and lead them to the Savior they seek. Allow us to see that You have us in the right place at the right time and to be willing to set aside our agenda to answer questions others might have and lovingly lead them to You. In Jesus' name we pray. Amen.

When was the last time you were called upon to share your faith? What happened?

_____
_____
_____
_____
_____

Pray for other opportunities to come your way.

Day 260 — *Annoyed*

> *"Let all bitterness and wrath and anger and clamor and slander be put away from you, along with all malice. And be kind to one another, tender-hearted, forgiving each other, just as God in Christ also has forgiven you."*
>
> Ephesians 4:32

Sometimes we have people in our lives who annoy us, but we must all realize that we also annoy others from time to time. In ministry, we may be called to work with those who have different gifts, talents, and ways to view and respond to what we do. Sometimes we'd prefer not to have to work with those who annoy us. Sadly, this is true even of Christians—in our Sunday schools, in our families, and in our work places.

Jesus is our ultimate example, showing us how to love the difficult people in our lives; and the word is where we will find how to deal with those who challenge us. We can try to make excuses and find reasons to treat others the way they treat us or to run away from the situation all together, but God is calling us to a higher standard. I have come to realize that I have nothing to gain by being mean and nothing to lose by being kind. I Cor.13:3–8 are the well known biblical passages on love. What a great chapter by which to pray and live!

Let's Pause for Prayer

Heavenly Father, thank You for the reminder in Your word that no matter what I do, even feeding the poor has little benefit if I don't love. I need to show love by being patient, kind, and unprovoked, not by taking into account a wrong suffered. As I review these scriptural reminders, help me, Lord, to respond in a loving manner to those who annoy me and challenge me. And let me forgive others as I'd want to be forgiven by them and as I am forgiven by You. Help me to know, as your scripture states in James 4:17: "Therefore, to one who knows the right thing to do, and does not do it, to him it is sin." Let me not demand my rights as I work with others, but let me recognize my responsibility so I treat others with the kindness and grace You have shown me. In Jesus' name we pray. Amen.

Can you think of someone who has been or is presently an annoyance to you? Without writing their name, share how you can pray for them.

Day 261

Variety

> *"Do not judge lest you be judged yourselves."*
> Matthew 7:1

I've always enjoyed the television shows that showcase people's talent. I especially enjoy performers who take the stage, but their voice or other talent is like nothing I expected!

I recall one woman, who was ridiculed as she walked on stage, and initially I couldn't help feeling sorry for her: first, because she didn't look the part all of us expected; then, because she had to listen to the jeering and sneering of the unforgiving crowd and judges. How impolite, rude, and mean! She certainly didn't look as if she'd be able to sing as she did, but she hadn't even been given the chance to prove herself before the laughter and jest ensued. She certainly showed us all what she had to offer. I was personally happy to hear the judges make an apology for the way they and the audience misperceived her!

The next time someone different from us crosses our paths, I hope we take the time to learn what they have to offer before passing judgment or criticizing.

Let's Pause for Prayer

Heavenly Father, help us to remember to see the good in others and to be patient to see it in its fullness. May we all think and speak well of others. Help us to see in another person what You see in them. We want to respond as You would—with love, caring, compassion, and concern. I pray we will be strong enough in You, Lord, to take a stand for others when they are mistreated and help them in whatever the difficult situation. Thank You for graciously caring for us so that we can do the same for others. In Jesus' name we pray. Amen.

Can you recall a time when someone was very much different from what you expected? What did you think and how did you react?

_____

_____

_____

How would you like to respond the next time a different, awkward, or uncomfortable situation occurs?

_____

_____

_____

_____

Day 262

Growing Older

"You are old and advanced in years."

Joshua 13:1

It's a privilege to talk with other women after the seminars and presentations I do. Often they are younger women. I am mentoring a number of younger gals in my life, and I just don't feel that much older than them. The twenty-, thirty-, or forty-year difference doesn't seem possible. But when I walk away from their pretty young faces without wrinkles or blemish and I catch a glimpse of myself in the mirror, I see the wrinkles, the changes in the skin, the changes in our bodies and minds—it all seems like a cruel joke. Time has gone by so quickly that we are left staring at an older person in the mirror, yet we feel so young.

Sometimes I feel excluded from youth-oriented conversations. As we experience numerous, rapid cultural changes in these next years, many cultures will be forced to reevaluate how they treat their older citizens, especially those in which respect for them has been compromised. We are all approaching old age. None of us is exempt.

Let's Pause for Prayer

Heavenly Father, help us to recognize in ourselves, what You saw in Your servant Joshua when You said to him, "You are old and advanced in years" (Joshua 13:1) so that we will not pretend to be young forever but take on the responsibilities you have for us in our later years. Thank you for helping David, who had reached old age, to prepare his son Solomon to be king over Israel (I Chron. 23:1). We desire to recognize that growing old gracefully can be done by accepting the changes we see as preparation for getting others ready to take our places as leaders of the faith. Instead of worrying about what we're losing, may we recognize what we have gained. As Job chided his accusers (Job 12:12), he did not take aging lightly when he told them, "Wisdom is with aged men, with long life is understanding." May we stay in Your word to gain wisdom to share with others as we grow older. May we be productive in later years as we share our faith, walk honorably with You, and leave a legacy to please You. In Jesus' name we pray. Amen.

How do you want to be treated as you grow older?

_____

_____

_____

Do you feel you treat those older than you the way you wish to be treated?

_____

_____

_____

Day 263 — *What Are We Saying?*

> *"We love because He first loved us."*
> I John 4:19

I didn't take it personally, but the sign on the back of the car said, "I HATE YOU!" That was someone I probably wouldn't go out of my way to meet, yet who knows? Loving and kind people may drive that car. After all, some Christians post signs on their cars and wear t-shirts advertising their Christianity but are unloving and unkind. I remember someone having a sign that said, "Beep if you are a Christian." Whenever people beeped, the driver would get upset, gesture at other drivers, and sometimes yell things out the window. Perhaps the driver had forgotten the message he carried on the back of his car!

I guess the question becomes, "What are we saying?" And does what we are saying match up with our actions and attitudes? If we want to show that we are Christians, we should follow John 13:34–35, which says, "A new commandment I give you that you love one another, even as I have loved you, that you also love one another. By this all men will know that you are My disciples, if you have love for one another." Three times He repeats "love one another" but emphasizes that we are loved by Him as well. He states that He Himself loves us in I John 4:7: "Beloved, let us love one another, for love is from God." This love is reciprocal and beneficial, the kind of love the world desires.

Let's Pause for Prayer

Lord Jesus, thank you for loving us first and for sending Your Son Jesus to die on the cross out of love for us. We want to be examples of love everywhere we go, and we want to reciprocate with the loving attitude and kind actions You taught us. Thank You for Your kind and loving example. We desire for others to recognize that we are Christians, not by the bumper stickers on or cars or shirts we wear, but by the way we genuinely show love to others. We look to you, our example, and pray that we will be faithful. In Jesus' name we pray. Amen.

Does an inconsistency in your life need to be changed?

_____
_____
_____

What do you want to say, and are you saying it?

_____
_____
_____

Day 264

Overload

"And to make it your ambition to lead a quiet life and attend to your own business and work with our hands, just as we commanded you"

I Thessalonians 4:11

Overload threatens our prayer lives. Being too busy to pray is simply being too busy. I sometimes catch myself in that overload cycle and generally ask myself what I am trying to prove. Sometimes we are just getting drawn into situations that keep us from other more important ones, like serving others and prayer.

When I find myself on overload, I intentionally take time to quiet myself, turn off the radio or TV, put my cell phone in another room, and do no work on the computer. Others might choose to put away other electronic devices, games, and distractions. When we make those choices, we are then free to seek the Lord in quietude and will likely hear from Him! When others say they don't hear from God, I suggest finding quiet for a lengthy period of time and seeking Him until they hear from Him. In the stillness of our hearts, we are led to pray for people and through situations with which we've struggled. Sometimes I am quite refreshed by praying out loud in the car when driving alone or when taking a walk alone, praying as I go. In countless ways we can find time to seek Him.

Let's Pause for Prayer

Heavenly Father, we pray that You would help us recognize when our schedules are just too full for our own good and need to quiet ourselves to hear from You. We apologize for those times when we allow our schedules to spin out of control and miss our time for Bible reading, prayer, and worship with You. We sometimes miss out on what we need most, and eventually we suffer for it. Help us to recognize quickly when we have not been in Your word. We know the importance of being in your word daily and want to hear from you throughout the day and daily. As we discipline ourselves to come to you daily for nourishment from Your Word, the Bible, help us desire more and more of it. In Jesus' name we pray. Amen.

How do you know when you are on overload? What do you do about it? Share ways that might work for you to keep from becoming overloaded.

Day 265

Does It Really Matter?

> *"They thanked me by committing adultery and lining up at the city's brothels. They are well-fed, lusty stallions, each neighing for his neighbor's wife. Should I not punish them for this?"*
>
> Jeremiah 5:7–8

Analyzing the fall of the latest politician or religious leaders to an extramarital affair, we hear some say, "He crossed the line. How could he do it?" Others ask, "Does it even matter that he had this affair? Does it really matter what he does in his personal life as long as he does his job well?" This discussion on national television as well as around dinner and pub tables have become commonplace. These kinds of questions should make us wonder about the morals and ethics we embrace or don't embrace as a culture.

I question why "we the people" trust any politician who lies to his wife by having an affair and actually believe he wouldn't also lie to the public. Do we want to be lied to? Anyone who's been through the devastation of spousal or parental abandonment would not take this notion lightly. If a man (or woman) finds it easy or convenient to lie and cheat on the person with whom they have the most intimate relationship, why would they think any differently when making decisions and choices with people they don't know personally? These kinds of people are not trustworthy, and when they call themselves Christians, it's a horrible blemish on and mockery of the cause of Christ. Perhaps these leaders fall because of sins like lust, pride, arrogance, and selfishness but more importantly because they don't have prayerful support or accountability to anyone.

Let's Pause for Prayer

Heavenly Father, You ask in Jeremiah 5:9, "Should I not avenge myself against a nation such as this?" Lord, our rebellion and sin as a nation are despicable. Our sin as individuals is no different, and we must not neglect recognizing our own sin. We pray for our leaders to live lives of obedience to you so they will be recognized as men as woman of integrity, honor, and truth. Call them to our minds to pray for them often. In Jesus' name we pray. Amen.

Have you felt frustration and disappointment in the spiritual and political leaders of our day? Explain.

_____

_____

It's easy to be the one to cast the first stone of accusation, but let's be the first to offer up a prayer for our spiritual and political leaders. Write out a prayer.

_____

_____

Day 266

Laughter And Tears

> *"Even in laughter the heart may be in pain, and the end of joy may be grief."*
>
> Proverbs 14:13

Who do you think said, "For every laugh there should be a tear"? It was Walt Disney. We all probably enjoy that thought for great books and storytelling, movies, and shows; but for real life, it seems we all would prefer to laugh and smile all the time. That makes life more fun and enjoyable, and, well—happy! But if all we did was laugh and if life were only about having a good time, I wonder how much we'd appreciate it. Sometimes I think we need those deeper valleys of sadness, grief, disappointment, and challenge to really appreciate the times when life is lighter, fun, and even outrageously wonderful.

The Book of Proverbs speaks to laughter and joy and how easily we might wear a smile on our faces yet feel underlying sadness and pain. Losing a loved one but laughing as memories of that loved are shared one or watching others with sadness in your heart as they do or accomplish things you never will because of your limitations, you still experience joy because you're genuinely happy for them. Life is difficult, but God gives us the joys and sorrows to balance life for us.

Let's Pause for Prayer

Heavenly Father, we thank You for knowing just what we need and for balancing our lives for us. According to Your word in Prov.11:1, "A false balance is an abomination to the Lord, but a just weight is His delight," so we thank you for always giving us just the right amount. Whatever you give is from Your hand of love for us. In David's Psalm 40:1–4, he shares the balance he experienced: "I waited patiently for the Lord; and He inclined to me, and heard my cry. He brought me up out of the pit of destruction, out of the miry clay; and He set my feet upon a rock making my footsteps firm. And He put a new song in my mouth—a song of praise to our God; Many will see and fear, and will trust in the Lord. How blessed is the man who has made the Lord his trust." Lord, may we trust You for all the sorrow, joys, laughter, and tears that you send our way. In Jesus' name we pray. Amen.

Share a recent sadness you smiled your way through.

_____

_____

_____

Share a recent joy that was a challenge because of a deep hardship with which you were dealing.

_____

_____

_____

Day 267 — Watch It!

> *"Watch over your heart with all diligence, for from it flow the springs of life."*
> Proverbs 4:23

We always have to watch it when going through airport security because it always proves to be interesting, but one time in particular we really had to "watch it"!

Joe put his computer, watch, shoes, and other things as well as Joey's items into the bins and sent them on their way. Joey, our son with special needs, knows he needs to find a seat to wait for us to put ourselves together and help him get situated. He obediently began putting on his shoes that we handed him. Once we were situated, and we'd tied his shoes, he started tugging at the back of his left shoe, saying, "It's not right." We checked the shoe and all seemed fine – it wasn't folded in the back and his foot was in, so we tied the shoestrings, and started moving him down the concourse to our designated gate. He mentioned several more times that it wasn't right, but we all kept walking.

On my way to get us something to eat, I asked Joe to please check Joey's shoe. Indeed something was wrong! Joe's watch wound up in Joey's shoe instead of his own passing through security!

Sometimes in our own lives we feel uncomfortable, and we can't quite explain why; but we just know something's not right. In the physical realm we need to make physical adjustments, and in the spiritual realm, spiritual adjustments likewise need to be made. When we sense something isn't right with the Lord or others in our lives and have that sense that God wants us to make spiritual adjustments, we need to "watch it!"

Let's Pause for Prayer

Heavenly Father, we recognize our need to watch for what You're trying to teach us. When we fail to recognize that You're trying to get our attention, we may go our own way, not listening to You or ignoring You all together. Help us to be discerning of the lessons You give us. When we're moving in the wrong direction, make us uncomfortable so we don't stray too far. When we are doing Your will, allow us to be at peace and enjoying contentment. In Jesus' name we pray. Amen.

How do you sense that the Lord is asking to be watchful? Share an example.

_____

_____

Write a prayer expressing your thoughts about being more discerning and ready for what the Lord is making you ready.

_____

_____

_____

Day 268 — *Just Make It Easier*

> *"Woe to those who are at ease."*
> Amos 6:1

A missionary family from Japan shared a very interesting thought in one of their prayer letters to us: "Japanese love rice, but because of the shortage of land, someone developed a way to grow rice underground. Somewhere under the world's largest city, they grow rice. Initially, the rice did not have much flavor. The reason, they discovered, was because the rice was not exposed to the elements outside—the scorching heat, the strong winds, and the summer downpours. So they began to simulate the weather outside. No matter what we might be going through right now, the heat and wind have a purpose—to make us 'tastier!'"

Such an observation on life! We want life to be easy, comfortable, and happy without a lot of effort! What makes us more useful and tastier, if you will, are the elements of life having their way with us. The scorching heat of hardship allows us to learn lessons we'd not learn otherwise, and when we yield to the Lord through those times we become beautiful examples to others of the way He can work in our lives. When sadness and disappointment come to us like a strong wind, we can learn to rely upon the One who can sustain us in the midst of turbulent times. When our tears pour like a summer downpour, it is the Lord who, according to Psalm 56:8, takes all of our tears into account and saves them in His bottle. In the end, God has a purpose for what He brings into our lives. Like the rice, we need to be made "tastier" in order to reflect who God is to others.

Let's Pause for Prayer

Heavenly Father, we don't usually want to be put into situations where we deal with hardship, sadness, and disappointment; but You allow those times in our lives so we can learn to rely upon You for what we need to sustain us and for what will make us more useful for Your work here on earth. We thank You for helping us through turbulent times and we are grateful that You don't leave us alone. You know better than to give us the easy way out. We'll learn to thank You through those hardships and challenging times. We know Your timing is perfect. Thank You, Lord, for using all things to accomplish Your purposes in and through us. In Jesus' name we pray. Amen.

Recall a time when you wished life could have been easier. What did you learn once you got overcame?

_____
_____

How do you feel now when you experience difficult times? Have you learned anything?

_____
_____
_____

Day 269 — *Bloom Where You're Planted*

> *"So then neither the one who plants nor the one who waters is anything, but God who causes the growth."*
>
> I Corinthians 3:7

As Joe and I drove downtown, he told me to be ready to see something unusual on the side of the road. On the busiest of highways grew a sunflower at least two feet tall!

How did it come to grow there? A cemented area with little soil grew this plant, yet just enough water was available for it to take hold and grow. How did it grow amidst the traffic and pollution? I guess, it did what we're to do—bloom where we are planted!

When we wonder how we ever wound up where we are, how the Lord allows us to be used in the place we are in, and how we are able to thrive and grow amid hardship and opposition of many kinds, we can be sure the Lord will use us where He puts us and will provide all we need to grow and have purpose.

Let's Pause for Prayer

Heavenly Father, we are amazed that You place Your children in some of the most unusual locations and under the most unusual circumstances to accomplish Your purposes. Thank you for placing us right where You want us, even when we question it. Thank you for showing us what You want us to do and accomplish where You have planted us and helping us to bloom there. Thank You for showing us that You are in control no matter where we are, no matter the challenges we face. We want our desire to be to serve You well where You have asked us to serve. And thank you for allowing us to bloom when we can see no humanly good reason to have done so. We know it's all from You and of You. We pray we will be faithful to Your call and content to serve where You have asked. As we were in awe with the sunflower growing in an obscure place, may onlookers be in awe of where You choose to put others. In Jesus' name we pray. Amen.

Do you feel God has uniquely placed and planted you where you are today? Explain.

_____

_____

_____

How do you sense God working in your area of service right now?

_____

_____

_____

Day 270

Special

> *"I will give thanks to Thee, for I am fearfully and wonderfully made."*
>
> Psalm 139:14

The right to life applies to more than unborn babies; it also applies to those with special needs whom others may feel have no quality of life. Some feel they should not be allowed to live. Those at the end of life, who are no longer productive citizens, are similarly considered by some unworthy to live because they do not produce and are not useful for any purpose. For those of us who have been in the presence of, raised, taught, or cared for people with special needs, they often make clear by their loving temperament that they enjoy a quality of life we only wish we had. Although some with special needs can be very challenging some or all of the time, they are very often caring individuals who love others unconditionally, would never say an unkind word about others, and simply take the day as it comes, going with the flow, without expectations or demands.

As a parent of an adult child with special needs, I can tell you that the challenges we experience are very real and often exhausting, but the joy and blessings have far outweighed the challenges. Today, if God were to visibly stand in front of us and ask if we'd like our son to be healed, I think my husband and I would likely say, "No, we like him just the way you created him, and thank you for using him to teach us lessons in life."

Let's Pause for Prayer

Dear Father, we thank you for how "fearfully and wonderfully" you make each human being according to Psalm 139. Thank you for giving to us children we need to help mold and who will help mold us to be more like You. Help all who have loved ones, friends, or neighbors with special needs to see the beauty and value in that special life. Please use the simple ways of those with special needs to lead those who think they are wise to know You. Thank you, Lord, for giving us the love and ability we need to care for those with special needs when others might think they should be disposed of or put away from society. Lord, help each of us care for those with special needs the way You would and the way You have called us to—showing dignity, value, and love. In Jesus' name we pray.

Have you or do you care for someone with special needs? How has doing so changed your life?

_____

_____

_____

Does someone who has a special need or is a caregiver come to mind for whom to pray? Pray.

_____

_____

_____

Day 271 — *Practice*

> *"Be diligent to present yourself approved to God as a workman who does not need to be ashamed, handling accurately the work of truth."*
>
> II Timothy 2:15

I enjoy attending a community symphony orchestra performance from time to time. A guest concert pianist played two pieces without any sheet music in front of him, each piece about 45 minutes long, one by Rachmaninoff, the other by Tchaikovsky. Each was played beautifully by this pianist and accompanied by the orchestra. He presented his skill impeccably. Truly, I was in awe.

I took piano lessons for eight years, and really enjoyed playing; but I did not study the piano as this man has and continues to do. I play the piano today but ever so simply by most standards and ever so poorly if compared to this master. I would not venture to play for an audience. This master entertained us in a way that seemed effortless; but we know this level of performance was achieved with much dedication, study, and practice.

Let's Pause for Prayer

Heavenly Father, we thank you for the excellence in which this pianist was trained and performs. Help me, help us, to be mindful of what we do for You, and whether or not we have given our life's work to You in a way that will cause others to be inspired to want to know. May we dedicate ourselves to the study of Your Word and apply it to everyday life. Father, we know this kind of service and surrender takes practice, diligence, faithfulness, and perseverance similar to one who masters an instrument. Let us be an instrument of Your love and a light in a dark place, wherever You have placed us and however You have gifted us. May we be faithful on the stage You've given us upon which to perform—for You. In Jesus' name we pray. Amen.

Have you ever developed a trade, skill, or other talent in such a way that you've mastered it?

_____

_____

_____

How diligently do you study God's word and make it a part of your everyday life?

_____

_____

_____

Day 272

Social Media

"Let love be without hypocrisy. Abhor what is evil, cling to what is good. Be devoted to one another in brotherly love, give preference to one another in honor"

Romans 12:9

Let's face it, social media is big! What started as a way for college kids to find one another and communicate has turned into a worldwide presence!

I love the informational parts, hearing from real friends and the ones who just hang out and share from time to time, playing Scrabble, and more. I am moved to pray when a need is shared. I enjoy reading blogs that are informative; finding people from high school and college; keeping in touch with current friends; meeting new people with similar interests and friends in common; seeing what they pin on their boards, what jobs their looking for, and what they tweet; and viewing the most recent pictures of grandchildren. All these are quite pleasant, yet the human touch is clearly missing.

One can't calculate the value of a shared cup of coffee, a casual dinner to "catch up," face-to-face communication, a hug, a tear, or a good laugh. The virtual world will never duplicate what happens in the real world of caring and compassion. God has given us relationships for a reason, and we should be mindful to care for them as He would want us to.

Let's Pause for Prayer

Lord, we thank You for the real relationships given to each of us, and we pray that we would be able to nourish them in ways that bring glory to You through them. We pray according to Romans 12:9–16 that we would love one another without hypocrisy; that we would abhor what is evil and cling to what is good, desiring devotion to one another, giving preference to others with honor, contributing to fulfilling the needs of others, serving friends and even strangers through hospitality, kindness, compassion, and words of encouragement; and that we would be of the same mind with one another, avoiding haughtiness and those who would do us spiritual harm. How wonderful to rejoice with people or offer compassion in grief for others through the challenges of trials of everyday life! Help us to exemplify what You want us to be for others. In Jesus' name we pray. Amen.

How do social media work for you?

_____

_____

How can you use social media to reach out to others in a more authentic way? Pray.

_____

_____

_____

Day 273

Taking The Plunge

> *"Walk in the manner worthy of the calling."*
>
> Ephesians 4:1

"I wish our church had a _____ ministry." Fill in the blank. Is it singles, college, single parents, other? My usual response is "Instead of wishing, hoping, and waiting for someone else to start a ministry to benefit your situation, why don't you start the group?" I guess the idea is this: If you have a need, if you see a need, if you can fill the need, then take the plunge and do it!

If you find in yourself a natural talent—providing a meal for someone in need, repairing cars, or other personal interests—it's possibly the very place God might be working in your life to begin a ministry. Someone in our church who was previously a restaurant owner, now a caterer, takes it upon herself to provide meals to families who have experienced the death of a loved one. She knows the state of mind people are in when they are going through a devastating time, recognizes the need, and prepares to meet it.

One doesn't have to search to find a need. I often say that if I ever have a day when I am bored (has not happened so far), I will go to our nearby nursing home and offer to serve water and have conversation with the residents there. I doubt that any of us who might do this would get past Room 1 or 2.

Let's Pause for Prayer

Lord, help us, according to Ephesians 4, to walk in a manner worthy of the calling with which You've called us. Help us walk in humility and gentleness, with patience, showing forbearance to one another in love, and preserving the unity of the Spirit in peace. When we recognize a need, let us be givers, not takers; workers, not relaxers; servers, not recipients. We will be called to be on the receiving end another time. Let's reject the notion that we have rewards coming to us or that we are deserving of reward. Instead, let's proceed with the thinking that we can be used of You, can help others in their season of need, and do acts of service and kindness without expectation of reward. Allow us to serve with a pure heart of love and devotion. In Jesus' name we pray. Amen.

If you were able to fill in the blank above, what ministry (current or past) was it?

_____

_____

_____

Did you or would you start it for the benefit of yourself and others? Pray about it.

_____

_____

_____

Day 274

Things Aren't Always As They Seem

> *"Jesus is the same yesterday, today, and yes, forever."*
>
> Hebrews 13:8

I remember reading *To Kill a Mockingbird* by Harper Lee in high school. I love the many stories told and lessons taught in this novel. The children of Atticus, an attorney, grow to understand that the world isn't always fair and that prejudice is a very real aspect of their world, no matter how subtle it seems. Through the events of the story and the injustices, his daughter Scout learns that no matter the differences or peculiarities, people of the world and of Maycomb County are all people. No one is lesser or better than anyone else.

My take on this story has another twist: Things aren't always as they seem. Many times in life, I've been led to understand a story one way, only to learn that it wasn't that way at all; or I've run with the notion that something is going to work out a certain way, and then it doesn't. As a believer in Jesus Christ, I'm learning that the only One who knows the real truth in all situations is Jesus himself. Although His justice is a comfort to me, injustice sometimes happens. Real life truth gets punished. Evil people get their way. Bad situations sometimes grow worse. I'd love to live in a world where evil is defeated, good always overcomes, and people ride off into a beautiful sunset and live happily ever after. But the reality is this: That's usually only in the movies.

Let's Pause for Prayer

Heavenly Father, we are most thankful that You know all things and that only what is sifted through your fingers will be permitted to touch our lives. Sometimes it actually feels impossible, but we desire in all ways to put our trust in You for the very simple injustices we face and for the devastating challenges You might have us walk through. Although we might not see the whole picture as You see it, will you give us the mindset to be able to trust and serve You through the trials and injustices of this life? Will you help us to stay focused on the truth of Your word and the purity of Your ways, never to doubt Your love for us? When we can't see clearly or when life isn't what it seems, let us present hope to others and live out the reality in our own lives, following Hebrews 13:8, which says, "Jesus is the same yesterday, today, and yes forever." In the trustworthy, honest, and loving name of Jesus, we pray. Amen.

Share an injustice you've encountered personally. How did you work, pray, and live through it and to what conclusion?

_____
_____
_____
_____
_____

Day 275

Pray – Study – Grow

"Devote yourselves to prayer, keeping alert in it with an attitude of thanksgiving."

Colossians 4:2

A study done for a well-known ministry showed some very interesting results. Basically, what caught my eye in this study was the direct correlation among one's personal time spent reading and studying God's word, prayer, and the results the individual saw in her or his personal ministry. In almost the exact same percentages, the person who had a consistent quality, daily, quiet time spent in Bible reading, Bible study, and prayer reported a consistent fruitful ministry. The persons reporting they did not spend time in God's word also reported they did not have what they themselves would call a fruitful ministry. All kinds of red flags popped up in my thinking.

First, I asked myself why someone serving in full time ministry wouldn't apply her or his time to the spiritual disciplines of studying the Bible and developing a rich prayer life. It seems logical to me that people wouldn't even consider full-time ministry unless they desired study, prayer, and personal growth and were, in fact, purposeful in that direction. It's difficult for me to wrap my thinking around the idea that someone who ministers God's word to others isn't in it!

Let's Pause for Prayer

Heavenly Father, as we serve You, let us first learn from Your word what that should look like in our own personal walk with You. Just as other relationships won't grow unless time is spent developing them, we know we can't and won't grow in our relationship with You unless we study in Your word, are in prayer, and seek after what You have for us. Lord, please speak to our hearts when we drift from You so that the call You have given us as our own personal ministry to serve You will not be diminished or—worse—taken from us. We don't want to neglect the gifts You've given us and the ability we've been given to serve You. For those who are weary, give them a new love for Your word so they will desire to serve with zeal and excitement. Give them a hunger for a consistent and quality prayer time with You. May we be faithful to study, pray, and minister using all that You have given us: time, energy, stamina, resources, and most of all, the love we have for You. In Jesus' name we pray.

Do you have a daily quiet time in God's word? If so, what is your daily routine? If not, why not?

_____

_____

_____

Do you have a sense that you and your ministry is growing? If so, explain. If not, why not?

_____

_____

_____

Day 276 — Get A Life!

"Thou wilt make known to me the path of life; In Thy presence is fullness of joy; In Thy right hand there are pleasures forever."

Psalm 16:11

"Get a life!" I'm often tempted to say that! As a young mom changing diapers I'd catch myself thinking, "I wonder when I'll get a life." When our son with special needs wasn't developing on schedule, doing the same therapy for what seemed the trillionth time, I'd think, "I just wish he'd get this, and get a life."

The grass is greener in someone else's yard, but do you ever feel trapped in yours?

I'd like to be able to participate in many activities in semiretirement, but I realize that finding care for our adult son isn't always easy. Many suggestions offered by others are neither comfortable nor viable options for us. Oh, if I could just get a life!

The grass often appears greener in someone else's yard, and I face the fact that my life differs from that of others around me. We have choices to make. For us (and you), choosing what is right means choosing what we value. For us the reality and choice was and is valuing and caring for our son with the knowledge that doing so would last a lifetime: either his or ours!

I've grown to realize I indeed have a life. It's caring for our son, who has brought so much to our lives. It's realizing that although we all want to get a life, we ultimately find that the phrase just needs to be reworked: "This is our life! And it's really pretty special."

Let's Pause for Prayer

Heavenly Father, thank You for the life you've given us to live, for the ways we can glorify You through frustrations and challenges. Help us to see that the life You've given is best for us and that we are examples to others because we live in service to You. Let us serve You by serving others, by relinquishing our rights and instead carrying out our responsibilities. We know it seems impossible from time to time, but we will rely upon You to be able to do that which we know is from You. Thank You for the strength, endurance, and perseverance You give to those who ask for it. In Jesus' name we pray. Amen.

Share a time you used the phrase "Get a life." Was it about your life or someone else's?

_____

_____

How are you able to live life amid the struggles and challenges you have?

_____

_____

_____

Day 277 — The Fool

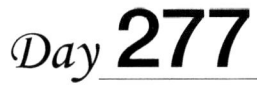

> *"The fear of the Lord is the beginning of knowledge; fools despise wisdom and instruction."*
>
> Proverbs 1:7

Occasional foolish behavior is something all of us must admit from time to time. When we feel that sting of foolishness (a.k.a. embarrassment), we should learn from mistakes, recall them the next time, and then use the situation as a wake-up call to avoid repeating that folly. Maturing people will learn from their mistakes and want to avoid folly, but real fools are, according to many verses in Proverbs, those who are unaware of their own foolishness, don't care, and don't care about the way their relationships are impacted. He wants and does his own thing, seldom open to anyone's counsel or suggestions. They're always right, and that means generally prideful. Few feel the need to own up to it, confess it, or repent from their foolish and hurtful ways.

Let's Pause for Prayer

Heavenly Father, please help us to see our sinful ways and make it our purpose to confess those sinful ways to You and to others when appropriate. Allow us to adjust our ways and then learn to make right choices. Let us recognize when we have been stubborn or even naïve and made mistakes that show us to be foolish. When others correct us lovingly, help us to accept that correction in the same way, and not repeat that folly. Help us as parents to teach our children to choose wisdom over folly. Let all of us learn to relate to others and not have the need to be right all the time. Let us treat others as more important than ourselves, and let us desire to live in harmony instead of discord. We desire to be maturing individuals who care about others, not just ourselves and having our own way. Show us when we err so that we can humble ourselves to come under Your authority and grow in Your wisdom daily. In Jesus' name we pray. Amen.

Share a moment of foolish embarrassment of your own and how you handled it.

_____

_____

Can you recognize a fool in your life? How will today's thought and prayer help you to deal with him or her?

_____

_____

Write a prayer for your next steps with this person.

_____

_____

_____

Day 278

Enlarge Your Tents

"'Shout for joy, O barren one, you who have borne no child; break forth into joyful shouting and cry aloud, you who have not travailed; for the sons of the desolate one will be more numerous than the sons of the married woman,' says the Lord. 'Enlarge the place of your tent; stretch out the curtains of your dwellings, spare not; lengthen your cord, and strengthen your pegs. For you will spread abroad to the right and to the left.'"

Isaiah 54:1–3

I count it a privilege to be a mom, but I've known numerous women who have never had children, some who've longed for them. Many have, as instructed in the book of Isaiah, "enlarged the place of their tents" so that their children and descendents would be more than of the women who bore children. They've "enlarged the place of their tents" by opening their hearts and homes to my children. Some are close family, some are dear friends, and some are women who have influenced me and my children and may not even know the full extent of the blessing they've been to our family.

Let's Pause for Prayer

Heavenly Father, I thank You for the women in our lives who've made themselves available to our children even while they've had no children of their own. Thank You for causing them to reach deep within themselves, often from a place of deep sadness and desire for children, to be used and useful in the lives of others. Thank You for those who've given us a break when we were ready to break. Thank You for those who've walked with us through our times of frustrations, even perhaps desiring to experience that frustration if it meant having a child. Bless them for taking the time to talk to, befriend, care for, meet the needs of, or listen to our children. I appreciate the women I listed and then told my children to talk to if they didn't feel they could come to me. What a blessing they have been! Please bless them in ways that they would know and understand that You are pleased with them and love them. We pray, Father, that women who are unable to bear children, would seek ways to open their hearts and homes to little ones. Perhaps for some it will mean adoption or foster care or for others helping in church settings or offering to help when they see a young mom struggling. We thank You for those who've answered a different call and been a blessing in and through it. In Jesus' name we pray. Amen.

Have you, or someone you know been unable to have their own children? Share the journey—how you'd like to see this journey continue—then pray.

Day 279

Proper Tools

> *"If the axe is dull and he does not sharpen its edge, then he must exert more strength. Wisdom has the advantage of giving success."*
>
> Ecclesiastes 10:10

I recently heard a story of two loggers competing in a log-cutting contest. One logger periodically took a rest. Even though he took time out, he was the one to win the contest. His competitor asked, "How is it that you could win when I spent more time cutting the log than you did?" The winner said, "Each time I rested, I sharpened my axe."

The Bible verse above makes me think about the importance of using tools that are in proper condition for the job. When our tools work properly, we don't have to work so hard. Consider the dentist or seamstress. The same is true for wisdom: If we use it properly, we'll have the advantage of success. Our wisdom comes from God's word; thus reading from it each day is a wise choice.

Let's Pause for Prayer

Heavenly Father, we are so thankful for Your word and for the opportunity to learn and glean from it. Help us make it a point to read from it daily and learn in a way that we will make changes in our lives for the better and for Your glory. As a logger repeatedly strikes a log until it's cut all the way through, let us repeatedly come to your word until You have taught us all that You want us to learn. Let us rest in Your word, and as we read it daily, help us to be able to share it with others, divide the word in a way that will help others understand it, and live it so that others will be drawn to it by watching us. Help us to be the Bible they might never read. Draw us to Yourself so that each day we desire Your word, come to it, read it, and then apply and teach it to others. May we not neglect, ignore, dismiss, disregard, or deny it. In Jesus' name we pray. Amen.

Are you in a career or profession in which proper tools must be well-sharpened or cared for in order for your job to be done properly, smoothly, and in a timely manner? Explain.

_____

_____

_____

Do you sense a need to know God's word better to be able to use it daily for yourself and to share with others? Explain.

_____

_____

_____

Day 280

Sin Makes Promises

> *"And He (the spirit) when He comes, will convict the world concerning sin, and righteousness, and judgment."*
>
> John 16:8

Sin promises happiness, but it can't keep its word. Sin never delivers what it promises. Sin also costs us a lot, and sadly, it's far reaching. It seldom affects only the sinner.

Take lying. Sinners who lie believe they'll benefit in some way if they deceive, misrepresent, or fudge the truth: Why else would they want to or feel the need to lie? But it doesn't stop there. They must lie to someone. That someone is now affected.

How about adultery? It's as prevalent in Christian circles as in the secular world. The adulterer and partner are seldom heard publicly to say how they feel that adulterous relationship will affect others. They just want what benefits them, and that's all that matters. Beyond the sin of adultery is the sin of pride and selfishness now left to ruin marriages, families, and sadly, even ministries.

Sin is never isolated.

We all struggle with sin, but God gives us a reset button; and it's called forgiveness. The reset button won't erase the damage, but it can start the repair process.

Let's Pause for Prayer

Lord, we confess to You our sin. We recognize the far-reaching results that sin, my own sin, can cause; and we want to be right with You and others. Help us to own our sin. As You show us our sin, let us be quick to confess it and repent (turn away from it). Please help us to make these corrections quickly so that we might be models for others to follow. Father, don't let us buy into the lie that someday when we get right with You, this will be our testimony showing Your love and forgiveness of a redeemed life. Yes, Your forgiveness is redemptive but may we not revel in our sin while we let it run its course of destruction in our lives and in the lives of others. Make us uncomfortable in our sin, and bring us to peace in putting that sin away. In Jesus' name we pray. Amen.

Is the Lord bringing to mind someone you need to ask forgiveness? Go to them. Call them.

_____

_____

If someone comes to you to request forgiveness, will you grant it?

_____

_____

_____

Day 281   *Life Changing*

> *"Nothing is too difficult for Thee."*
> Jeremiah 32:17

As couples plan, prepare, and approach their weddings, they feel much anticipation of the wonderful and festive day and a life "lived happily ever after."

Couples exchange vows: "For better or worse, for richer or poorer, in sickness and in health, to love and to cherish until death do us part." When a couple says those words on their wedding day, few are prepared for the "worse, poorer, and sickness" parts and the degree to which marriage will change their lives! Through tears a few years back, Joe and I renewed our wedding vows. Tears because we'd live through the worse, poorer, and sickness parts! Those of us who've made it that far realize the hard work marriage is and can through tears be thankful for what the Lord has brought us through.

Let's Pause for Prayer

Heavenly Father, we are so thankful that those of us who know You as our Lord and Savior have You as the glue that holds our marriages together. Thank you for being there to help marriages succeed and as we put our trust in You to help us see your hand in each and every situation. Help newlyweds take as much or more time in preparing for the marriage as they prepare for the wedding day. We pray they will have You as the center of all they will plan and as the center of every single part of their marriage so that when inevitable difficulties come, they'll be prepared to weather those storms with You guiding and strengthening them. Thank You for bringing each marriage to various points of need, recognizing our dependence upon You for the next step. Thank You for protecting us and bringing us through the difficulties so we can be an example to others of Your love for us. In Jesus' name we pray. Amen.

For married couples: What will we do when those challenging times come?

_____

_____

_____

For everyone: For whom can you pray as you watch a new marriage budding or perhaps one that is falling apart?

_____

_____

_____

Day 282

Is That Not Enough?

"Let your way of life be free from the love of money, being content with what you have; for He Himself has said, "I will never desert you, nor will I ever forsake you."

Hebrews 13:5

I engaged in battle with some birds and what they were doing to and around our house. The first battle started with robins slamming into our back windows. They hit the windows so hard, I thought for sure I'd hear broken glass any minute. The second battle was with some tiny little birds that I thought were so cute until I realized the noise I heard for much of one morning while working in our ministry room was their pecking away at the stucco on the front of the house. It was not until I left home to run an errand and returned to see that the noise I heard was their song as they made a hole the size of my fist in the façade. I didn't really know what they were doing, but they have a substantial piece of wooded property behind our home to do their pecking, and my question to them was this: Is that not enough? Why must you mess with my house when all those trees are yours?

It made me think of our own human nature. What we have is often enough, but once we achieve one goal, we want to go for the next. We purchase an item, and before long we feel the need for the updated version: clothing, games, cars, homes, and sometimes even spouses. We're all guilty to one degree or another.

Let's Pause for Prayer

Father, we admit that we often find ourselves in a place of discontent. In this economy, if we have a job, help us to find contentment with our wages. Thank You for always being there for us and for our being able to trust You to give us just what we need, not necessarily what we want. We pray we would appreciate all that comes from Your hands and be content. In Jesus' name we pray. Amen.

Whether or not you know your weak spot, let's pray about what we're sensing isn't quite enough in our lives. When you desire something more, how will you handle it?

_____

_____

_____

_____

_____

Day 283

Happy To Work

> *"Keep deception and lies far from me, give me neither poverty nor riches; feed me with the food that is my portion, lest I be full and deny Thee and say, 'Who is the Lord?' or lest I be in want and steal, and profane the name of my God."*
>
> Proverbs 30:8

Recession, job loss, reduction of wages, downsizing, loss of homes. In the midst of this difficult time for many people, we have a golden opportunity to show what we trust in, Who we rely upon, and on what we'll depend.

For the first time in many years, I heard, "I'm not finding the job I have to be fulfilling, but I'm just so happy I have a job." One person I know was without a job for 30 months. She endured, as she put it, "months of unemployment or underemployment"; she said, "I am happy that He has provided a job for me. It was not easy at times, but I am so glad that He was holding me up." Many friends prayed for her. It was a difficult time of waiting for her and for those of us who prayed her through that time. I learned from her that she had great trust in her Lord and Savior and that she depended upon Him to meet the obligations she had each month.

Let's Pause for Prayer

Lord, we are so thankful that we have a caring God like You, who knows every detail of our lives and can answer any prayer we pray in a split second; yet You also know us so well that You'll often challenge and stretch us in ways that will draw believers to grow closer to You and unbelievers to want to know more of you. May we be faithful to You, Lord, and serve as good examples to those who are watching us so that others will desire to follow after You. May we appreciate and enjoy the work You've given us, and for those looking for work, may they find jobs that will offer satisfaction and provision. In Jesus' name we pray. Amen.

Have you gone or are you going through a difficult situation looking for work?

_____
_____
_____

Have you gone or are you going through a time when you didn't enjoy your work?

_____
_____
_____

Pray for work and provision—for yourself or for others.

Day 284

Selfish

> *"Everyone who is called by My name, And whom I have created for My glory, Whom I have formed even whom I have made."*
>
> Isaiah 43:7

Do you enjoy serving or do you prefer to be served? People who serve tend to grow more beautiful with every act of service. They just glow because what they do is often done to share the love they have for the Lord. They are warm, welcoming, and wonderful!

Those who prefer to be served are often ones who like to be pampered, like to have their own way. I don't need to describe them much further as I'm sure you already have the picture of someone who popped into your mind. In contrast to the server, the one who prefers to be served wears on, drains, and maybe even jangles our nerves. If we stick around long enough, we'll notice that their "circle of friends" grows smaller and smaller all the time.

According to Isaiah 43:7, the goal of "everyone who is called by My name, and whom I have created for My glory, whom I have formed even whom I have made" should be to glorify God. We can't do that and serve ourselves at the same time.

Let's Pause for Prayer

Heavenly Father, thank You for Your word in Matthew 6:24, which reminds us, "No one can serve two masters." Help us to take our eyes off ourselves and focus them on You. Show us where our focus is wrong. Nudge us to move from a self-centered, selfish person to a vibrant believer who desires to serve You and others. Thank you, Lord, for coming to serve and giving Your life for me and for my sin. Let us not be free to serve others as an extension of Your love for us. May we not be comfortable seeking our own comfort and ease but in serving others for Your glory. In Jesus' name we pray. Amen.

Let's address the question once more. Do you enjoy serving or do you prefer to be served?

_____
_____
_____

Do you sense that You are serving others and God in the way you should be and in the way He has called you? Do you sense any selfish motives or ways about which you can pray?

_____
_____
_____

Day 285

Reach Out

> *"Like a shepherd He will tend His flock, in His arm He will gather the lambs."*
>
> Isaiah 40:11a

I had written a Pause for Prayer for my radio segment about social media and the importance of maintaining face-to-face and one-on-one time with others. Following that Pause for Prayer segment, someone from the listening audience asked me to be her friend on Facebook. Every once in a while we'd share a thought or two between us. About six months later I was putting together a group of women to do a Bible study and had invited people personally as I spoke with them, via email as I emailed friends, and then I sent an invitation via Facebook. My WCRF friend mentioned she might like to be a part of the study. Of our group of 17, we had six churches represented, one woman Skyped with us from Cincinnati, and our ages ranged from the mid 30s to mid 60s. It was a great group and fun to meet my Facebook friend face to face! What I liked most was watching this diverse group of gals connect with one another and connect with the Lord as we learned, grew in our faith, and found freedom in the unique ways God had made each of us. It was a little taste of what heaven might be like: many backgrounds, different passions, different gifts, varied values, and diverse personalities, yet all there to serve and worship One God.

Let's Pause for Prayer

Heavenly Father, what a gift You give us when we gather with other believers! Thank you for gathering us to Yourself and tending to us. Thank You for the diversity of gifts within the body of believers, which allow for Your work to be accomplished. We thank You for our being able to express those gifts diversely as we minister in our various churches and neighborhoods. We pray, Lord, that as we learn and grow in our knowledge of Your work, that we would share our faith and pray for others and take the time to meet with others to teach them Your ways. What a blessing to be called for your purposes. Thank You for the reminders that despite the diversity among us, You are the glue that holds us all together in unity. In Jesus' name we pray. Amen.

Is it easy for you to reach out to meet with others, or does it take a bit of effort?

_____

_____

_____

Can you reach out this week and meet someone face to face just once or perhaps consider opening your home to study God's word? Pray.

_____

_____

Day 286 — Our True Character

"Discretion will guard you; understanding will watch over you."
Proverbs 2:11

Some people define character as "qualities that make someone or something interesting or attractive." I've also heard it said that character is who we are when no one is looking. I'm sure that if God is pleased with our characters, then others and we would be, too. I often consider the little acts I perform like returning a grocery cart instead of leaving it in the middle of the parking lot or putting an unwanted item back on the shelf where it belongs as a small indication of my character. Traits that others don't see like honesty in sharing information accurately show who we really are when no one knows whether our words are truthful.

As the children grew up, I recognized that they learned both directly and indirectly from me, and I had to check in my mind everything I did and said. Sometimes I'd catch them imitating behaviors of mine that I didn't want them imitating—character check—or using words or phrases I didn't want them using—character check. Kids are great mirrors, aren't they? We became great accountability partners as we all did character checks, and now that they're grown, we have the freedom to call one another on traits or actions that might not show godly character.

Let's Pause for Prayer

Heavenly Father, we desire to be men and women of godly character. We want to act in private situations just as we would publicly when we know others are watching. It may seem to us that no one is watching because no one is around, but we know You always see us. Let us be mindful that we are examples to someone. Help us not to take short cuts in becoming the people You want us to be. Show us areas of our character that need work. Reveal the flaws, and may we be willing to work on them. We pray that our thought life would show us to be people of character, letting our minds dwell on the good and the pure. We pray that our words would uplift and encourage others. We pray that our actions would match our thoughts and words in such a way that we present to You the whole package of one desiring to follow after You in spirit, truth, and goodness. May we mirror You and be found to be attractive in our character. In Jesus' name we pray. Amen.

When you consider a person of character, how would you describe her or him?

_____
_____

Do you fit into that same description? Why or why not? What will you do if you don't fit?

_____
_____
_____

Day 287

What Is Mine To Do

> *"And I do all things for the sake of the gospel, that I many become a fellow partaker of it."*
> I Corinthians 9:23

Traveling to the Pacific Northwest for vacation allowed for a visit to Victoria, British Columbia, and a tour of the Butchart Gardens. I can say with certainty that I've never seen so many flowers so beautifully situated in gardens, colorful and fragrant; nor have I ever seen so many huge bees in one area!

Although our son is a grown man, his special needs are such that he very childlike; and thus, he was quite fearful of all the bees. They were clearly visible, but the buzzing and humming sounds they made were very loud and more intimidating than just their appearance. I moved our son to a place away from the flowers to watch the bees and told him that they were so busy doing their job of getting nectar from the flowers that he was of little interest to them. I took him closer and closer until we were both quite close to the loud, busy, buzzing bees.

Being so busy doing what God has called us to do that we wouldn't need to be concerned at all about others' comments or disruptions would be quite advantageous for us as Christians. We would simply work without distraction!

Let's Pause for Prayer

Heavenly Father, You have fearfully and wonderfully made us (according to Psalm 139) in such a way that we have a specific role to play and job to do during our time on earth. We want to serve, work, praise, and worship without worrying or wondering about how others might view us, what others say about us, or what others think we should do differently. Find us doing the work You have given us. Thank you for gifting, equipping, and guiding us in specific ways to accomplish Your will. Help us to keep our minds set on You, focused on the work You've given us and steadfast in all ways to accomplish it for Your glory. We desire to ignore the distractions that would hinder us from the call You've given. As you make us aware of distractions, give us the perseverance to continue on for Your name's sake. In Jesus' name we pray. Amen.

What easily distracts you from doing what God has asked of you?

_____

_____

_____

How can you reengage and ignore the distractions all around you?

_____

_____

_____

Day 288

Transparency

> *"And art intimately acquainted with all my ways."*
>
> Psalm 139:3b

Touring the Boeing Factory in Seattle, Washington, the largest building in the world, is quite impressive. From the tour balcony we watched the stages of assembly of the 787, 777, and 747. Although the scale of everything we saw seemed so large in so many ways, every detail of assembly is impressively recorded and documented. If the team detects any problems, inconsistencies, mistakes, or issues as they take a plane for its first flight, they are able to locate in this documentation in the form of a DVD and CD what needs correction. When the airplane is completed and all testing is done, the final documents and plane are received by the owners. Total transparency characterizes this process. Both Boeing and the owners see every detail of the assembly and corrections and have the documents that provide proof.

With the Lord we have total transparency. He sees every detail of our lives. He knows every error, mistake, or sin we commit; and He is there to help us make life-changing corrections so that our lives will run smoothly and with integrity.

Let's Pause for Prayer

Father, we know we can hide nothing from You, and we need Your help to make the kinds of choices and decisions that reflect our desire for transparency. We want to be totally open to You and totally used by You. When we sin, please call it to our attention so that we can ask forgiveness of You and others. When we make a mistake or err in some way, help us to be men and women of integrity so we can own up to it and change our ways. When we say, do, or think what is wrong, we ask You to call us on it and redirect us. May we be open to that transparency so that others will see You in our lives. Someday when we meet You face to face, we want the record of our lives to reflect total transparency with You. In Jesus' name we pray. Amen.

How do you test yourself for the accuracy and transparency in your life with God?

_____

_____

_____

What corrections need to be made so you have total openness with God?

_____

_____

_____

Day 289 — *Making The Correction*

> *"O Lord, lead me in Thy righteousness because of my foes; make Thy way straight before me."*
>
> Psalm 5:8

With travel as a family whose members are now all adults and can handle last-minute changes and longer trips, we sometimes don't plan our hotels or restaurants ahead of time. We want to try new places. We have two basic rules:

1. We find a hotel whenever we get tired and need to rest.
2. We dine only at restaurants if we don't know the name (i.e., no chain restaurants or coffee shops).

This can prove to be, shall we say, interesting! At the end of our trip, we review our favorites and least favorites of both! And we can tell a lot of stories to go along with those!

Once we wound up at a hotel at a good location near where we wanted to be. We were tired and needed rest. They had one room left, and we took it. It seemed clean and fit our needs just fine, but what we noticed shortly after settling in was that it wasn't level. The floor slanted in the bedroom area, the sliding door to the balcony tilted, and the bathroom door literally did not stay open and eventually came away from the hinge because of the gravitational pull on it. After spending some time in the room, Joe and I experienced a bit of vertigo! We became sensitive to the slight difference to the normal balance of life, making the correction the next night in a new location!

Let's Pause for Prayer

Heavenly Father, we pray that we would always be sensitive to what isn't right or level, to what might be off course in our personal lives and in what is happening around us. Please show us when personal corrections need to be made. When we need to ask or grant forgiveness, flee from sin, or just steady our course, will You be the One to direct us? When we see what is happening around us jump off course, will You keep us headed in a direction away from danger, error, sin or discord? Thank You for alerting us to what isn't right. Thank You for helping us to change course if we haven't gone too far off the path You've asked us to travel. In Jesus' name we pray. Amen.

How are you able to tell whether you are out of balance or off course? What are the markers for you?

How do you make the correction to get back on course?

Day 290

Practice

> *"I press on toward the goal for the prize of the upward call of God in Christ Jesus."*
> Philippians 3:14

I've enjoyed watching a number of Olympic gymnastics competitions, and I think I could perform as well as any of those competitors. I've also watched a number of cooking programs, and I think I could make those gourmet meals having simply paid attention to how the chefs did it. I'm also very sure I could compete in some of the singing shows because I've listened to the voices for so long.

Preposterous! Don't you agree?

First of all, I'm past the age when beginning some of those activities is feasible; but most importantly, I wouldn't ever have been able to be skilled in any of them just by watching. I would have needed to study, learn, and practice; and after many years of doing so, I would have become proficient in those activities. Simply observing will not allow us to excel at much.

So, when it comes to prayer life, that is, an obedient life as a Christian following Jesus, having right responses when others mistreat us or when engaging in any other biblical discipline, we must study, learn, and practice before we can ever be close to accomplishing our godly goals to the fullest.

Let's Pause for Prayer

Heavenly Father, we realize we can't sit on the sidelines of life and expect to learn to walk closely with You without putting forth some effort as we practice what we'd like to accomplish. Help us, Lord, to study Your word daily that we might present to You a heart of wisdom (Psalm 90). Help us to study in such a way that we learn little by little to hear from You as we choose obedience over our own way. And then help us to practice over and over what we learn so that our walk with You becomes consistent and strong. We desire to teach others through our example. Let us not be foolish to think or believe we can learn simply by watching. Allow us to take action steps forward little by little. In Jesus' name we pray. Amen.

What area of your Christian walk should take little to no practice to accomplish?

_____

_____

_____

How do you practice Christian life?

_____

_____

_____

Day 291

It's Just The Thing To Do

> *"God is a righteous judge."*
> Psalm 7:11a

Without going into statistics, perhaps you've sensed that many young couples (Christian and non Christian) live together but do not marry. Some of them say it's for financial convenience, some for sharing a bed. Some say it's OK once they're engaged, and others say, "It's the thing to do." Even older folks (including the 70–80 and older set) say they live together as though they were married because they don't want to lose their social security income or the pensions provided them following the death of a spouse.

God's word says, "Do not be deceived, God is not mocked; for whatever a man sows, this he will also reap. For the one who sows to his own flesh shall from the flesh reap corruption, but the one who sows to the Spirit shall from the Spirit reap eternal life" (Galatians 6:7–8). Scripture also says in Hebrews 13:4, "Let marriage be held in honor among all, and let the marriage bed be undefiled; for fornicators (having sex and not married) and adulterers (having sex outside marriage) God will judge." God's word is simple and clear. It's up to us whether we want to be obedient to it or not.

Let's Pause for Prayer

Heavenly Father, we are thankful for the truth and power of Your word and the way it convicts of sin. Help those cohabitating to read, understand, and then obey Your word. For those who counsel young couples, help them clearly teach from scripture and not avoid or evade the issue of couples living and sleeping together before or outside marriage because they are embarrassed or feel they are out of step with the culture but instead speak straightforwardly in step with God's word. Allow those who obey to sense that You are pleased with their obedience and bless them in ways that they will recognize those blessings are from You. In Jesus' name we pray. Amen.

Where do you stand on sexual relations outside marriage? Use scripture to support that stand.

_____

_____

_____

Compose a prayer that speaks to the heart of this issue.

_____

_____

_____

_____

Day 292

Worry

"And do not seek what you shall eat, and what you shall drink, and do not keep worrying. For all these things the nations of the world eagerly seek; but your Father knows that you need these things. But seek for His kingdom, and these things shall be added to you."

Luke 12:29

Recently at a business meeting around my kitchen table, Renee shared this statement with the group, "If you're going to pray, then don't worry. If you're going to worry, then don't pray." Wow! How fun to hear such wisdom in a business meeting, but even taken a bit further, let's apply that to our everyday lives!

So often I catch myself wondering (i.e., worrying) how plans will turn out, perhaps even fretting or feeling concerned or thinking about them. But worry? Of course not! I shy away from the word, but all I'm doing is avoiding the truth of it: Worry in the first degree!

We have a mighty God, who is interested in every detail of our lives, and we have no need to worry but to trust.

Let's Pause for Prayer

Father, we come to you in trust for what overwhelms us in our minds and in our lives. Help us to give worries over to You, knowing that You will give us what we need. Although we may think You're late in answering our earnest prayers, we know in our hearts that Your timing is perfect in every way. Thank You for allowing us to learn new ideas, experience new ways of trusting You, and have a testimony to share because of the time we've patiently waited to hear from You. We thank You in advance for how we will learn and grow by trusting in You. In Jesus' name we pray. Amen.

What do you worry about?

_____

_____

_____

Have you been able to turn your worries over to God? How does that look for you?

_____

_____

_____

Day 293 — Only The Beginning

> *"I love those who love me; and those who diligently seek me will find me."*
> Proverbs 8:17

Although some have said, "How nice that the work is now done" when one finishes a book, the truth is that the work has just begun. The time and effort it takes to write a book is only the start. The book then needs to get out into the hands of people whom the author hopes it will help and encourage and not just sit on a shelf somewhere collecting dust.

Thus it is with our walk as Christians. Sometimes it takes a while for someone to come to faith in the Lord. The efforts of many may be necessary to lay the groundwork for one to understand what it means to make a decision to follow Christ, but when that decision is made and the person becomes a Christian, it's just the beginning. The new believer who wants to follow God has work to do!

Let's Pause for Prayer

Heavenly Father, we are so grateful that coming to faith in You is not the end of our journey but the beginning. We desire to share the excitement and reality of our faith with others who don't know You. We purpose to share our faith and what we're learning about You with others. Will you be the guide we need to know when to share, when to lead, and when to be silent? Let us not become comfortable sitting in the pew thinking this is all we need to do as a believer, collect dust, if You will. Guide us to others to show Christlike love, lead us to people who need to understand the love You have for them, and allow us to be purposeful about our own walk, encouraging others, helping them, and loving them in the name of our Lord and Savior. In Jesus' name we pray. Amen.

When did your journey of knowing Christ begin to unfold?

_____
_____
_____

Where are you in the journey?

_____
_____
_____
_____

Day 294

Dismissed

> *"But I say to you who hear, love your enemies, do good to those who hate you, bless those who curse you, pray for those who mistreat you."*
>
> Luke 6:27–28

That feeling of being dismissed, ignored, or even interrupted in ways that make us feel as if someone has just told us to shut up are like the sting of a bee. Perhaps it was the call that someone never returned on purpose and you know it, the time someone left you out of an activity when you were in on the planning from the outset, the time someone took you out of the ministry spot you had without saying a word to you as another filled your shoes, and each instance left you wondering what to say or do without gossiping or hurting others but resolving the situation. If we can quickly come to the true realization that Jesus knows all the details that others will keenly try to hide; He will be the One to take us in.

Let's Pause for Prayer

Heavenly Father, we are so thankful that You will always take us in. You will always care for and comfort us when others dispose of and dismiss us. Correct others who have been dismissive and allow us to see whether and when we are doing the same. May we desire to serve and bless one another instead of being unkind or cursing one another. Give courage to people who choose to talk to those who've wronged them and humility to the ones who caused the wrong so no divisiveness will damage the body of believers. Let us be kind and caring, and when we need to correct, may we do so with love and in a way that will be respectful, helpful, and kind. Help us to be the type of Christian others would want to emulate. In Jesus' name we pray. Amen.

Do you know the feeling of being dismissed? Share a time it happened to you.

_____

_____

_____

How have you handled some of these hurtful moments in your life? What would you, could you, or should you change?

_____

_____

_____

_____

Day 295

Not Making The Cut

"I am the vine, you are the branches; he who abides in Me, and I in him, he bears much fruit; for apart from Me you can do nothing."

John 15:5

Gardening and yard work give Joe and me a bit of time together. In fall, every so often we'd look at a leaf and say, "Oh this one is such a pretty color." When our daughter taught in Florida, we'd save a few to mail her to show her little first graders who knew only all green! Other times we'd look at a leaf and drop it back down, basically saying, "You're not the chosen one." Similarly when we trim and prune, we have to decide what would stay and what would go. In each of these scenarios, we made judgment calls on what would make the cut.

Our oldest daughter learned the same lesson when she didn't make the volleyball team in middle school. The youngest, who graduated with a degree in musical theater, has had her share of not making the cut for plays for which she auditioned. It happens in so many places—not getting the job, not winning the prize, not being chosen for a team—and none of it is easy.

God, however, has a plan that allows each of us to make it to heaven to be forever with Him. John 14:6 says, "Jesus said to him, 'I am the way, the truth, and the life; no one comes to the Father but through Me.'" To *abide* means "to dwell, remain, and last." We might not make the cut in the eyes of the world, but God never puts us aside.

Let's Pause for Prayer

Lord God, we are so thankful that when we come to You, we are accepted just as we are. We don't have to earn Your favor or do a certain amount of good to make it to heaven although we desire to serve You because of all You've done for us. We are so thankful that we simply need to come to You. And once we do, thank You that we are never to be separated from You because we abide with You. Lord, it seems so simple, and yet Your Son's death for us was not. Thank You for Your Son's work on the cross, for loving us unconditionally, and for the security we have in knowing we've made the cut and will be with You forever. In Jesus' name we pray. Amen.

Share a time when you didn't make the cut and how you felt. How did you handle that disappointment?

_____
_____
_____
_____
_____

Day 296

The Choice Is Ours

> *"And if it is disagreeable in your sight to serve the Lord, choose for yourselves today whom you will serve,... but as for me and my house, we will serve the Lord."*
>
> Joshua 24:15

Every so often we feel a sense of overwhelming happiness and perhaps even ease. If that's happened to you, did you find yourself enjoying the moment or find it kind of scary?

Someone once asked me, "How are you doing?" It was one of those rare times when life was really good. I answered, "You know, we are in a very nice season right now. Everyone seems to be doing well, and life is pretty good. Thank you for asking! I almost don't want to turn around in case the train is comin' down the tracks!" My friend said, "Well, what will you do if the train is coming?" I said, "I guess I have three choices: move, get hit, or hop on. I'm hoppin' on!"

We all have those options in life when a trial comes our way. We can either let it knock us over and really get down and out about it, or we can move over and let life take its course. But if we hop on and engage the battle, struggle, or challenge, we are likely to find that God has some very exciting surprises for us along the way! I can attest to knowing that in the midst of raising a child (now an adult) with special needs, having some severe back issues, the deaths of five family members in a 10-year span, and other things in life, at times moving over and walking away would be at the top of the list of responses; but when we experience God in the midst of these struggles, we can find blessings beyond what we might ever have tried even to imagine.

Let's Pause for Prayer

Heavenly Father, we are waiting for our next marching orders from You, knowing that we may be called to enter into a challenging time. We know that if we do, You are with us. We know from Your word that You will never leave nor forsake us, so we choose to hop on the train that is coming down the tracks, knowing it's not just about the destination but also about the journey. Help us to recognize the good You are showing us in the journey You have planned. The kind neighbor or good friend who helps us, the person we hardly know who prays for us, the family member who steps up and does something to serve when we least expect it. Allow us to be appreciative of the lessons from You and the help from others. In Jesus' name we pray. Amen.

Where are you right now in life? Enjoying the ease or in the midst of challenges?

_____

_____

What kinds of choices are you making as you deal with these challenges?

_____

_____

_____

Day 297 — Best Of Intentions

> *"Man's steps are ordained by the Lord; how then can a man understand his way?"*
>
> Proverbs 20:24

I sometimes wonder whether I'm obeying as I should. When other Christians act in ways that obviously aren't right—like being manipulative or divisive—I often wonder whether they really think they're obeying God. I know it's not my concern to judge them, but nevertheless I wonder. Are we obeying God when He asks us to act or perform in some way but the request doesn't sit well with us and we question it? I also wonder—when God calls me to do something but I don't do it because I didn't sense that call, have I missed the mark totally or will He redeem the situation in time?

It's confusing sometimes. I know we can judge sin, but I'm thinking about those instances where a question remains about a situation. I'm thankful to have come to a place as a Christian to realize that God probably takes my best intentions even when I'm not totally on His page for me and allows good to come of it when I have pure intentions but lack understanding. I'm not talking about sin. Sin is sin, and we must call it that and confess it. I don't believe He'll ever bless those blatant acts of disobedience but will allow the consequences to teach us. If our desire is truly pure, I trust that He will make the course right for us, turning us in a different direction or showing us in some way that we're off course.

Let's Pause for Prayer

Lord, we recognize we don't have license to sin or to see whether we can disobey and get away with sin. You know the intentions of our hearts. We trust that You will make good what happens when we might be off course! Thank You for leading us and speaking to us; we can hear You in our hearts and obey. When we aren't listening well, please gain our attention that we might obey in truth and purity. We love You and desire clear directions the first time so we can do everything according to Your will for Your glory. In Jesus' name we pray. Amen.

Can you look back to a time when you thought you heard God and did His will but later learned you were terribly off course? How did you recognize you were off course, and how did you get back on course?

What is happening in your life right now that you might question? Seek Him!

Day 298

Frustration

> *"As in water face reflects face, so the heart of man reflects man."*
> Proverbs 27:19

It was late and everyone traveling looked tired. I could see it on a few faces: They were thinking as I was. "I see those families with little kids. I hope they're running around now and get out all that energy so the plane ride is quiet while they sleep." You know where I'm going with this, don't you? Indeed, one child screamed and wiggled for the two solid hours of the flight. People surely could not easily watch a movie, listen to their music, much less read as that child wailed.

I honestly tried to pray during that flight even though I was among the frustrated and tired. Perhaps my prayers were answered as I didn't see anyone huffing or puffing, saying anything negative, nor asking the attendants to "do something about that child."

I wanted to read or close my eyes. Neither were options. As I recognized that bit of selfishness for what I wanted, I asked the Lord to remind me of times I tried to quiet one of my children in a restaurant or on a plane to avoid ruining a meal or trip for others. It didn't take me long to remember a time or two, and He supplied the memories well over that number. I asked the Lord to comfort that mom and quiet the baby. It only took two hours until the Lord answered my prayer. In the last 30 minutes of the flight—as we were beginning to descend—the toddler ran out of energy and fell asleep.

Let's Pause for Prayer

Father, when we're frustrated at the behavior of others around us that is obviously cutting into our personal time or space, help us first to come to prayer to You. Help us understand and sympathize with people and situations instead of demanding our way, want, or need, quiet, or time alone or saying something we might regret! Help us to remember times when we might have been the reason or cause of frustration to others and we couldn't do anything to change it or perhaps were oblivious of it at the time but remember it now! Lord, make us sensitive to show love and patience and do so through prayer. In Jesus' name we pray. Amen.

How do you handle this level and kind of frustration?

_____

_____

What is your typical response when you're frustrated? Now pray!

_____

_____

_____

_____

Day 299

Making Me A Willow

> *"He breaks me down on every side, and I am gone; and He has uprooted my hope like a tree."*
>
> Job 19:10

Even though we might think we know the directions we should go, goals we should state, plans we should establish to be better at this thing called life, it is true that life will bend us. I remember my mother-in-law telling me, "You were born an oak, but God is making you into a willow." Through the trials of life we'll endure, we can yield to what God is teaching us (bending to accommodate the teaching), or we can reject and deny it and break under the pressure of the branch bowing. When we accept His journey for us and as we learn to rest in Him, it can become a beautiful trip during which we can admire the wonderful scenery along the way through His eyes; or we can cross our arms, bend our heads down like pouting two-year-olds unwilling to learn, and miss what He has for us along the way.

Let's Pause for Prayer

Heavenly Father, we want to be flexible and bendable to Your will in our lives. We know You are the Potter, and if we are to be the clay, we must be easy to work with, pliable, and moldable. Help us to see where we need to make changes in our lives to accommodate that which You're teaching us. Help us to realize that while we think we have Plan A all figured out, You might choose to teach us through Plan B, or even C to make us a better fit for what we are to accomplish for Your glory here. Allow us the flexibility in our minds to go with Your plan over ours, Your goals over ours, Your will and Your way over ours. In Jesus' name we pray. Amen.

At this moment are you bending or breaking? Why?

_____

_____

_____

How is the Lord making you into a willow?

_____

_____

_____

_____

Day 300 — House Of Prayer

"And He began to teach and say to them, 'Is it not written, "My house shall be called a house of prayer for all the nations?"'"

Mark 11:17

My conclusion would be that if a church does not have prayer, it's not a house of God; but have you noticed that prayer meetings are one of the hardest events to which to attract large attendance?

Prayer should be a priority, publicly in church and privately in our hearts. That is the beauty of this discipline. We can practice it in a small or large group, and we can practice it quietly alone; yet sometimes we'd prefer to serve in some practical and physical way instead of take time to stop and pray. I've even heard people say, "I don't do the kinds of things so-and-so does, so I don't think my prayer or what I do is counting for the kingdom." I recognize this comment as indicative of the mindset of a person who says, "If people are noticed for what they do, it counts." But have you ever considered the importance of people praying for those who are noticed or who have been called to more public work? What would those people do and what would they even accomplish if not for the prayers of those who support them? It might just be that the greater work of prayer is that which we'll someday find was the greatest of all.

Let's Pause for Prayer

Heavenly Father, Your scripture tells us in I Peter 3:12, "For the eyes of the Lord are upon the righteous and His ears attend to their prayer." Please attend to our prayer now, and speak to our hearts individually about the need to be fully attentive to Your word. Speak to those who feel their ministry of prayer is not worthy. Help them to realize the importance and need for it. Help each of us to hear from You so we know when to pray and for whom to pray. Let us lift up those who have a more public work than we do. Let us recognize Your hand in the answering of our prayers. We are thankful for the desire, ability, and willingness to pray. Thank You for showing Yourself faithful even to the tiniest and shortest of prayers prayed in confidence and with boldness. Use us, Lord, in Your mighty work with the simplicity of our prayers and the obedience of our hearts as we follow Your lead. In Jesus' name we pray. Amen.

What do you consider to be the ministry God has given you?

_____

_____

_____

Do you have a team of people who pray for you and the ministry? If not, why not? Ask a handful of people to commit to praying.

_____

_____

Day 301   Servant Heart

"Just as the Son of man did not come to be served, but to serve, and to give His life a ransom for many"

Matthew 20:28

As a child, I remember Mom serving Dad and the four of us kids before taking her portion of the meal. It wasn't that we didn't have enough; it was her servant heart. Both she and my father had grown up with very little. I recall Mom telling us about days when an egg or a potato was all they had for the entire day. Dad, whose mother died when he was nine years old, lived with relatives as a boarder and was not permitted to eat until the family with whom he stayed was finished. Thankfully, my parents provided for our family in a way that we never had to struggle as they did as kids; but they taught us the lesson of sharing, no matter how much or how little we had—food, candy, earnings, time.

The valuable lesson of sharing and serving is something I feel fewer and fewer people comprehend. Popular mantras like "all for me," "I'm first," and "I'm entitled" drown out generosity, which would allow others to recognize us as Christians.

Let's Pause for Prayer

Heavenly Father, we thank You for being the perfect example of generosity by sending Your Son to serve in exemplary ways. We want to and need to stop making excuses for failing to share and serve and just get busy and do so. Help us to recognize needs and meet them. Help us to see when someone is struggling and offer to help. Perhaps others will become curious about You when we show them how much we care. Thank You for caring for us first. In Jesus' name we pray. Amen.

Share a few ways you have put others first, serving them before yourself. How did it feel?

_____

_____

_____

Consider a few ways you can make this an action point and improve your service to others.

_____

_____

_____

_____

Day 302 — Grandparenting

"Grandchildren are the crown of old men, and the glory of sons is their fathers."
Proverbs 17:6

It's called "grand" parenting for a reason. Grandparenting is often so much easier than what we were called to do as parents, when we were always tired and clinging to the thought that someday we'd be able to take a nap. As grandparents we have the luxuries but not the liabilities, yet in this role that has little power but lots of perks, we are called to be the influencers of the next generation. Many in this stage have "been there, done that, don't want to now" and choose instead travel, golf, or naps over spending time with the little ones. Many of us are still relatively young and healthy and have many years to help mold, guide, and influence the next generation. The only stumbling block is our willingness.

Let's Pause for Prayer

Heavenly Father, what joy You've given. You've allowed our children to have children and extended the blessing of grandparenthood. Thank You for the privilege of influencing the next generation to know and serve You and teaching young children to follow You and to delight in You. May we be examples to our grandchildren. Lord, allow us to make and take the time each of our grandchildren will need to learn and grow under our love and care. We know it's not our job to take over parenting when their parents are able to do what is expected of them, but help us to guide our grandchildren as an extension of what their parents are already teaching them. Give those who have neither children nor grandchildren people in the neighborhood or at church to whom they can impart wisdom and in whose lives they can invest. Thank you for the privilege. May we take our roles seriously and give generously of our time, talents, and treasures for their development. In Jesus' name we pray. Amen.

How can you invest in the lives of your own grandchildren, or if you're a young parent, how can you engage your parents in grandparenting?

_____
_____
_____

If you've not had children, to whom can you impart wisdom? With whom can you share time?

_____
_____
_____
_____

Day 303

Judging Intentions

> *"Do not judge lest you be judged yourselves."*
> Matthew 7:1

The coach in *Facing the Giants* addresses one of his players saying, "You judge [him] by his actions and you judge yourself by your intentions." How easily we give grace to ourselves but are harsh in our thoughts, judgments, or deeds directed at others.

We can and often do justify what we say, make excuses, rationalize, defend, and account for our actions, but the bottom line is this: We give ourselves more latitude than we are willing to give others. I've been trying to catch myself when I make assumptions about another's intentions or motivation. I'm trying not to play out the worst case scenario in interpreting the actions of others but instead give them the benefit of the doubt in situations when I have no way of knowing their real intentions nor the reality of a given situation. We often fabricate explanations that are far from the truth.

Let's Pause for Prayer

Heavenly Father, we desire to treat one another kindly, generously, and graciously. Help us to see when we are making assumptions without basis in fact, when we are dwelling on fiction that isn't reality. Show us the error of our ways and teach us to extend grace and mercy to others in our lives. Let us give one another the benefit of the doubt as often as we are able, and instead of making unwarranted assumptions if we question someone's actions, allow us lovingly to confront, question, and inquire of others so that we can all be on the same page with attitudes of compassion, understanding, and love. Show us how to work out questionable or uneasy situations so that we can work in harmony with friends, family, ministry partners, and coworkers. In keeping our minds and hearts focused on You and Your ways, may we respond as You would. In Jesus' name we pray. Amen.

In what ways have you found yourself judging the intentions of others?

_____

_____

_____

_____

Are you willing to ask the Lord to alert you when you judge another and allow Him to show you how to extend grace to that person?

_____

_____

_____

Day 304 — Modern Day Lion's Den

"But the goal of our instruction is love from a pure heart and a good conscience and a sincere faith."

I Timothy 1:5

Driving a stretch of highway to and from my daughter's college, I saw numerous billboards for the Lion's Den Adult Superstore. Seeing them gave me many opportunities to pause to pray. First of all, how appropriate that a place that sells pornography would be called the Lion's Den. I seem to recall that most people didn't make it out of the lion's den alive. It's not much different with pornography: It's killing our marriages and destroying our families.

As Joe and I travel the country speaking on behalf of marriages, we can't tell you how many marriages are hanging by a thread because of addiction to pornography. And by the way, although many men are addicted, we must understand it "takes two"; and many women find themselves in the same den. Pornography addiction occurs at epidemic proportions in the Christian community as well as the secular. I remember reading an article showing the affects of pornography and how it destroys the brain in ways similar to drug addiction. The addiction is as powerful as chemical dependency on cocaine.

Let's Pause for Prayer

Heavenly Father, we pray that those addicted to pornography, even though they may deny it and say they see no wrong in it, would have a sense of conviction from You that what they are doing is wrong, sinful, despicable, and worthless. Give the spouse of an addict who is married the courage to address this issue and to stop denying it even though it might bring hurt and challenge to their marriage. We pray for families who know the reality of the pain and devastation this sin causes but don't want to rock the boat to create an opportunity for change. Help us protect the young and innocent, keeping them from the effects of this addiction. Allow the sex addict to be honest with the God who forgives and with fellow believers who are strong and capable of helping and to work this through no matter how long it takes. We pray that the addict will call this addiction by name and recognize it as the absence of any true relationship in this addiction. In Jesus' name we pray. Amen.

If this is currently a problem in your life, whom can you seek out today to get help? Don't wait. Get help today.

_____

_____

_____

If this is not an issue for you, pray for someone you know who is dealing with the devastation of this sin.

Day 305 — Power, Prestige, Control

> *"And as for you, you meant evil against me, but God meant it for good in order to bring about his present result, to preserve many people alive."*
>
> Genesis 50:20

It continues to amaze me and I'm thankful that one can read something from God's word over and over and each time learn something new. I was very impacted this time around with the story of Joseph, who endured so much opposition and hardship, often from those he most loved and knew best. His envious brothers tried to kill him; he was sold into slavery, falsely accused by his master for a wrong done to his master's wife, and sent to jail. While there, the chief cup-bearer promised that when he was released, he'd remember Joseph and work toward his release, but he didn't. Through all these obstacles and hindrances Joseph remained faithful and was placed in a position of honor—second in command in Egypt. He didn't let the circumstances in life get in his way of faithfulness and living life honestly.

Let's Pause for Prayer

Heavenly Father, may we be honest and forgiving of others no matter how we have been slighted, dismissed, forgotten, or deceived. May we take each step forward, believing You will have Your way with us and with others according to the deeds and hearts of each. We pray that You will keep our hearts pure and seek only Your best for others. We recognize from Joseph's life that people often want power, prestige, and control no matter the cost. Show us the error of our ways when striving to make life go our own way, when our sin makes outcomes look as if someone else was at fault, or when we accuse others who are innocent, or when we make choices that jeopardize another's future, shamefully doing so at their expense. Speak to the hearts of all deceivers, anyone who deceives and knows it. Let no individuals escape the realization that You are speaking to them, and may they own up to wrong motives and deception, and ask for forgiveness for hurting others. In that way, may the body of Christ be made whole. In Jesus' name we pray. Amen.

Have you observed a time when you or someone you know has been on the receiving end of mistreatment? How did you get through it?

_____

_____

_____

_____

_____

If someone comes to mind for whom to pray, pray for them now.

Day 306 — *Directionally Challenged*

"Call to Me, and I will answer you, and I will tell you great and mighty things, which you do not know."
                                            Jeremiah 33:3

When you have a decision to make, a question to answer, a new direction in which to go, or a choice among several good options, how do you make the decision? Do you talk to people first, or do you first pray to God? Do you search articles, blogs, and books, or do you spend time researching God's word? Doing what is easy and at our fingertips seems easier than seeking spiritual means to finding an answer, but along with the one above, here a few scripture verses that encourage us to seek God and His word before people and the books they write.

Matthew 6:33:
"But seek first His kingdom and His righteousness; and all these things shall be added to you."

Matthew 7:7:
"Ask, and it shall be given to you; seek, and you shall find; knock and it shall be opened to you."

Let's Pause for Prayer

Heavenly Father, we want to make a habit of coming to You first and always when we have decisions to make. As we come to You, please guide us through Your word and through our prayer times with You; and show us the direction You want us to take. We want to learn to rely upon You because You would never steer us in a wrong direction or tell us to do what isn't pure and right. Thank You for giving us Your word to enrich our lives and decisions and for inviting us to call upon You any time of day or night as well as in crisis or in calm. When we feel no answer forthcoming from You, help us to be patient and listen carefully and well. Show us how to be still and calm when situations around us seem to move quickly yet You tell us to wait. May we be able to look back on the decisions made and know that You have been the One to answer in Your own time. In Jesus' name we pray. Amen.

Do you have a decision to make that requires you to be quiet and wait patiently? Pray to the Lord and ask Him for direction.

Day 307

Who Will We Become?

"A joyful heart is good medicine, but a broken spirit dries up the bones."

Proverbs 17:22

One day Joe and I visited three elderly women in their late 80s to early 90s whom we'd known for 30 to 35 years. The first visit was with someone I hold dear and have known from my church. Recovering from an illness at home, she needed some help we could provide; so we stopped over. My conversation with her was lovely and God-centered. It was a delight to spend time with her.

The next visit was to a nursing home, where my friend's mom was in rehab. As tired and ill as she was that day, her face just shone as she talked about Jesus. She asked us how we were and was so pleasant.

The third visit also took place in a care facility. After a brief hello, our elderly friend talked nonstop about her frustrations regarding some games she was playing, people not visiting, and disliking her nail polish. To my knowledge she doesn't know the Lord, but for certain, she was not pleasant to visit. I learned some important lessons that day.

Let's Pause for Prayer

Heavenly Father, we recognize who we are now becoming and who we will become. Help us to praise You with our lips at all times, to have pleasant thoughts that we will share with others about Your goodness, and to desire to bless others as we visit with them day to day. Let us practice kindness to others now so that in our later years kindness will be second nature to us. Let us offer words of encouragement to others today so in our tomorrows such words will come naturally to us. Lord, please remind us when we are complaining how awful we sound and what a poor example it is when we should be showing gratitude and appreciation of all You've done for us. We know we'll never be perfect, but help us develop the kinds of skills now that will allow our words to bless, to encourage, to give thanks, and to show kindness so that we will be people of gratitude. Thank you Lord for all You've done for us. We are so appreciative. In Jesus' name we pray. Amen.

Are you able to catch yourself when you complain? When did you last complain?

_____

_____

_____

Share the way you can turn a complaint into a prayer of thanksgiving and gratitude.

_____

_____

_____

Day 308

With Me

"Be strong and courageous, do not be afraid or tremble at them, for the Lord our God is the one who goes with you. He will not fail you or forsake you."

Deuteronomy 31:6

Should we even try to pursue excellence? How do we know whether we are indeed pursuing excellence? Who really cares about the pursuit of excellence? It's my thinking that most of us desire to be good at a particular skill. Sadly, even those proposing to do evil want to be good at it. But in terms of a positive personal pursuit of excellence, I believe we are pleased when God is pleased; and He is pleased when we are doing what He has asked of us. He is always with us to help us succeed and achieve excellence.

Let's Pause for Prayer

Lord, we are here to serve You and others whom You've put into our lives. We know that when we seek to honor and please You instead of seeking personal attention and accolades, You are pleased. As we choose good deeds over evil, Your will over our own will, and excellence over ordinary, we acknowledge who You are and Your steadfastness. From acknowledging who You are, we come to know You, and when we know You, we should desire to serve You. As we serve You, we often do so by serving others. May we serve others in ways we'd like to be served, in ways that will bless others, and in ways that will meet needs. May we serve others and ultimately please You. And Heavenly Father, as we choose right actions, may we do so with excellence in all ways. Show us where those needs are, and then give us the desire to meet them as we love well. Keep us from selfishness and wanting or seeking attention, allowing us to depend only on You. Keep us from proceeding in wrong directions and missing Your instruction to pursue excellence as it pertains to knowing, serving, and pleasing You. In Jesus' name we pray. Amen.

Can you recall a time when you felt as if you wanted to take credit for something you did or accomplished?

_____

_____

_____

How did you handle it, and would you handle the situation any differently today?

_____

_____

_____

Day 309 — Who Or What Is More Important?

"Do nothing from selfishness or empty conceit, but with humility of mind let each of you regard one another as more important than himself; do not merely look out for your own personal interest, but also for the interest of others."

Philippians 2:3–4

Thinking isn't the same as doing. Sometimes I think I've written a thank you note until I see the note card still sitting on my desk. Sometimes I think I followed through on an email I needed to send until I check my out box. Sometimes I think I answered that phone message but realize it's not checked off my list. We all do this from time to time, but following through is a must. In some situations, however, we fail to be the kind of people we need to be as Christians. When we don't say thank you, when we don't follow through with others who have asked something of us, when we choose not to return a call to someone—I believe those times show we do not appreciate them. Worse yet, we say we are more important than they are because we choose to ignore them. Purposely neglecting to follow up on a task or purposely ignoring someone is rude.

Let's Pause for Prayer

Heavenly Father, thank you for the instruction Your word gives us. Help us, Father, to put others first by following through with that which we know is right, and help us to show appreciation and gratitude to others whenever we have opportunity. We don't want to be selfish people who think only of ourselves, our convenience, and our comfort but desire to offer to others what we hope they would offer to us. Please help us to be mindful of following through with what we say we'll do and what we promise—the simple ways of showing kindness as we do what we say. Help us to extend grace to those who have let obligations truly slip their minds as they've forgotten. Let us be the example of forgiveness and grace. In Jesus' name we pray. Amen.

Do you follow through with what you've been asked to do? If a person to call or job to finish pops into your mind, follow through today.

Day 310 — *Isolated And Defeated*

> *"He who separates himself seeks his own desire, He quarrels against all sound wisdom."*
>
> Proverbs 18:1

I've heard it said that "an isolated Christian is a defeated Christian." Isolation seems to happen the same way a wall is built—one brick at a time. For each wrong done toward a person, whether perceived or real, if that person is not careful to forgive quickly, she or he can stop moving forward in relationships and thus add a brick to the building of a wall of separation from others. After a time, that wall is so high that it will take years before it can come down.

The need for power and prestige can also cause isolation, desiring one's own way for personal gain. Soon, with no one to hold an individual accountable, isolation occurs at the top, where it's easy to fail in some aspect of the Christian walk. This isolation takes place in friendships, marriages, church relationships, and even in local and national ministry relationships.

Let's Pause for Prayer

Heavenly Father, thank You for good friends, close family, and ministry partners who will hold us accountable to staying in fellowship with the body of Christ and to working through difficulties that involve plans and people and who will keep our feet on the straight and narrow. Give us open minds to accept constructive criticism and even reproof from those who are giving it to us in a loving and gentle way. Let us be wise to the attempts of others who want power and prestige when they attempt to put people in their place solely because of their evil and wrongful attempts to secure position. Allow us to discern these tactics and solely surrender to doing Your will, no matter what. Keep us in fellowship with like-minded believers who have surrendered and are desirous of serving You with a pure heart. Keep us from isolating others and keep us from isolating ourselves when we sense that is the path we are taking. We never want to be isolated from You. In Jesus' name we pray. Amen.

Do you feel isolated and defeated now or did you sometime in the past? Describe the situation.

_____
_____
_____

How would you or how do you keep from becoming isolated from others?

_____
_____
_____

Day 311 — *Express Yourself*

> *"Be on the alert, stand firm in the faith, act like men, be strong. Let all that you do be done in love."*
>
> I Corinthians 16:13–14

People in this country have the right to protest in public and in nonviolent ways in order to share their feelings about various issues and in the politic arena. These expressions are permitted in our free country and for that we should be thankful. As Christians take part in these public displays, we should remember to be Christlike in all ways: in our words, our actions, and our attitudes. Some people will neither publicly protest nor verbally share their views on issues or candidates, but they will enter the voting booth and there express their views and thoughts. What a blessing to have these opportunities to express our views!

Let's Pause for Prayer

Lord, in a day and age when many want to voice their opinions publicly, many others are uncomfortable doing so and privately make their opinions known through prayer and voting at the poll. Thank You for giving us both types of freedom in our country, and may we always be grateful for that freedom. As we exercise our freedom to publicly share our thoughts and as we take seriously our right to vote, please give us the right attitudes and discernment to do either with Your wisdom and insight. May we research and educate ourselves. Please silence the voices that share false information and spread lies. Point us in the direction of truth and help us to find needed nonpartisan information so that we can be clear in our thinking, prayerful in our seeking, and clear in the direction in which You are pointing us. In Jesus' name we pray. Amen.

Have you ever protested or shared your views in a public setting? How did it go?

_____

_____

_____

Whether or not you've shared publicly, how can you privately make your position known in the public arena? Prayer and voting are just two ways. What else?

_____

_____

_____

_____

Day 312

Experiencing Loss

> *"Weeping may last for the night, but a shout of joy comes in the morning."*
>
> Psalm 30:5b

(Excerpt from *A Grace Disguised* by Jerry Sittser)

When we experience a loss, justice is not always served. Bad people get away with doing bad things. If we insist life is fair, we will be disappointed. People will fail us and will not pay for doing so. The process of forgiveness begins when we realize nothing can reverse the wrong done or the loss. Forgiveness is costly. We must give up the right to get even. The supreme challenge to anyone facing loss involves facing the darkness of the loss on the one hand and learning to live with renewed vitality and gratitude on the other. This challenge is met when we learn to take the loss into ourselves and to be enlarged by it so that our capacity to live well and to know God intimately increases. To escape the loss is far less healthy and realistic than to grow from it. Loss can diminish us, but it can also expand us. It depends on choices. Each of us has experienced loss. It's our choice what we do with it.

Let's Pause for Prayer

Heavenly Father, we trust in Your word. Sometimes it's very hard to grasp it when we're going through a challenging loss in life. Please meet us in our loss and mourning, whether a job loss, a medical diagnosis we just received, the death of a friend or loved one, the unfaithfulness of a spouse, or the betrayal of a friend, family member, coworker, or ministry partner. Father, we know we have the choice of whether or not to forgive others, and we want to choose the right direction so that we aren't missing out on the good that will come if we do what You ask. We desire to live with renewed vitality, gratitude, and freedom so that we will sense You using us through our example as we trust in You. May we know You more intimately through our pain as You comfort and guide us. In Jesus' name we pray. Amen.

What was the greatest loss you ever experienced? Share the way you worked through it in your own heart and with His help.

_____

_____

_____

_____

_____

_____

Day 313

Borrowed But Missing

"For if you forgive men for their transgressions, your heavenly Father will also forgive you. But if you don't forgive men, then your Father will not forgive your transgressions."

Matthew 6:14-15

As I began preparing this manuscript, I decided I would take a hymn and concentrate on each of the verses and then pray it back. Before I arrived at that point, I had to first ask forgiveness and then grant it. You see, one of the songs I wanted to use was missing from the binder I've had since 1976. I had lent it out a while ago, and when I requested its return, I learned not only was that hymn missing, but a total of 33 hymns were missing. I wasn't too happy, but as God does, He worked through my heart from my sadness about the loss and my displeasure with the person who likely has them (but denied it) to praying that the person who has them will use them for His glory. I first asked God to forgive me for being so upset and then grant forgiveness to those who have my music! Sometimes frustrations and disappointments in life serve as opportunities and lessons from which to learn how to respond to God.

Let's Pause for Prayer

Heavenly Father, thank You for teaching us through the frustrations and disappointments that life brings. I know I learn better through times of frustration and disappointment better than I do in the times when life goes my way. Will you help each of us to confess to You when we are frustrated and lack grace toward others? Thank you for redirecting us when our plans are disrupted; we just need to listen carefully for what disruption means for us. Thank You for allowing us to let go—even before we know or see the whole picture—and offer and extend forgiveness. In Jesus' name we pray. Amen.

When have you had to ask for and grant forgiveness in one action?

_____

_____

_____

Share how God has worked in your life through an act of forgiveness on your part.

_____

_____

_____

_____

Day 314

Our Daily Bread

> *"Give us this day our daily bread."*
>
> Matthew 6:11

We have freezers and refrigerators packed with food, closets stuffed with clothing and shoes, and schedules brimming with people to see and places to go. How can we even comprehend the beginning of the Lord's Prayer that prays for the temporal, daily needs like "our daily bread"? With such excess, we can't possibly recognize our needs when they've already been met.

Thus, we must train ourselves to recognize the little things we take for granted, the necessities in life that are already provided even before we realize they are needed and before we even consider getting on our knees to ask for them. In addition, we should ask ourselves whether we are willing to offer our excess to others who might be in need.

Let's Pause for Prayer

Heavenly Father, thank You for abundantly blessing our lives by giving us what we need and often so much of what we desire. We are thankful to You because most of us joining in this prayer today have no worries about where our next meal will come from or what we will wear today or tomorrow. You have provided all we need before we even needed to consider asking, and for that we are most grateful. Will You help us recognize when others are in need and out of our abundance and generosity share with them? May we obey and offer it with an attitude of generosity and humility? And if it's to give when we don't have abundance, may we also give cheerfully and generously. Thank You for Your daily provision. May we appreciate everything You provide. May we offer our thanksgiving freely and genuinely. May we never take for granted Your goodness to us. In Jesus' name we pray. Amen.

Have you ever been in a situation when you've had to ask for your daily bread because you truly had none? How did the Lord meet you in that situation?

_____

_____

_____

Do you generally give out of your abundance? Have you ever given so generously that you really felt it? Share it. If you never have, pray, and possibly try it!

_____

_____

_____

Day 315 *Desperation*

> *"Only two things do not do to me, then I will not hide from Thy face: Remove Thy hand from me, and let not the dread of Thee terrify me."*
>
> Job 13:20–21

The desperation we feel when we experience loss is very real. We can't raise that feeling when we are in a good place in life. We might remember past difficulties, but we can't summon the feelings. Similarly, if we experience physical pain for a time, it's hard to remember ever feeling good. But when the pain is gone and healing is restored, it's difficult to remember how bad we felt. And we have no idea what another is experiencing unless we, too, have experienced it. C. S. Lewis said this about his grief in the death of his wife (*A Grief Observed*): "I had been warned—I had warned myself—not to reckon on worldly happiness. We were even promised suffering… and I accepted it. I've got nothing that I hadn't bargained for. Of course, it is different when the thing happens to oneself, not to others, and in reality, not in imagination."

Let's Pause for Prayer

Father, allow me to be compassionate to others in their loss. May I be equally empathetic in the loss of a job, the loss of a friendship, dismissal from a group, or the death of a loved one because no matter the loss, it is real to the one experiencing it. Use me, Lord, to listen and care. Allow others to sense that what they're going through matters to others. Help us not to dismiss another's pain because we see it as less than our own. Lord, be with us as we walk through painful parts of life—ours and those of others. Show us how we can learn and grow in the midst of loss and pain and become a more beautiful reflection of You. We are grateful that our best times of growth often come when the pain and loss are the deepest. Allow us to turn to You in those times and seek after You, not choosing instead to turn away and deny You. May we welcome the learning and cherish the growth that we know comes from You and that You have allowed to enter into our lives. In Jesus' name we pray. Amen.

Share a time when you felt totally helpless and perhaps totally alone.

_____

_____

_____

Did you experience physical pain? Did you suffer? Did you come to a point of acceptance? If so, how? If not, why not?

_____

_____

Day 316

With Cheerfulness And Joy

> *"But a cheerful heart has a continual feast."*
>
> Proverbs 15:15b

When I began writing and airing my Pause for Prayer spots on June 15, 1998, under the tutelage of Katie Williams, I wondered how long one untrained person like me might last! Katie was always gracious as I turned in my manuscripts. When I look back on them, I see so many points she might have told me to do better, correct, or perfect. But because her emphasis was on prayer, I think she just let the Lord work on my writing skills as He worked on my heart!

I have reduced the three hours it used to take me to write a two-minute spot (about 350 words) to between an hour and a half and two hours from start to finish for each segment, including the prayer, thinking, writing, and practice time. With well over 800 manuscripts on file, I figure I've enjoyed this process between 1,200 and 1,500 hours total; and I can't think of a time that I didn't want to do it. It's something from which I derive much joy, and it's something I do with cheerfulness.

Let's Pause for Prayer

Lord, thank You for giving each and every one of us a purpose to which You've called us in service to You. May we embrace the ministry opportunities You send our way, and might we recognize them so we don't ignore the way You can and will use us if we are but willing. Thank You for giving each of us different gifts, talents, and treasures that we hope will reach and touch others in ways we never imagined. May we all take that next step even if we feel unprepared, unworthy, or unable: We want to be willing. Thank You for moving us in life in such a way that we don't often plan or purpose to do some of the tasks we've been chosen or asked to do. As we look back at how You have paved the way by giving us different experiences—meeting people along the way to help us, allowing circumstances that have led to opportunities to learn and grow—and most importantly obedience, may we give You all the credit and thanks for putting us in places that we wouldn't have dreamed of finding ourselves. Wherever You've asked us to serve, may it be done with cheerfulness of heart, and may we be faithful to the call. In Jesus' name we pray. Amen.

What has the Lord given you to do in ministry, and do you enjoy it?

_____

_____

_____

Share how you got started and who was helpful to your success? Pray for them in thanksgiving!

_____

_____

_____

Day 317

The Best Day Of My Life

> *"[You] art intimately acquainted with all my ways."*
>
> Psalm 139:3b

"What was the best day of your life?" What a fun question to answer! Was it an amazing play you made in a game? Was it someone you met? Was it the day you married or the day you put your trust in Jesus Christ?"

My daughter was about eight years old when she asked, "How do people know what the best day of their life is?" I explained that the answer would probably change over time but that we should live every day as if that day might be our best so that we'd always have an answer!

Let's Pause for Prayer

Lord, You tell us that You already know how amazing our every move, each of our moments, and our entire life will be. You already know which days will be some of our best, and You already know which days will present very big challenges. Thank You for allowing us to turn to You in both types of situations, knowing You will guide us and direct us through each. As we weep during times of challenge and crisis, may we look to You for comfort. As we rejoice in times of great joy and excitement, may we remember that You are also with us. Sometimes we forget to thank You during those times when life seems smooth and carefree. And we know (Psalm 138:8) that you will accomplish in our lives just what we need. We pray that with these insights we would look to every day and choose to live in it as if it may be our very best day ever or even as if it might be our very last. No matter what each day brings, may we serve You fully and faithfully so that someday we will be able to see the best days You've given us and that You helped us through the tough ones. May all that happens please You in the process. In Jesus' name we pray. Amen.

Share your best day ever so far.

_____

_____

_____

Share a prayer of thanks for this day, the people in it, and the moments that made it special.

_____

_____

_____

_____

Day 318

Healthy Relationships

"And be kind to one another, tender-hearted, forgiving each other, just as God in Christ also has forgiven you."

Ephesians 4:32

According to Dr. Leslie Vernick healthy relationships are mutually caring, mutually honest, and mutually respectful. Although we can have relationships of varying degrees of intensity, they will be healthy only when all three of those ingredients are present mutually. One person cannot carry the relationship and keep it healthy. These statements are helpful in keeping one's marriage healthy and in making sure investments in friendships are worthwhile; when a relationship isn't mutually caring, honest, and respectful, both individuals involved need to improve their understanding of how to handle it so both of them remain vital participants.

Let's Pause for Prayer

Lord, we are thankful for all the relationships you give us and for helping us understand more about them. Guide us to knowing what is healthy and what honors You. We recognize that we have a responsibility to be the ones who can initiate healthy relationships, the ones who notice when relationships are unhealthy, and the ones who know how to handle each. Help us to recognize when we are uncaring, dishonest, or disrespectful to others, and show us ways to correct our poor and sinful behavior. When others act in unhealthy ways toward us, give us the grace to be kind and firm in setting our own healthy boundaries that will serve as examples to help lead and instruct others to healthier living. Let us not be haughty know-it-alls who have nothing new to learn. Let us always learn to have closer, deeper, and more meaningful friendships, marriages, and walks with You that will mirror Your image and reflect who You are to others. Instruct us and change us so that others will know change is possible; and that healthy relationships are possible and worthwhile. In Jesus' name we pray. Amen.

Seek and ask the Lord to help you see what we need to change to promote healthy relationships. List what He brings to mind.

_____

_____

_____

_____

How will you act upon what you just prayed about and felt directed to do?

_____

_____

_____

Day 319 — *Constructive Criticism*

> *"And the Lord's bond-servant must not be quarrelsome, but be kind to all, able to teach, patient when wronged, with gentleness correcting those who are in opposition, if perhaps God may grant them repentance leading to the knowledge of the truth."*
>
> II Timothy 2:24–25

Most people have at one time or another been on both the giving and receiving ends of criticism, but more than likely we recognize harsh criticism because of the way it makes us feel, especially if the one giving it is uncaring. Hurt and wounded feelings are indicators letting us know when we've been spoken to harshly. Harsh criticism is difficult to swallow, but when someone who cares for us, loves us, and gives us constructive criticism, it can be very positive; and it's from there that we can learn and grow to become better people. How that criticism is delivered is very important to the way our hearts receive it.

Let's Pause for Prayer

Lord, our hearts tell us whether criticism is harsh or constructive, but even when engaged in the challenge of facing criticism, it's good for us to take a moment to check our heart attitude with You and determine whether You want us to learn something from the difficult words people use with us or the way they criticize. We recognize that we've sinned when we harshly criticize another, and we want to change that behavior. We ask You to check our hearts and help us to use our words wisely and kindly when we need to deliver criticism. We want to be people of truth but also of grace. We never want to be unkind, mean, or nasty. Give us truthful, kind, and caring words. When we receive criticism, help us to sift out what parts are true and which ones are not. Help us to use what is true to make needed changes, not only in our hearts but also in our lives, and to dismiss what is hurtful or untrue or a situation another person is dealing with that is not ours to change. We don't want to carry another's jealousy, envy, or other sin if their criticism comes from a sinful place. Let us be very discerning and careful. Let us be wise and firm. Give us open hearts and minds to receive what we need to hear. In Jesus' name we pray. Amen.

Share a time when someone harshly corrected or criticized you and how you handled it.

_____

_____

Share a time when you harshly corrected or criticized someone. What you would do differently if you could?

_____

_____

Pray for the way you will seek the Lord in these situations in the future.

Day 320 — *Maturity*

"For this reason also, since the day we heard of it, we have not ceased to pray for you and to ask that you may be filled with the knowledge of His will in all spiritual wisdom and understanding, so that you may walk in a manner worthy of the Lord, to please him in all respects, bearing fruit in every good work and increasing in the knowledge of God."

Colossians 1:9–10

A discussion ended in these words: "A sign of maturity is individuals' consideration of others before themselves." Adults wanting their own way, demanding attention, and expecting others to meet their needs are examples of situations when immaturity and selfishness as well as the failure to notice others dominate. On other occasions simple rudeness or lack of having been taught may be the cause. It's not always something we notice at first, but as time passes, patterns emerge and before long, we see that some people haven't grown up to be mature adults because they don't know how to put others first; sometimes it's not even clear whether they even think of others at all.

Let's Pause for Prayer

Lord, we ask You to show us when we have chosen to act immaturely. Help us to recognize when we have carried a conversation as a monologue instead of as a discussion or dialog. Show us when we have talked only about ourselves or gone on and on about a topic we know something about for too long. Give us a nudge to welcome others into the conversation by asking them questions, showing interest in them, and listening well to their answers without wanting to jump back in with our thoughts and agenda. May we maturely deny ourselves and not always expect our own way or make demands, expecting others to be flexible while we remain inflexible. Allow us to see others first and to prefer their needs over our own. Let us ask questions, consider ahead of time what needs others might have, and then make it a point to serve them accordingly. We want to be others-oriented, not selfish. We want to choose to be others-centered, not self-centered. We want to choose to serve as You served. We know that will take practice, so we thank You for Your patience as we take baby steps in learning to put others first. As we grow, let us recognize how considering ourselves second feels and looks. Give us great joy as we do what we know is right and godly. In Jesus' name we pray. Amen.

How mature do you think you are? Explain.

_____

_____

_____

Ask the Lord to grow you up to maturity in Him. Be specific.

_____

_____

Day 321 — Bad Decisions

> *"Teach me, and I will be silent; and show me how I have erred."*
>
> Job 6:24

It's no stretch to see that each of us is but one step from a bad decision. It's amazing, but many of us justify a wrong and bad decision simply because we

- feel we've been wronged,
- want to get even with someone,
- choose to retaliate because we didn't get our way,
- are unhappy, or
- want something better or more, and we don't care whom we hurt.

In reality we make decisions all day long. Some will be frivolous decisions that make little difference, right?

- What should I wear today?
- Where will I go to lunch?
- Who will I hang out with later?

Wrong! Our every decision makes a difference because we are always inching our way to that fine line between what I used to tell my children is fun vs. foolish and right vs. wrong.

Let's Pause for Prayer

Lord, we sometimes take for granted that our little decisions just might have big consequences. Please help us individually to include you in all our decisions. When we feel wronged or we want to get even with someone or we're simply unhappy, help us to recognize the overall vision of what You might be doing in our lives—the sin you're exposing and letting us see and recognize. Help us consider the next steps and what will happen if we make certain decisions. Will the way we dress be a problem for someone else because we cause them to be drawn to look at us in a certain way, or will our decision about whom we'll spend time with be a problem when we play out what that time will look like? Help us, Lord, to be mindful of the stumbling blocks of sin that are in our path. Give us wisdom to look beyond the moment. In Jesus' name we pray. Amen.

Consider the most recent poor or bad decision you made. Why do you think you made that decision—think of the process—and what did you learn, if anything?

_____

_____

_____

_____

Day 322

Crossing The Line

"For Thou art my rock and my fortress; for Thy name's sake Thou wilt lead me and guide me."

Psalm 31:3

So what if we make a bad decision, you ask? The problem is that we sometimes just don't know when we cross that line from fun to foolishness or from right to wrong. Consider the following:

- It doesn't matter what we wear—unless we're wearing an outfit because we want someone to notice us or if we're calling attention to something we shouldn't. That single decision can make or break the next choice we'll need to make.
- It doesn't matter where we go to lunch unless we're meeting someone whom we shouldn't.
- It doesn't matter with whom we're hanging out, but if they're a bad influence, it will certainly matter! If it's the kid who points us to trouble; men or women unhappy in their marriages and looking for something new and different, looking to us to fulfill a need (emotional or otherwise); or a friend who doesn't have the guts to call us out when we sin, we might not have the right influences to help us.

Let's Pause for Prayer

Father, we recognize that we don't always see ahead to the way our words or actions might affect us or others. Please help us to recognize both the obvious and the hidden. Give us the wisdom that only You can give, that helps us to work out where we are and to see just where we want to go with certain decisions and choices. We don't want to be in situations that will cause us to sin and poorly reflect You, so please give us spiritual vision to see ahead of the decisions we make. Give us discernment to recognize what isn't evident in the moment. Help us to play out in our minds scenarios that could or might happen, depending on our choices. Help us teach others also to be wise in their choices. We know that sometime the choices we make will be examples to others, and we want the examples to be wise and good ones. In Jesus' name we pray. Amen.

When have you crossed the line from fun to foolishness?

_____
_____
_____

How will you be able to avoid stepping over that boundary from fun to foolishness next time?

_____
_____
_____

Day 323 — *Grow Up*

> *"Take pains with these things; be absorbed in them, so that your progress may be evident to all."*
>
> I Timothy 4:15

Sometimes we are heading in the wrong direction when we are in the process of making little decisions. It happens so subtly we don't always notice that we are being swept somewhere we hadn't planned on going! We don't always think ahead to where that somewhere is. Sometimes we think if we've made a wrong decision, we cannot turn back; but that is wrong thinking as well.

Why do we take steps, knowing that we're wrong, knowing that we're hurting others and God? Why don't we make right decisions? Perhaps because we

- are afraid we won't be liked,
- think it's impolite to disagree with someone else's politics,
- want to be happy and think making a particular decision will fill a void, or
- are unable or don't know how to stop.

As I see it we all need to grow up.

Let's Pause for Prayer

God, we know that You want us to learn from our mistakes and sin and grow to Your likeness. Help us to remember that You will not be mocked. "Do not be deceived, God is not mocked; for whatever a man sows, this he will also reap." We know that we can't plant apples and expected oranges. Our choices and decisions are the seeds planted today that will come to fruition tomorrow. We want what we sow to be precious to You and approved by You. Help us to seek your wisdom and discernment in everyday decisions as well as the more significant ones that might yield more serious consequences over time. We want to please You, Lord, and in doing so, we know that we will sense Your pleasure and approval. Help us not to be more concerned about pleasing other people, but about pleasing You. Show us when we are worried or fretting over political positioning and just stand firm in what we know is true of You and about You. May our every decision be rooted in wanting to honor Your name. In Jesus' name we pray. Amen.

What progress do you want to see as you mature spiritually? How do you intend to make that happen? Write out a prayer to the Lord.

_____

_____

_____

_____

_____

Day 324 — What We Need To Learn

> *"Like a dog that returns to its vomit, is a fool who repeats his folly."*
>
> Proverbs 26:11

We simply can't expect all good, warm, fuzzy, happy, positive results when we make poor choices. Consequences will inevitably follow. God will not be mocked.

The Bible says, "Like a dog that returns to its vomit, is a fool who repeats his folly" (Proverbs 26:11). This verse should make us think about the wrong decisions we're making, and then we should go to the Book of Proverbs in the Bible to study and underline all occurrences of the words *foolish*, *wicked*, and *folly*; then follow those up by underlining words like *wisdom*, *counselor*, and *good*. But truth be told, we'll only look up these words when we're

- willing to stop mocking God,
- serious about dealing with our sin,
- ready to ask Him for forgiveness and make things right,
- desiring to make restitution for our sin, or
- wanting to make right again relationships that we ruined (or are in the process of ruining).

Let's Pause for Prayer

Lord, You have shown us that the way of a fool is wicked and full of folly. We don't want to wander down that path, so we ask You to keep us focused on You and not silliness that leads to nothing or sin. Help us to surround ourselves with people who are godly and willing to help us walk the walk of faith. We want to be purposeful and intentional in choosing wise friends who will give us good and godly counsel about both simple and difficult choices. We want friends and family who have good intentions and desire and wish the best for us to help guide us as we choose to follow You. We will trust You to guide us to the right people who will call us on our sin and foolishness; who will tell us what we need to hear, not just what we want to hear; and who will look after our best interests because they know how much we want to serve and follow You. In Jesus' name we pray. Amen.

Have you taken God's word and direction for granted, thinking it's not quite written for you?

_____

_____

Are you ready and willing to deal with your sin and immaturity and do right? Write out a prayer sharing your willingness to follow Him.

_____

_____

_____

Day 325 — *Small Choices And Where They Lead*

> *"When I was a child, I used to speak as a child, think as a child, reason as a child; when I became a man, I did away with childish things."*
>
> I Corinthians 13:11

We can play out many scenarios in our minds as to how we got to where we are: adultery, lying, cheating, drugs, addictions, pornography, gossiping, hateful actions, murder, _____ (fill in the blank). How did we get to the point of committing the kinds of sins I just listed? We got there through a series of small poor decisions, wrong choices, and wanting our own way instead of God's way.

No one can force us to make a good decision. That's the choice we individually have to make, and during numerous times throughout our day and week, we have opportunities to keep us on the right track or to take that one step that leads us to a bad decision. When we understand that both large and small decisions will impact our lives and our serving as examples for others, we can recognize the importance of making good, honorable, and right choices.

Let's Pause for Prayer

Lord, we need Your help. It's so easy to want our own way and even to justify our actions to make them sound as if we deserve to have our way, thinking that we are right when we are clearly wrong; or to act in certain ways that are clearly harmful to ourselves and others. Please give us Your wisdom. We ask You to fill us with Your spirit so that we can have Your wisdom. We know that in and of ourselves, we'll probably make many bad choices, so we take this step to ask You to help us. Help us to see where one wrong and foolish choice will lead us. Help us to play out scenarios so that we will not ultimately hurt ourselves and others in the process of wanting or demanding our own way. We want to seek You, Your way, and Your will for us. We want to be examples that others would desire to follow. We thank You for caring enough to help and guide us, and we will be listening! In Jesus' name we pray. Amen.

Do you feel you make childlike or adultlike decisions?

_____

_____

What will help you make your adult/grown up/big choices the right ones? Write a prayer.

_____

_____

_____

_____

_____

Day 326 — Aging

"For he will not often consider the years of his life because God keeps him occupied with the gladness of his heart."

Ecclesiastes 5:20

Aging can be difficult. At some point we can look back at certain decades and identify the ones we liked or didn't. Some decades that were particularly difficult may not inspire as much fondness as those that were more carefree and fun. But through each one, if we can find that doing what God wants us to do brings us gladness, we should be able to look back with fondness instead of sadness or regret. At some point we may say, "It's amazing how little time we really have in this life."

Ecclesiastes 5:20 makes it clear that we won't even worry about our age if we're doing what He has asked of us. We'll be so busy doing His will we won't think about how old we are because we'll be happy doing it.

Let's Pause for Prayer

Lord, time flies. When we were young, we looked to the future but too soon found it's the past. We know You can slow down, speed up, and even stop time if You wanted to; but we simply want to be faithful to appreciate each moment You've given us to live in each moment with joy-filled appreciative hearts. Let us live vibrantly with excitement, with gusto, with happiness as we serve You. We pray we would look at life positively and embrace every part of it. May You give us many years to serve You, and as we do so, may we see the joy and fun in life even amid trials and tribulations. We need a sense of appreciation for what You've given us to do so that we will carry it out with excellence and obedience. Thank You for the gift of life, the gift of aging, and the appreciation of how You work through our lives. In Jesus' name we pray. Amen.

How old are you, and how do you feel about being this age?

___

___

Are you able to find joy and gladness in your days with the work He's given you? If not, why not. How will you pursue being occupied in such a way?

___

___

___

___

Day 327 — Use Us Til We're Used Up!

"He who watches the wind will not sow and he who looks at the clouds will not reap."

Ecclesiastes 11:4

I don't know about you, but I don't want to be found sitting around waiting for life to happen. I love to stay busy, not for the sake of busyness but for the sake of feeling I've accomplished something in my day—primarily for the Lord. I love to wake with a plan, and I like to have a direction, knowing that I write it out in pencil and give the eraser to the Lord!

Neither my husband nor I want to retire. We want to be used every day in whatever way the Lord guides and directs. We are aware that at times (and have experienced plenty of them) when what we plan is rearranged—perhaps because someone has a need we didn't anticipate or perhaps because someone in our family is ill and in need of care. When that happens, we trust that we will be redirected because the Lord has another plan. We want Him to use us until we're used up!

Let's Pause for Prayer

Lord, we want to sow, reap, and see the fruits of our labor—if they are first directed and determined by You. Help us to listen to you closely and carefully as we pray and read from Your word so we can seek Your direction daily. We know that You give the work to be done, and we desire to do what You ask. Guide our thoughts and steps with Your vision so that we may accomplish the tasks to complete Your work. We are thankful for the purpose you have for each of us, and we want to be clear about what it is. Encourage us as we seek You. Give us rest when needed to become refreshed. Give us seasons of respite when we need rest. Give us strength in times when we feel too weak to continue serving. We desire to be in the center of Your will whether in rest or in service. Bless our time, efforts, talents, and treasures for Your glory and to accomplish Your good. In Jesus' name we pray. Amen.

Are you waiting for life to happen as you watch it pass by?

_____

_____

_____

Are you actively pursuing service to the Lord? How does that look for you?

_____

_____

_____

_____

Day 328

He Supplies

"And if we know that He hears us in whatever we ask, we know that we have the requests which we have asked from Him."

1 John 5:15

I have experienced times, though rare, when I recognize an immediate answer to prayer. Other times, I see that He answers but more slowly.

After the death of a dear friend's mother, I remember praying as I ran errands, telling the Lord I was available for anything my friend needed. In moments I began weeping, so much so that I needed to return home. The following week my friend told me that on that very day (and time) the burden of grief had been lifted from her, and she was able to tend to things that had been difficult to do.

Let's Pause for Prayer

Dear Lord, we recognize that prayer is a time for seeking Your approval and direction regardless of our own plans. It's in the quiet closet of prayer where ministry leaders are lifted up, where families are embraced and cared for, and where our connections to You, the Creator, are made. We recognize we should never act without prayer behind our actions. Help us to avoid jumping into action based on our own strengths but instead to come to You first for direction and guidance, and thus sense Your presence and our place in the center of Your will. May we rely on You for every thought and action as we prayerfully consider each. Let us not be slow in following where You lead us in prayer, and may we see prayer as the work—not just the preparation for the work—and then do it. Prepare us for what You have in mind. Break our hearts for what breaks Yours. Help us to recognize and feel the needs of others. Meet us in the place we least expect, but let us see it's You and recognize Your hand. In Jesus' name we pray. Amen.

What gets you praying like nothing else?

_____

_____

_____

Do you pray in anticipation of events or mainly in crisis?

_____

_____

_____

Day 329

Keeping It Simple

> *"Then some children were brought to Him so that He might lay His hands on them and pray; and the disciples rebuked them. But Jesus said, 'Let the children alone, and do not hinder them from coming to Me; for the kingdom of heaven belongs to such as these."*
>
> Matthew 19:13–14

A while ago one of our grandsons was sick while he stayed at our house. Joey, our adult son with special needs, overheard the conversation and came to me with his hands folded, and said, "Let's pray." I said, "Go ahead, you pray." He insisted, "No, Mom. You pray." Joey is mentally challenged (very much like a child) and has very limited speech as well. He can't formulate all the words, but I know his heart formulates the need for prayer just fine. In childlike faith he came to me to ask for prayer. Today, consider something the Lord has put on your heart and pray.

Let's Pause for Prayer

Lord, some of us may have heavy hearts as we pray for deep needs in our lives or in the lives of our family. We lift up to You these needs that we might not even be able to share with others or that we can't even formulate into words to You. Hear our hearts, Lord. Hear our needs. Help us to understand what You want us to learn through these challenging times and let us reflect You to others through these times. Others of us may have simple issues in life that we know could use prayer and that You also care about. We lift those situations up to You as well. We know You care for every detail of our lives, whether it's the simplest of problems or the deepest of needs—and everything in between. We know we can't hide from You the needs we have, but sometimes we neglect or forget to come to You. Today, we want to share it all. We want to recognize our need for You and the need for prayer in our lives. We want to submit to You as we commit our heartfelt prayers to You. We desire to simply come to You. In Jesus' name we pray. Amen.

When you come before the Lord in prayer, do You keep it simple or feel the need to pray eloquently?

_____
_____
_____

How will You pray today to meet the Lord right where you are? Will you keep it simple?

_____
_____
_____
_____

Day 330

To Serve Or Be Served—That Is The Question

"As each one has received a special gift, employ it in serving one another, as good stewards of the manifold grace of God."

1 Peter 4:10

The aroma of turkey, the taste of delicious mashed potatoes, and the enjoyable fellowship with family and friends are some of what I love best about Thanksgiving.

But let's land on this thought: "Will you serve or be served?" Even if we are an invited guest at someone's home, we can be a servant. An older person might need a little help getting food. The host and hostess might appreciate your assistance as those last-minute preps come together. You could also sit somewhere waiting to be served. No matter what your choice, you might just be doing what God has asked of you. Always remember Mary and Martha in the Bible. God may ask of you to take part in helping, or He may have you seated beside someone to listen to, care for, and minister to them. Wherever God has us celebrating Thanksgiving, let's ask Him to guide us as to how He may want us to serve.

Let's Pause for Prayer

Heavenly Father, we thank You for the many blessings You've bestowed upon us. Even if we are experiencing a challenge at this very moment in time, we can still recognize Your goodness to us in the midst of it. May we also find ways to thank You as we meet with others this day or perhaps as we are alone. Show us how we can serve through our actions in helping others with the meal, cleaning up, listening to others share their hearts, or sharing with others our love for You. Let everyone recognize and understand that each person will have a role to play at Thanksgiving dinner, and may we all be appreciative, thankful, and show gratitude for the way others have chosen to take part on this day. In Jesus' name we pray. Amen.

As you anticipate Thanksgiving, are you drawn to serve in some way? Share.

_____

_____

_____

Perhaps this year you are the one who'll need help or aren't able to serve for some reason. Share how you'll graciously receive help.

_____

_____

_____

Day 331　　　　　　　　　　　　　　　　　　　　　*Heart Of Gratitude*

"So then, as we have opportunity, let us do good to all men, and especially to those who are of the household of the faith."

Galatians 6:10

Many enjoy Thanksgiving as their favorite holiday. I think I most enjoy it because it's very casual, the food is always good, and commercialism hasn't ruined it. Food preparation is time-consuming, but we don't have the excesses that come with the purchasing and giving of gifts or other aspects of consumerism.

We understand that the pilgrims set this day aside for the giving thanks for the food that they harvested as newcomers to this land. No doubt they experienced many challenges for which they might have complained, but they chose to give thanks. It's my hope that we won't omit prayer before the meal, lacking the cultural understanding of what this holiday is all about and celebrating it just as a time to get together.

As we enjoy a meal with family, we often share reasons for our thankfulness. Because our family is sometimes scattered for this occasion, visiting other family members, we sometimes celebrate it on a different day just to be together. We enjoy being together, but the most enjoyable part is sharing what makes us thankful.

Let's Pause for Prayer

Heavenly Father, we give You thanks. Thank You for the health You've given, the blessings of warm homes, and food on the table. We are so appreciative that You are the greatest giver of gifts and You do not withhold. Thank You for the ministry opportunities You supply, to share with others our relationship wtih You, to share Your word, and to tell of Your gifts, grace, and mercy. Help us to be the beacon of light to others so they notice our appreciation of You as we share our thankfulness to You. May we extend that appreciation and thankfulness to others as we become a reflection of You. In Jesus' name we pray.

Will you be home for Thanksgiving or traveling? Share your plans for this special day, and write a prayer to pray your way through this day.

_____
_____
_____
_____
_____
_____

Day **332** *Giving Thanks In All Things*

> *"Always giving thanks for all things in the name of the Lord Jesus Christ to God, even the Father."*
>
> Ephesians 5:20

I'm looking forward to Thanksgiving as I do every year. I love it because it's a time for families to gather and simply give thanks to a loving God. I know the day is a lot of work, but I very much enjoy its inherent simplicity. I most enjoy the giving of thanks. Certainly we can and should praise and thank Him daily, but setting aside a day to make a point of it is indeed a blessing. We have so much for which to give thanks, and yet we often neglect doing so. Making a special time to recognize our blessings and be thankful is the essence of Thanksgiving.

Let's Pause for Prayer

Heavenly Father, we delight in knowing You, the Holy One. "Holy, holy, holy is the Lord of hosts, the whole earth is full of His glory" (Isaiah 6:3). We rejoice in knowing You personally. Lord, may all who gather around a Thanksgiving table this year pray together and thank You for the many blessings You've bestowed upon us. Thank You, Lord, for your abundant generosity and for providing for all of our needs. We can't take for granted Your love and care for us for which we give You thanks. In Jesus' name we pray. Amen.

List below what makes you thankful:

1. _____
2. _____
3. _____
4. _____
5. _____
6. _____

Pray through each one as a prayer of thanksgiving.

Day 333 *Waiting With Thanksgiving*

"I praise and honor You, Father, because You are a God who loves to answer prayer and who begins to answer even before I pray."

Isaiah 65:24

Thanksgiving is the perfect time of year to take inventory of the many blessings we have as Christians. God takes such good care of us even when life is difficult and challenging. He doesn't just forgive us and allow us to be saved and leave us there. He continues to watch over us, guide us, sustain us, provide for us, give us joy, and answer our prayers. Thanking Him is such a small act for us to perform in appreciation. We deserve so little, but He offers so much.

Let's Pause for Prayer

Heavenly Father, You are mighty and care for us in every way, for which we give You thanks. You are a forgiving God, and we appreciate it. Nehemiah 9:17 says, "I want to bless You with praise, Father, because 'you are a forgiving God, gracious and compassionate, slow to anger and abounding in love.'" We don't deserve Your goodness, but we enjoy it. Thank You for being here with me whenever I need You and even when I don't know I need You. You protect me before I even know I need it. I often sense Your hand of blessing upon me, and I know it surpasses what I see today. I can enjoy Your blessings today and forever. You are always a step ahead of me, even as I pray. Your word confirms it. Thank You for Your love and faithfulness, which I can't understand fully but appreciate and enjoy deeply. In Jesus' name we pray. Amen.

Have you ever waited long for the Lord to answer a prayer? What was the situation, and in the end were you glad you had been made to wait?

_____

_____

_____

Why do you think God made you wait?

_____

_____

_____

_____

Day 334 *Usual, Customary, Reasonable*

"Know therefore that the Lord your God, He is God the faithful God, who keeps His covenant and His lovingkindness to a thousandth generation with those who love Him and keep His commandments."

Deuteronomy 7:9

Sometimes in our daily prayers we can be heard to thank God for what is usual, customary, and reasonable. We settle into a pattern of reciting our list of thanks, and eventually it doesn't sound sincere because it's the same list we've been reciting for quite some time. God never gets tired of hearing our thanks. I don't tire of hearing my husband and family thanking me for dinner or for other tasks I routinely perform. And I hope my husband never tires of my thanks and appreciation of him for providing for us and taking care of us.

When I think about the vastness of God's love for us and how much He has done for us, it's difficult to wrap my mind around it all. Certainly, great is His faithfulness—for all the big things and all the usual, customary, and reasonable things, too.

Let's Pause for Prayer

Dear Lord, we recognize You as a faithful God. Deuteronomy gives us a glimpse of Your faithfulness for which we give thanks. When I think of all You have done for me, for us, I know I can't understand it in real terms, so I want to thank You for all Your provisions and faithfulness. Great is Thy faithfulness. You never stop blessing, giving, sharing, teaching, and loving us. Your mercy is limitless: "The Lord's lovingkindnesses indeed never ceases, for His compassion never fails. They are new every morning; great is Thy faithfulness" (Lamentations 3:22–23).

What are the usual, customary, and reasonable prayers you often pray?

_____

_____

_____

How do you see God from a perspective of mercy and compassion?

_____

_____

_____

_____

Day **335** *Really? Give Thanks For That?*

> *"In everything give thanks; for this is God's will for you in Christ Jesus."*
> II Thessalonians 5:18

The telephone rang as the oven buzzer went off, letting us know dinner would be served momentarily. The telephone call was from someone who had previously declined our dinner invitation but was now able to come. I wish I could say I was delighted. I wish I could tell you my first response was rejoicing in serving this guest. Because no one knew I had taken the call, no one really knew what was going through my mind. But as quickly as the negative thoughts came, I asked the Lord to show me just what He wanted me to do—and He did!

With the table fully set, no additional seating available at tables, and name cards for each guest, I quickly turned mine inside out and wrote the name of our last-minute guest on the other side. Not audibly, but to my heart the Lord seemed to be telling me to serve with joy because my table was full: "Serve with love because someday there would be an empty seat. Serve with your whole heart and allow everyone to enjoy the day and leave feeling refreshed."

I was so thankful I obeyed. The following Thanksgiving my father-in-law was no longer with us. In just a few more years we had four more empty seats: my brother's, my Dad's and Mom's (they passed away within five days of each other), and then my mother-in-law's.

Let's Pause for Prayer

Heavenly Father, we are so thankful that we have homes to open to others this holiday. Many will be missing loved ones. Help us to meet their needs, serve them with joy, and allow them to leave refreshed. Let us be gracious as we warmly welcome others to our tables. May each guest feel wanted and welcomed. We know that refreshment will come from You, and we will rejoice that You have refreshed our guests. In Jesus' name we pray. Amen.

Consider how you will welcome and serve guests in your home. Whom will you invite?

_____

_____

_____

What will you do to actively serve with joy "as unto the Lord"?

_____

_____

_____

Day 336

Gifted

"Therefore encourage one another, and build up one another, just as you also are doing."

1 Thessalonians 5:11

The biggest shopping day of the year is Black Friday. I will stay home! I can enjoy the crowds and the hustle and bustle more when I'm not trying to find gifts for those I love. I admire those who enjoy this day, truly I do. I wish I liked it. But we're all made differently, and it's good to know our strengths, weaknesses, and gifts. I'll be staying home.

As we prepare for the upcoming CHRISTmas season, I'd like to draw our attention to gifts: how God has given each believer a particular gift to be used to accomplish His will. Whether we are gifted in evangelism (sharing the gospel), hospitality (welcoming others to our homes), exhortation (being of encouragement), serving, or other gifts, we need to be sure that we use our gifts for His glory, not our own.

The one gift given to us will be the motivating factor in much, if not all, of what we do. I believe my gift is exhortation, which is encouraging others. But God doesn't let me off the hook and say, "Cindi, you don't have to share the gospel because it's not the particular gift I gave you." No, God will use the gift of encouragement and enable me with the help of the Holy Spirit to encourage others as I indeed share the gospel. Exhortation (encouragement) is what nudges me to do all that He asks me to do.

Let's Pause for Prayer

Heavenly Father, please reveal to us the gift You've given us with which to serve You. Help us to be willing to use that gift with boldness and confidence as we step out to use it as You lead us. Allow our minds to be open to Your leading even if we are asked to work out of our comfort zone. We pray to be found willing and able to serve whenever You call upon us. May we not procrastinate, deliberate too long, or delay acting in obedience when You give us direction. In Jesus' name we pray. Amen.

How about you? How has God gifted you, and how to you use that gift?

_____

_____

_____

How will you use that gift throughout the holiday season?

_____

_____

_____

Day 337 — *Presents Or Presence?*

> *"And an angel of the Lord suddenly stood before them, and the glory of the Lord shone around them."*
>
> Luke 2:9a

Presents or presence? You've seen it before. You receive an invitation, and the inside reads: "Please come to the party to honor 'so and so.' Bring no presents, just your presence." Of course, most of us read that and say, "I can't show up to the party and honor the guest without bringing some kind of gift!" So present in hand we make our way to the party, the guest saying, "Oh, you didn't need to do that. The invitation said no presents!"

As we prepare to celebrate the birth of our Lord, I wonder how the inside of an invitation to His party might read. "You are invited to the birth of the Savior. Please, don't bring a present. After all, He is the gift. He doesn't need a gift—only you. Won't you consider just coming and offering yourself to Him? It's really all He wants."

His birthday is almost here. You probably have a gift list made and some checked off. You might even be waiting for this very invitation to come to you. Well, it's here. He wants you. He wants your heart. Don't wait any longer. Don't put off giving the one item that you don't have to purchase. He already purchased your salvation with His death on the cross. Your account says "paid in full" upon receipt of this gift from Him. Will you offer yourself to Him as we Pause for Prayer?

Let's Pause for Prayer

Heavenly Father, I want to give myself to You and thank You for Your death on the cross to pay for my sins. I thank You for not requiring me to list my good deeds, figure out how much money I donated, or convince myself or others what a great person I am. You already see me as clean before You because I have confessed my sin to You and accepted Your provision of salvation through Your Son's birth, death, and resurrection. I surrender myself to You and ask You to help me from this day forward to obey You and walk with You. Here I am, Lord. In Jesus' name we pray. Amen.

Have you given your heart to Jesus? Share that time or ask Him into your heart this moment by writing a prayer of acceptance of Him.

_____
_____
_____

In light of your relationship with Jesus, what would your gift of yourself look like?

_____
_____
_____

Day **338**   *It's Beginning To Look A Lot Like Christmas*

"And they came in haste and found their way to Mary and Joseph, and the baby as He lay in the manger."

Luke 2:16

Yes, it's beginning to look a lot like CHRISTmas because we are

- not getting enough sleep with so much to do,
- feeling discouraged because we don't have time for everything on the list,
- feeling emotionally and physically drained because of the strain of the schedule that is already full even without CHRISTmas added

I've wondered whether Joseph, Mary, the shepherds, or the angels experienced some of the same emotions we experience but for different reasons. For instance, consider the following:

- Tired and perhaps emotionally and physically drained, Joseph and Mary likely lacked sleep. They were making their way to their hometown to be registered in the census that Caesar Augustus had decreed (Luke 2:1–7). They couldn't find a place to rest. That couldn't have been easy to handle while preparing for the birth of a child.
- Scripture tells us that the shepherds made their way "hastily" to find Jesus (Luke 2:16). I wonder how they handled the emotions surrounding the change in plans when they were keeping watch over their flocks by night (Luke 2: 8–9).

We need look no further than a few verses later in Luke 2:17–20: "And when they had seen this, they made known the statement which had been told them about this Child… But Mary treasured up all these things, pondering them in her heart. And the shepherds went back, glorifying and praising God for all that they had heard and seen, just as had been told them."

Let's Pause for Prayer

Heavenly Father, please help us develop the right perspective on celebrating this CHRISTmas season. Help us to ponder in our hearts Your goodness and treasure it. May we be able to glorify and praise you as the shepherds did, and may it be with the same kind of obedience so that others around us will realize that it is indeed beginning to look a lot like CHRISTmas! In Jesus' name we pray. Amen.

Will you respond to the demands of this season by being emotionally frazzled or seeking Him in obedience as did the shepherds, Mary, and Joseph?

_____

_____

_____

_____

Day 339 — *Poor Me*

> *"My help comes from the Lord, Who made heaven and earth."*
>
> Psalm 121:2

This can be a very happy and memorable time of year, but it can also be a most challenging and sad time of year. Not everyone has wonderful childhood memories of Christmases past. Some may even be struggling with Christmas present—the recent loss of a loved one, no one with whom to spend the holidays, a relationship that has been severed this past year, the loss of someone through death, or the inability to get out and enjoy the holidays.

In some situations we must learn to accept that nothing can be changed and simply tell God that we're sad and lonely or even frustrated. But if we're creative, in other situations we can actually do something to prevent the holiday blues.

- We can reach out to others who might be in similar circumstances and find ways to celebrate in a new way: remembering the past with loved ones but looking to the future when we will be able to accept their loss, not forgetting them but remembering them.

- We can stop rehearsing our own sorrow and disappointment and reach out to others who have been hurt or disappointed as we have and start from a new place.

- We can try to rekindle that severed relationship if it is healthy to do so. It might mean humbling ourselves to ask for forgiveness.

Let's Pause for Prayer

Heavenly Father, thank You for bringing issues to our attention and helping us to see that others may have similar or greater needs than we have. Help me reach out to another and show Your love, Your healing power, and Your forgiveness. Help us reach out even from our own needs so we don't get caught up in the "poor me" narrative during this time of year. Let me not wait to make the first move. In Jesus' name we pray. Amen.

So what do you think? Would you like to give reaching out a try? How will that look for you?

_____
_____
_____
_____
_____

Day 340 — Setting Priorities

> *"Cease striving and know that I am God."*
>
> Psalm 46:10

CHRISTmas is coming soon! Some people are frantically trying to finish all the tasks on their list. They realize they don't have the money to buy all the specific gifts their loved ones requested, they are running out of time even faster than money, and they are finding themselves irritable, overwhelmed, and anxious. Does that sound like you or someone you know?

Some of these problems can be realistically conquered by

- ✔ sticking to our budget, not spending more than we have;
- ✔ prioritizing our gift list and the time we have to realistically shop so we won't be overwhelmed;
- ✔ getting proper rest so we won't be so irritable and anxious.

Where is the reason for the season in all of this? Can we reach out to others in need as Jesus did? Grant forgiveness as Jesus did to someone who has hurt us? Pray for others as Jesus did, especially for those who are lost and without a Savior?

Let's Pause for Prayer

Heavenly Father, we tend to become so wrapped up in all the busyness of this season that we forget why Your Son came to earth and what He accomplished here. Thank You for reaching out to those in need—like me. I appreciate that You loved me enough, that even though I hurt You with my sin, You forgave me. Thank You for allowing me to see that I was less fortunate and needed a Savior—Your Son. Thank you for being the Way, the Truth, and the Life. Help me this CHRISTmas season to share Your truth with others so that I might point them to You. And thank You for the peace that You have given those of us who know and serve You. In Jesus' name we pray. Amen.

How can you personally slow down and make this time of year count for something of real value beyond the cost of gifts, food, and parties?

_____

_____

_____

Do you need to mend a particular relationship?

_____

_____

_____

Day 341

What Are You Waiting For?

> *"Behold, this Child..."*
> Luke 2:34

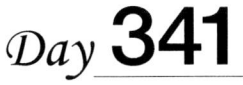

What are you waiting for this CHRISTmas season? Are you waiting for a special gift, a family member to return home from the armed service, someone visiting from out of town, or might you be waiting for the Messiah?

Simeon waited a long time, anticipating his Messiah. Here is the account from Luke 2:25–35: "And behold, there was a man in Jerusalem whose name was Simeon; and this man was righteous and devout, looking for the consolation of Israel, and the Holy Spirit was upon him. And it had been revealed to him by the Holy Spirit that he would not see death before he had seen the Lord's Christ (the Messiah). And he came in the Spirit into the temple, and when the parents brought in the child Jesus, to carry out for Him the custom of the Law, then he took Him into his arms, and blessed God, and said, 'Now Lord, Thou dost let Thy bond-servant depart in peace, according to Thy word, for my eyes have seen Thy salvation, which Thou hast prepared in the presence of all peoples, a light of revelation to the Gentiles and the glory of Thy people Israel.' And His father and mother were amazed at the things which were being said about Him. And Simeon blessed them, and said to Mary His mother, 'Behold, this child is appointed for the fall and rise of many in Israel, and for a sign to be opposed—and a sword will pierce even your own soul—to the end that thoughts from many hearts may be revealed.'"

Let's Pause for Prayer

Heavenly Father, we pray that those waiting for You and seeking after You will recognize You. We pray that You would reveal Yourself uniquely to those who desire to know You so that they might find You and accept Your provisions! As we pray for someone You have put in our path this CHRISTmas season, help us faithfully to share with them the wonder of Your Son's birth, love, death, resurrection, and Your salvation. Let us not withhold the sharing of the Good News that Jesus Christ, Your only begotten Son, is born this day! In Jesus' name we pray. Amen!

Some still await the Messiah. Let's pray for them to recognize Him this day.

_____

_____

_____

What was the turning point for you to recognize that Jesus is the Messiah?

_____

_____

_____

Day 342 — Not So Important

"And it came about when the angels had gone away from them into heaven, that the shepherds began saying to one another, 'Let us go straight to Bethlehem then, and see this thing that has happened which the Lord has made known to us.'"

Luke 2:15

Are you feeling pressured right about now? Do you still have a stack of cards that need to be signed and stamped even though they might be received after Christmas? Do you still have a few decorations to finish up, or do you have a few more gifts to buy, gifts to wrap? Oh, and food to prepare a bit ahead of time so there's not so much to do on Christmas day? And cleaning the house for all the company expected. And we can't forget to be sure all the holiday clothes are cleaned, pressed, and ready to wear. And what about planning to go to the church Christmas program?

With so much left to do, it's a wonder we can really stop and enjoy the event for which we are planning. How can we do it? Are any of those tasks left to do really all that important? It's hard not to stop. We want everything to be perfect. We want to make special memories. But the most special memory to be made is that impression on our hearts that God sent His only Son to be born among us. Luke 2:15 tells us, "And it came about when the angels had gone away from them into heaven, that the shepherds began saying to one another, 'Let us go straight to Bethlehem then, and see this thing that has happened which the Lord has made known to us.'"

Let's Pause for Prayer

Heavenly Father, we're sorry when like a train out of control we speed ahead in preparation and planning and yet do not take the time to thank You for sending Your Son to earth to save us. Thank You, Lord. Thank You for loving us so much that You came to save us from our sin. Thank you for the great news of salvation You have brought to us. Help us to share the good news of that salvation with others. We stop and pause in preparation of the celebration of Your Son's birth, to thank You for all You have done for us. May we set aside the pressures, striving, and planning of what is not so important and take a moment to reflect upon the importance of You. In Jesus' name we pray. Amen.

What planning and preparation do you find important at this time of year? Make a list.

How will you make Jesus the most important aspect of this season?

Day 343 — *Stop Grumbling And Complaining*

"Offer hospitality to one another without grumbling. Each one should use whatever gift he has received to serve others, faithfully administering God's grace in its various forms."

I Peter 4:9–10

God's word instructs us in Romans 12:13, "Share with God's people who are in need. Practice hospitality." I enjoy having company in my home. I enjoy having close friends and family over to our home to share a holiday meal, and if they are from out of town, I enjoy having them stay overnight. I enjoy practicing hospitality, especially with people who are special to me; but I need to challenge myself with the other part of that scripture as well. Am I sharing with God's people who are in need?

I suppose I could rationalize by recognizing that everyone has some need, but I wonder whether I'm supposed to take one more step beyond that usual comfort zone.

Another verse about hospitality is from I Peter 4:9–10 (see above.) If we know our spiritual gift, we probably enjoy using it to serve others. And what a great time of year to share our spiritual gifts and reach out to others by showing the love of Christ.

Let's Pause for Prayer

Heavenly Father, we pray that you would bless our times of hospitality as we have fun and fellowship. May we show Your love to others and share Your word and gospel with those that don't know You. Allow us to use our spiritual gifts as you bring friends and family to our homes. Let us help those who have needs. Help us to be gracious, caring, and loving as we celebrate Your Son's birth this Christmas! In Jesus' name we pray. Amen.

What does it mean to practice hospitality? Are you willing to pursue it?

How will it look to pursue hospitality this CHRISTmas season?

Day 344

Here's To Tradition!

"So then, brethren, stand firm and hold to the traditions which you were taught, whether by word of mouth or by letter from us."

II Thessalonians 2:15

This is a wonderful time of the year to enjoy the traditions that have been established in our families over time, sometimes over generations. Some may enjoy baking together, having family get-togethers, reaching out to neighbors and those who are homebound, volunteering at city missions, or reading holiday cards and letters that arrive each day. Those are all great ways to celebrate the season of Christ's birth. Serving and celebrating in these ways are fun, memorable, and meaningful.

One type of tradition that could be started during the holidays is teaching the children in our lives about character building. For a given number of days, you might talk about what it means to be worshipful, retelling the story about Mary worshipping the Lord. Another day you might talk about joyfulness, sharing the idea that happiness on the outside can differ from the joy we feel in our hearts. We could stimulate conversation and learning by discussing why the shepherds were worshipful and joyful, whether or not we think Joseph and Mary were joyful, why the angels were singing and praising God. As we read through scripture, we can teach about character traits through various words like *thankfulness, wisdom, love, belief*—we have many to choose from.

Let's Pause for Prayer

Heavenly Father, thank You for Your word, which we can use to teach others. Help us take the lead at this wonderful time of year to teach about You and to learn to build character into our lives by studying Your word. Thank You for the children whom You've put into our lives: children, grandchildren, nieces, nephews, friends, and neighbors. May we share meaningful dialog and teaching opportunities about You with those you have placed in our lives. In Jesus' name we pray. Amen.

Share a favorite tradition you enjoy specifically during the CHRISTmas season.

_____

_____

_____

What would you like to add to make your traditions more meaningful?

_____

_____

_____

Day 345

Captive Audience

> *"How beautiful are the feet of those who bring glad tidings of good things."*
>
> Romans 10:15

Do you send out Christmas greetings? Do you have a goal in sending them out? We do, and for us the main goal or purpose is to include a scripture verse that will help us share the gospel with those who might not know the Lord along with updates of our year. We generally just share a verse or two that relates with the theme of our letter. For those who know we are Christians and are Christians themselves, the letter is probably more informational and, we hope, enjoyable. For those who don't know the Lord, our hope is that the verse will cause them to ask themselves whether they know the living God as we do.

For instance, one year our theme had to do with feet: the places our feet have taken us, the steps we made, and the ways we were able to do the things God asked us to do. Our scripture verse was Romans 10:15, "How beautiful are the feet of those who bring glad tidings of good things." We shared the places we had gone, areas where we'd served Christ, and we ended with our thanks for the way God walks with us to teach us and allows us to grow to be more like Him. We tried to make it clear that our growth sometimes comes in baby steps and sometimes in giant leaps but that God is the one with us, helping us in each and every step.

At this time of year, we have a captive audience. Most people receive greetings and hear Christmas carols, even sing the name of Jesus. What a great time to initiate conversation when the whole season centers on Christ! After all, his name is what CHRISTmas is all about.

Let's Pause for Prayer

Heavenly Father, we pray that you would show us unique ways to share with others our relationship with You this CHRISTmas season. May we take this opportunity and not be shy about telling others about our Savior. Lord, help us to use the gospel in the cards and letters we send out, in our listening to the words of songs, and as a conversation starter in sharing what you have done for us. Help us to share that excitement with others. In Jesus' name we pray. Amen.

In what ways do you share news about the Lord with others during this season?

_____

_____

_____

If you don't, how might you share and show that Christ is the essence of CHRISTmas?

_____

_____

_____

Day 346

Don't Miss Opportunity

"Let your light shine before men in such a way that they may see your good works, and glorify your Father who is in heaven."

Matthew 5:16

You know the words all too well: "'Tis the season to be jolly"! But those words can present quite a tall order for some people. Unfortunately for some people, Christmas and New Year's celebrations are very difficult. Being jolly is far off their radar screens. Depression is often a part of some people's holidays, and for some it's a part of their postholidays.

For those who have lost loved ones, the first Christmas without them is difficult; but sometimes the second Christmas is even more difficult because the numbness has turned into reality, and no numbness is left to hide behind. It seems every holiday turns into a new way of celebrating, taking time to adjust, and making having a jolly attitude difficult.

Although seeking professional help with clinical depression and taking ample time to mourn losses are important for people, one remedy for sadness, depression, and loneliness is purposing to find something to do for someone else. We may be going through a time that is less than jolly, but others are suffering, too; and helping them can sometimes comfort our own ailing hearts.

Let's Pause for Prayer

Heavenly Father, we pray for those who experience depression, loneliness, and sadness. Please help us to think of ways we might brighten someone's difficult times. Help us bring the light of Jesus Christ to someone's hurting heart. Remind us of ways that others helped us and allow us the opportunity to serve others. Father, we pray that we would be quick about doing what You ask, that we avoid delay in blessing another. In Jesus' name we pray. Amen.

When you faced challenges during this season, did someone reach out to you?

Does someone who is hurting come to mind whom you might be able to serve or help in some way this year?

Day 347

Purposeful Christmas

"But when you give alms (deeds of charity), do not let your left hand know what your right hand is doing that your alms may be in secret; and your Father who sees in secret will repay you."

Matthew 6:3–4

When I set out to do Christmas planning and preparations, I ask myself the question, "What is my purpose?" As I buy gifts, write out cards to send, decorate, and plan hospitality, I make active choices to incorporate my purpose into all the preparations. For me, my purpose is to keep Christ and others at the center of all that went on throughout the season. I later take inventory of the memories made and relationships that were built or strengthened. Perhaps you can ask yourself the questions I ask myself:

- ✔ Did I show my family and friends how special they are to me and more importantly how special they are to Jesus?
- ✔ Did I serve meals in such a way that others knew it was a pleasure to serve them because I was doing it for the Lord and for them?
- ✔ Would people around me say that I showed the love of Christ as I drove in parking lots and on busy streets in heavy traffic?
- ✔ Would fellow customers browsing in stores and waiting in lines say that I was patient like Jesus and kind, too?

The answers to these questions are important in determining whether I really had a successful Christmas. Ultimately, it only matters what Jesus thought of everything I did. He knows my true heart motives. In some cases we may have done fairly well. In others, we probably have room for improvement, some possible good ideas for our New Year's resolutions!

Let's Pause for Prayer

Heavenly Father, we thank You for the beauty of the Christmas season and pray that we reflect a true image of who You are to others. We pray that as you show us areas where we need to improve and change, we would have the courage to make those changes with Your help and guidance. May our New Year be centered on You and how we can serve You and others. In Jesus' name we pray. Amen.

What are your main purposes as you celebrate CHRISTmas? Write ways you can make your purposes come to life and put them into action.

_____
_____
_____
_____
_____

Day 348

Pondering The Season

> *"But Mary treasured up all these things, pondering them in her heart."*
>
> Luke 2:19

'Tis the season to realize that for many Christmas has its downside. Crowded stores, unexpected guests, last-minute shopping, and a long gift list with too little cash. I have found holiday stress mainly centers on the big three: time, energy, and money.

We attempt to expend too much of each of these at this time of year, by trying to cram everything into the month of December instead of pacing ourselves throughout the year. We simply try to fit too much in, and nothing else in life stops to accommodate all the additions! When we do that, the month of January shows us to be depleted in time, energy, and money. Not a great way to start off a New Year!

As we ponder the coming of Jesus and plan our time according, I think we might better plan how to spend the holidays and find ourselves looking back and realizing we indeed enjoyed them. For me one important remedy is to simplify. Stress indicates to me that I have too much on my schedule and something has to change. I have to think back and remember my purpose and focus on that purpose! Likely no one will notice whether the tree isn't fully decorated or whether I left boxes of decorations in storage (as I've done a few times). They will notice, however, if the stress of misusing my time, energy, and money is getting to me!

Let's Pause for Prayer

Heavenly Father, please help each of us to use the time, energy, and money You have given us to glorify You this CHRISTmas. Please help us to choose a purpose in our holiday celebrations that will please and honor You and will keep us at peace so we can point others to You. We want to remember that this is a celebration of Your Son's birth. Allow us to ponder the true reason for the season and act accordingly. In Jesus' name we pray. Amen.

When you ponder CHRISTmas, what comes to mind?

_____

_____

_____

How will you turn your thoughts about the true meaning of CHRISTmas into reality?

_____

_____

_____

Day 349

The Perfect Gift

> *"I am the way, the truth, and the life; no one comes to the Father, but through Me."*
>
> John 14:6

Buying gifts for some people is difficult. We can look and look and never find just the right item, but God knew the perfect gift to send us. When God offered the gift of Jesus to all humanity, He offered that gift to one and all. He does not defer to wealth or poverty. He does not favor good looks or plainness. He is not impressed with human intelligence, nor does he look down on those who lack intelligence. He does not favor someone who holds a high-paying job over one who takes home a small paycheck. He offers His gift to people of every nation, ethnic and racial group, and social status.

Interestingly, the gift God gave—Jesus—is not only offered to all humanity: It is needed by all humanity. In spite of the threat to our own independence, all of us need this gift because its equivalent can't be earned. No one can merit eternal life. We can't deserve forgiveness of our sin nor adoption into the family of God. According to Roman 3:23 and 6:23, "all fall short of the glory of God"; and "the wages of sin is death, but the free gift of God is eternal life in Christ Jesus our Lord."

Let's Pause for Prayer

Heavenly Father, I thank you for sending Jesus Christ as a gift to all humanity. I accept you as my personal Lord and Savior and ask you to reign over my life. I desire to live for you and thank you for the eternal life you have given me. In Jesus' name I pray. Amen.

Do you recognize Jesus as the perfect gift? Have you accepted Him? Write out a prayer in which you ask that others in your life for whom you're praying know Jesus as the perfect gift.

Day 350

What I Want For Christmas

"For by grace you have been saved through faith, and that not of yourselves; it is the gift of God, not of works, lest anyone should boast."

Ephesians 2:8–9

At this time of year, people make lists of what they want for Christmas. Some even say, "I deserve that special gift!" But the gift that is most special and that no one deserves is the gift of eternal life that God gives us when we accept Jesus Christ as our Lord and Savior.

We don't deserve the gift because we have been so resistant to God, and we cannot earn the mercy, love, or forgiveness He alone offers. The gift that can't be earned has been paid for in full and in our name. All debts can be cancelled as soon as we accept the offer: Christ's life for our life, His righteousness for our wrongs.

But in order to claim that gift, we must accept it by faith. We must believe God wants to give life and forgiveness and family relationship to all who believe that Christ died for their sins. Without faith, this gift cannot be received. Only those who trust God know He is their only hope for both time and eternity.

Let's Pause for Prayer

Lord, we thank You that You have given the gift of your Son Jesus, which can't be deserved, which is already paid for, and which I now accept by faith. Thank You for being my only hope in this world and in the next. I desire to know You better through Your word, through living for You, and through serving You. Help me to do what I need to do. In Jesus' name we pray. Amen.

Does CHRISTmas hold the meaning of the manger and the cross for you? Explain.

_____

_____

_____

How can you help others to understand the meaning of the manger and the cross?

_____

_____

_____

_____

Day 351   *Strings Attached*

"Do not fear, for I am with you; do not anxiously look about you, for I am your God. I will strengthen you, surely I will help you. Surely I will uphold you with My righteous right hand."

Isaiah 41:10

If you have accepted the gift of Jesus Christ from God the Father, did you know strings were attached? Well, not quite in the way you might be thinking!

Those who receive the gift of Jesus Christ cannot walk away without obligation. By entrusting themselves to God, the recipients of God's grace become His children, His servants, new people who are owned and empowered by His Spirit. By receiving the gift, we are subject to the lordship of Christ and to His correction. Although God's gift of Jesus Christ is a free gift that can't be earned or deserved, we must recognize that acceptance of the gift of Jesus comes with obligations and responsibilities.

Let's Pause for Prayer

Heavenly Father, although we have the choice to choose for or against You (our heavenly Father) at any time, we recognize that we owe You our very lives because of what You gave us through Jesus Christ. We desire to serve You with sincerity, love you passionately, and obey you with a sense of urgency and responsibility. Thank You for always being with us and for being a Father to us, a Father who cares and is interested in our well-being. In Jesus' name we pray. Amen.

Have you ever received a gift and felt as if strings were attached?

_____
_____
_____
_____

When you accepted Jesus, did you recognize the uniqueness of that gift and all you received at that moment?

_____
_____
_____
_____

Day 352

Gifts

> *"For a child will be born to us, a son will be given to us; and the government will rest on His shoulders; and His name will be called Wonderful Counselor, Mighty God, Eternal Father, Prince of Peace."*
>
> Isaiah 9:6

Many gifts can be received merely for one's own enjoyment and enrichment, but the gift of Jesus Christ is of such value and accessibility that to withhold information about where others can find it is an insult, not only to the gift itself but also to the Giver. Nothing is more important than pointing others to the only place they can find rest, peace, and hope for their souls. It's not too late to pick up the phone or make plans for one more holiday visit in order to share the gift of Christ. It's a gift that will never run out or wear out. It has no end, and it is available year round!

Let's Pause for Prayer

Heavenly, Father, I thank You for giving me the gift of eternal life through Jesus. If You desire me to tell someone about You, please bring her or him to mind and give me the boldness to share my faith with this individual. I desire to be obedient and will trust You as you lead me. I know that many are floundering and in need of a Savior. I pray I'd have the opportunity to share that need with others. In Jesus' name I pray. Amen.

What was the very best material gift you were ever given? Does that gift have any comparison to the gift of salvation and eternal life?

_____
_____
_____
_____

With whom might you share the gift of Jesus?

_____
_____
_____
_____

Day 353 — Peace

> *"The steadfast of mind Thou wilt keep in perfect peace, because he trusts in Thee."*
>
> Isaiah 26:3

So much is going on at this time of year: cards to send, gifts to buy and wrap, decorations to put up, places to go, and people to see. But what if you don't feel like it? What if you can't? It is not a festive time of the year for everyone! This time of year can be stressful and depressing for many people.

For some people, depression keeps them from fully enjoying the holiday festivities; some are homebound because of illness and would give anything to be able to go out and enjoy some fun but experience loneliness. For others, the bills are mounting out of control as they try to make Christmas meaningful by buying and spending, but they experience frustration instead.

One of the names given to the Lord is "Prince of Peace." How many of us experienced His peace this year? Yesterday's verse is a reminder of that peace. Isaiah 9:6 says, "For a child will be born to us, a son will be given to us; and the government will rest on His shoulders; and His name will be called Wonderful Counselor, Mighty God, Eternal Father, Prince of Peace." If Jesus is strong enough to have the government rest on His shoulders, why do so few of us come to Him for the strength we need to have peace—perfect peace?

Let's Pause for Prayer

Heavenly Father, we are so sorry for failing to trust in You to meet our needs. Help us to focus on what is really important at Christmastime—Christ. Lord, I pray that those around us who are experiencing depression and loneliness would put their full trust and faith in You and that they would claim Philippians 4:7: "And the peace of God, which surpasses all comprehension, shall guard your hearts and your minds in Christ Jesus." Allow them to experience the joy that comes from You alone. Help us to make Your Son Jesus the reason for the season! In Jesus' name we pray. Amen.

If you are experiencing frustration, depression, anxiety, or other negative emotions this Christmas, can you come to the Wonderful Counselor, Mighty God, and ask Him how to focus on what is of most importance this season?

Share a prayer and express your heart.

Day 354

The Giver

"He who did not spare His own Son, but delivered Him up for us all, how will He not also with Him freely give us all things?"

Romans 8:32

As the song says, "It's a most wonderful time of the year," that is, if you enjoy all the extra responsibilities that are added to your to-do list! Of all of the responsibilities added to my job description at CHRISTmastime, one task that is most difficult to accomplish is buying gifts. I don't mind shopping, spending money, or wrapping gifts with paper that I know will be ripped off and thrown away! What I do mind, however, is that I think our ideas about gift giving have gone off track! It seems all of us, including me, try to get the best deals, try to get done quickly so we aren't bothered at a busier time nearer Christmas day; but we don't always consider what the recipient desires or needs.

When God gave Jesus to us as a gift, He knew exactly what we needed—a Savior who would be willing to pay the ultimate price, that is, to die for our sins. He didn't find a cheaper or counterfeit way to provide for our needs. He provided and sacrificed His own Son. That is the ultimate in gift-giving! He fulfills so many roles: provider, healer, prince of peace, comforter, wonderful counselor. He can provide for our needs even before we ask.

Let's Pause for Prayer

Lord Jesus, You are the perfect gift giver and the perfect gift. Thank You for your death on the cross, which paid for my sins. I want to be Yours to use for your glory. At this Christmastime I want to dedicate and rededicate my life to You so that I can do the work You have set out for me to do. Thank you for all the ways you have provided for me even before I even ask. In Your Name we pray. Amen.

Jesus is the Giver. How has He provided for you this year (healed, comforted, other)?

Consider the ways He's given to you, and take a moment to reflect upon His goodness as you write out a prayer.

Day 355

Christmas: Real Or Fake

"Therefore if any man is in Christ, he is a new creature, the old things pass away, behold new things have come."

II Corinthians 5:17

Decorating our new home for the holidays a number of years ago made for fun finding a new place for the old possessions. We had a few hand-me-down artificial trees along the way, so we placed them in the family room and basement and the mini trees in the children's rooms.

Our daughter Kristina and boyfriend (now husband) Cos made a plan for a real tree. Does he mean the kind you have to cut down, try to put straight in a stand, water, and care for? That was exactly what he meant! I had rather enjoyed the artificial trees with the ease they provided. And I liked the stairway decorations for the same reason.

Some of our lives are like the artificial decorations we have. We put on our nice clothes at Christmas and go to church, making good impressions (if not on others, certainly on ourselves); but everyone knows it's a pretense. Then we put ourselves back into storage until next year.

Let's Pause for Prayer

Lord, like the smell of that fresh Alberta spruce, beautiful lights, and other decorations that added new life to the other decorations around it, may our lives in Christ do the same for others around us! We desire to come to know You personally and entrust our lives to You. It takes a new life in Christ to be the sweet fresh fragrance to those around us, creating the desire in others to know You. In Jesus' name we pray.

What does it personally take to be real, not fake, to others so they'll see Christ in you?

_____
_____
_____

How will you do the same as you prepare your heart for the Christmas season?

_____
_____
_____
_____
_____
_____

Day 356

No End To Peace

> *"There will be no end to the increase of His government or of peace."*
>
> Isaiah 9:7

I love the festivities that surround this time of year—the celebration of the birth of Christ, exchanging gifts as we remember the gift that God gave to us in Christ Jesus, and the time that we are able to spend with loved ones—yet I much prefer the peaceful side of this holiday!

It takes planning at this time of year to ensure that we will have a peaceful Christmas holiday. When we add decorating, baking, shopping, entertaining, hospitality, and gift wrapping to our already busy lives, it's easy to neglect, if not to completely forget, the real reason we take time to celebrate! We need to remind ourselves why He came and what He can provide for us.

Let's Pause for Prayer

Heavenly Father, we thank You for being a Mighty God and the Prince of Peace. Please help us to keep that in mind as we plan and prepare for this Christmas. Keep us from neglecting Your word daily as we pursue peacefulness in our own lives. May we show kindness, gentleness, and Your peace to others as we add the many additional responsibilities of the season to our already busy lives. Let us tell others the reason we celebrate and be personally mindful that Jesus is the reason for the season! In Jesus' name we pray amen.

How does perfect peace look to you?

_____

_____

_____

How will you intentionally work toward that perfect peace this CHRISTmas season?

_____

_____

_____

_____

Day 357 — *Share With Everyone*

> *"But sanctify Christ as Lord in your hearts, always being ready to make a defense to everyone who asks you to give account for the hope that is in you, yet with gentleness and reverence."*
>
> 1 Peter 3:15

Sharing one's faith isn't always easy. It's sometimes uncomfortable and difficult because sadly, we don't do it often enough to have the confidence; and then we lack the boldness. CHRISTmastime is a time when we have opportunity to share our faith, pointing others to our Savior with the obvious tools around us: sharing scripture in our CHRISTmas carols, the nativity, the star of Bethlehem, angels, Jesus as our gift, and so much more! If we don't take this opportunity now, we'll likely miss less obvious opportunities to share our faith throughout the year.

We can gently guide conversation to the topic of Jesus when we talk about the words we hear in a Christmas carol, sharing that He is our gift—the gift of salvation. Asking people about how they celebrate the holidays can lead to our sharing how we celebrate ours. The opportunity this CHRISTmas might be the last or only time you'll get to share with some people.

Let's Pause for Prayer

Lord God, we want to be open about sharing our faith in You as we walk through this CHRISTmas season with family, friends, coworkers, and acquaintances. Help us to encourage meaningful conversations. Show us how to guide a conversation about spiritual matters, inviting others to be a part of it instead of carrying on a monologue. Give us boldness when we fear what others might say about this season or You. Help us gently and kindly share the hope we have in You and the hope they might have in You as well without condemning but instead understanding and caring. When we take steps to share, please give us right answers to questions others might ask, grace when others might be confrontational, and love if we are challenged. Allow us to shine for You as we share the hope we have within us. In Jesus' name we pray. Amen.

Is it with ease or difficulty that you share your faith in Christ with others?

_____

_____

_____

Think of one lead-in comment or question to use as a conversation starter.

_____

_____

_____

Day 358

Go Tell It On The Mountain!

"How lovely on the mountains are the feet of him who brings good news, who announces peace and brings good news of happiness, who announces salvation, and says to Zion, 'Your God reigns!'"

Isaiah 52:7

I love planning, creating, and sending our annual CHRISTmas card. I think about it all year long! I love to think of a theme and have fun with it as I share our year. Some years I share a scripture; other years I'll add a handwritten note telling the recipient when we prayed for them. It's the one time of year others will read scripture or listen to the things of the Lord with an open mind and heart. Not everyone likes cards that tell about someone else's year, but for me, it's my way of telling it on the mountain. I'd be writing the same thing to each person, and this makes it easier (and more fun for me) to make one card for all. I love hearing from others about their year and often wonder how they are doing when a card bears only a signature. This is such a great time to greet others by mail and pray for those in our lives.

Let's Pause for Prayer

Dear Lord, let us use this time of year as a way of telling others about You, sharing from Your word, and then praying for others throughout this season and as we begin the new year. We want to make every opportunity count as we celebrate Jesus' birth. Let us not miss our chance to share with others that Your Son is the gift given to us and You are the gift giver in a world that desperately needs what You have to offer: peace, hope, encouragement, and salvation. As we use this precious and priceless opportunity to share openly from Your word and about who You are, let us do so with gentleness, boldness, love, and sincerity. We pray that others would be curious about a new life in Christ by asking us questions, seeking from Your word, and then trusting in You. Show us the opportunities You set before us, and let us show Your love. Thank you for the loving gift of Your Son, Jesus Christ. In His name we pray. Amen.

Do you enjoy receiving and sending letters in or as your CHRISTmas greeting? What do you share?

_____

_____

_____

What will be your way to go tell it on the mountain this year?

_____

_____

_____

_____

Day 359 — *Say It With Prayer And Care*

> *"And everything you ask in prayer, believing, you shall receive."*
> Matthew 21:22

We have tried to create unique ideas for prayer as we focus on the holidays. One year I made a stocking, and we called it our prayer stocking. Everyone who entered our home was given a 3x5 card and was asked—if they wanted to—to write down a prayer request; and we would pray for them throughout the new year. They had the option of signing their name to the prayer request or remaining anonymous.

One particular year a young extended-family member shared this prayer request: "Please pray for me. I am always getting into trouble, and I know I shouldn't do these bad things." So we did. We prayed for this family member throughout the year even though we did not know who wrote it. Sure, we had a feeling, but we did not know for sure! The following year, the family member said, "I know you were praying for me! Every time I thought about doing the wrong thing, I just had to do the right thing because I knew you were praying for me!" It was a wonderful opportunity to focus on prayer and more specifically, praying for the needs of others. Please join me as we Pause for Prayer.

Let's Pause for Prayer

Heavenly Father, thank you for allowing us to make prayer a focus despite the many tasks to be accomplished throughout the holidays. Let us not neglect praying for others, and let us have a real excitement about being in prayer for the holidays. Thank you for helping us extend that prayer into the new year as we pray for others whose lives we have touched. In Jesus' name we pray. Amen.

How might God show you how to focus on prayer this Christmas season? Come up with a few ideas and list them.

_____

_____

_____

_____

_____

_____

_____

Day 360

Secretly Giving

"Ask, and it shall be given to you; seek, and you shall find; knock, and it shall be opened to you."

Matthew 7:7

Years ago when the children were very young, we had a CHRISTmas bank made of tin. All year long we filled it only with quarters. At the end of some years, we had a significant amount of money. We prayed throughout the year about who would receive a surprise gift from us. Every year, the Lord brought to our minds and hearts someone with a need, often someone who would never know who we were because we didn't know them either. We decided what to do with the money to specifically bless the person or family and would find a way to give that gift anonymously. It was such fun.

We felt blessed because we were not looking to do it for attention or thanks. We did it simply to bless, and in the process we were blessed.

Let's Pause for Prayer

Heavenly Father, please make me an instrument to bless others. Please speak to my heart and direct me to one who needs a blessing this year. Even if it is as simple as a kind note, please let me know just whom you would like me to bless. Help me to do it without expecting attention or thanks. May I do it to glorify you! In Jesus' name we pray. Amen.

Ask the Lord how He might use you this CHRISTmas season to be a blessing to someone who in need. Write out a prayer.

_____
_____
_____
_____
_____
_____

Whom has He brought to your mind, and how will you follow through?

_____
_____
_____

Day 361 — Saying Thank You For Our Gifts

"Always giving thanks for all things in the name of our Lord Jesus Christ to God, even the Father."

Ephesians 5:20

Have you ever given someone a gift but received no thanks for it? You took the time to think about the perfect gift for the occasion, shopped for it, wrapped it, and then delivered it. The gift was received and opened, but the recipient never acknowledged receiving or appreciating it. Ouch! That hurts. I know some might say we should not expect a thank you and we should give without expecting anything in return—and I agree—but from the perspective of manners, I'm saying the receiver should show appreciation verbally or in a written note.

Our heavenly Father sent us a gift that we all need, whether we have come to realize that need or not. He sent the gift of Jesus because He knew for all eternity that we would need it. We needed someone who could make us right with God, and that was Jesus. He knew that none of us could afford this perfect gift, and although we would never even deserve it, He loved us so much that He sent us Jesus to die for our sins as the perfect gift. As we look back over CHRISTmas and look to the new year, let's appreciate and thank Him.

Let's Pause for Prayer

Heavenly Father, thank You for Jesus, who was born to be the Savior of the world and who lived a perfect life as an example and comfort to me. Thank you, Jesus, for dying for me. I appreciate and honor You all the days of my life. I want to serve, pray, and know You better day by day. Even as we enter into a new year, we want to prepare our hearts to be appreciative and thankful at all times and in all ways. In Jesus' name I pray. Amen.

Think back to the gifts you received this CHRISTmas. Do a mental inventory of whether or not you adequately thanked the givers. If you didn't thank them, give them a call or write them a note of appreciation and thanks. Make notes for yourself here.

_____

_____

_____

_____

Share a prayer of thanksgiving for who the Lord is in your life. Include how and why you appreciate Him.

_____

_____

_____

Day 362 — New Year's Eve Encouragement

"Therefore encourage one another, and build up one another, just as you also are doing."

1 Thessalonians 5:11

As we look back over the past year, let's take a moment and think about someone for whom we are thankful and who cared, took the time to meet a need we had, or even prayed with us. When someone cares about us and shows it by encouraging us, praying with and for us, and helping us when they see some practical way to help, we feel as if our load has been lifted or lightened and that we can go on. It might be someone we least expected who comes alongside us and helps us get to the next point, the point we didn't think we could reach alone. Such people are often the ones who make us feel appreciated and loved; they may even give us a renewed sense of purpose or worth. We all need words of encouragement—words that give life.

Let's Pause for Prayer

Heavenly Father, You are the great encourager. Help us to rely upon Your word as the source of encouraging others. Give us the words that fit in each and every situation to encourage one another, not words that are fluffy flattery but words that will give life to others who need a boost to go on, who need to recognize that they have a sense of worth and purpose, and who need to persevere. May we lighten the burdens of others with kind words so they feel loved and appreciated. Allow us to be of help, not a hindrance; to give words of life, not death; to grant forgiveness, not withhold it; and to be there when someone has a need. Father, please use me for Your glory. In Jesus' name we pray. Amen.

Who has encouraged you this year? Perhaps thank him or her.

_____
_____
_____

Who will you consider encouraging this next year, someone who possibly needs a verbal boost?

_____
_____
_____
_____

Day 363 — Brevity Of Life

"Lord, make me to know my end, and what is the extent of my days, let me know how transient I am. Behold, Thou hast made my days as handbreadths, and my lifetime as nothing in Thy sight, surely every man at his best is a mere breath."

Psalm 39:4–5

We're all saying it, so won't you join me in the chorus of the day, "Where did this year go? It has just flown by!" Well, it's certainly a reality, isn't it? It's also very sobering. I remember hearing Billy Graham's answer when he was asked, "What has been the biggest surprise to you in your lifetime?" He answered, "The brevity of life."

When we think about how quickly this year has flown, how we've all turned another year older, how we've achieved some goals and made some mistakes, how we've moved three steps forward in some areas and sadly shuffled four steps backward in others, we get a sense that life can be full of surprises, challenges, victories, and regrets as time rushes on. But as we look back over this year, instead of looking ahead and making the goal to lose weight or change some habit, I wonder whether we could take some time to review the ways the Lord has worked in and through us to make us more like Himself and the ways He has used others to help us achieve some goals and enjoy some victories in life. It might be fun to listen to the top songs of the year and recognize top entertainers and famous people, but God has used each of us to accomplish His will in ways that are lasting and important.

Let's Pause for Prayer

Heavenly Father, thank you for working in our personal lives this year. Help us to recall the wonderful things You accomplished in and through us. We pray that we were faithful in obeying You and that Your will was accomplished because of our obedience and willingness to follow You. Thank you for leading us in creative ways to pray for and help others; and we are grateful that You have used others to meet our needs, encourage us, and help us in many ways. Please help us to evaluate our sins and the mistakes we made so that we don't repeat them. Also please help us to listen carefully to the goals and desires You have for us to accomplish this coming year. In Jesus' name we pray. Amen.

Consider how the Lord used you to meet the needs of others, the times you put others first and desired to do the will of the Father. List your most rewarding moments of this past year.

_____

_____

_____

_____

_____

_____

Day 364

Success

"If the axe is dull and he does not sharpen its edge, then he must exert more strength. Wisdom has the advantage of giving success."

Ecclesiastes 10:10

We must prepare in advance to accomplish the goals we're planning for next year. I often use today's verse as I'm teaching goal setting. When giving it a practical spin, it sounds something like this, "If the scissors of a seamstress are dull and she doesn't sharpen them, it will be harder and more work for her to cut the fabric easily. If she is smart, she'll sharpen her scissors for her fine fabric." Another practical spin might be, "If the tools of a gardener are dull and he does not sharpen them, his work will be even harder. He must do what he knows will help him and get his tools sharpened, which will likely allow him to use less energy and get the work done sooner."

Let's Pause for Prayer

Heavenly Father, we ask You to show us what we need to do to have success in accomplishing our goals for this coming year. Father, help us to sharpen the areas of our lives in which You are asking us to concentrate. We know You will gently but firmly be our Guide if we but ask You, so we ask for direction, clarity, and help as we do that which You direct us to do. Father, if we are not being sharp, not being wise in the way we have set out to reach our goals and resolutions, please stop us in our tracks now and turn us around to where we need to be going so that we will be wise and successful. Help us to see where we err or behave foolishly, and grant us Your wisdom to plan ahead so that our goals can actually be accomplished. If that help comes from others who can guide and direct us, then may we be open to learning from them and growing; but we don't want to neglect hearing from You first. In Jesus' name we pray. Amen.

What do you feel you need to do to be successful in the eyes of the Lord?

_____

_____

_____

_____

What skills do you want to sharpen in the coming year?

_____

_____

_____

_____

Day 365 — *The Next Step*

> *"Rise and enter the city, and it shall be told you what you must do."*
> Acts 9:6

As we continue pursuing the goals and direction God has for each of us during this new year, let's wrap our minds around the concept that we don't need the whole year mapped out; we must simply watch and listen to the way God will direct us one day and one step at a time. As Saul breathed threats of murder against the disciples of the Lord, he approached Damascus with some men traveling with him when they saw a light from heaven flash around Saul, blinding him. He heard a voice: "Saul, Saul, why are you persecuting Me?" As Jesus identified Himself, He gave Saul (and those with him) direction to "rise and enter the city, and it shall be told you what you must do." For three days and nights they did as they were told and waited without eating or drinking. Ananias was the messenger sent to Saul, who then opened his eyes to see, both physically and spiritually.

Let's Pause for Prayer

Heavenly Father, we desire to hear from You on the road we're traveling. As we believe You've called us to certain resolutions, plans, goals, ministries, and new patterns for the new year, please give us direction so that we will know what step to take next without running ahead of You. As you gave Saul only the next few acts to perform and not the whole picture all at once, help us to be patient, to wait upon You, and to listen when You show us that next small step to take. Help us to realize that Your hand is upon us each step of the way and that we need not worry or fret for tomorrow or even two days from now but to act in obedience to the present request and direction You give. As we learn to trust you in the baby steps we take along the way, help us to then trust You when You ask us to wait longer than we think we should. Allow us to listen, trust, and obey, no matter how long we need to wait to hear Your direction for our lives. In Jesus' name we pray. Amen.

Do you usually try to plan out the year, or will you take this year step by step?

How will you wait upon the Lord for the next step?

To connect with Cindi or to consider her to speak for your group or event visit
www.cindiferrini.com